The Black Celts

The African Substratum Theory

Volume One

IBRAHIM ALI

ISBN: 978-1-9998543-1-7 (paperback)

Front cover design by© Ibrahim Ali.

Images: All photos of Cardiff Castle Roman Wall mural (Silures) taken by Ibrahim Ali; copyright Ibrahim © 1997-2021; Maps designed by Ibrahim Ali; Foot shape outlines created by © Ibrahim Ali 1997-2021; Pict (N.E. Scotland) foot outline: based on Phyllis Jackson notes & private communications. Stonehenge image attributed to TheDitalArtists/ via

Pixabay license. Stonehenge image attributed to Fotobias via Pixabay license. For images in the public domain, wiki common license CC; all attributions are given underneath the individual images.

Flag of Wales, attribution Unknown Vector graphics by Tobias Jakobs, Public domain, via Wikimedia Commons

Published by ACECAA (Afro-Celtic Education, Culture & Arts Association) UK

***Email**: blackcelts2016@gmail.com*

***Follow** on Twitter: Ibrahim_Ali@Black_Celts @black_celts*

***Follow** on Academia.edu for current articles from the author.*

[visit; //troglodytescavedweller.academia.edu]

Sword from Awfat, Harar Province, East Africa.
© Ibrahim Ali

DEDICATION

This book is dedicated to
my
Mum & Dad
&
To my amazing daughter Nabeela

"The world exists as you perceive it.
It is not what you see, it is how you see it.
It is not what you hear,
But how you hear it.
It is not what you feel,
But how you feel it."
-Rumi.

CONTENTS

ACKNOWLEDGMENTS

The past decades of research on this topic have allowed me to travel an unconventional road. It has allowed me to collect data through my own anthropological surveys of these islands. Phyllis Jackson's pioneering work on foot-shape inspired me to conduct similar research between 1997 and 2005. It was with her assistance that I was able to learn how to interpret the data I had collected. I am also indebted to Professor Wesley Vernon, the UK's leading expert in forensic podiatry, for sending me some of Phyllis Jackson's papers in his possession. I hope that Phyllis Jackson's work will reach a wider audience and inspire 'unconventional' research. I would like to thank all those individuals who allowed me to document their foot-outlines over the past two decades; they are now immortalized in this edition. I am also indebted to the Internet Archive, an independent and non-profit charity that provides much needed digital library access to researchers, historians, scholars, and the public. A service that needs to be supported, so that it can continue.

This work was inspired by Bob Quinn's amazing Atlantean documentaries. He kindly sent me the fourth documentary in the series. Also, way back in the 1990's, I was fortunate enough to screen Bob Quinn's Atlantean in Cardiff's Tiger Bay. He had kindly sent me copies of the three documentaries that had been aired on Channel 4 and S4C (Sianel Pedwar Cymru). The Atlantean Quartet, which is available at www.conamara.org., is an incredible piece of work; and is essential viewing. I have encountered many obstacles in getting this work completed. However, inspired by Bob Quinn's forth documentary in the Atlantean series, I was determined to produce this edition.

A special acknowledgement to my amazing daughter Nabeela - who has been by my side during this journey; without whom I would have never completed this project. When she was born, I spontaneously proclaimed the Azzan - the same Azzan that started Bob Quinn's journey of exploration.
Ibrahim Ali May 2021 United Kingdom.

1 AUTHOR'S NOTE

Have an open mind; maybe all the things you have been taught about the 'Celts' has been incorrect. Maybe the 'Celts' or Gauls did not inhabit these islands. Imagine, for a moment, that Abbe Paul Yves Pezron (1639-1706), a Breton theologian from France invented this fake 'Celtic' identity. Have the Gaels, Scots, and Cymry been fooled into accepting a false identity?

Add to this the 19th century 'Celtic' revival when the fake 'Celtic' identity was firmly adopted. This 'alien' identity was cleverly imposed on the people and embraced by co-operative academics. Through a grand conspiracy, an 'alien' identity was imposed onto the Gaels, Cymry, and Scots. An identity that was composed of tall, blond Aryan 'Celts' with blue eyes, arriving in waves from Central Europe. The new arrivals were supposed to belong to an 'Aryan' race and were supposed to be cousins of the Anglo-Saxons This narrative still dominates academia and forms the backbone of the current Eurocentric 'colonial' syllabus. However, the colonial British Empire's representation of the Irish people was very contradictory. Let me bring to your attention the 19th century British publications, such as Punch and The London Illustrated News, produced cruel caricatures of the Irish people. They were depicted as apes, a tactic aimed at shaping public opinion by propagating hatred: the same tactic used by Giraldus Cambrensis a thousand years earlier. At the same time colonial academics successively promoted the idea of the ancient 'Celts' as Aryans - while at the same time dehumanizing the modern Irish. The colonial attempt at eradicating the Irish language was primarily designed to be the coup de grâce - the final blow to Irish identity. However, the Gaeltacht regions survived and still flourish today.

Many scholars have challenged the colonial narrative. Bob Quinn's contribution is the most important because it documents how an Irishman rejected this fake 'Celtic' identity that was imposed on them.

Scientific Racism

Drawing by: H. Strickland Constable. 1899, Ireland from One or Two Neglected Points of View; [public domain]

shows an alleged similarity between "Irish Iberian" and "Negro" features in contrast to the higher "Anglo-Teutonic." The accompanying caption reads "The Iberians are believed to have been originally an African race, who thousands of years ago spread themselves through Spain over Western Europe. Their remains are found in the barrows, or burying places, in sundry parts of these countries. The skulls are of low prognathous type. They came to Ireland and mixed with the natives of the South and West, who themselves are supposed to have been of low type and descendants of savages of the Stone Age, who, in consequence of isolation from the rest of the world, had never been out-competed in the healthy struggle of life, and thus made way, according to the laws of nature, for superior races."

James Joyce [celebrated Irish writer] was aware of the British Empires' narcissistic treatment, and racist stereotyping of the Irish people. In Stephen Hero, Joyce's Madden speaks of those *"old stale libels; the drunken Irishman, the baboon-faced Irishman, that we see in Punch."* [p33, Vincent J Cheng, Cultural Margins, Race and Empire]

I have focused on the Iron Age, in this edition, because it is during this era that the fictitious 'Celts' are supposed to have arrived in these islands. In an attempt to end this fake myth of 'Aryan Celts', I have presented a detailed examination of the Iron Age, which undeniably shows that the inhabitants were not 'Celts' from either the La Tene or Hallstatt Cultures - there was no significant human migration from central Europe. The evidence contained in this book unveils the close links between the ancient people of Britain, Ireland, and Africa. The evidence is over-whelming but is largely ignored by academics.

The story starts with sean-nós and its similarity to the Muslim Azzan. An intriguing story worth exploring. The connections are certainly fascinating. I have researched the Gaelic lament for many years and its magnetic spiritual contents, which I hope to publish elsewhere.

The publication of the *'Genetic and Population Studies in Wales'* (University of Wales Press) captured the attention of the Guardian Newspaper, which had the headline *'Arabs may have been the first Welsh' by Tony Heath*. The South Wales Echo had the heading *'A mongrel race - and here's the proof' by Peter Underwood.*

Professor Bernal's *'Black Athena'* caused a bit of a stir within academic circles. But it is Bob Quinn's open and honest rejection of the label 'Celt' that deserves the most praise.

My aim is simply to show that the indigenous inhabitants of these islands were not 'Celts' - instead, we have evidence supporting the existence of a multicultural society, that was populated by diverse groups who shared a common identity.

This edition allows me to share my favorite research tool - the variation of the cuboid bone in ancient and modern feet. This new branch of ethnoarchaeology was pioneered by podiatrist Phyllis Jackson, who inspired me to undertake my own research in this subject. Many people who think they are Anglo-Saxon will be surprised to find out that the shape of their cuboid bone might place them in a different 'ethnic' group. The reader is welcome to contribute to this research by submitting their own foot outline so that a more comprehensive knowledge of human migrations can be reconstructed across the globe.

2 NOT CELTIC

The Gaels (Irish) and the Cymry (Britons/Welsh) are not 'Celts'. This is the first point the reader needs to clearly understand. Bob Quinn, through his 4-part documentary series 'Atlantean' and his book *'The Atlantean Irish: Ireland's Oriental and Maritime Heritage,'* boldly rejected the label 'Celt.' His work was decades ahead of its time. It offers a unique perspective; an Irishman who realized that his people were never 'Celts' - unfortunately, the label 'Celt' is still widely used and has not been abandoned. Most Irish, Welsh and Scots are still under the illusion that they are 'Celts'. Add to that around 40 million Irish Americans who still think they are 'Celts' - an inappropriate label invented only 250 years ago. In today's language it would be considered 'fake news' - a made up identity, created by 18th and 19th century academics.

The latest edition of my book aims to bring the 'Black Celts' up to date. Recent progress in strontium isotope analysis has helped identify the original homeland of some of the ancient settlers. This edition also gives me a chance to review the valuable contribution made by other scholars in this field. I am especially excited to share my foot shape research - inspired by the pioneering work of Gloucestershire podiatrist Phyllis Jackson. I was lucky enough to get her valuable opinion on a series of foot-shapes that I had carefully collected from different communities. This new branch of ethnoarchaeology has enabled the tracking of tribal movements and helps distinguish the ancient Britons, newly arrived Anglo-Saxons, and other 'ethnic' communities.

The ancient books of Ireland and Britain are full of characters with different skin colours. This book proves that ancient Britain was a cosmopolitan, multi-racial society - it raises the question - *'what is Britishness or Irishness?'* The answer is rather surprising - and it is for the reader to decide.

The Afro-Celtic Series

The Afro-Celtic series was born with the launch of the Black Celts. It produced a lot of reviews in both the UK and across the Atlantic in the USA. Bob Quinn was kind enough to send me copies of his documentary, which I proudly screened in Cardiff Bay (the oldest multicultural community in the UK). A few years later I produced more titles and then decided to primarily focus on research. Today many school children are beginning to discover the true contribution that black people have made to British and Irish history. However, politicians still attack multiculturalism. Former UK Prime Minister David Cameron made a venomous attack on multiculturalism with the following words:

"We have allowed the weakening of our collective identity under the doctrine of a state multiculturalism." [David Cameron, former PM of the United Kingdom]

He failed to inform his audience that colonial England has never encouraged a 'collective' British identity as the Cymry (Welsh) and Scots know full well.

In 1747, the Act of Proscription banned the teaching of Scottish Gaelic and prohibited the Highlanders from gathering. In the same year, The Heritable Jurisdictions Act forced Highlanders, who owned land, to either accept all English rule or have their land confiscated. Even the inhabitants of Ireland's Galway were instructed to teach their children English unless they incur the high displeasure of King Henry VIII. Irish Gaelic speakers were regarded by the English as disloyal, and parents were encouraged to speak to their children only in English. The English colonists wanted to remove Gaelic culture all together. *[see p117, The Politics of the Irish Language Under the English and British Governments, Sean Cahill & Seán Ó Cathail]*

The Welsh also suffered greatly under English domination. The 'Welsh Not' or 'Welsh Stick' was intended to stigmatize any child speaking Welsh, and it continued well into the 20th century. Any pupil heard speaking Welsh was admonished and given a stick with the initials WN. If another pupil was heard to speak Welsh, they would be given the stick. At the end of the day, whoever possessed the stick was beaten. These tactics were designed to terrorize Welsh speakers; the sole intent was to eradicate the indigenous languages spoken in these islands.

Historical Revisionism

Can this book be classified as historical revisionism? First, we need to define historical revisionism:

> Historical revisionism usually involves challenging the 'orthodox' (established, accepted or traditional) views held by professional scholars about a 'historical event' or time-span or phenomenon, introducing contrary evidence, or reinterpreting the motivations and decisions of the people involved. The revision of the historical record can reflect new discoveries of fact, evidence, and interpretation, which then results in revised history. [https://en.wikipedia.org]

In the light of new research and contrary evidence, the 'Celtic' theory can no longer be accepted. Although the concept of 'Celtic' identity has been rejected by some academics - unfortunately, most people have been fooled into accepting this 'fake' identity. The 'Celts' or Keltoi are a not the same as the ancient Gaels and Cymry (Britons).

There is a need for a revisionist approach, especially for history, anthropology and even genetics. When language classifications were being developed, Africans were not allowed to sit at the table to share their opinions. Consider the classification of Somali, Oromo, and Afar as Cushitic languages. We know that Nubia was Cush and in the Old Testament we also have *'Cush begot Nimrod'* (in Mesopotamia). So why did European language experts, such as Joseph Greenberg, encourage the label Cushitic for East African languages. Cush and the Horn of Africa are separated by a distance of 1335 miles. The appropriate name for the languages of East Africa should have been Punt; a name that encompassed the entire Horn of Africa and also extended south as far as the African Great Lakes (including the Mountains of the Moon, Tanzania, Arabic *Jabal al-Qamar* or *Jibbel el Kumri*); an area referred to by the ancient Egyptians as the land of the Ancestors or God's Land. The languages classified as Nilo-Saharan should have been called Cushitic. The reason for these strange naming systems is because Eurocentric's were uncomfortable with a sub-Saharan African Punt - the ancestral homeland of the ancient Egyptians. Eurocentric's tried to place Punt in Southern Arabia. However, all evidence points to East Africa, especially since the animals and plants indicate an African land. The ancient Egyptians noted that when it rained in Punt, the Nile would flood. This obviously places the homeland of the ancient Egyptians in sub-Saharan Africa.

The terminology used by Eurocentrics is inconsistent. The equator runs through Uganda, Kenya, and Somalia. These countries use to be collectively referred to as East African countries; Mogadishu is 140 miles from the equator, and yet Eurocentrics have introduced the term north-east Africa which does not make sense. These countries are East African countries that are closely interlinked historically, geographically, and culturally.

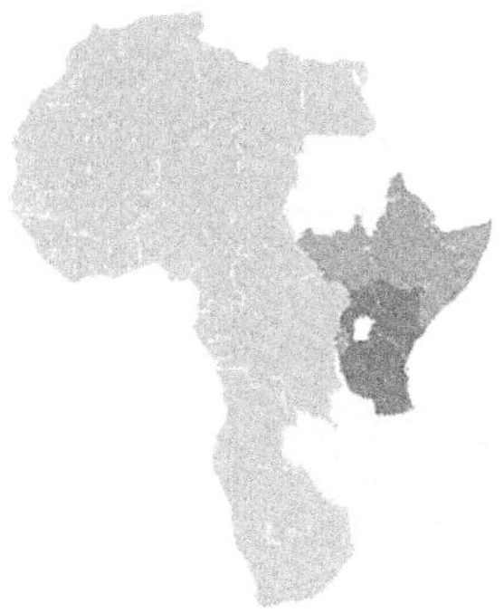

A Map of East Africa showing countries always included in East Africa (darkest green), Normally included in East Africa (medium green), and Sometimes included in East Africa (light green).
(Attribute to Leviavery, CC0, via Wikimedia Commons)

The term Hamito-Semitic and Afro-asiatic are strictly used as linguistic terms. In my previous edition, I replaced this term with Erythraic languages - since these languages are believed to have originated somewhere around the Red Sea. Virtually all the literature and research papers available have use the term 'Hamito-Semitic' or 'Afro-asiatic'; using my preferred term, 'Erythraic', would simply confuse the reader, and reference searches using the term Erythraic would not produce any fruitful results.

Roger Blench gives a concise history of these classifications:

> The name 'Semitic' was proposed in 1781 by von Schlozer. Berber and some of the Chadic languages, notably Hausa were added during the course of the nineteenth century. The earliest version of Afro-asiatic as presently understood probably appears in Müller (1876- 87) who linked Egyptian, Semitic, Berber, Cushitic and Hausa, the only known Chadic language at the period. A phylum under the name Afro-asiatic goes back to Joseph Greenberg (1963). Previously, the preferred name was "Hamito-Semitic", an unfortunate conjunction both clumsy and redolent of suspect racial theories. Hamito-Semitic is by no means expunged from the lexicon: hence the confusion in titles of various collections of conference

> proceedings (cf. Bynon 1984). Even disregarding the "Hamitic hypothesis" Hamito-Semitic gives a primacy to Semitic that is entirely without linguistic justification. Other proposed names include Afrasian, Lisramic (Hodge 1976) and more strangely, Lislakh. These have not been widely adopted...Greenberg (1963) was responsible for the establishment of this phylum in its present form. His particular contribution was the dethronement of Semitic from its formerly central position. and the emphasis he placed on its relations with the languages of Africa. [Roger Blench, The Westward Wanderings of Cushitic Pastoralists]

The term Afro-asiatic is very misleading; four out of the five languages within this family are found exclusively in Africa; only one, Semitic is found outside of Africa. The name wrongly implies that the languages are equally distributed in Africa and Asia. Hamito-Semitic is not the most useful name; however, this term dominates the existing literature along with Afro-asiatic - for ease, both terms will be use together in this book.

The term Semitic is often used incorrectly. It should not be used as a racial classification. The speakers of Semitic languages have every skin colour imaginable. The oldest of the Arabs are referred as 'Al-Arab al-Ariba' (العرب العاربة) and are said to have come from Yemen: the phenotype and skin colour of the Mahra, Qara, Soqotri, and Hadrami tribes (and many others) closely resemble their neighbors across the Red Sea in Africa.

Yemen Socotri Tribe, Children, Socotra Island
Attributed to Rod Waddington from Kergunyah, Australia, CC via Wikimedia Commons

Yemen, Soqotri Tribe, Fish Market.
Attributed to Rod Waddington from Kergunyah, Australia, CC BY- via Wikimedia Commons

The aim of this book is to put forward the case for an African substratum in Ireland and the British Isles. The ancient Irish and Britons had a close affinity with Africa and the Mediterranean; they were not related to the Continental Hallstatt or La Tene Celts. I believe the evidence presented in this publication overwhelmingly supports this theory.

I have come to the conclusion that the Gaels (Irish) and Cymry (Britons) did not speak an Indo-European language originally - they adopted an Indo-European language from mainland Europe as a result of close trade connections during the Iron Age. The ancient people of Britain and Ireland were not the descendants of 'Celts' from central Europe; in fact, they had more in common with Africa and the southern Mediterranean. The evidence reveals a vastly different picture of history.

The British Isles was comprised of cosmopolitan communities, with every skin colour imaginable. It was a vibrant society connected through commerce with many distant lands. It raises the question, **'How do we define British and Irish identity?'**

3 A CELEBRATION OF BOB QUINN

Bob Quinn's Atlantean, a four-part documentary series explores an Irishman's rejection of the 'Celtic' identity - It is a fascinating journey that explores the connection between the Gaels, Africa, the Middle East, and even reaches the land of the Tartars. In the fourth film, the journey takes him to Russia. When Bob Quinn initially undertook his journey, in the mid 1980's, DNA analysis had yet to be developed. We now know that many Tartars share the same male y-DNA haplogroup as the Gaels and Cymry. Bob Quinn adamantly rejects the label 'Celtic' - his work is incredibly accurate and was so far ahead of the scientists and historians.

Bob Quinn drawn by © Ibrahim Ali.

Bob Quinn started out as the head of Irish state television, Radio Telefís Éireann (RTÉ). His time at RTE was marked by challenges. Quinn's approach has always been unique. His book the Maverick is worth reading *[see Maverick: A Dissident View of Broadcasting Today, by Bob Quinn]*. His career with RTE and his rebellious flight to the West of Ireland was truly fortunate because it resulted in the birth of the Atlantean series. With some seriousness he thought, *"If I am Irish, then I should live somewhere Irish is spoken."* In 1969, he left Dublin for the Gaeltacht region of Conamara, in the West of Ireland, making his home in Carraroe (An Cheathrú Ruan), overlooking the Atlantic Ocean. In that year Bob Quinn left RTE and wrote a letter that still has relevance today. Before re-visiting Bob Quinn's letter from 1969; it should be noted that in 2019 the Irish Language Commissioner's investigation found that RTÉ had failed in its statutory obligation to the Irish language, and was in breach of the Broadcasting Act:

> Only 1 per cent of programming on RTÉ Radio One and RTÉ 2FM was in Irish, with just 0.1 per cent on RTÉ Lyric FM. Those figures are lower than many commercial and community radio stations and are in line with the commissioner's finding that only 0.7 per cent of television output is in Irish. [Dr John Walsh, Lack of money no excuse for RTÉ's paltry Irish programming, Irish Times, 10th April 2019]

Could there be a conspiracy against the Irish language? On leaving RTE in 1969, Bob Quinn's letter warned of this monolith:

> ..... What can one person do? When confronted by a monolith which proposes to eat you, even in the nicest possible manner, you must do something. The worst thing to do is to allow the monolith to define the terms of battle. Ignore its pleas for logic, because it uses logic to obscure the truth; ignore its calls for reasonableness, the assumptions and premises of which are entirely questionable; query its sacred cows, its gods and its liturgies, its systems, its impeccable phrases imported from the respectable corruption of business management. Ignore above all its offers of a comfortable place in the technocratic womb, its bribes of security, status, and free burial service. Having ignored all of these expressions you will now find yourself out of a job. And you can't afford this because you have a mortgage, an overdraft, a hire-purchase agreement, and a realization that you were never free. So, you will not follow the advice in the preceding paragraph. That is when the organization laughs.
>
> And what do I propose to do about it?
>
> Mine is a personal philosophy of responsible irresponsibility. It attempts to counter the organization's pseudo-philosophy of irresponsible responsibility. If you follow me. I propose to

> get a boat and sail off, Charlie-Bubbles-like into the setting sun. All contributions will be tolerated and appreciated if they're in the form of moral support. [Bob Quinn Letter to RTE 1969, for full account see http://www.indymedia.ie/article/92261]

After leaving RTE, Bob Quinn settled in the village of Carraroe where he founded the film-company Cinegael. His pioneering film Poitin (1979) was the first Irish film drama produced completely in the Irish language. Since then, he has produced over sixty films and he certainly deserves the title 'father of Irish Film' - والد الفيلم الايرلندي.

Bob Quinn noticed, 'the response from conservative academics and particularly 'Celtic' scholars was silence, while silently attacking the thesis.' An exception was Professor Barry Cunliffe, who Quinn says, 'was pleased that a hitherto-repressed perspective on Ireland had seen the light of day.' Through his determination and dedication to the subject, the establishment has recognized Bob Quinn's thesis and his book received official support by the Irish Heritage Council [see https:www.conamara.org, Cinegael - Bob Quinn - Atlantean]

Some of the early reactions to Atlantean are captured in Bob Quinn's book. However, criticism from an unexpected source did leave me bewildered, and is addressed directly by Bob Quinn:

> The same airy disregard was shown recently in The Journal of Music by Dr. Lillis O'Laoire, who attacked O'Riada's and my ideas on the music as 'exoticization'. How many of us - apart from the late Hubert Butler - realized, before the sickening war in the Balkans, the extraordinary proportion of Muslims who are native to and still reside in these European regions? [Bob Quinn]

Lillis O'Laoire, a well-known sean-nós singer from Donegal, wrote an article where he expressed his discomfort with connecting sean-nós with other singing styles from around the world (a disguised attack on Bob Quinn's Atlantean), He wrote:

> One aspect of the notes that disturbs me, however, is the insistent exoticization claimed for traditional Gaelic song, likening it to Flamenco, North African, Asian or Indian singing. Such a strategy is meant to be sympathetic, but it deliberately removes this kind of singing from the real, and places it in one hermetic, a historical, timeless, category,

> rendering it mysterious, eastern, and non-European. The roots of such an imaginary can be traced at least to the eighteenth century and are uncritically presented here as truth more than opinion. Such claims are highly exaggerated. Affinities of approach between various kinds of non-western singing and Irish traditional singing, while they may exist, are no proof of common origin, but this suggestion continues to be advanced, as if it somehow bestows some ineffable quality of superiority on the tradition. [Lillis O'Laoire, Sean-nós Singing & Exoticism, Journal of Irish Music, 1st Jan 2003]

Lillis O'Laoire's comments are disappointing for many reasons. His contribution to Sinead O'Connor's documentary *Sean-nós Nua* was excellent and his description of how Sinead O'Connor performs Singing Bird is worth mentioning:

> Ah yeah, the long note she belts that out, she shares that with the old singers as well. That longing, that absolute want, it is like wanting to be re-joined with a lover. Like in the Sufi tradition, the Muslim tradition it is wanting to be re-joined with God who is imagined as the lover. [Lillis O'Laoire, The Making of Sean-nós Nua, Sinead O'Connor]

The comments he expressed in The Journal of Irish Music seems to contradict the views he expressed in the Sean-nós Nua documentary. Add to this, O'Laoire is from Gort, Donegal, the homeland of the African Formorians. He grew up only 85 km from the coastal area known as 'Bloody Foreland' or Cnoc Fola, literally 'The Hill of Blood'; the place where the African Formorians battled with the Tuatha de Danaans (both rather exotic tribes?).

Ireland's legendary Seán Ó Riada, remembered as Ireland's most talented composer and arranger of traditional Irish music, was the single most influential figure in the revival of Irish traditional music.

On the origin of Sean-nós, Seán Ó Riada said:

> There is not a European musical classical tradition in this

> country [Ireland], there is on the other hand a highly developed traditional music. Which because it is orally transmitted should not be considered folk music. For example, in the Orient you have music that is orally transmitted but is still highly developed, You have the court music of Japan for example.... here we also have a highly developed traditional music, very complex, very sophisticated. But it is more Oriental than Western ......the main part of it is vocal, the song in Irish, many of which can be traced back four or five centuries in their origins. It involves a very highly complex linear ornamentation so that people hearing ot for the first time think that it sounds Arabic music or Persian music. [Seán Ó Riada, Danish television in 1970.]

Seán Ó Riada

(Public domain, via Wikimedia Commons)

Liam Ó Maonlaí, an Irish singer and member of the band Hothouse Flowers, gives a truly hypnotizing rendition of the sean-nós song *Sadhbh Ní Bhruinneallaigh (Bhruinnealla),* which I highly recommend. I will briefly share a story here of when I first encountered this song.

In an interview with Claddagh Films in a Galway restaurant, Liam explains the meaning behind the song. He says, *"A boatman falls in love with Sadhbh (Ní Mhuinghile) from Inis Gé, off the Mayo coast, and he tries to gain her hand in marriage."* She says to the boatman, *"When you get the call to the sea, you'll be gone."* The boatman looking at Sadhbh's clothes, proclaims that he will be able to take care of her, if she elopes with him.

After watching this brief interview, I searched for a longer performance by Liam Ó Maonlaí. I stumbled on a Highland Session with Liam O Maonlaí on vocals and whistle, Kathleen MacInnes - harmony vocals, Allan Henderson – fiddle, Steve Cooney – guitar, Allan MacDonald – harp, Jim Sutherland - drum-box and bodhran, and Neil Johnstone – cello. The performance was truly magnetic and captivated me and is something I will not forget. Especially since listening to Liam's voice, I was able to use my intuitive Sufi skills to read his voice and pick up on any relevant ancestral memories. For a whole week this song could be heard on replay in my house, as I enjoyed the Sufi visions that were accessible through the tune. Visions of Liam in Mali kept appearing in my 'minds-eye' – so vivid, like a movie. A week later I decided to try and find out if there was a connection between Liam and Mali; and to my surprise my visions were accurate:

> Dambé: The Mali Project is a documentary film directed by Dearbhla Glynn (Dublin to Gaza), and produced by Vanessa Gildea. The film documents as the Irish musicians Liam Ó Maonlaí and Paddy Keenan embark on a musical adventure to Mali in West Africa. Travelling over 3,000 miles they meet and collaborate with people from musicians (Afel Bocoum, Toumani Diabaté) to nomadic herders, culminating in a performance at the remote musical festival 'Festival au Désert.' [Wikipedia]

This is proof that sean-nós has a powerful hidden message, that connects people in unusual ways. In an interview with German NRW live, Liam Ó Maonlaí carefully explained his thoughts on sean-nós:

> Our culture is a living culture, a network of music and unspoken philosophy – the philosophy is within the music, and then its linked to the language as well, so its ancestry. On our national radio we don't get to hear much of our traditional culture. It is marginalized like Native American culture and dissed.... this stands up in the world, its yours Irish people and for the whole world; it can fuel their own DNA. [Liam Ó Maonlaí, interview on NRW live Teil 1]

Unfortunately, academic still have not dropped the label 'Celtic' -a name that should not be applied to the Gaels or Britons. This edition provides a chance to evaluate the current 'Celtic from the West' hypothesis, proposed by Professor Barrington Cunliffe and Professor John T. Koch, et al. At the same time, I unashamedly promote in this edition an alternative theory that clearly points to Africa and the southern Mediterranean as the homeland of the

Gaels and Cymry.

This edition also provides me with an opportunity to share, for the first time, the foot shape research I conducted over 20 years ago. Phyllis Jackson's pioneering work on foot shapes created a new branch of ethnoarchaeology. Her work was first published in Current Archaeology. She advised me on the foot shapes that I had collected, and shared aspects of her research with me that have not been previously published.

It is important at the outset to remember that the Gaels & Cymry (Britons) never referred to themselves as 'Celts'; a label created 250 years ago. It was a grand conspiracy; aimed at turning the ancient Gaels & Britons into blond, blue-eyed Aryans. Even olive-skinned Mussolini adopted this 'comical' Aryan model in the 1930's, so as to please his German Nazi allies.

Tacitus commented on how the Britons varied in their shape, skin colour and appearance. The first Gallic tribes to arrive in these islands only arrived a few centuries before the Romans arrived.

The language today know as 'Celtic' seems to have spread across Western Europe without an equivalent human migration. Thus, the language arrived before the 'Celts' or Gauls arrived in these islands. Recent evidence suggests that the language spread due to commerce rather than the movement of a people. Modern 'Celtic' languages were adopted by diverse groups across Western Europe. This language encountered African Hamito-Semitic (Afro-asiatic) languages which resulted in the hybrid languages we now called modern Insular 'Celtic'.

So, let's get back to Bob Quinn's Atlantean.

He boldly states, "The Irish are not Celts, but they are not Arab either."

This is certainly true!

Bob Quinn is adamant that the Irish, Cymry, and Scots should never be referred to as 'Celts' - a label invented by Abbe Paul Yves Pezron (1639-1706), a Breton theologian from France.

Carol M. Davison gives a good summary, in 'Scottish Gothic: An Edinburgh Companion, on how the name 'Celtic' was adopted:

> 'Celtic' separatism was properly inaugurated in 1703, when Paul Pezron published his L'antiquite de la nation et de la

> langue des Celtes, autrement appellez Gaulois, translated in 1706 by David Jones as The Antiquities of Nations; more particular of the Celtae or Gauls, taken to be originally the Same People as our Ancient Briton.....That suggestive subtitle, 'the Celtae or Gauls, taken to be the Same People as our Ancient Britons, was Jone's own contribution - and his own invention.....Pezron's aim was to construct an Armorican national myth for France, with the Bretons as the aboriginal French race and, in doing so, proposed the Celts as the forefathers of both the Gauls and Ancient Britons........The Keeper of the Ashmolean Museum in Oxford, Edward Lhuyd, who had encouraged Jones to translate Pezron, published his own Archaeologia Britannica in 1707 and took the cause of 'Celtic' separatism further by linking the Cornish, Irish, Manx, Scots and Welsh language to Breton: these languages, he decided, were "Celtic'/k' and the people who spoke them 'Celts'. Although Cunliffe suggests that Lhuyd only adopted such terms because 'Gaulish' sounded too French and implied Jacobite and Catholic sympathies. [p20]

Simon James in his book Atlantic Celts (1999) hints at a conspiracy when he comments:

> 'It is, at very least, a remarkably fortuitous coincidence that the concept of 'Celtic' speakers, and by implication ethnic Celts, in Britain, Brittany and Ireland was first published in 1707. That was the very year that the Treaty of Union between England and Scotland saw the official creation of a new political identity called British......with the signing of the Treaty, then, the name was appropriated for all subjects of the new English dominated superstate.'

Edward Lhuyd's work gained so much academic support, the natives of these islands would now be called 'Celtic' even though the 'Celts' or Gaul reached Britain only a short time before the Romans. The Welsh Triads firmly proclaims that 'the Galedin [Gaul/Celts] would only become Cymry (i.e., Britons] after 9 generations in this island, however, they would not have any claim to the land.' They were tribal newcomers - Pezron's motives were simple; as a Frenchman he aimed to extend the name 'Celtic' to Britain, thereby giving Breton Nationalism a much-needed injection of self-esteem and prestige. Lhuyd's acceptance and propagation of this new idea was foolish.

While the Irish and Cymry were converted into 'Celts' overnight - something even stranger was happening in London. The Royal House of England and the English aristocracy started to claim descent from the Royal House of David in Palestine. The Anglo-Israelites or Hebrew Anglo-Saxons started to become an adopted identity amongst the English aristocracy. Even Ireland's most sacred site at Tara was claimed and excavated (1899 & 1902) by the English Anglo-Israelites. However, William Butler Yeats, George Moore, and Douglas Hyde, opposed this and demonstrated openly against this violation of Ireland's most sacred burial site. Mairéad Carew's fascinating book *'Tara and the Ark of the Covenant'* is worth reading. It seems the colonist will always re-write the past to justify the oppressive actions they have been guilty of.

When reviewing Bob Quinn's four-part documentary series Atlantean, it should be remembered that the DNA evidence was not available back then. Not so long ago, the BBC Weather Broadcasts did not include the Irish Republic.

Bob Quinn humorously noted:

> "the colonizer has even edited Irish out of the weather.' He asked, "has this happened with written histories" [Bob Quinn Atlantean Documentary]

The answer is an overwhelming YES.

The BBC Weather Broadcasts did include the weather over France, Belgium, Spain, and even Iceland. The Irish Republic, only a few hundred miles away, was excluded. The only news that we consumed in Britain was coverage of the 'troubles' - the struggle between the Irish Republican Army, Loyalist Paramilitary Groups, and the occupying British Army - nothing else was covered by the British media.

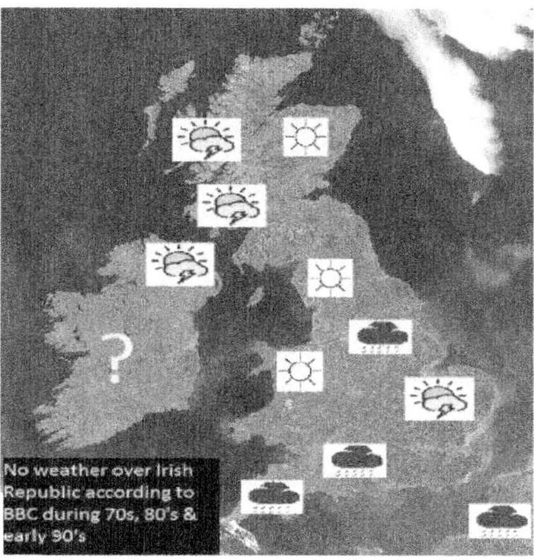

No Weather over the Irish Republic
according to BBC News in the 70', 80's & early 90's

The Gaeltacht (Irish speaking) region of Ireland was the only place that made sense to him. In the documentary he recalls how school told him he was something called a 'Celt' - he realized he was suffering from a colonized mind.

What started him off was the Azzan - the Muslim call to pray and it's striking similarity to Irish sean-nós; the traditional unaccompanied singing style still practiced in the Gaeltacht regions of Ireland. There are different styles of singing across Ireland. The Conamara style (my favorite) has an amazingly soft, ethereal approach, illustrated by Róisín Elsafty. Róisín's performance of *Seoithín, seo hó*, an old Irish lullaby, is a fine example of her talent. Conamara sean-nós is powerful because of its ability to transmit ancestral memory embedded deeply within the tunes. Contained within these old songs are powerful memories; that can be unlocked by intuitive people with open hearts. I believe the heart can translate these songs through visions; taking the listener back in time to re-live the experiences of previous generations. Empathic listeners cannot resist the hidden emotions that inhabit sean-nós. Julie Henigan has the following conclusion about sean-nós:

> Sean-nós, in conclusion, cannot be reduced to a single definition; rather, it has many different levels of meaning, depending upon the context in which the term is used. It may be used to describe distinct performance styles - or to refer to the singing tradition as a whole. In this larger sense, sean-nós embodies the many interrelated aspects of the tradition, including performance style, performance context, social function, and repertoire. On a personal level, sean-nós has as many meanings as there are members of the tradition - and as

> many functions. It can serve at once as a form of entertainment, as an emotional release, and as a means of communication, expressing life as it enriches it, creating connections with the community and with the world at large.

Sean-nós connects Ireland with its spiritual past and ancestral memory. It preserves the language and allows the release of emotions trapped within the cellular memory and aura. The experience of the past comes alive; through a mechanism called epigenetics. Music unleashes memories which have a profound influence on human DNA. Human memory can turn genes off or on; trauma can be passed down, as well as blessings. Even if one does not speak Gaelic, it is possible to absorb the meaning through intuition and empathy; it allows anyone to enjoy this ancient music.

In 1947 BBC Radio Wales produced a program dedicated to exploring the connection between the Welsh hwyl and the Muslim Azzan. The Welsh hwyl is a melodic chanting style used by Welsh preachers. Even Giraldus Cambrensis (12th century AD) had something to say on this:

> In their musical concerts they do not sing in unison like the inhabitants of other countries, but in many different parts; so that in a company of singers, which one very frequently meets with in Wales, you will hear as many different parts and voices as there are performers, who all at length unite, with organic melody, in one consonance and the soft sweetness of B flat. In the northern district of Britain, beyond the Humber, and on the borders of Yorkshire, the inhabitants make use of the same kind of symphonious harmony, but with less variety, singing only in two parts, one murmuring in the base, the other warbling in the acute or treble. Neither of the two nations has acquired this peculiarity by art, but by long habit, which has rendered it natural and familiar; and the practice is now so firmly rooted in them, that it is unusual to hear a simple and single melody well sung; and, what is still more wonderful, the children, even from their infancy, sing in the same manner. As the English in general do not adopt this mode of singing. [p498, The historical works of Giraldus Cambrensis Thomas Wright 1894]

Giraldus further speculates as to where the Britons (Cymry) acquired their boldness and confidence in speaking:

> The English also, although placed in a distant climate, still retain the exterior fairness of complexion and inward coldness of disposition, as inseparable from their original and natural character. The Britons, on the contrary, transplanted from the hot and parched regions of Dardania [Troy] into these more temperate districts, as "Coelum non animum mutant qui trans mare currunt," still retain their brown complexion and that natural warmth of temper from which their confidence is derived. [Thomas Wright, 'The historical works of Giraldus Cambrensis', p500,1894]

Ronald L. Lewis in his book 'Welsh Americans: A History of Assimilation in the Coalfields' gives the following description of the Welsh Hwyl:

> Welsh preachers became known for their dynamic preaching and Welsh hwyl. This distinctively Welsh characteristic was often the subject of comment. One writer described it this way: The best description I can give of this peculiarity is this: it is the application of sentences in a chanting style to portions of the minor scale. The minister is never at a loss how to apply the words to the melody; they appear to run together as by mutual attraction. The sentence is started, for instance, on E minor. The minister has his own peculiar melody. It ranges here and there from the first to the fifth, often reaching the octave, and then descending and ending in a sweet cadence on the keynote. I am sure that in the genuine hwyl the intonations are always in the minor mode. The introduction and the deliberate parts are in the major, and the voice continues thus until the emotional point is reached; then it glides triumphantly into a thrilling minor, which generally continues to the close. [p143]

The Norman invasion brought devastation to Ireland. There was a clash of cultures. Giraldus gives a deeply offensive, and unfair portrayal of the Irish. They are demonized by the Normans; a tactical approach to justify the brutal invasion of Ireland. Bob Quinn commented on how a similar tactic was used when Iraq was demonized just before it was invaded by the 'Western' countries. Irish civilization was more advanced than Anglo-Saxon England - the most important center of Christianity in England, Lindisfarne, was founded by Irish monks in AD 635. Giraldus Cambrensis' character assassination of the Irish was intentional and part of a colonial strategy to occupy the country.

Giraldus Cambrensis portrayal of Irish men - the start of anti-Irish propaganda c.1188 A.D. The historical works of Giraldus Cambrensis Thomas Wright 1894 public domain

Giraldus Cambrensis portrayal of an Irish woman. More anti-Irish propaganda from the Normans c. 1188 A.D

The description of Ireland given by Giraldus Cambrensis was designed to demonize the Irish and justify an English invasion. He unfairly accuses the Irish of being very ignorant of the rudiments of the faith:

> The faith having been planted in the island from the time of St. Patrick, so many ages ago, and propagated almost ever since, it is wonderful that this nation should remain to this day so very ignorant of the rudiments of Christianity. It is indeed a most filthy race, a race sunk in vice, a race more ignorant than all other nations of the first principles of the faith. Hitherto they neither pay tithes nor first fruits; they do not contract marriages, nor shun incestuous connections; they frequent not the church of God with proper reverence. Nay, what is most detestable, and not only contrary to the Gospel, but to everything that is right, in many parts of Ireland brothers (I will not say marry) seduce and debauch the wives of their brothers deceased, and have incestuous intercourse with them; adhering in this to the letter, and not to the spirit, of the Old Testament ;* and following the example of men of old in their vices more willingly than in their virtues. [p135, The Historical Works of Giraldus Cambrensis, Thomas Wright, 1894]

Quinn's brief look at the exotic and the mysterious carvings called Síle na Giġh [pronounced Sheela nah Ghee] is fascinating. They are prominently displayed on many old Churches and Castles. These pagan fertility symbols have also been found in many parts of Africa and the Middle East - where they date back to the Neolithic and Bronze Age era. Astonishingly, the Síle na Giġh in Ireland and Britain, that openly adorn many Christian Churches, were introduced by the Normans. These crude figures were not in line with Brehon Law, and belong to the Normans rather than the Gaels.

The Sheela na gig project, which has carefully documented the distribution of these carvings across both Ireland and Britain, states that these carvings are normally found on Churches built by Normans and are of Romanesque design. They have also been found on secular buildings and can also be found on many castles.

The Austerfield Sheela na gig (Yorkshire, England) is described in the as follows:

> The present church was built in 1080 AD by John de Bully .... as a Chapel of Ease for the people of Austerfield. They had previously been making a 12-mile round trip every Sunday to attend Blythe Priory. John de Bully lived from 1054 to 1089 (?), since the church would have been built between these dates or soon after, it places the carving of the sheela firmly in a Norman context but one which is quite early for a UK sheela na gig. This of course assumes that the sheela was carved at the time of building. Even if the sheela is a later addition the pillars are still Norman work (12th century?). Whichever century the pillars belong to it still firmly places the figure in a Norman context. [sheelanagig.org]

The Sheela na gig embedded in the walls of churches across Ireland and Britain raises a lot of questions. Why do we find these occult symbols on every Norman Church?

Brehon Law and native Irish customs were directly opposed to Roman customs. The cultural practices observed amongst the Irish peasants, such as the belief in the existence of the evil eye, polygamous marriage, and the belief in spiritual beings (*the shee* or 'The Good People') all have more in common with Sufi Islam than with Romano-Christianity.

Quinn succinctly says, *"A Roman version of a Palestinian religion."*

Did pre-Christian Ireland have more in common with Sufi Islam?

The Muslim proclaim *'Alhamdulillah'* and the Irish always say, *'God Bless.'* Both invocations are intended to ward off the evil eye. The Irish and the Muslims both believe that if you see something that pleases you must immediately say aloud *'God Bless'* - so that the evil eye is not cast upon the person or animal admired. Both cultures believe babies and children are particularly susceptible to the evil eye. Irish women wore headscarves, as protection against the glance of envy (the evil eye).

The Irish sidhe are identical to the *jinn* in Islam. They are a separate distinct people (of different density), with families and clans, and special dwelling places. Eddie Lenihan, a folklore expert from County Clare, has spent decades researching and collecting old folk stories about these unseen people. He has studied the life of the famous healer Biddy Early, who is said to have come from Carraroe. She was gifted with second sight and had the extraordinary ability to heal people. She had knowledge of herbs and was said to be able to get advice with the help from the unseen *'Good People'* - the same tradition is held by Muslims who call these spirits jinns. In Islam, the jinns are very diverse; some obey God and help mankind, while others are mischievous and cause havoc.

Every village in Ireland had traditional healers. Biddy Early became famous across Ireland, and regularly came into conflict with the Roman Catholic priests. This was a vastly different Ireland. It was a place where a man could have more than one wife; saying God bless helped ward off the evil eye; piseogs (i.e., people who cast spells) where banished and not killed; priests were afraid of healers with second sight; and it was normal for ordinary peasants to see the unseen people (sidhe/jinns) and not be regarded as *'crazy'*. This was a vastly different Ireland; indeed, as the song says, 'Once upon a time there was, Irish ways and Irish Laws.'

Based on our knowledge of Irish healers and their traditions, the Sheela na gig seem to be out of place and directly opposite to the beliefs held by the Irish peasantry. The Evil Eye and piseogs were outlawed by Brehon Law. If a person was found guilty of performing black magic, or guilty of spreading the 'evil touch' - they were banished from their community. These beliefs have continued into modern times. A report in the Farming Independent proclaimed, "Even today land blessing traditions survives as farmers seek to ward off piseogs." [see Caitriona Murphy, Farming Independent, 3rd May 2011].

Eddie Lenihan's account of a farmer who suspected his neighbor of being a piseogs is enthralling:

At dawn, he watched as the old woman crept into his field and searched for a cow pat. Crouching over it, she drew a reaping hook through the dung repeatedly, chanting "All for me, all for me, all for me." The furious farmer confronted the old woman and his cattle never pined again. *[Eddie Lenihan,*

Irish folklore expert]

This gives us a clue as to the real nature of the Sheela na gig and the piseogs. Menstrual, feces, and other impure liquids were used by piseogs to harm people - a form of Babylonian magic.

Before you dismiss this as 'mumbo jumbo', consider for a moment the powerful influence menstrual can have on people. Scientists have discovered that pole dancers earned more money during their menstrual cycle:

> The fact that tip earnings peak during estrus suggests that men can detect female fertility more accurately than the "concealed ovulation" model suggested. [Geoffrey Miller, et al., 2007, 'Ovulatory cycle effects on tip earnings by lap dancers: economic evidence for human estrus?']

Irish and Scottish folklore lore boldly states that piseogs (and oculists) went to Spain and Italy to learn black magic.

The Gaels had a different relationship with the unseen. Ireland was a nation dominated by healers and wise women gifted with the power of second sight. Sadly, the famine brought a complete change to Irish society. By the mid 1800's the Church started to have more of a presence in the west of Ireland. The Roman Church was able to extend its control into areas which had remained opposed to the church's doctrine. The Roman Church was fervently opposed to the healers and forbade all priest from performing any traditional healing. When the Penal Laws were relaxed, the Church began its expansion into the Gaeltacht region; giving them control of the schools. Most of the peasants did not attend mass before the famine - it was only after the devastating famine that the Church managed to gain real influence over the rural Irish.

Ireland was the home for many different faiths. According to legend St Patrick drove out the snakes from Ireland. Bob Quinn has a vastly different interpretation. He believes that Naas, in County Kildare, was the scene of a showdown between the Naasenes, from North Africa, and the Roman Church. The Hebrew word for serpent is nāḥāš. Interestingly, the town motto of Kildare is *'Prudens un Serpens'* meaning 'the wisdom of the snake.' Ronnie Kinnane, a local historian, told reporter Nuala Woulfe that 'Kildare and Nas, in particular, were associated with St. Patrick.' *[see Snakes on a terrain in Kildare, The Irish Examiner, 16th March 2005].*

An expert on this subject, William Cooper, devoted his life to unveiling secret societies. His radio show, Hour of The Time, and his book Behold the Pale Horse revealed many things about the Babylonian Mystery School: The transcripts of William Cooper's Mystery Babylon series make fascinating reading.

> Gnosticism, which practices initiation, ecstasy and some rituals which have been said to resemble those of the Freemasons. [And of course, they do, because they are. (laughs) In every Masonic temple you will see somewhere up on the wall a big letter 'G'. And you will see it in their symbology, in their books. You will see this letter 'G'. And if you ask a Freemason, being bound by the oath never to tell you or reveal you the secrets to the profane—which is what they call those who are not initiates, or adepts in the Mysteries—he will tell you it's for God, but that is a lie. That does not stand for God, for I have researched it deeply, all the way up the ladder of the stages of initiation. And at the top, those adepts known as the Priesthood know this large letter 'G' to represent Gnosticism. And it is an admission that they are indeed the recipients of the ancient Gnostic. They are Gnostics, and they are looking to attain the gnosis, through which they will receive Apotheosis. And they believe that they are the only ones in the world who possess truly mature minds and, thus, the only ones in the world capable of ruling the rest of us, whom they refer to as cattle—cattle. [see Transcripts of William Cooper's Mystery Babylon Series, The history, the dogma, and the identity of Mystery Babylon. [see hour of the time website for Bill Cooper-mp3 collection]

Ironically, William Cooper's controversial research suggests that the Mystery Babylonian religion, also known as the Luciferian faith, has infiltrated many aspects of modern society. All the Norman Churches and Castles found scattered across Britain and Ireland, have embedded in the wall's strange phallic symbols and Síle na Giġh (*the Hag*); both are obvious signs of a secret Babylonian religion.

In 'old' Ireland, the serpent worshippers of Nas would have been referred to as piseogs; people that practiced 'dark occult' witchcraft [like the Tuatha de Danaans]. The Síle na Giġh (pronounced Sheela nah Ghee) embedded in old Church walls, clearly resemble the menstrual flux of the 'goddess' Kali in many South Indian sculptures. Is it a coincidence that Shelagh was also the folkloric "wife of St Patrick"? [see website, Satan in The Groin, exhibitionist carvings on medieval churches]

Herodotus mentions in his 'Histories' the shameful occult Babylonian custom that took place in their Temples. The cult of the Shelagh na Ghee is connected to '*a demonic*' marriage' or offering to the 'deity' *Betis* ("the lady") of the Phoenicians or the Babylonian *Mylitta/Ishtar* - hence, their Temples were places of forced prostitution and abuse:

> 199. The Babylonians have one most shameful custom* Every woman born in the country must once in her life go and sit down in the precinct of Venus, and there consort with a stranger. Many of the wealthier sort, who are too proud to mix with the others, drive in covered carriages to the precinct, followed by a goodly train of attendants, and there take their station. But the larger number seat themselves within the holy enclosure with wreaths of string about their heads, and here there is always a great crowd, some coming and others going; lines of cord mark out paths in all directions among the women, and the strangers pass along them to make their choice. A woman who has once taken her seat is not allowed to return home till one of the strangers throws a silver coin into her lap, and takes her with him beyond the holy ground. When he throws the coin he says these words " The goddess Mylitta prosper thee." (Venus is called Mylitta by the Assyrians.) The silver coin may be of any size; it cannot be refused, for that is forbidden by the law, since once thrown it is sacred. The woman goes with the first man who throws her money, and rejects no one. When she has gone with him, and so satisfied the goddess, she returns home, and from that time forth no gift however great will prevail with her. Such of the women as are tall and beautiful are soon released, but others who are ugly have to stay a long time before they can fulfil the law. Some have waited three or four years in the precinct. 2 A custom very much like this is found also in certain parts of the island of Cyprus. [Herodotus, Histories vol 1, G. Rawlinson, 1910]

The Anglo-Normans left a trail of Shelagh na Ghees in regions they occupied, they adorned their castles and churches with the '*hag*', a clear linked to the pagan occult:

> Scholars disagree about the origins of the figures. James Jerman and Anthony Weir believe that the sheela na gigs were first carved in France and Spain during the 11th century; the motif eventually reached Britain and then Ireland in the 12th

> century. Jerman and Weir's work was a continuation of research begun by Jorgen Andersen, who wrote The Witch on the Wall (1977), the first serious book on sheela na gigs. Eamonn Kelly, Keeper of Irish Antiquities at the National Museum of Ireland in Dublin, draws attention to the distribution of sheela na gigs in Ireland to support Weir and Jerman's theory; almost all of the surviving in situ sheela na gigs are found in areas of Anglo-Norman conquest (12th century). The areas that remained "native Irish" have few sheela na gigs. [https://en.wikipedia.org/wiki/Sheela_na_gig]

Note: it is worth noting that the Babylonians did not have any knowledge of healing. Herodotus tells us:

> 197. The following custom seems to me the wisest of their institutions next to the one lately praised. They have no physicians, hut when a man is ill, they lay him in the public square, and the passers-by come up to him, and if they have ever had his disease themselves or have known anyone who has suffered from it, they give him advice, recommending him to do what- ever they found good in their own case, or in the case known to them; and no one is allowed to pass the sick man in silence without asking him what his ailment is.

[Brehon Law had healing at its core, while the Roman Church persecuted healers such as Biddy Early. Why?]

Not many people are aware that Coptic Egyptian Christians settled in Ireland long before St Patrick:

> Coptic influence in Ireland has understandably led many to adopt a theory of direct Coptic activity. A. S. Atiya, in analyzing the missionary activities of the early Coptic Church, states that there is "little doubt" regarding the arrival of Coptic monks in the British Isles "on the edge of medieval Europe." Such faith in the missionary ability of Egyptian monks is certainly strengthened by the historically documented tenacity of these cenobites to seek isolation. Fortunately, in the case of Switzerland, a specific Coptic monk, St. Mauritius, may be named as a possible cultural link. Martyred with the Theban legion in A.D. 285 in Switzerland, Mauritius became an object of local veneration, and his statue presently stands in St. Moritz. Three of his companions, Felix, Regula, and

> Exuperantius, were believed to have reached the Lake of Zurich, where they baptized converts until they were beheaded by Roman officials........ Other Coptic saints in Switzerland include St. Warina of Garagos (Upper Egypt), venerated at Zurich at Aargau, and St. Buqtor (Victor) whose relics were taken to Geneva in the fifth century. Further evidence for the presence of Egyptians in Switzerland has been noted in the atypical predominance granted within that country to St. Anthony, the founder of Egyptian monasticism. [Robert K. Ritner, Jr., Egyptians in Ireland: A Question of Coptic Peregrinations']

Quinn mentions the presence of Egyptian monks in Ireland. The settlement of Coptic Egyptians and the spread of Coptic Christianity into Ireland occurred long before St. Patrick. Robert K. Ritner, Jr. in his paper, '*Egyptians in Ireland: A Question of Coptic Peregrinations*', comments about these Egyptian settlers:

> As late as 825, the Irish monk and geographer Dicuil in his De Mensura Orbis Terrae speaks of having learned the geography of Egypt from a fellow brother. Indeed, actual reference to Egyptians in Ireland is contained in the litany of St. Oengus in the Book of Leinster: "Seven Egyptian monks in Disert Ullaigh, I invoke unto my aid through Jesus Christ." The "disert" or "desert" in which we find these monks represented is an isolated hermitage, so styled in Ireland in memory of their Egyptian desert origin. [Egyptians in Ireland: A Question of Coptic Peregrinations]

Tau Cross and West Pier Toraigh, Tory Island, Ireland. Showing Coptic Influence. (Attributed to David Baird creative commons via Wikimedia Commons.)

W. G. Wood-Martin [1892] confirms the Egyptian influence in Ireland. He states, *'evidently part of the lid of a flagon, bears a human head in profile, with ornaments, the style of which shows the workmanship to have been influenced by Egyptian ideas.'*

Egyptian influence in Ireland W.G. Wood-Martin, Traces of the elder faiths of Ireland: a folklore sketch; a handbook of Irish pre-Christian traditions

Brehon Law and the beliefs held by Irish peasants had more in common with Sufi Islam than with the Roman version of Christianity. The Gaels were not colonized by the Romans. Many different religions and sects found refuge in Ireland. Gnostics, Coptic Christians, and even Muslim Moors found a safe place in Ireland. The Moorish Science Temple of America believes Ireland was once part of the Moorish Empire. They believe that the 'Celts' were Moslem, and that black-moors from northern Africa settled in Ireland. The belief that the Irish use to be Muslim is very widespread. *[see Peter Lamborn Wilson, Moorish Pilgrimage to Ireland]*

Quinn mentions the Blue Men or *Fir Garem.* He explains that the word used to describe a man from Africa is not black-man but blue-man; and that even the northern town of Ballymena was settled by seven Egyptian monks in the 10th century. Could this be memory of Gormund The African?

Geoffrey of Monmouth, in his book *'The History of the Kings of Britain'*, gives an account of Gormund the African who landed in Ireland with 100,000 troops. He launched an invasion of Britain, conquered Loegria (now central England), and then gifted the land to the Saxons. This Loegria then morphed into Mercia, which was ruled by King Offa from 757 AD to 796 AD.

Why did this Anglo-Saxon King produced Islamic Coins proclaiming *'There is no God but Allah alone' - the Shahadah?*

King Offa defeated the Cymry (Welsh) and pushed them further west.

Did he recruit African mercenaries and make an alliance with Gormund the African?

Russia was the focus of the fourth film in the Atlantean series. Commenting on the music of the Tartars, Brian O'Ruairc says, "*I've heard lots of music from different countries, but that's the closest to sean-nós I've ever heard.*"

Quinn makes the long journey to Kazan, the capital of Tatarstan, to find out why they sang in the same style as the people of Conamara. DNA analysis has shown that the Tartar Bashkir share the same DNA as the Irish and Welsh. The dominant Y-DNA haplogroups frequency for Bashkir males is haplogroup R1b (R-M269 and R-M73), found in around 47.6%. This R1b haplogroup arrived in Ireland during the Bronze Age. It spread from the Pontic-Caspian steppe and swept down across the southern Mediterranean Sea; finally arriving in the Iberian Peninsula.

Trying to unravel these migration patterns is key to understanding the origins of the Gaels and Britons. New research has completely changed our understanding of ancient human migration patterns. The addition of strontium isotope analysis has assisted in the unravelling of this complicated mystery.

'Celtic' art, Quinn reveals, did not have its birth in Central Europe, but had its inspiration in Egypt, Syria, and other eastern nations. The Egyptian Coptic interlacing pattern inspired the patterns that would later appear in the Book of Kells and other similar works. These interlacing patterns are also found further south in East Africa and the Azanian coast of Tanzania.

Nora Chadwick in her book *'The Age of Saints in Early 'Celtic Church'* believed there was strong connection between the British Isles and the eastern Mediterranean:

> We must postulate a strong intellectual influence from the East Mediterranean whether directly or indirectly, possibly through Aquitaine or Spain......We know from the personal letters of the fifth century of the lively intercourse of Saint Jerome and the exchange of books with Saint Augustine and the other scholars of the North African Church........For us the most important results of the pronouncement of these art historians are that the 'Celtic' manuscripts of this early period exhibit art forms wholly independent of Merovingian style, and closely related to those of Coptic and Syrian manuscripts; that certain individual features are found also in somewhat later Spanish manuscripts though unknown elsewhere; and that certain of these early features of manuscript illumination are found also on the cross of Carmdonagh and Fahan Mura in then north of Ireland........Britain and southern Ireland shared the literary culture of Aquitaine at this period. In particular there are indications that southern Ireland was in active communication with the outside world, especially Aquitaine and North Africa. [p51-53, Nora Chadwick, The Age of Saints in Early 'Celtic' Church]

What is important about Bob Quinn's work is that he is not afraid to challenge the Eurocentrics. He says, *"I want to challenge the lies of history. Eurocentricity, racism, and intellectual treason."*

The subject of Charlemagne, the Vikings and Islam makes Quinn ask the question, *"What was the extend of Arab cultural influence a thousand years ago? The dollar brings Coca-Cola, Dallas, and Consumerism. What baggage did Arab silver bring a thousand years ago."*

In what was a great piece of detective work, Quinn asks, *"Did Islam finance the revival of Charlemagne's Christian Empire in Europe? If so, what was the reason for this?"*

Many people do not realize that Charlemagne was a Unitarian Christian, sharing much in common with Muslims: Jesus was regarded as human and not divine, also both did not accept the trinity. Muslims naturally regarded Charlemagne's people as allies (people of the Book). The Muslims were motivated by the desire to assist the spread of Monotheism and thus promote Christianity.

Quinn's conclusions are remarkably refreshing; simply ahead of everybody else:

> The Dark Ages were a Euro-centric fiction.
>
> Gaelic Ireland and Arabic Spain were the civilized world at that time.
>
> The revival of Christianity in 8th and 9th centuries was financed by Islam.

Quinn concludes:

> "The Dark Ages did exist, but they only applied to post Roman, Central Europe - while language, art, and culture still flourished like a river around edges of Europe. Sean-nós singing is the missing soundtrack, it must be heeded."

We can see that Bob Quinn's journey of exploration was so far in advance of others. He did not have the advantage of DNA studies and yet he was able to intuitively search for the truth.

Most schools and universities teach the old 'Aryan' model: the Hallstatt-La Tene model, where blond 'Celts' arrive in Britain and Ireland during the Iron Age (*starting c.800 BC*).

'Celtic from the West' proposed by Professor Cunliffe and Professor Koch, et al., places the 'Celtic' homeland in Iberia. The problem with this theory is that there is no evidence of any significant migration of 'Celts' into these islands.

The African Substratum Theory, that I lay out in this edition, proposes an African homeland for the Gaels and Cymry (ancient Britons). They spoke an African language that most likely belonged to the Hamito-Semitic (Afro-asiatic/Afrasian/Erythraic) language family. They eventually adopted an Indo-European language, during the Iron Age, mainly through extensive trade and commerce with Iberia.

There was no large-scale migration of Indo-European speakers until the Angles and Saxons appeared in the 5th century AD. Modern Insular 'Celtic' languages developed and spread due to the growing commerce between the Atlantic 'fringe' countries; it became the lingua franca of the Atlantic zone. The people of Iron Age Britain and Ireland show a close affinity with the African Guanches, Copts of Egypt, Pompeiians, and the Etruscans.

Obviously not Celts!

Bob Quinn's conclusion is needed more today than ever; the world needs to pay more attention to his wise words:

Bob Quinn said,

> 'The Irish have a more exotic past than they think……our traditional shamrock, for example, comes from the Arabic Shamrakh (شمراخ) which signifies any three-leafed plant.'

Shamrocks-
(Image attributed to Jill Wellington from Pixabay)

4 ETHNICITY IN THE ANCIENT WORLD

The word 'ethnic' is used frequently in the media. The term is relatively new; it was only included in the Oxford English Dictionary in 1972. The modern usage of this term is accredited to Sociologist David Riesman in 1953. The Greek word 'ethnos' originally meant pagan or heathen. Thomas Hylland Eriksen mentions how the term has a negative context:

> In the United States, "ethnics" came to be used around the Second World War as a polite term referring to Jews, Italians, Irish and other people considered inferior to the dominant group of largely British descent.........In everyday language, the word ethnicity still has a ring of "minority issues" and "race relations", but in social anthropology, it refers to aspects of relationships between groups which consider themselves, and are regarded by others, as being culturally distinctive. Although it is true that "the discourse concerning ethnicity tends to concern itself with sub-national units, or minorities of some kind or another" (Chapman et al., 1989: 17), majorities and dominant peoples are no less "ethnic" than minorities. [Thomas Hylland Eriksen, Ethnicity and Nationalism Anthropological Perspectives, third edition, 2010]

Lisa Bond's article, 'The Problem with 'Celtic' Ethnicity', and its misinterpretation, gives an interesting insight into this term:

> Material culture (in culture-historic archaeological terms) is

> assigned to a tribe or ethnic group based on the premise that their religious or cultural norms are prescriptive, and any innovative change is slow unless contact with a more creative group introduces change. This is the 'Diffusionist' approach; the spread of culture change was initiated by a biologically superior race (Jones 1997, 24-25). This had a far-right political implication and was open to abuse, such as the work of Kossinna and the Nazi Party in the 1930s with their attempts to create a national identity through the material record to justify invasion and ethnic cleansing (Trigger 1996). In the history of archaeology importance has been placed on constructing identities by assigning material culture to past ethnicities and the distribution of material culture to migration and invasion theories (Jones 1997, 1).

Lisa Bond draws attention to the fact that the archaeological record does not support the idea of 'Celtic' migrations into regions such as Italy, which has very little recovered material. Many areas that have been presumed 'Celtic', have no evidence of cemeteries or settlements.

The word 'ethnic' is frequently used in confusing ways. The concept of 'race' is a social construct, a product of colonialism and European expansion. The rest of the world has different concepts and ideas about 'ethnic' identity - hence, there is no universally accepted definition of ethnicity.

Ancient Egyptian iconography colourfully depicts the tribes and nations they encountered. Having studied these faces from the past with awe, matching the faces with modern nationalities can be an interesting exercise. It should be remembered that the ancient Egyptians regarded all these nations as foreign; the only exception is the Land of Punt, which the Egyptians regarded as 'God's Land' or 'Land of the Ancestors'.

The Concept of Kinship

The concept of 'race' did not exist in the ancient world - it is a social construct. The recent development of DNA analysis has led some people to suggest that humans can be divided into genetic populations. However, data interpretation can be influenced by the 'cultural' background of the investigator.

Q: When is sub-Saharan DNA not sub-Saharan DNA?

A: The answer is: When it is found in Europe.

The E1b1 y-DNA haplogroup (male) originated in East Africa - where it is classified as sub-Saharan; however, when it appears in Greece and the Balkans, in the form of E1b1 E-V13, it miraculously no longer qualifies to be sub-Saharan by Eurocentric scientists. I wonder, as an E1b1 individual writing in Britain, does my DNA morph from sub-Saharan to European or Eurasian DNA? A rather comical approach by Eurocentrics who currently dominate genetic research.

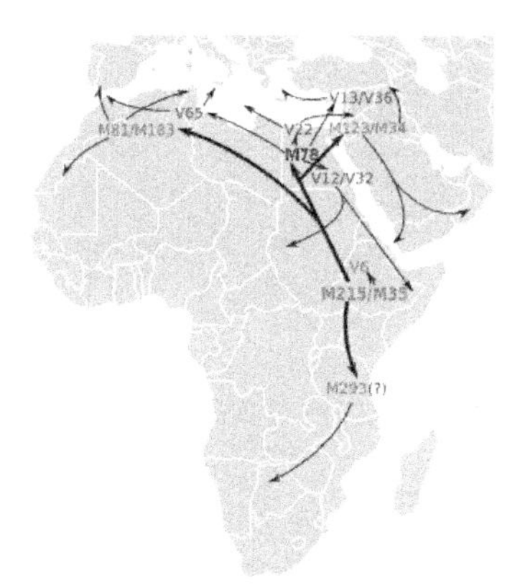

E3b1 and its haplogroups E-M81 and E-M78 and E-M123 out of Africa; Andrew Lancaster creative commons via Wikimedia Commons.

As soon as 'African' haplogroups leave Africa (through human migrations), and then return back to Africa - it is strangely labelled, by Eurocentrics, as a 'Eurasian' – back-migration', a strange use of language. Sergi's 'Eurafrican' theory was abandoned during the late 1920's and 1930's as a result of the rise of fascism in Europe. The term 'Eurafrican' or 'Afro-Mediterranean' was developed by Sergi (the Father of European Anthropology) to describe prehistoric groups of dark-skinned people that migrated from Africa into Europe. Sergi credits these people with the founding of all civilizations in the Mediterranean (i.e., Greece, Italy, Crete, Egypt, etc.).

A published genetic study was able to confirm the substantial gene flow from sub-Saharan Africa into ancient Greece. The paper, *'The Origin of Palestinians and their Genetic Relations with Other Mediterranean Populations'*, throws light on the genetic profile of the Palestinians using human leukocyte antigen (HLA) gene variability and haplotypes. The study unveils some surprising revelations:

> Greeks are found to have a substantial HLA gene flow from sub-Saharan Ethiopian and Black people……This could have occurred when hyper-arid Saharan conditions became established and large-scale migrations occurred in all directions out from the desert. In this case, the most ancient Greek-Pelasgian substratum would come from a negroid

> stock. A more likely explanation is that at an undetermined time during Egyptian pharaonic times a Black dynasty with followers were expelled and went towards Greece where they settle. [Arnaiz-Villena A, et al., Hum Immunol. 2001 Sep;62(9):889-900]

The paper illustrates *[see fig 5]* how the HLA frequencies for the Greek (Aegean), Greeks (Attic), Amhara, Fulani, Oromo, Moss, and Rimaibe are all related according to the HLA-DRB1 allele frequency data. The author then concluded that the data fitted with the account given by Herodotus who mentioned the daughters of Danaus migrating from Egypt in great numbers and settling in Greece.

This paper was later retracted, why?

Ancestry testing is now extremely popular and affordable. People are now able to locate ancestral matches from across the world. This proves that 'race' is a social construct - whereas kinship is the main basis on which society was built. Kinship establishes how individuals and groups are connected through bonds of blood relationships or marriage. For example, the ancient Egyptians and the Hittites eventually made peace after the battle of Kadesh. To seal the peace, Ramesses II married the daughter of the Hittite King Maathorneferure. This created new ancestral ties and bonds. When the Phoenicians were asked by the Persians, under Xerxes, to wage war on the Carthaginians, they refused and replied, '*We cannot wage war on our children.*'

From the earliest of times Irish society was organized around kinship groups. Irish clans consisted of those related by blood and also included individuals who were adopted into the clan. All members, whether blood-related or adopted, bore the same surname.

The concepts of 'ethnic' identity varies around the world. The comedian Wonho Chung was born in Jeddah, Saudi Arabia, and raised in Amman, Jordan. His father was South Korean and his mother Vietnamese. Wonho's upbringing was Arab, and he is proficient in five languages. This comedian's description of an encounter with an Arab taxi drive in the UAE illustrates the different concepts of 'ethnicity' that exist around the world:

> Once I was on the way back from Abu Dhabi to Dubai in a taxi and the driver happen to be Arab. He started talking to

> me .... after an hour's drive we get to Dubai, he turns to me and says: "Are you Syrian?" I said, "No, I'm Korean." He said that was my second guess. I was thinking either Korean or Syrian. [Wonho Chung comedy special Friday Night Live]

The reader may think this is unusual - but people familiar with different phenotypes regularly come to the same conclusion. So, Syrians are sometimes confused with Koreans; and interestingly, the reverse has been known to happen:

> Shin Hyun-joon is a South Korean actor. He is best known for his roles in Barefoot Ki-bong, Stairway to Heaven and the Marrying the Mafia sequels, and as the photographer in the popular music video "Because I'm A Girl" byKISS. In the Korean press he is nicknamed as 아랍왕자 ("Prince of Arab") due to his foreign look and long eyelashes. [wikipedia.org/wiki/Shin_Hyun-joon_(actor)]

It is wildly acknowledged in Korean that Shin Hyun-joon looks Arab. How could Koreans and Arabs be related?

Ancient Syria and Lebanon (Shams) was a melting pot of diverse tribes. The point of this story is to make the reader aware of the diversity of the ancient Mediterranean - it is worth having a brief look at the diverse phenotypes of these tribes.

Faces from the Past

The ancient Egyptians were challenged by a confederation of tribes, known as the Sea People. The two 'super-powers' of the ancient world were the Egyptians and the Hittite empire. The Egyptians faced their Hittite enemy in Syria. Another serious threat came from the north, from a coalition of 'sea people'. Egypt was faced with a coalition of nations that joined together with a single aim – to destroy Egypt.

The Irish Annals mention the Danaans migrating from an island off the coast of Egypt; the Milesians became mercenaries and supported the ancient Egyptians, and the Cymry fled from Italy to Mauretania. Putting faces to some of these characters is a worthwhile task. Ancient people varied in skin colour and phenotype. 'Race' had not been invented yet. Societies were based on kinship ties and not colour. Ancient Egyptian iconography gives a glimpse of what people looked like thousands of years ago. The ancient world was populated by diverse groups that freely mixed with each other.

Keftiu is associated with Caphtor in the Old Testament. In the Table of Nations, they are regarded as being descended from Ham. Most sources tend to associate Keftiu with Crete or Cilicia. They closely resemble the ancient Egyptians; they have the same skin colour and dress in the same manner. The island of Crete plays an important role in Irish folklore. The Tuatha De Danaans were forced out of Crete by the ancient Egyptians. Is this another clue to their real identity? If it is, then they are far removed from 'Celtic' Hallstatt or La Tene culture, currently propagated throughout most universities and schools.

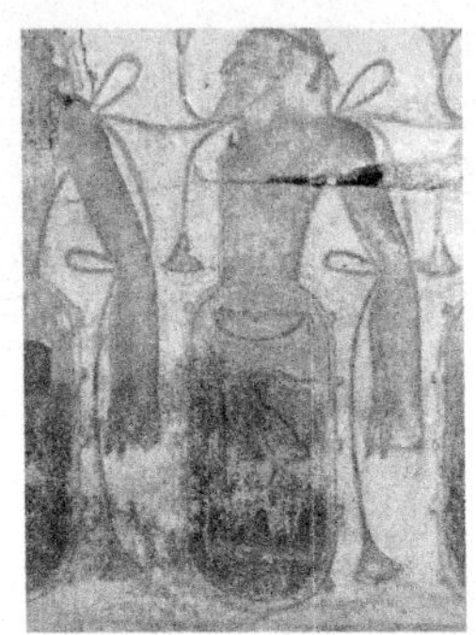

Name-Keftiu-(Cretans)at-Abydos-Ramses-Temple (attributed to HoremWeb, CC via Wikimedia Commons)

The ancient Egyptians encountered a myriad of different tribes. The Hittites, who spoke an early Indo-European language, dominated Anatolia (modern Turkey) and much of the Near East. The genetic analysis of Bronze Age Anatolia indicates that the most common male lineages were J1a, J2a, J2b, and G2a; and to a less extend the male lineages H2, T1a. and E1b1. The phenotype of the Hittites is rather interesting. They clearly have features comparable to south-east Asian populations, particularly Mongolians and Koreans. On close examination, others show African phenotypes. This leads one to question the validity of the Indo-European language classification.

Should the Indo-European language family be regarded as fake? Angela Marcantonio, associate professor of Linguistics at the University of Rome La Sapienza, has raised some important questions about the Indo-European Language Family and its status. This will be discussed in the chapter on 'Pre-Celtic' Languages. From the iconography, the diversity of the population can be seen easily.

From my point of view, the Philistines look like the Fulani or Wodaabe; Ynuamа Syrians (Canaanites) from Retenu look like Koreans; the Damascus Syrians (Canaanites) look like East Africans; some Retenu (Canaanites) look like southern Sudanese; the Sea People have unique features with sloping forehead, large protruding lips, facial-scarification-tattoos, and prominent noses -an interesting combination. A remarkably diverse group of people.

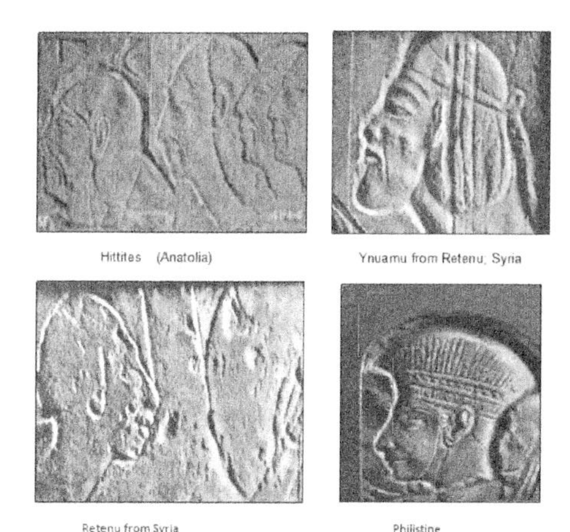

Top left Hittite; top right Syrian; bottom left Syrian; bottom right Philistines. (Flinders Petrie, and Sayce, Public domain.)

Sea People; Shakalashu, Mashauasha, Sherdana, & Shashu. (Petrie public domain)

Philistine, Medinet Hebu Temple

Relief of Hatshepsut's expedition to the Land of Punt attributed to y Σταύρος via wikicommons public domain.

Men fromDamascus - Syria (identical to East African Punt?) [Sayce]

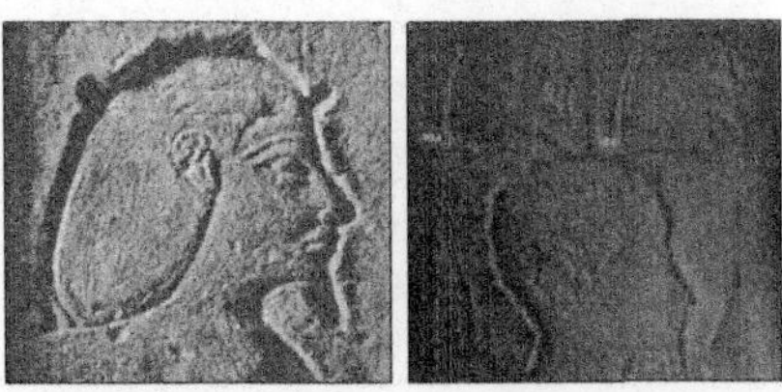

(*Left*) Man fromPunt; (*Right*) Three men from Punt (East Africa) [Sayce]

Men from Syria and men from East Africa Punt

Chief Farehu of Punt
(Hatshepsut expedition to East Africa)

Is the term sub-Saharan African racist?

Eurocentrics use the term sub-Saharan in an inconsistent and racist way. The term was invented with the intent of cleaving ancient Egypt away from Africa. The French and the British divided Africa along artificial Eurocentric concepts, which started with Napoléon's invasion of Egypt in 1798 AD. Napoléon Bonaparte invaded Ottoman controlled Egypt. His aim was to disrupt the British Empire's lucrative control of trade from India. France's control of Egypt only lasted until 1801, when they were ousted by the British. The short-lived occupation of Egypt by the French resulted in an interesting legacy:

> France's presence in Egypt was short-lived. But another aspect of the invasion has left a lasting impression up to the present time. In good French cultural fashion, Napoléon was accompanied in his 1798 invasion by an entourage of 150 prominent scholars and scientists. The intellectual efforts of this group were combined with some 2000 artists and technicians to produce the magisterial Description de L'Égypte (Description of Egypt). Over a twenty-year period, these scholars, scientists, and artists examined and meticulously documented almost every aspect of contemporary and ancient Egyptian civilization, including the flora and fauna. The end result was twenty volumes of texts and plates compiled to make up the Description. These writings and engravings have become the most comprehensive record and inventory of Egypt's landscape,

monuments, and people. [Description de L'Égypte produced by the Bibliotheca Alexandrina in conjunction with the International School of Information Science

This encounter with ancient Egyptian civilization was the beginning of Europe's attempt to impose a 'white' hierarchy onto Africa. They even started looking for a 'white' Prester John of Ethiopia. The real reason for the invention of sub-Saharan Africa was to elevate ancient Egypt into a 'white' Mediterranean civilization; regardless of the fact that Egyptians do not base their identity on skin colour – their identity is based on kinship/tribal affiliations. The tribes of Egypt vary in their colour and features; the Copts, Bisharin, Siwa Oasis tribes, Nubians of Aswan and Luxor, have considerable internal variations.

Neighbouring Libya consists of three main geographical regions, Tripolitania, Fezzan, and Cyrenaica. The inhabitants are equally mixed and show a range of skin colours – the Fezzan is populated by very dark-skinned people, while the coastal region is lighter – however, they are thoroughly heterogenous.

(left) President Anwar Sadat of Egypt, public domain.
(right) President of Libya (2014)Abdul_Hamid_Dbeibeh_(15-04-2021) Government.ru, CC via Wikimedia Commons.

The Libyan President, to the right has an 'Irish look', while the late Egyptian President Anwar Sadat has features typical of the Nile population.

Eurocentrics have created an artificial hierarchy that does not really exist; each person is loyal to his tribe and kinship group, not colour. Geneticists have also played the Eurocentric 'game.' North Africa is genetically identical to East Africa, which is dominated by sub-Saharan (E1b1 DNA). The Tuaregs of central Algeria have black skin and have E1b1 y-haplo DNA, identical to their East African cousins; and yet Algeria is labelled 'white' by the Eurocentrics.

The Sahara has been used by Europeans as an artificial barrier that cuts Africa into two. Geneticists, economists, policymakers, and academics constantly use the term in bizarre ways. An article in the Economist, 'What is sub-Sharan Africa?', acknowledged the inconsistent use of the term:

> The answer might seem obvious. Anywhere south of the desert is, geographically, "sub-Saharan". The first problem is that some countries, like Mauritania, are mostly in the desert itself. And the confusion runs deeper. Consider Somalia and Djibouti, both in the Horn of Africa. They are south of the Sahara, but the IMF oversees them from its Middle East and Central Asia department. The World Bank used to include both countries in sub-Saharan Africa, before moving Djibouti to the Middle East and North Africa in 2000. Meanwhile Eritrea, to the north of both of them, is considered sub-Saharan. And whereas the World Bank includes the Arabic-speaking states of Mauritania and Sudan in sub-Saharan Africa, the IMF does not. [What is sub-Saharan Africa? by L.T. | KAMPALA, Economist, 7th Marc 2019]

The reader can see the nonsense propagated by Eurocentrics. Mauretania located directly in the Sahara is defined as sub-Saharan, even though it is not located south of the Sahara. Geneticists use the term in an incorrect way since Moroccan males have 85% sub-Saharan E1b1 y-haplo DNA – identical DNA to their East African cousins. Scientists suffer from cognitive dissonance when they encounter sub-Saharan E1b1 DNA in Europe. Greece, Italy, Albania, Bulgaria, and Romania have considerable sub-Saharan E1b1 DNA, reaching 50% in some parts. Whenever they discuss this male haplogroup, they conveniently delete any reference to sub-Saharan Africa.

The IMF plays its own games. Suddenly, Djibouti an exceedingly small East African country, was moved from sub-Saharan to Middle East. And yet Eritrea, to the north of Djibouti, is classified as sub-Saharan by the World Bank? A very confusing situation.

The distribution of sub-Saharan Haplogroup E-M78 (Y-DNA), illustrated by the following map, shows that the population of northern Africa is closely related to groups living south of the Sahara.

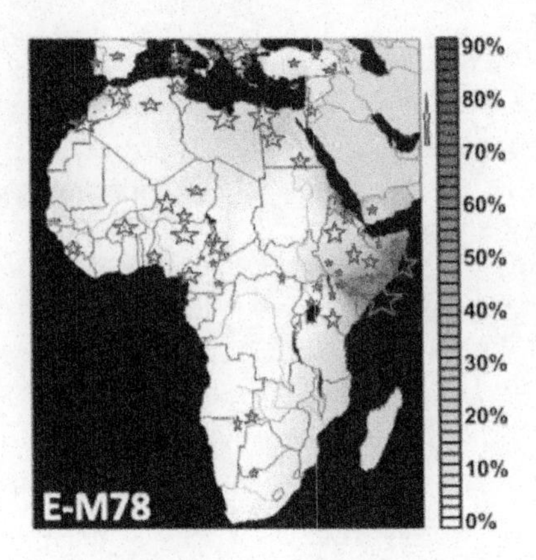

Geographical frequency distribution of Haplogroup E-M78 (Y-DNA) [modified by the author to emphasize cluster with red stars; original available at wikmedia: Attributed to Eugenia D'Atanasio, Beniamino Trombetta, Maria Bonito, Andrea Finocchio, Genny Di Vito, Mara Seghizzi, Rita Romano, Gianluca Russo, Giacomo Maria Paganotti, Elizabeth Watson, Alfredo Coppa, Paolo Anagnostou, Jean-Michel Dugoujon, Pedro Moral, Daniele Sellitto, Andrea Novelletto & Fulvio Cruciani, creativecommons.org/licenses CC via Wikimedia Commons.

5 CELTS BLACK OR WHITE?

The term cognitive dissonance refers to a strong emotional or mental discomfort that arises from having two conflicting beliefs, values, or attitudes. Humans need consistency in their beliefs and perceptions, so this conflict causes feelings of unease or discomfort. School children across Ireland, Scotland and Wales are taught that their ancestors were tall blond-haired 'Celts.' These dark-haired children are supplied with books illustrated with tall, yellow-haired, pale warriors. This results in a disconnection from their own real ethnicity. The 'Atlantic Fringe' countries are believed to have been originally populated by 'Afro-Mediterraneans' [G. Sergi]. Famous examples are Tom Jones, Piers Brosnan, George Clooney, and Catherine Zeta-Jones.

Tom Jones became the focus of international news when the media started to debate his ethnicity. The Daily Mail Online headline on the 1st of November 2015 was, *'I am having a DNA test to see if my ancestors are black, says Sir Tom after being told he is just passing as white.'* The article explained how his thick, curly black hair and his deep voice led people to believe he was black. Tom Jones was born Thomas Jones Woodward in Pontypridd, South Wales. His mother was Welsh, and his father had English ancestry.

Many African Americans have openly ask if Tom Jones had black ancestry. Tom Jones discussed the matter in an interview with CNN's Larry King. *"When I first heard It's Not Unusual,"* Larry King recounts, *"I thought you were black, and many people thought that."* King continues, *"Are you thinking of checking if you have any black ancestry in your DNA."* Tom Jones then opened up and informed King that he was approached by a reporter who asked him if he would be opposed to taking a DNA test. Tom Jones simply replied, *"No I would not be opposed to it."* The reporters then rushed to print *'Tom Jones is*

Taking DNA Test to See If He is Black or Not' - great headlines but not accurate. During the interview Tom Jones did say he thought he might have some black ancestry. Larry King interjected, *"They thought the same about Frankie Lane."* Tom Jones shared how he always sang in that style - *"In school the teacher would ask why he sang the Lords Pray as if it was a 'Negro' spiritual."* Larry King ended this part of the interview by saying, *"It was a great compliment by the way."*

The comments about this interview on social media are worth noting. Some compared him to Ryan Giggs, a Welsh footballer whose grandfather came from Sierra Leone; other said he looked like Smokey Robinson (a famous African-American singer), and most simply thought he was of mixed ancestry.

Comparisons with Frankie Lane is remarkably interesting. His parents were from Monreale, Province of Palermo, Sicily. The similarity between the Cymry, the Italians, and other Mediterranean people is a continuous theme in this book. South Wales singer Tom Jones regarded being thought of as Black as a compliment. His love for 'black' music and the artists he has worked with is genuine. He is greatly respected in the music industry and admired by Black musicians he has worked with for decades.

Sir Tom Jones, Welsh Singer
Attributed to Ralph PH the Queen's Birthday Party (cropped-2), CC wiki common license.

However, when is black not black? Tanay Hudson posted (9th August 2020) on Twitter, *'Just Realized Rita Ora Isn't Black'* - this Albanian singer, regarded by some as 'White'; even though her skin colour, and features make her look like an Ethiopian Amhara. Albania has the highest frequency of the sub-Saharan haplogroup E1b1 in the whole of Europe:

> Haplogroups in the modern Albanian population is dominated by E-V13, the most common European sub-clade of E1b1b1a (E-M78). E-M78 most likely originated in eastern Africa. The peak of this haplogroup is in Kosovo. [Wikipedia/Origin of the Albanians]

Race is a social construct. Anthropologist and ethnologists make up the rules to fit their own cultural bias. They tend to be committed to the outdated, racist, and hierarchical model; where the mythical 'Aryans' (now disguised under the term Indo-Europeans) must stay free of any connection with 'darkest' Africa. Sergi's Eurafrican classification is totally ignored; while the term Eurasian heavily populates the world of academia, genetics, and linguistics. For example, 'Western' geneticists constantly use the term Eurasian DNA, but the term Eurafrican DNA does not exist. Why?

Anyone who has travelled extensively in Europe will be aware of the differences in skin colour. However, the differences in skin colour amongst the inhabitants of the British Isles receives very little attention. Clearly a taboo subject. However, an online forum had the following topic heading: *'Having olive skin, dark hair and eyes but being 100% Welsh.'* In this forum a range of comments were exchanged about the olive skin colour of Catherine Zeta Jones and other famous Welsh celebrities. In addition to this, Welsh contributors mentioned their own skin colour and how they were perceived by others. The comments reveal a lot about the variance in skin colour. Examples from the site include:

> I am Welsh but people ask if I am mixed-raced'; 'I have olive skin and dark eyes, and people ask if I am from the Philippines'; 'In Japan they wouldn't believe my Welsh friend was British, because he looks Asian'; Grandfather was always mistaken for a Middle Eastern, as were my sis and bro'; Nana looked American Indian with a flat face, high cheek bones, dark hair, dark eyes, olive skin and small in stature. [Having olive skin, dark hair and eyes but being 100% Welsh, source: internet forum]

Obviously, kinship is not based on colour. It is based on blood and marriage bonds. White, Black, Brown, and Olive coloured people have always mixed. A simple analysis of the reader's family tree would reveal every colour imaginable. 'Race' is a recent invention - the 'Celts' have conveniently become 'Aryans' - invented by Lhuyd and his English colleagues in London.

Enya, a singer from Donegal, produced her first solo album 'Enya' in 1987. The BBC used some of the tracks for the documentary 'The Celts' - which was aired in 1992. Her album was renamed 'The Celts' and was re-released in 1992 by WEA Records in Europe and Reprise Records in the USA. The raven-haired artist from Donegal *(headquarters of the African Formorians)* made the name 'Celts' even more recognizable around the world. It is interesting to note that the name Enya is the anglised version of Eithne - her full name being Eithne Pádraigín Ní Bhraonáin - a name she shares with Eithne, the granddaughter of Balor, the African Formorian ruler of Ireland, who had his headquarters on Tory Island. Enya's hometown of Gweedore is situated in the Gaeltacht district of Donegal, which has the famous landmark Bloody Foreland (Brinlack Point). It is here that the famous battle between the African Formorians and the 'cruel-cold-hearted' Danaans took place.

The examples just quoted show how various nationalities have different perspectives on ethnicity. This is an especially important point. The *'one drop'* rule has persisted in the USA. This social and legal definition classified individuals as Black if they had one Black ancestor. The dominant 'White' American society defined anyone with mixed ancestry into a subordinate group. - even one Black ancestor would be enough to place that person into the 'Black' category, regardless of skin colour. This one-drop rule was adopted as law in the USA during the 20th century.

Research from Harvard University by Arnold K. Ho, published in the Journal of Personality, [113(5), 753–768,] revealed that the USA's 'one-drop rule' still did not regard Biracial individuals as equal members of both parent groups. Biracial individuals are still seen as belonging more to their minority parent group. The racial hierarchy in the USA assigns the highest status to 'Whites' and the lowest status to 'Blacks.' As a result of this discrimination only 8.24% of Black–White Biracial self-identify as White. An example of Black-White Biracial who identified as 'White' was J. Edgar Hoover *(head of the FBI)*. Millie McGhee, the author of *'Secrets Uncovered'*, discovered that J Edgar Hoover's grandfather and great-grandfather lived in a segregated black area of Washington and were classified in a census as 'coloured.'

J Edgar Hoover (first director of FBI), Black or White?
Attributed to Underwood & Underwood, Public domain, via Wikimedia Commons)

The definition of ethnicity is vastly different in Russia. Jonathan Steele, writing for the Guardian Newspaper, wrote an article asking the question:

> 'What is white in America and black in Russia?
>
> The answer is 'the colour of Caucasian skin.'

His article demonstrates clearly how different nationalities have different views on who is 'White' and who is 'Black'; he described his experience as follows:

> "Put down Caucasian, I remember being told in Washington when I applied for a driver's license. In Moscow that would not do. Here they call anyone from the real Caucasus - Georgia, Armenia, Azerbaijan, and Checheno-Ingushetia as "black." [Jonathan Steele, article 'From the USSR', The Guardian]

The Irish, Scots, and Welsh are taught that they are 'Celts' - a message that was repeated so many times, it is no longer questioned by the average person. The word 'Celt' refuses to go away - even though the Irish and Cymry were never called 'Celts' or Keltoi by any ancient writer. Those familiar with Asterix the Gaul (or Celt) cartoon character will notice that he has long blond hair and pale skin. The opposite phenotype is dominant amongst the so-called 'Celts' of Wales, Ireland, the Western Isles, and the Scottish Highlands - areas where raven-black hair is the norm. This obviously indicates cognitive dissonance: a new belief was created (by Pezron and Lhuyd) where tall blond Celts became the desired 'racial type' for Ireland, Scotland, Wales, and Brittany. The modern Britons and Gaels have been fooled into thinking they are 'Celts' - their national identity was changed beyond recognition, and it all started because of Abbe Paul Yves Pezron (1639-1706). Eventually a fake identity was successfully propagated by the likes of Oxford scholar Edward Lhuyd (1660-1709) and other academics. This resulted in people becoming detached from their real heritage and adopting a new 'false' identity.

During that period, some scholars challenged Lhuyd's 'new 'Celtic' construct. The 'Orientalists' (as they were known) held alternative views. They believed the Gaels and Cymry came from the East and had affinities with the Phoenicians, Cushites and Arabians.

The most dynamic of these 'Orientalists' was General Charles Vallancey (1725-1812), who stated firmly:

> 'the learned Lhuyd has, in my humble opinion of the Irish language with Basque; between which I say there is no affinity; but between the Irish and the Punic (Canaanite) I think I may affirm there is a greater affinity, than between the Irish and any other ancient language whatever.' [Charles Vallancey, 'An essay on the antiquity of the Irish language]

The 'white-washing' of Roman & Greek Statues

The numerous Greek and Roman statues prominently displayed in European museums were originally painted with rich, colourful paint. This fact has been suppressed for a very long time. Margaret Talbot writes:

> "For centuries, archaeologists and museum curators had been scrubbing away these traces of colour." [see, The Myth of Whiteness in Classical Sculpture, by Margaret Talbot, October 22, 2018]

Margaret gives the examples of Aphrodisias, a thriving city in Greek Anatolia. In the 7th century AD, it was destroyed by an earthquake. In 1961 archaeologist began excavating the ruins. Margaret Talbot, staff writer at the New Yorker, comments:

> In 1961, archaeologists began systematically excavating the city, storing thousands of sculptural fragments in depots. When Abbe arrived there, several decades later, he started poking around the depots and was astonished to find that many statues had flecks of colour: red pigment on lips, black pigment on coils of hair, mirrorlike gilding on limbs. For centuries, archaeologists and museum curators had been scrubbing away these traces of colour before presenting statues and architectural reliefs to the public. "Imagine you've got an intact lower body of a nude male statue lying there on the depot floor, covered in dust," Abbe said. "You look at it up close, and you realize the whole thing is covered in bits of gold leaf. Oh, my God! The visual appearance of these things was just totally different from what I'd seen in the standard textbooks—which had only black-and-white plates, in any case." For Abbe, who is now a professor of ancient art at the University of Georgia, the idea that the ancients disdained bright colour "is the most common misconception about Western aesthetics in the history of Western art." It is, he said, "a lie we all hold dear." [The New Yorker, Oct 22, 2018]

The practice of scrubbing ancient statues until all the paint is removed, leaving a shiny white colourless object was an act of 'Eurocentric Vandalism.' This was practiced for centuries in secret by the custodians of the museums throughout Europe, a truly shocking revelation.

(above) Head of the Troyan helper (figure E-IX) of the east pediment of the Temple of Aphaia, ca. 485–480 BC. Attributed to -DSC04447_Istanbul_-_Museo_archeol._-_Testa_dal_frontone_di_Egina_-_Foto_G._Dall'Orto_28-5-2006

(below) reconstruction

Figures of the pediments of the Temple of Aphaia were found in 1811, and acquired in 1813 by Ludwig I of Bavaria for the Glyptothek. Attributed to Glyptothek, Public domain, via Wikimedia Commons.

Female head partially imitating a vase (lekythos) - 325 - 300 BC. Apulian, discovered at Calvi in Campania, and acquired by the British Museum in 1859. British Museum - GR 1859-2-16-4 (Terracotta D194). Patrice78500, CC via Wikimedia Commons

The vast amount of pottery created by the civilizations within the Mediterranean region seem to have escaped the 'white-washing' antics of Eurocentric archaeologist.

Poseidon holding a trident. Corinthian plaque, 550–525 BC. From Penteskouphia.

The statues, pottery, and paintings of Roman and ancient Greece exhibited a vast range of skin shades. Herodotus' observations confirm the cosmopolitan and multicultural composition of the ancient world. The Colchians, he remarked, 'have black skin and crinkly curly hair like the Egyptians. 'This ancient tribe from the Caucasus mountains', he states, 'could be equally related to other nations who have the same features.'

6 OLD HALLSTATT AND LA TENE THEORY

The old 'Celtic' model was based on the idea that the Hallstatt Iron Age culture that emerged in central Europe, was attributed to a people called 'Celts' - this culture was conveniently divided into Hallstatt A, Hallstatt B, Hallstatt C, and Hallstatt D. This culture was named after Hallstatt, a village in Austria, south-east of Salzburg. The term Hallstatt was first used by Swedish scholar H. Hildebrandt and was subsequently made popular by German archaeologist Paul Reinecke. The term covers the end of the Bronze Age and beginning of the Iron Age in Central Europe. The early period is called Hallstatt A (1200 – 1050 BC) and Hallstatt B (1050 – 800 BC), which was confined to central Europe. From 8th Century BC the La Tene Culture develops out of the Hallstatt Culture - with Hallstatt C (800 – 500 BC) and Hallstatt D (620 – 450 BC) crossing the Alps into Italy, spreading southwards into the Iberian Peninsula, and crossing the British Channel into Britain and Ireland. *[see chapter 10, Justyna Baron, The Hallstatt Period in Śląsk]*

The development of the first urban centers north of the Alps took place between 650 BC and 400 BC in southern Germany, Bohemia, and Central France. Urban sites such as Heuneburg developed rapidly. It is quite often regarded as the first city north of the Alps. Was the catalyst for the development of these new Iron Age, urban settlements due to contact with the Mediterranean world, in particular the Etruscans and Phoenicians?

Heinrich Härke comments on the early Iron Age and the impact of southern influences:

> Continental archaeologists have traditionally interpreted this process of social differentiation in Hallstatt D as a 'Celtic' reaction to Greek and Etruscan influences reaching Central

> Europe through long distance trade, mainly from the Greek colony of Massalia (founded around 600 BC) near the mouth of the Rhone.

Heuneburg developed rapidly from 600 BC onwards with major constructions using new building techniques not seen in this part of the world before:

> Around or soon after 600 BC the Heuneburg was completely restructured, an act that is to be interpreted as the result of a planned political decision (Periods IVb– IVa). A fortification that was unparalleled and quite unique north of the Alps was constructed along the circuit of the Heuneburg, replacing the old earth and timber rampart; it consisted of mudbricks set on a stone foundation (Gersbach 1995). It has been estimated that approximately 500,000 mudbricks were required, which were then plastered with daub and then whitewashed with lime. The wall was 3 meters wide, and probably 5 meters high, including a timber parapet, the charred remains of the beams of which were found. Masonry plinths and mudbricks were widespread in the Mediterranean from the Bronze Age, but no other examples of this construction technique are known from the Early Iron Age in central Europe to date. [Heinrich Härke, Early Iron Age hill settlement in west central Europe: patterns and developments, Oxford Journal of Archaeology May 1982]

Heuneburg 600 B.C., Germany
Attributed to Kenny Arne Lang Antonsen, creative commons via Wikimedia Commons.

The impressive mud-brick wall was inspired by Phoenicians, Greeks, and Etruscan influences. The adobe mud brick walls used at Heuneburg Hill fort indicate intimate contact with the southern Mediterranean; these techniques were not previously used in central Europe. Confirmation of southern contact has come from the discovery of Greek Attic sherds and pottery produced in the eastern Mediterranean and Levantine region (over 1,000 miles away). Did this impressive fortified urban settlement - a massive hill fort, with 17 towers projecting along both the west and north side of the plateau, owe its birth to the Phoenicians and other Hamito-Semitic (Afro-asiatic) speakers? The site had it's beginning around 600 BC and flourished until around 450 BC - when the site was burned downed and abandoned.

The Hallstatt D culture flourished mainly due to the trade in high value goods, especially those obtained from the Mediterranean due to contact with Phoenicians and Etruscans:

> The success of Hallstatt D clearly points to that 'prestige goods economy' through which Celts monopolized trade, not only in Hochdorf, but also in eastern neighbours like Vače, in Slovenia. Besides Hochdorf, there are other places of immediate vicinity that provide further evidence, like Hohmichele, the second largest early Iron Age cluster of mounds ....The whole array of grave goods previously discussed suggest that Hallstatt D became the wealthiest era in all Europe, but where a specific genre (male) did not necessarily have to control the power, as it has been demonstrated that women could also inherit valour and honour like in Hohmichele grave VI, and this implies that burials cannot be reduced to a single interpretation: Hallstatt was (archaeologically and temporally) based on diversity and social distinctions. [Adriadna Belmont, The Emergence of the Hallstatt "Princely' Graves in the Context of the Development of "Celtic" Society, 2019]

It appears that imported Mediterranean pottery was strongly associated with these central European Iron Age hill forts. The elite warrior burials show a remarkably close links with the Mediterranean:

> The volume of trade with the Mediterranean world increased sharply in the Hallstatt phase Ha D2-3, in absolute terms approximately dating between 530/520 and 450/440 BC. It was in this phase that trade with the Greek colonies of the French Midi started, and only now did the supply of Etruscan bronze vessels become regular. The upsurge of trade must be explained primarily by the receptivity and mounting power of

> the West Hallstatt elite. The spread of elite burials and settlements to the Saone valley in Ha D2-3 meant that the distance separating the West Hallstatt elite from the Greek colonies became much smaller. [Christopher Pare, Furstensitze, Celts and the Mediterranean World, Proceedings of the Prehistoric Society 57, part 2,1991, pp. 183-202]

This proves that increase commerce was the stimulus for the development and eventual spread of Iron Age technology from central Europe into western and south-Western Europe. Academics have tried to identify the Hallstatt culture as the eponymous ancestor of the 'Celtic' people. This was mostly based on the assumption that the spread of art styles and artefacts must have been accompanied by an equivalent human migration. The Hallstatt Culture was followed by the La Tene Culture which spread into France and Spain. The evidence suggest that people of different 'ethnic' origins adopted this culture and then adapted it to their own indigenous styles, without any major colonisation or take over taking place. The Phoenicians were the first to begin the exploitation of silver in the Iberian Peninsula. Diodorus Siculus gives a detail account of how the Phoenicians monopolized this trade:

> 33.Now the natives were ignorant of the use of silver, and the Phoenicians, as they pursued their commercial enterprises and learned of what had taken place, purchased the silver in exchange for other wares of little if any worth. And this was the reason why the Phoenicians, as they transported this silver to Greece and Asia and to all other peoples, acquired great wealth. So far indeed did the merchants go in their greed that in case their boats were fully laden and there still remained a great amount of silver, they would hammer the lead off the anchors and have the silver perform the service of the lead. And the result was that the Phoenicians, as in the course of many years they prospered greatly, thanks to commerce of this kind, sent forth many colonies, some to Sicily and its neighbouring islands, and others to Libya, Sardinia, and Iberia.......36. But at a much later time the Iberians, having come to know the peculiar qualities possessed by silver, sunk notable mines, and as a consequence, by working the most excellent and, we may say, the most abundant silver to be found, they received great revenues. And although many are the astounding features connected with the mining just

> described, a man may wonder not the least at the fact that not one of the mines has a recent beginning, but all of them were opened by the covetousness of the Carthaginians at the time when Iberia was among their possessions. It was from these mines, that is, that they drew their continued growth, hiring the ablest mercenaries to be found. [p204, Diodorus Siculus, 03]

Material Culture

The material culture of what is referred to as 'Celtic' evolved as a direct result of trade with people from the southern Mediterranean. The Phoenicians had a massive impact on the inhabitants of the Iberian Peninsula, the central European Alpine region, and the British Isles. Other southerners, such as the Etruscans and Greeks, also had an impact on the tribes of southern Germany and the Alpine regions. The expansion of Etruscan trade into the Alps brought new innovations in material culture:

> It has been said that La Tène art had no genesis; it came into the world in fully developed form, with a distinctive personality. It is evident, however, that Ionian Greek colonizers in the south of France and Etruscans in northern Italy supplied the models that ignited the creative skills of Celtic craftsmen. The wine trade from these areas acted as the catalyst, introducing, besides the liquid itself—in great quantity—the goblets, flagons, cauldrons, mixing bowls, and all the appropriate equipment for its proper consumption.....Spectacularly rich burials in parts of Germany, France, and Switzerland have yielded the finest objects, one outstanding piece now in the museum of Besançon in France (probably taken from a plundered burial). This Etruscan bronze flagon was transformed by a master artisan through the addition of a web of finely engraved ornament—including palmettes, S scrolls, comma leaves, even the yin-yang symbol—around its sides and on the base. [encyclopedia.com/humanities/encyclopedias-almanacs-transcripts-and-maps/la-tene-art]

The fusion of different cultures resulted in new creative styles, especially in metal work. Although the La Tene style became popular in parts of Western

Europe, however, it was strangely absent from some regions. The style tended not to use the human form, except the human head which was the focus of many rituals. The use of animal imagery occurs, especially that of birds, boars, and griffin like creatures.

The Snettisham Hoard, gold torc from the Snettisham Hoard.
c.100BC England. British Museum, CC via Wikimedia Commons

Celtic Head, Northern England (Romano-British), CC creative commons,
Migration period, 2nd-3rd centuries
Sandstone with traces of original red paint
The Cleveland Museum of Art. The Cleveland Museum of Art Handbook. Cleveland, OH: The Cleveland Museum of Art, 1958. Mentioned and Reproduced: cat. no. 89
archive.org. Gift of Dr. and Mrs. Jacob Hirsch 1955.555

The art seems to have spread erratically and cannot relate to a human migration from central Europe. The growth in elite burials in central Europe during this period was a direct result of the massive increase in trade from southern Mediterranean. Insular Art.

The complicated spread of this art form is described by Jennifer Paxton, in 'THE CELTIC WORLD Insular Art: The La Tène Style of Art and Its Influences':

> What we find in Britain and Ireland is a bit complicated, though. The art of this style that we find is broadly similar, so you find artifacts all over this region that have broadly similar designs, whether they come from Britain or Ireland. The spiral shape, known as the triskele, is a common motif found in La Tène style of art in both Britain and Ireland. For example, you might find a brooch from the north of Ireland that looks remarkably similar to a shield mount from the south of Britain. Both pieces might use the same motif, such as the spiral shape known as the triskele. So, in some way, this art was using older motifs and creating a broadly coherent style across a wide geographical area. But here's the odd thing. Even though there are similarities between objects found in northern Ireland and southern Britain, just as we found on the continent, this art style in Britain and Ireland is not evenly distributed. It's not found everywhere. It's much more solidly attested in the north of Ireland than the south of Ireland, which is somewhat surprising since you would think that the south would be more open to trading contacts, but we must be seeing the evidence of trade routes that operated in ways we cannot otherwise recover. The point is that this is not an Irish style or a British style. It's not even a southern style or a northern style. It's a style that some groups of people living in these islands adopted, and others did not. And we may never know why.
>
> [www.thegreatcoursesdaily.com/insular-art-the-la-tene-style-of-art-and-its-influences/ by Jennifer Paxton, Ph.D., The Catholic University of America]

Celtic from The West

Professor Cunliffe's 'Celtic from The West' explores the idea that the 'Celtic' language emerged in the Atlantic Zone during the Bronze Age. Cunliffe explains his hypothesis as 'a major departure from the long-established but increasingly problematical scenario in which the ancient 'Celtic' language and people called Keltoi (Celts) are closely bound up with the archaeology of the Hallstatt and La Tene culture of Iron Age west-central Europe.' [B. Cunliffe, et.al., 'Celtic' From The West 2]

Professor Cunliffe's 'Celts from The West 2' (ed. 2017) has some new controversial elements. It has contributions from some very accomplished academics, including John T. Koch, J. P Mallory, and Colin Renfrew. According to this theory, the 'Celts' originated in south-western Iberian Cunliffe, Koch, et al., have revised 'Celtic' chronology by placing the 'Celts' in Bronze Age Iberia and the Atlantic by 3000 BC. According to theory they spread throughout Ireland, the British Isles, and western regions of France. After an initial spread along the Atlantic coast of south-west Europe, they then spread into central Europe and further.

The real ethnicity of many tribes shown on the map, *[the overview of the Hallstatt and La Tène cultures]*, is simply not known. Academics have assumed that certain tribes were of 'Celtic' origin, but there is no evidence of this. Were the Belgae really Germans? And were the Galatians really 'Celtic'?

Anthony Durham & Michael Goormachtigh [2012] asked the question - 'Were the Galatians really 'Celtic'?' They challenged the idea of the Galatians settlers of Anatolia, ever speaking a 'Celtic' language:

> Saint Jerome's AD 386 remark that the language of ancient Galatia (around modern Ankara) resembled the language of the Treveri (around modern Trier) has been misinterpreted. The "Celts", "Gauls" or "Galatians" mentioned by classical authors, including those who invaded Greece and Anatolia around 277 BC, were not 'Celtic' in the modern sense of speaking a 'Celtic' language related to Welsh and Irish, but tall, pale-skinned, hairy, warrior peoples from the north. The 150 or so words and proper names currently known from Galatian speech show little affinity with 'Celtic' but more with Germanic. [Anthony Durham & Michael Goormachtigh, 'Was Galatian Really 'Celtic'' 2012]

Overview of the Hallstatt and La Tène cultures.
The core Hallstatt territory (800 BCE) is shown in solid yellow, the area of influence by 500 BCE (HaD) in light yellow. The core territory of the La Tène culture (450 BCE) is

shown in solid green, the eventual area of La Tène influence by 50 BCE in light green. (Attributed to Dbachmann, creative commons via Wikimedia Commons.)

This article, 'Was Galatian Really 'Celtic', highlights some interesting questions. The paper questions the accuracy of the translation of many Galatian names:

> However, those translations are almost always much the same as in other European languages or else they look less plausible than alternatives based on Greek, Latin, or Germanic. It follows that our original three-part working hypothesis can be summed up in one even more provocative suggestion: the entire concept of "Continental 'Celtic'", outside Iberia, Caesar's 'Celtic' part of Gaul, and some 'Celtic' travelers inside the Roman Empire, is one huge fallacy that has led historians and linguists astray. A slight crumb of comfort for the old view lies in tantalizing hints from linguistics (Isaac, 2010) and genetics (Oppenheimer, 2010) that proto-Celts originated in the eastern Mediterranean. However, Cunliffe and Koch (2010) have now united behind the view that 'Celtic' really expanded as a distinct language branch only after seaborne traders broke out of the Mediterranean in search of metals, and then expanded back eastwards up major rivers. [p26, 'Was Galatian Really 'Celtic'' 2012]

The Greek language spread rapidly through the Mediterranean as a result of the establishment of trading posts on Europe's southern coastline; allowing them to dominate strategic islands such as Sicily, Balearic Islands, Corsica, and Sardinia. The 'Celtic From The West' theory proposes that the 'Celtic' languages formed in Iberia and then spread outwards because of increased commerce in the region.

James Patrick Mallory, an American archaeologist, and an emeritus professor at Queen's University (Belfast), explored the Indo-Europeanization of Atlantic Europe. The 'Celts' cannot be found in Neolithic Iberia. The expansion of impressed ware or cardial culture into southern Europe, was closely associated with males carrying sub-Saharan E1b1 y-haplo DNA. The introduction of farming into Europe during the Neolithic era can be attributed to famers with specific y-DNA haplo groups (male), such as E1b1, G2a, and T. The Chadic R1b1 V88 haplogroup was also present in Europe, however, it was a legacy from an earlier Mesolithic period; long before any so-called 'Celtic' R1b subclades appeared in Europe. Even the Basques do not make an appearance in Iberia until the Bronze Age (at the earliest) - male Basques are predominantly R1b. The genetic make-up of the Basques is interesting. 86% of the Basque y-DNA (male) belong to haplogroup R1b3*-M269 with a detection of a minor African male component (1.2%) confirmed by the lineages E3*-P2 and E3b2-M81.

Santos Alonso, et al., exploring the place of the Basques in Europe, reveals:

> 'Contrary to previous suggestions, we do not observe any particular link between Basques and 'Celtic' populations beyond that provided by the Paleolithic ancestry common to European populations.' [European Journal of Human Genetics (2005) 13, 1293–1302]

The paper concludes, 'Basque DNA data do not show any signs of long-range diffusion of Basque Y-chromosome haplogroups into North Europe associated to the retreat of the last Glacial Maximum, as has been suggested for mitochondrial DNA.'

The introduction of Cardium pottery (impressed ware) marked the beginning of the introduction of Megalithic monuments, c. 4700 BC., into Iberia. This culture extended from the Adriatic Sea to the Atlantic coasts of Portugal and south to Morocco. This eliminates any chance of associating the spread of Megalithic culture with the so-called 'Celts' or 'proto-Celts' since the dominant Neolithic male y haplogroups during this period has been found to be E1b1, J, T, and G2a.

Another controversial aspect of 'Celts from The West' is John T. Koch's hypothesis that the ancient Tartessians of south-west Iberia spoke a 'Celtic' language.

Diodorus Siculus gives an indication of where the Celts lived:

> And now it will be useful to draw a distinction which is unknown to many: The peoples who dwell in the interior above Massalia, those on the slopes of the Alps, and those on this side the Pyrenees mountains are called Celts, whereas the peoples who are established above this land of Celtica in the parts which stretch to the north, both along the ocean and along the Hercynian Mountain, and all the peoples who come after these, as far as Scythia, are known as Gauls; the Romans, however, include all these nations together under a single name calling them one and all Gauls. [p184, C. H. Oldfather, Diodorus Siculus, 03]

The Gaul or 'Celts' that settled in the Iberian Peninsula intermarried with the Iberian tribes, creating a new group that ancient writers referred to as Celtiberians. How they came into being is described by Diodorus Siculus:

> Now that we have spoken at sufficient length about the Celts, we shall turn our history to the Celti-Iberians who are their neighbors. In ancient times these two peoples, namely, the Iberians and the Celts, kept warring among themselves over the land, but when later they arranged their differences and settled upon the land altogether, and when they went further and agreed to intermarriage with each other, because of such inter-mixture the two peoples received the appellation given above. And since it was two powerful nations that united and the land of theirs was fertile, it came to pass that the Celtiberians advanced far in fame and were subdued by the Romans with difficulty and only after they had faced them in battle over a long period. And this people, it would appear, provide for warfare not only excellent cavalry but also foot-soldiers who excel in prowess and endurance. They wear rough black cloaks, the wool of which resembles the hair of goats. As for their arms, certain of the Celti-Iberian carry light shields like those of the Gauls, and certain carry circular wicker shields as large as an aspis and about their shins and calves they wind greaves made of hair and on their heads, they wear bronze helmets adorned with purple crests. The swords they wear are two-edged and wrought of excellent iron. [p188, C. H. Oldfather, Diodorus Siculus, 03]

Tartessian - the Merchants of Tarshish

The 'Celtic from the West' theory relies heavily on Tartessian being Indo-European. This could be regarded as premature, since Tartessian is only known from around 70 inscriptions found on stone slabs. Most linguists have classified Tartessian as a non-Indo-European language, that has probably borrowed some words because of commerce. Jose Antonio Correa first proposed the connection with Celtic based on the presence of some Celtic names absorbed with a non-Indo-European language. John T. Koch, a professor at the University of Wales Centre for Advanced Welsh and Celtic Studies, goes further and has proposed Tartessian as the first attested 'Celtic' language - allegedly going back to the 7th century BC.

Professor Koch describes the technique he used as follows:

> I describe the method with which I initially approached the SW corpus as, 'essentially fishing for any further Celtic forms within a corpus of inscriptions in which a few promising examples had already been recognized' (Koch 2013a, 5). This is not a slip betraying a methodology inferior to that claimed. 'Fishing' is what needs to be done, casting the net as wide as the full range of possibilities for an Ancient Celtic language. The classification question cannot be approached encumbered by unexamined assumptions about what an Ancient Celtic language should look like or eagerness to settle unresolved questions in a particular way. Once a catch of Celtic-looking forms is hauled in, it is then time to ask whether they look Celtic in a grammatically and phonologically consistent way—consistent with each other and also consistent with what we actually know about Proto-Celtic and Proto-Indo-European. [John T. Koch, On the Debate over the Classification of the Language of the South-Western (SW) Inscriptions, also known as Tartessian]

One could argue that the African Substratum Theory is guilty of the same technique of 'fishing' for any similarities between 'Celtic' and African/ Arabian languages; however, in this case I have 'cast the net far and wide' in the opposite direction to Professor Koch. It is very surprising that Professor Koch has not explored the African substratum within the British Isles and Ireland; especially since he is based in Wales.

Tatyana A. Mikhailova, Institute of Linguistics, RAN (Moscow), is quite balanced in her approach to this topic:

> Interestingly, those who believe Tartessian to be non-Indo-European accept the presence of Indo-European and even Celtic names borrowed into it over the course of long-term contacts. The proponents of the 'lost Indo-European language' may see these names as either borrowed from Celtic or as native cognates, often close to Celtic or Italic. Thus — I would stress it once more — Koch's idea that the language of the SW inscriptions is Indo-European and presumably Celtic is not totally unsubstantiated. [Tatyana A. Mikhailova, Celtic origin: location in time and space? Reconsidering the "East-

West Celtic" debate]

Tatyana A. Mikhailova goes even further, questioning why some academics presenting Celtic Tartessian as fact:

> Should I feel concerned that the Atlantic theory and the recognition of Tartessian as Celtic are moving from the field of academic debate to the field of firmly established facts, deserving popularization? Or, on the contrary, relief on seeing that the Cunliffe-Koch theories are being expelled from the field of mainstream academic discussion and reduced to the confines of marginal popular books? [Tatyana A. Mikhailova, Celtic origin: location in time and space? Reconsidering the "East-West Celtic" debate]

Strong opposition to 'Celtic from The West' comes from Dr. Blanc Maria Prósper, University of Salamanca. Prósper's approach is very refreshing:

> I shall begin by saying I find no a priori reason to rule out a Celtic classification of Tartessian. But it is important to note that this idea, originally put forward by José Antonio Correa, rests on the interpretation of a large number of words as Celtic personal names (in fact, a third part of the corpus in Koch's approach). As is obvious to nearly every linguist (including Koch, but interestingly not some of the works on Lusitanian that he quotes), proper names are not diagnostic of the genetic appurtenance of the language in which the text is conducted. This is why –briga place names mentioned in indigenous Lusitanian inscriptions contribute nothing to the study of Lusitanian. People travel, and the allusion to persons bearing Celtic names in ancient epigraphy, whether Celtic or not, is entirely unproblematic. ……….. nearly a third part of its contents consists of Celtic personal names, these may have been borrowed (or simply consigned in writing) long after the dawn of literacy, and consequently may reflect the actual synchronic phonetics of SW Celtic dialects more faithfully than the non–Celtic appellative vocabulary which is constrained by writing tradition. [Blanca María Prósper, Some Observations on the Classification of Tartessian as a Celtic

Language, The Journal of Indo-European Studies, vol 42, 2014]

Dr Prósper's paper makes some valid points which challenge the 'Celtic from The West' theory':

> *Koch has not displayed a full-fledged phonological and morphological account of Tartessian, which is imperative in this kind of work.
>
> *Prosper challenges Koch's overall conclusion that 'ancient' Celtic and its closest kin were in close quarters and interacting with each other in the Iberian Peninsula. There is no evidence whatsoever that Celtic had 'closest kin' anywhere; Lusitanian has mostly Italic comparanda.
>
> * The Lusitanian indigenous inscriptions cannot be classified as Celtic.
>
> * There is no reason to accept the idea that only one Celtic migration was responsible for all the Indo–European speaking peoples in the Iberian Peninsula.
>
> * Celtiberian defies Koch's description of Tartessian in that it is attested much later but looks much more conservative.
>
> * Koch's efforts to demonstrate the Celticity of the royal name Arganthonius is unconvincing. Even if Tartessian had a word arganto– 'silver' this might only mean that this was a loanword from the Baeturia Celtica or Celtiberia itself, as IE terms for metals frequently are (including, of course, English silver).
>
> *The proliferation of personal names of Celtic ancestry is disturbing. But it is highly likely that only the names of the local aristocracy have been handed down to us. (As can be seen in Mitannian royal names and the Hurrian languages of their subjects).

Lusitanian is one of Europe's least know language. It has been reconstructed from a small number of inscriptions such as from Cabeco das Fraguas, in Portugal. Dr. Blanca Maria Prósper's examination of these inscription has shown it not to be Celtic, and it does not fit into any existing Indo-European family:

> Inspection of the inscription doesn't encourage us to consider Lusitanian Celtic language: on the contrary, it is not amenable to inclusion in any IE family, but it bears some phonetic and lexical resemblances to Italic *for more of these.......and also some lexical correspondences to Baltic, Germanic and Greek which are absent from Celtic. Typically, Lusitanian features are sometimes difficult to extricate from those belonging to a substrate language probably belonging to the Alteuropaisch stock notably /a/ < IE/o/. [Blanca Maria Prosper, The inscription of Cabeco das Fraguas revisited. Lusitanian and Alteuropaisch populations in the west of the Iberian Peninsula, 1999]

Tartessians in the Ancient World

The men of Tarshish were famous for being a great trading nation. Prophet Jonah (asw) sought refuge in Tarshish, The Bible confirms that 'Jonah rose up to flee unto Tarshish from the presence of the LORD. He went down to Joppa, and found a ship going to Tarshish.' [Jonah 1:3]

The exports from Tarshish included gold and silver, ivory, apes, and peacocks. Sir E. Tennent points out that some of the names of these exports (peacocks, apes, and ivory) are identical to names used by Tamils of southern Indian. Gibson makes an interesting observation:

> Silver would suit Tartesus in Spain, but the other exports do not. None of the named exports of Tarshish are prominent as items from the British Isles of antiquity. Neither do these exports make one think of Carthage or any other North African port, nor of any place adjacent to the Mediterranean, nor yet the European coasts. Ships would not sail down the Red sea to reach Spain or Britain. If Solomon wanted to reach any place to the west, he had seaports in his own land right on the Mediterranean coast, Joppa (II Chronicles 2:16), Dor, Accho, etc. Indeed, Solomon could have arranged with his friend Hiram the King of Tyre to send ships out from Tyre itself. But no, his ships had to be launched in eastern waters to meet his designs and plans. Neither do we find any linguistic support to link the exports of Tarshish with a western proposal. [David J. Gibson, The Ships of Tarshish A survey and evaluation of the historical references to the "Ships of Tarshish" with suggested solutions for various problems and issues, 2012]

It is evident that the Phoenician sent out expeditions to Ophir. Journeys to Tarshish occurred once every three years. Gibson claims Tarshish was in India. Psalms 48.8 mentions fleets of Tarshish ships serving King Hiram and prophet Solomon (asw) in the Mediterranean and the Red Sea. The description is vague and could be interpreted as 'ships of the Tarshish type' set sail to various destinations in both the Mediterranean and Red Sea.

The Phoenicians/Carthaginians had mapped the coast of Senegal; they knew it was parallel to the cinnamon producing land (modern-day Somalia); but they did not have a clue where cinnamon really came from (i.e., Sri Lanka and Indonesia). The African Trogodytes (the Barbara) had a complete monopoly on this trade. If Tarshish was Sri Lanka, why is cinnamon never listed as an export?

[Note: The original spelling was Trogodytes. Some classical authors later misspelt the word and used the term Troglodytes, probably due to the similarity to the Greek word trogle (hole or cave), and dyein (to go in) resulting in the incorrect translation of Cave dweller.)]

The Tyrian King Hiram I sent fleets of ships to Ophir from the southern port of Ezion-Geber on the Gulf of Aqabab (Red Sea). The list of products from this land included gold, silver, sandalwood, pearls, ivory, apes, and peacocks. Sandalwood naturally occurs in Sri Lanka, India, and Indonesia. The southern provinces of Tamil Nadu, Karnataka, and Kerala produce around 85% of Indian's sandalwood. From this we can see that Tarshish, and Ophir seem to be in opposite directions.

On the other hand, the journey mentioned by Pliny informs us of how the African Trogodytes sailed on rafts across the Erythraean Sea to gather cinnamon: the whole journey took 3 years. For thousands of years the source of cinnamon was kept secret by the African Trogodytes.

The Tartessians or merchant of Tarshish, the Phoenicians, the Troglodyte Barbara of Punt, and the Dedanites were all trading partners. It is highly unlikely for Tarshish to have been 'Celtic' - the evidence points to them being either an African or Arabian tribe that borrowed some words from 'Celtic' and Italic.

Tarshish clearly represents a geographically imprecise and vague location. Several different locations have been suggested over the years.

Examples are:

> * Cadiz (Southern Iberia) has abundant deposits of silver and copper which were exploited by the Phoenicians and the local tribes.
>
> *Nora (Sardinia) Solinus wrote, 'argento Sardinia' or 'silver from Sardinia' - a country with a long history of mining and metal working. The 9th century Phoenician inscription on the Nora Stone locates the toponym Tarshish at ancient Nora,

> Sardinia.
>
> * Cyprus derives its name from Kúpros (Copper) - the ancient Cypriots were expert miners, producing gold, iron pyrite and silver.

The Phoenicians spearheaded the spread of metal technologies across the Mediterranean. The exact location of Tarshish is uncertain; the best fit is Sardinia. However, regardless of its exact location - it can be concluded that the Phoenicians played a crucial role in spreading new technologies across the Mediterranean.

The classification of the so-called Palaeohispanic languages; Tartessian, Iberian, Celtiberian, and Lusitanian (southern Tartessian) have been the subject of disagreement amongst scholars. E. R. Luján explored Lusitanian in the chapter *'Language and writing among the Lusitanians'* - published in the book Palaeohispanic Languages and Epigraphies, 2019:

> The prevailing opinion is that Lusitanian was not Celtic. It must have diverged from western Indo-European dialects before the kernel of what would evolve into the Celtic and Italic families had been constituted.
>
> The Iberian Peninsula was originally populated by tribes that spoke languages classified as non-Indo-European. These tribes were the Basques, the Aquitaine, and the Iberians; they mixed with and absorbed new incoming tribes from beyond the Pyrenees.

Names such as Briga are regarded as possibly 'Celtic.' The fact that it has been found on the Lusitanian stelæ, Blanca María Prósper concludes, *'contributes nothing to the study of Lusitanian (southern Tartessian).'*

The funerary monument for a 'Celtic' leader has the inscription begin with *'lokooboo niiraboo too aŕaia i kaaltee'* - which means 'Invoking the divine Lug of the (Galician) Neri (tribe)' *[Southwest Palaeohispanic script, via Wikimedia Commons]*

The Lusitanians dominated much of central Portugal. The origin of the Lusitani is worth noting. The original name for this tribe was Belitanian or Beal-I-tanos, which was transformed into Lusitanos - obviously close to the Semitic Phoenician Bel-tane. It is possible that they were an Iberian tribe that later adopted an Indo-European language.

DNA studies have raised many questions - such as *'where are the Hallstatt Celts?'* Whoever they were, they do not seem to be present in Iberian:

> It is still uncertain what the exact haplogroup composition of

the Hallstatt Celts would have been, except that they surely possessed a large percentage of R1b-U152. They might also have carried G2a3b1 and J2b2 lineages, among others. Oddly enough, while R1b-U152 is found everywhere in the Iberian Peninsula, its frequency never exceeds 5%. [Maciamo Hay, Genetic History of the Spaniards, and the Portuguese, Eupedia, 2013 (updated 2107)]

The Tartessian Fonte Velha inscription (Bensafrim)
Tartessian Stele User Papix, Public domain, creative commons via Wikimedia Commons. Ethnographic Iberia via Wikimedia Commons public domain.

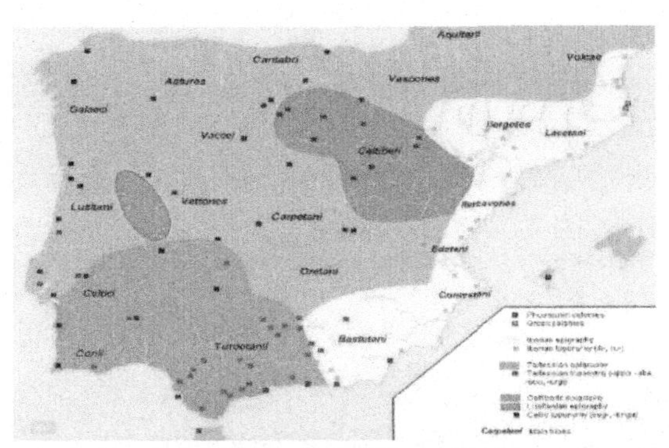

Languages of pre-Roman Iberia
attributed to Sugaar at English via Wikipedia commons, public domain.

The Ethnicity of Lusitanians

On a final note, on this topic, it is worth analyzing the ethnography of the region. If 'Celtic' developed in south-western Iberia and then migrated to both Ireland and Britain, there should be some similarities in phenotype between these regions. The inhabitants of Luso (an abbreviation of Lusitania), a few miles north of Coimbra, should be descendants of the ancient Lusitanian tribes. Luso is situated in the Serra do Bucaco mountain range which rises to 1801 feet. It is famous for its therapeutic springs. These mountainous tribes were famous for their independent and warlike nature.

The term Celti-Iberian was used by ancient authors to describe a distinct ethnic group that comprised of a mixture of 'Celtic' and Iberians. They were defined by their language, rituals, and names. The mountain tribes of Luso differ from the tribes that inhabited the lowlands. This was pointed out to me during a visit to the region, by my Portuguese guide. *'Look they all have long heads,'* said my guide. In contrast, my guide had an extremely broad, brachycephalic head, a with an index of at least 84. There seem to be nothing 'Celtic' about these mountain people; in-fact their faces could be compared to some Egyptians?

Indigenous inhabitants of Luso, central Portugal, photo taken by © Ibrahim Ali.

The brachycephalic population is remarkably interesting in that they tend have black-raven hair; similar in this aspect to the long-headed inhabitants. The genetic history of Iberia is complex. However, there is a high degree of bias which under-values the genetic contribution from Africa. The following extract from an article in The New York Times, *'A History of the Iberian Peninsula, as Told by Its Skeletons'* by Carl Zimmer, illustrates how the African contribution is regarded as a 'novelty':

> A skeleton from an elaborate grave in central Spain about 4,400 years old belonged to a man whose ancestry was 100 percent North African.
>
> "That's crazy," said David Reich, a geneticist at Harvard Medical School and a co-author of the paper in Science. "We

> double-checked it because it was so weird."
>
> Another striking result emerged when the researchers studied the DNA from a 3,500-year-old woman. They concluded she had a North African grandparent.
>
> These findings suggest that people were moving into Iberia from Africa more than 3,000 years before the rise of the Roman Empire. "These are cosmopolitan places," Dr. Reich said. About 4,500 years ago, still another wave of people arrived, profoundly altering the make-up of Iberia. [Carl Zimmer, A History of the Iberian Peninsula, as Told by Its Skeletons, Matter Column, The New York Times]

The reaction of David Reich, a geneticist at Harvard Medical School, is surprising. Why does he find the African genetic contribution weird? The genetic make-up of the early western European hunter gatherers population known as the Villabruna people (northern Italy) had the same genetic make-up as the Chadic speaking tribes of western and central Africa. The discovery of a 14,000-year-old individual from Villabruna revealed Y-DNA haplogroup R1b-V88. It seems that scientists are guilty of being too selective in what information they share.

> Does cultural bias affect how genetic data is interpreted?
>
> I would say *Yes*.

7 FOLKLORE OF THE CYMRY (WELSH)

Folklore and oral traditions are extremely important. They need to be kept alive, since they are a valuable connection to the past and give people a sense of identity, allowing a deeper bond with the land. I came across Irish folklore at an early age. The old copies of the Annals of The Four Masters and The Annals of Clonmacnoise provide a wonderful account of tribal invasions, epic battles, magical duels, and provide us with the location of important burial places.

Folklore can be an important tool in understanding the origin of communities. Most geneticists carry out research without any knowledge of the folklore and oral traditions of the people they are studying. They fail to make the connection between the ancient past and the current population. The so-called 'Celtic' Renaissance, towards the end of the 1800's, tried too hard to embrace a new identity. Jason Marc Harris in his 'Folklore and the Fantastic in Nineteenth-century British Fiction' highlights this duality:

> The 'Celtic' Renaissance's employment of folklore is conflicted. Motivated by visions of Irish and Scottish nationalism, writers hoped to reclaim their suppressed traditions of native artistry, but these sophisticated artists were sometimes uncomfortable with what they considered the ignorant or irrational aspects of folk beliefs and narrative. Consequently, a gap lies between the narrator in the work that contains folklore and the informants who serve as characters; a similar distance often occurs in the handling of folk collectors and their informant. W.B. Yeats for example, often adopts an ironic tone, which is far from an endorsement of

> the "peasantry" conceptions of the world. This ironic distance sometimes seems condescending, witty, or humorous.........they are using the domains of the "peasantry" without granting this worldwide view an autonomy that frees it from the interest of their literary feudal lords. This uneasy rapport between Anglo-Irish writers and the folkloric material of their "subjects" (in both the literary and semi-feudal sense) is characterized by tensions of power and cultural identity.

The best storyteller in the whole of Ireland is County Clare's Eddie Lenihan. He has the unique ability to capture any audience's attention with his dramatic expressions, and unconventional performances. His connection to the story is deeply authentic, mainly because he gives them the respect they deserve. He reminds the audience that these stories are very real. They represent a living culture, not just stories to be found in an old book. He is gifted and is able to capture the attention of young and old alike. He is a storyteller who makes the past come alive. References to skin colour in Irish and British folklore is abundant and gives us a hint of how diverse the ancient inhabitants were. The following example illustrates the openness with which colour difference appears in the literature:

> All the MacCodrums of North Uist had been brown-skinned and brown-haired and brown-eyed and herein may have lain the reason why, in bygone days, this small clan of Uist was known throughout the Western Isles as the Shochd-nan Ron, the offspring of the seals." [p180, Jason Marc Harris, Folklore and The Fantastic in Nineteenth-century British Fiction]

Victorian scientist became obsessed with measuring the variation of skin colour across the British Isles. They developed the Coefficient of Racial Likeness (CRL) and Index of Nigrescence (a complicated statistical equation used to measure skin colour). They eagerly started to classify the British and Irish population according to these rather bizarre and detailed measurements. This was quickly abandoned when the results did not fit with the artificial racial constructs. The results revealed that the so-called 'Celts' were overwhelmingly darker than the Anglo-Saxons, and were generally characterized by black-raven hair, especially in the westerly regions of these islands.

The Cymry

Throughout the Middle Ages, the word Cymry was used to describe the Welsh people. The older term Brythoniaid was used up to the 13th century AD and encompassed all the Britonnic people (Cymry, Loegrians, etc.). After this period, the term Cymry became the most widely used name for the indigenous Britons. The term Cambrian is a Latinized version of Cymry, and it can be found in place names such as the county of Cumbria (NW England), Cambrian Mountains in Wales, and other placenames throughout the British Isles.

The word Welsh is derived from the Anglo-Saxon Walha, which means foreigner or dark one. The obvious difference in skin colour between the Germanic Anglo-Saxon tribes and the indigenous Britons was significantly more visible 2000 years ago compared to current times. The correct name for the natives of Britain during the 5th and 6th century A.D was Cymry, which is derived from the Brythonic word Combrogi which signifies a fellow Countrymen or Compatriot. In modern times, the English have used the word Welsh or Welch in a derogative manner. Take the example of the modern English saying, 'to Welsh on a bet' - this meant to signify a dishonest person who goes back on his/her word. The *'Adventurous History of the Word Wales'* websites has the following explanation:

> More clearly than in other languages, Walha took on the meaning not just of foreigner but of 'the other' in Old English; it became a term for an inferior race, worthy of enslavement. Without mercy or shame, the Anglo-Saxon invaders gradually forced the Welsh from the rich, arable plains of the East to the rough, barren mountains in the West. And these are still the regions where the English 'Celtic'- speaking minorities live to this day. Wales '(the land of the) foreigners' and Cornwall, with Corn- referring to the original tribal name of the inhabitants and-wall from Old English 'foreigner.' Welsh comes from the corresponding adjective, welisc, wælisc, 'foreign.' Subsequently, the Old English word Welsh even allowed for its interpretation as 'slave.' The word wealh is also used in a racially discriminatory sense in the Laws of King Ine of Wessex from the late seventh century. The law assigns - even to free wealas - a lower social rank than to an Englishman, as the compensation paid for killing them was lower for the former than for the latter. [see The Adventurous History of the Word Wales, http://old-engli.sh/trivia.php?ID=Wales]

The folklore of the Cymry has many comparisons with Irish legends. The Irish are generally regarded as having arrived in these islands before the Cymry. Although the ancient books of the Cymry are not as detailed as the Irish Annals, they do add independent confirmation of the arrival of Africans, Arabians, and tribes from various parts of the Mediterranean.

Trioedd Ynys Prydein

The Triads of the Island of Britain

The compiling of information into triads is very common in Irish and Cymry folk traditions. Kuno Meyer produced an extensive Irish collection, the *'Trecheng Breth Féne'*, over 100 years ago which resulted the completion of the brilliant scholarly work Triads of Ireland in 1906.

Welsh literature owes an enormous debt to Rachel Bromwich who compiled a very comprehensive edition of *'Trioedd Ynys Prydein'*. She started in 1961 with her first edition and produced her third edition in 2006. She was the leading expert on the triads and there is no one who comes close to matching her expertise.

Rachel Bromwich's masterful translation of the medieval manuscripts *'Trioedd Ynys Prydein'* (Triads of the Island of Britain) has preserved details of early Cymry traditions. The Welsh Triads, which are basically a collection of ancient poems grouped and themed in three. A rather intriguing example is the fascinating account given of the "Three Invaders" of Britain. The account begins with the Three Red Ravagers of Britain:

> There were 'Three Red Ravagers' Britain – The first was Arthur, the second was Rhun, son of Beli; and the third was Morgant. One of these 'three savage men' of Britain, who performed some assassination, was Iago, son of Beli. A recurring theme in the Triads is the tax that the ancient Britons were forced to pay. This tax was imposed on the people of Britain by Caswallawn, son of Beli. This Caswallawn is said to have driven out the Romans and succeeded in driving them back as far as southern France. He is also said to have conquered many neighboring islands. The story of Beli and his sons is extremely important in the Welsh traditions. Ancient documents mention three tribes that oppressed the ancient Britons after the departure of the Romans.

The first group to invade Britain was a tribe called the Coraniaid from Arabia. The second invaders were the Gwyddyl Ffichti or the Picts. The last group to oppress the Britons were the Saxons under the leadership of Hengist and

Horsa. Rachel Bromwich, was the leading expert on the Welsh Triads (Trioedd Ynys Prydein) has the following:

> translation of triad 36:
>
> Three Oppressions That Came To This Island,
>
> And Not One Of Them Went Back:
>
> One of them (was) the people of the Coraniaid,
>
> (The Coraniaid (y Corr(y)anyeit) may be the Tylwyth Teg)
>
> who came here in the time of Caswallawn (=Lludd?) son of Beli:
>
> and not one of them went back. and they came from Arabia.
>
> The second Oppression: the Gwyddyl Ffichti
>
> (The Gwyddyl Ffichti are the Picts).
>
> And not one of them went back.
>
> The third Oppression: the Saxons, with Horsa and Hengist as their leaders.

Bromwich gives more information about triads 35 and 36 in her notes:

> R substitutes porth 'an army (in aid)' to designate the first host, and Pen. 16 employs kymorth, a compound of porth in 1.3 where R has dygyfuor. In favour of cyvor as the original word in the triad is the fact that triads 35 and 36 form a contrasting pair; the use of cyvor to designate an (outgoing) flood, a draining of their resources of the Island of Britain, is balanced by that of gormes in triad 36 to designate an incoming invasion. It is difficult to account for R's substitution of porth in item a, since this stresses the idea of assistance which has no counterpart in triad 36 (triad 36 is in fact omitted from all texts of the WR version). [p84]

The second oppression was from the Picts; a people whose origin are shrouded in mystery. They do not appear to have spoken an Indo-European language. The Picts once inhabited most of Scotland and the surrounding islands. The Picts are referred to as the Papes or Pents by the Vikings. They are described as the first inhabitants of the Orkney Island. The early Irish Christian hermits in Iceland were also known by the name Papes. The *Historia Norwegie* written c. 1211 AD gives an interesting insight into their origins:

> Originally those islands were inhabited by Pents and Papes. One of these races, the Pents, only a little taller than pygmies, accomplished miraculous achievements by building towns, morning and evening, but at midday every ounce of strength deserted them and they hid for fear in underground chambers. At that period these islands were not called the Orkneys but rather Pentland, so that the sea which separates the islands from Scotland is still known by the natives as the Pentland Firth............ Of the place where these Pents came from, we know nothing at all. The Papes were so called on account of the vestments in which they clothed themselves like priests, and for this reason all priests are known as papen in the German tongue. One of the islands is still named Papey from them. However, as the appearance and letter-forms of the books they left there behind them testify, they were from Africa and clove to the Jewish faith. [Edited by Inger Ekrem and Lars Boje Mortensen Translated by Peter Fisher, Historia Norwegie, 2006]

The arrival of Hengist and Horsa at Ebbsfleet (449 AD) is well documented. Irish tribes such as the Desi colonized much of Wales and south-west Britain; they were famous for their fierce raids. The arrival of the Arabian Coraniaid is shrouded in mystery. The Welsh Triads seem to add support to Geoffrey of Monmouth's account. Gormund The African and his 100,000 men conquer Ireland, invaded Loegria (central England/Midlands); drove the Cymry into the western parts of the Island, and then granted permission for the Anglo-Saxons to settle the region:

> The Coraniaid and the Saxons united, and by violence and conquest brought the Loegrians into confederacy with them; and subsequently took the crown of the monarchy from the tribe of the Cambrians [Cymry]. And there remained none of the Loegrians that did not become Saxons, except those that are found in Cornwall, and the commot of Carnoban in Deria and Bernicia. In this manner the primitive tribe of the Cambrians, who preserved both their country and their language, lost the sovereignty of the Isle of Britain on account of the treachery of the refuge-seeking tribes, and the pillage of the three invading tribes." [Iolo Morganwg translation (1807)]

The name of this tribe could be derived from the Hamito-Semitic (Afro-asiatic) 'carn' meaning horn. This tribe is strongly associated with the people of Beli. The Coraniaid, Cornii, and Coraniaid tribal name is found in Cornwall, Midlands of England, further north in Scotland, as well as in southern Spain.

Beddoe's remarks on the physical characteristics of the people who now inhabit areas associated with the ancient Coraniaid tribe is worth mentioning here:

> They are supposed to have occupied the counties of Lincoln, Nottingham, Derby, Leicester, Rutland, and part of Northamptonshire ; and in these counties I can find no Roman station whose name appears to be Teutonic; while the important town of Margidunum, near Southwell, in Nottinghamshire, bears a name almost certainly 'Celtic', and Ratis Corion does the same ; and Nottingham would seem to have remained 'Celtic' long enough for its Welsh name not to have been altogether forgotten even in the time of Alfred ; for Asser says it was called in Welsh, Tigguocobauc. Again, if the Coritavi were Germans, and were overlaid by successive strata of Angles and Danes, one may reasonably expect to find the Teutonic physical type prevalent over their whole area to a degree not found elsewhere in Britain. Now, in the northern part of the Coritanian area it is really very prevalent, but in the southern (Leicestershire and Northamptonshire) there is, if I may judge by the colours of the hair and eyes, a strong non-Teutonic element. The following table shows a great difference between Lincoln and Leicester, Nottingham, and Northampton, in these respects, there being a much larger proportion of dark hair in the two more southern towns.

The observation of the dark phenotype is a recurring theme in Beddoe's work:

> Professor Phillips, than whom no ethnologist was a keener observer, once visited Leicestershire, with the expectation of finding a strongly marked Scandinavian type predominant there; but he was surprised to find a dark-haired type, which he supposed to be 'Celtic', equally prevalent. This may easily be accounted for, and that without treating the traditions

> about the Coranied as altogether spurious, as Lord Strangford thought them, if we suppose the Coritavi to have been a Colony of 'Celtic' Belgae; but, unless we throw aside the evidence of physical type, we can hardly conceive how this can possibly have been Germans. Moreover, the silence of Tacitus respecting any suspicion of there being Germans in the island, except the Caledonians, is of weight on the same side. [Beddoe]

On closer inspection, the Cymry clearly state that three tribes came to Briton as guests; the Caledonians, the Irish tribes who dwell in the Highlands of Scotland, and lastly the Galedin (Gauls or Celts). These three tribes could only become Britons after nine generations, and they would have no claim on the land of Britain. The Triads have the following:

> There were three refuge seeking tribes that came to the Island of Prydein and they came under the peace and permission of the tribe of the Cymry, without arms and without opposition. The first was a tribe of Caledonians in the north. The second was the Irish tribe, who dwelled in the highlands of Scotland. The third were the people of Galedin, who came in naked vessels to the Island of Wight, when their country was drowned, where they had land granted them by the tribe of Cymry. They had no privilege of claim in the Island of Prydein, but they had land and protection assigned to them under certain limitations; and it was stipulated that they should not possess the rank of native Cymry until the ninth of their lineal descendants. [p620-621, Trioedd Ynys Prydein Triads of The Isles of Prydain, The Word: Welsh Witchcraft, the Grail of Immortality & the Sacred Keys, T. Enion Vawr,]

The clues start to mount up. The tribe led by Beli is known to have driven out the Romans. The Welsh Triads describe how the Roman Emperor Maxen fought Beli, son of Manogan. Belinus, the son of Lud, led the people of Britain into war against the Romans. Also, early Welsh genealogies trace the Cymry back to an eponymous ancestor called Beli Mawr (Mawr= big). All ruling dynasties of the Cymry traced themselves back to the family of Beli.

The expulsion of the Romans or Romano-Britons seems to have involved people from Africa and Arabia. Geoffrey of Monmouth brings them out of Ireland under Gormund, while the account in the triads name them as the Coraniaid Arabians. The mysterious Coraniaids were gifted with the ability of being able to hear a single whisper across the land (similar to the Formorians under Balor).

DNA analysis of population of Abergele (Conwy, North Wales) found that over 40% of the male population had haplogroup E1b1 (E-V13). This sub-Saharan male DNA migrated out of Egypt into the Balkans around 5000 years ago. Interesting, the area known as Loegria (Midlands), from where the Africans drove out the Cymry, has been labelled by scientist as an 'E1b1 hole.' Steven C. Bird has suggested that the West Midlands and South Midlands of England (Loegria) underwent complete population replacement because the genetic profile of this region (male DNA) is very similar to Friesland, making it very Anglo-Saxon. Steven C. Bird paper, *'[Haplogroup E3b1a2 (now E-V13) as a Possible Indicator of Settlement in Roman Britain by Soldiers of Balkan Origin']*, opposes the theory that E-V13 arrived in Britain during the Neolithic. He attributes the presence of this DNA type, found in very high concentrations in North Wales, to Roman soldiers from the Balkans. He writes, *'If E3b1a-M78 had in fact arrived during the Neolithic era by water routes from Iberia and the Mediterranean, there would not appear to be any obvious reason for it to be distributed so unevenly between Britain and Ireland.'*

The distribution of E1b1 subclades such as E-V13 has not receive much attention from modern geneticists. Bryan Sykes in his 'Blood of the Isles' gives only a brief paragraph to this particular topic:

> Lastly, I have found a tiny number of very unusual clans in the southern part of England. Two of these are from sub-Saharan Africa, three from Syria or Jordan. These exotic sequences are found only in England, with one exception, and among people with no knowledge of, or family connections with, those distant parts of the world. I think they might be the descendants of Roman slaves, whose lines have kept going through unbroken generations of women. If this was the genetic legacy of the Romans, they have left only the slightest traces on the female side. I have not found any in Wales, or in Ireland and only one in Scotland. There is an African sequence from Stornoway in the Western Isles, for which I have absolutely no explanation. [Sykes, Bryan. Blood of the Isles (Kindle Location 4206)]

Geoffrey of Monmouth

The early Welsh triads and Geoffrey of Monmouth's 12th century account of the History of Britain are two sources that independently confirm the arrival of Africans and Arabians. Geoffrey of Monmouth was descended form a family of Normans, Bretons, and Franks who formed the ruling elite after the conquest of William the Conqueror in 1066 A.D. Geoffrey of Monmouth states that his book was based on ancient books found in the land. Geoffrey's History of The Kings of Britain begins with the tale of the Trojan hero Brutus. Aeneas and his son, Ascanius, escaped to Italy after the Trojan war. Geoffrey of Monmouth credits Ascanius with the founding of the city Alba, on the river Tiber. One day, while hunting Brutus accidentally killed his father, and was subsequently banished from Italy. He then travelled to Greece and joined up with some Trojans. Brutus became the leader of this group, organised them, and set sail towards Africa. They passed by the 'Altars of the Philistines' [Lepcis Magna, Libya] and the salt-pan lakes [Tunisia]. After a hazardous journey, they finally reached Mauretania [modern Morocco]. Brutus and his followers, according to Geoffrey of Monmouth, travelled into north-western Africa, and ravaged Mauretania. Next, they sailed through the Pillars of Hercules [the Straits of Gibraltar], and into the Atlantic Ocean.

The Irish version of the Historia Britonum of Nennius gives a similar account:

> Afterwards the Scythians went, with their children, into Africa, to the altars of the Philistines, to the wells of Salmara, and between the Ruiseagdse, and Mount lasdaire, and across the River Mbalb through the Mediterranean Sea to the pillars of Hercules, beyond the sea of Gadidon to Spain; and they dwelt in Spain afterwards, until the sons of Miled (Milesius) of Spain came to Erin, with thirty boats, with thirty couples in each boat, at the end of a thousand and two years after Pharaoh was drowned in the Red Sea. [p55, Todd, James Henthorn, 1805-1869; Irish Archaeological Society, Irish version of the Historia Britonum of Nennius, 1848]

The story continues with Brutus joining Trojan exiles led by Corineaus. Cornwall was the first part of Britain settled by the progenitors of the Cymry and was named after Corineaus. This group departed from Africa and sailed for Aquitaine in south-western France. The Picts were already in possession of this region and the Cymry were defeated in a series of battles. The Cymry then retreated and set sail towards Britain.

On landing in Cornwall, the Cymry were opposed by Giants. The most famous of these giants was Gog Magog. Corineaus, who was famous for his wrestling abilities, defeated this Giant and Britain was freed from this mysterious race of giants. The Trojans settled in Britain, and their leader Brutus married Ignoge. They had three sons: Loegria (Locrinus), Cymru (Kamber), and Albanactus. The eldest son Loegria governed what is now England and was called Loegria after him. The Cymry (or Welsh) take their name from Kamber, the second son of Brutus, who was given Wales to govern. The youngest son, Albanactus, was allowed to rule Scotland, which in ancient times was called Albany.

The significance of this story recorded by Geoffrey of Monmouth is that he describes the migration of the Cymry from the interior of northern Africa. The journey from Mauretania and then finally reaching south-western Britain is the same route taken by the proto-Irish. According to the Welsh triads, a collection of ancient poems, the Welsh came from the Land of Summer. Is this a reference to Mauretania? (notice how they did not land in Iberia). When they landed in south-west Britain, the Welsh renamed that region *Gwlad yr Haf* or the Land of Summer - now called Somerset, after the ancient Cymry homeland (Mauretania?).

After the Romans left Britain, Aurelius Ambrosius, a Romano-Briton, became the ruler of the island. Geoffrey of Monmouth recounts how this monarch set out to build a monument for fallen war heroes. The famous druid Merlin instructed Aurelius to go to Ireland and bring back the Giants Ring, a group of exceptionally large standing stones. Merlin stated that in ancient days the Giants from Africa, who inhabited Ireland, brought these stones from that continent. These Africans, he states, used these stones to cure their ailments.

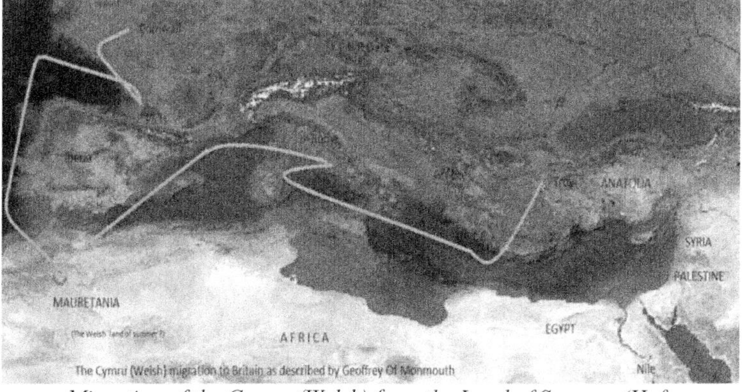

Migration of the Cymru (Welsh) from the Land of Summer (Haf), modified by the author.

This story reflects a trend in both Irish and Scottish folklore that constantly refers to the ancient megalithic structure scattered across these island as having been built by Africans. For example, in the folklore of the Scottish Highlands, the standing stones of Callanish are said to have been built by tall black men who wore robes made of feathers, These Western Isles of Scotland are associated with the African Formorians who are said to have had their base in the Hebrides. It was from these northern islands that the African Formorians frequently raided Ireland.

Clochan na bhFomharach [stones of the Fomorians]
(Attributed to A Quinn (ambquinn) from Pixabay)

Gormund the African Conqueror of Britain

There is an intriguing connection between the establishment of the Anglo-Saxon tribes in Loegria (Central England) and Gormund's African troops or Blue-men (*fir-Gorm* of Irish tradition or *fir ghorma* in Scottish Gaelic). Between the 7th and 8th century A.D., the kingdom of Mercia suddenly makes an appearance; fully formed – it appears out of nowhere!

Did the blue men from Africa drive the Romano-Britons out of central England, and then hand over the land to the Anglo-Saxon tribes?

The landing of Hengist and Horsa, the leaders of the Saxon tribes, are mentioned by Geoffrey of Monmouth; however, the detailed description of the invasion of Gormund and his 1000,000 African soldiers that are said to

have decimated the Romano-Britons has been largely ignored by Historians.
When Constantine III ruled Britain, the Angles and Saxons (pagan Germanic tribes from northern Germany) constantly made raids on the southern British coast that lay opposite France. Flavius Claudius Constantinus was Western Roman co-emperor from AD 409 - 411. In his reign the province of Britain was in open revolt. During this period there was significant tribal movements. Tribes such as the Vandals, the Burgundians, the Alans and the Sueves were crossing the Rhine and overwhelming the Romans.

The newly arrived Germanic tribes were a minority in south-eastern Britain. Brythonic (Cymry) speaking tribes inhabited the entire region along with tribes descended from the Bronze Age period. A revolt by the Saxons was crushed by Constantine III. The next ruler of Britain was Keredic. He was also faced with increasing attacks from the Saxons, but unlike his predecessor, he was unable to maintain the independence of Britain.

Did an African invasion force Keredic to seek refuge in the city of Cirencester? Corinium was the old name for Cirencester, it was also known as the City of Sparrows. Gormund and his African warriors are said to have destroyed this city and forced Keredic to flee to Wales. The entire Midland region (Loegria) of Britain was conquered by Gormund and his Africans. The story then takes a fascinating twist. The Africans then encouraged the Saxons to settle in the Midlands (Loegria). The remaining Romano-Britons fled to the remotest parts of the Island and some sought refuge in Armorica; also referred to as Brittany or little Britain. The Bretons are classified as one of the six so-called 'Celtic' Nations, i.e., Ireland, Scotland, Wales (Cymru), Cornwall, Isle of Man, and Brittany.

These manuscripts give an account of Africans initially conquering Ireland, landing in Britain, and then forcibly driving the Romano-Britons into the western parts of the island. After this, the Africans invite the Angle and Saxon tribes to settle in Loegria (Central England).

1346 battle of Caen English troops attacking fortified Caen, France.
Notice there are many black faces on left side.
(Attributed to Jean Froissart, Public domain, via Wikimedia Commons.)

1346 battle of Caen English troops with black-skinned mercenaries.
(Attributed to Jean Froissart, Public domain, via Wikimedia Commons.)

Who was Gormund?

And are there any independent sources that also mention him or an African invasion?

It is worth noting that this is not the first time the English have had African allies. In 1346 King Edward III launched an attack on the Frenchtown of Caen, situated in Normandy. The large English army, estimated at 15,000 men, attacked, and captured the town. The troops used by King Edward III seem to have been made up of large numbers of men with 'black' skin.

The eldest son of Edward III took part in the military campaigns across

France. A point of interest, he is remembered by the name the Black Prince (15 June 1330 – 8 June 1376). Does his portrait indicate a swarthy coloring; maybe its for the reader to decide?

The Edward, Black Prince (1330-1376), black or white?

Edward, The Black Prince
(Attributed to Unknown author,
Public domain, via Wikimedia Commons.)

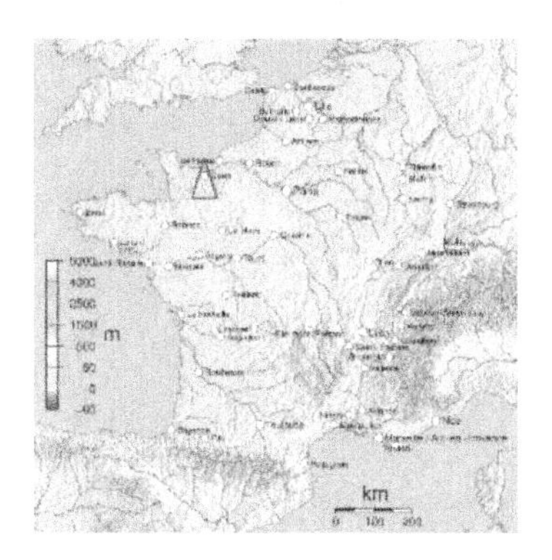

Location of Caen shown in a relief map of Metropolitan France,
showing cities with over 100,000 inhabitants.
(Attributed to David Monniaux, creative commons Wikimedia Commons,
Modified by the author to show location of Caen in red).)

The account given by John Major (1521 AD), translated from the Latin by Archibald Constable (published in 1892 AD), is worth consulting:

> [CHAP. VIII.] Concerning the arrival of Gormund, first in Ireland then in Britain, and his cruel dealings with both lands; also, of the rule of the Saxons in Britain under Gormund:
>
> About this time a man of Africa named Gormund, famous for the cruelty of in war, a heathen too, but aiming at new territories, made his descent into Ireland with a large army, and brought into subjection a great part of that island. And when the Saxons in the perfidy of Britain came to hear of this, being inferior to the Britons, they Saxons. sent an embassy to Gormund the African, praying him to come to Britain, and promising to confer on him the supreme power. Whereupon he lands in Britain, and, with help of the Saxons, wrought indignity on the churches and on all that pertained to the Christian religion, and so restored the heathen the established way and infidel worship among the Britons. But Gormund heathenism. tarried no long time in Britain, but led all his African train into Gaul, that by land he might return to his own; and to the Saxons who had been at his bidding in the war against the Saxon rule. Britons he made over their territory, and so the heathen came to hold that part of Britain which the Saxons call England. One may believe, however, that with them some Britons were mingled. Hence it is plain that among the Britons the Christian religion flourished in Britain, and often times was overthrown by the unbelievers. [by A history of Greater Britain as well England as Scotland John Major edited and translated by Archibald Constable, 1892]

More details about Gormund can be found in Theodor Fluri's 1895 publication 'Isembart et Gormont. Entwicklung der Sage und historische Grundlage' (translation: Isembart and Gormont, Development of the legend and historical basis):

> [Brut of Layamon III, p. 156-160.] Then was in Africa a king, exceeding powerful; he was an African, named Anster; he had two sons, brave knights both; Gurmund hight the elder, and Gerion hight the younger. The old king died, — his days were passed, — he gave his son Gurmund his good realm. But

Gurmund despised it, and have it he would not, and thought all another thing, and gave it to his brother; and said that he would not possess any realm, unless he it won with weapon and with men, but with battle he would possess a kingdom, or nevermore would he have one! Gurmund was a champion approved in might, and he was the strongest man that any man looked on. He began to send over all the land, into Babylonia, into Macedonia, into Turkey, into Persia, into Nubia, into Arabia; and bade all the youths over the heathen lands, that they should procure them worthy weapons, and he would forth right make them knights, and afterwards go with them, and seek where he might win kingdoms, with his strong warriors. It came toward Africa from many a kingdom the son of many a mighty man, many a heathen person came to Gurmund, the heathen chief. When this host was assembled, and his folk numbered, then were there told, knights most bold, a hundred and sixty thousand, freely weaponed without their archers, that before should press, and without the craftsmen, that came to Gurmund. Forth they marched innumerable host; to the sea they came, then had they fair wind; into ship embarked the heathen warriors. Seventeen there went, that were kings' sous, there were eight and twenty of earth offspring swept from the land; seven hundred ships in the foremost flock, without the ships following! Forth floated with the waves innumerable folk; all the islands that they before them found, all they went in hand to the king Gurmund. Many a king he fought with and they all yearned his peace, and all the lands he won that he looked on. And then at the end he came to Ireland.

[Wace v. 13973-84. Layamon III, 170] Gurmund made castles about Cirencester; three he committed to three heathen knights, himself he held the one, Isembart the other. Gurmund made a tower, therein he built a chamber, therein he played his play, that men loved in those days, therein he had his mawmet, that he held for his god. [Note: This is the archaic form of mammet; used in Middle Ages as a reference to Muslim worship]

Say me, lord Gurmund, — thou art king very powerful, — how long wilt thou lay about this burgh? "What will thou give me, if I give thee the burgh, and all that is within, to do thy will, that nought shall be left, for all thou shalt possess?" Then answered Gurmund, the mighty heathen king, I will give thee an earldom, ever to possess, on condition that thou quickly deliver me the burgh. This agreement was made anon, — few men it knew. Then this heathen knight up arose forth- right, and sought nets woven exceeding narrow, and the tools there to, and cut them very narrow; and there before he can pour draft and chaff and oats. Thus, can he it delight; and sparrows thereto alighted, and he at the first draught very many he caught; and he took them in safety from the ground, so that all their wings were not injured. Then sought he nut-shells, and caused it to be put in the shells, and before the night brought fire therein, and fast knotted them to the sparrows' feet. These he let go forth, very many sparrows; the sparrows took their flight, and flew to their holes over the burgh, where they were inhabiting, in the eaves they clung, so they did in the mows. Anon as the fire was hot, as the sparrows inner crept, the wind came with the night, and the fire kindled, and the burgh in many places her to burn; in the east side and in the west side, — woe was to the Britons there, when they weaned to be sure; and they fled into one end. Then arose the fire anon, before, and behind. Gurmund caused horns and trumpets to be blown; fifteen thousand brought to the blast. The Britons burn, the Britons can but run; they leapt out of the walls, and men slew them all.

[Wace v. 14029-36, Layamon III, 175-176]. And many winters afterwards, the folk that there dwelt called it Sparrow-Chester in their popular speech; and yet so do some men call it, to commemorate the old deeds.

[Wace 14055-82, Layamon III, 178]: Beside Alemaine is a land named Angles, there were born the same that were chosen to whom Gurmund gave all this kingdom in hand, as he had promised to them in covenant, if he should it win. All his promise he fulfilled to them of Angles they came, and thereof they took name, and caused themselves to be called, full truly, the folk that was English; and this land they called Angle-land, for it was all in their hand. After first the Britons came to this land, Britain it was named, of Britons took name, until this folk came that this name took from it.

> [Wace v. 13931-48, Layamon III, 168—6]. It was on a day that Gurmund with his folk, — heathen thanes, — rode a hunting. Then came there a man riding to Gurmund the king; he was named Isemberd, in France was his native land; he was Louis's son, the king of the country. His father hat driven him out of all his kingdom, so that he might not where dwell in all his sovereignty; he fled to this land to Gurmund. He had for companions two thousand riders, and he became Gormund's man; he might no worse do, for Christ himself he forsook, and to the Worse he took and there he deserted Christendom and heathenism took on him.

The account found in the Rambles by Rivers Thames by James Thorne (1849) gives us even more details:

> To Cirencester, through which town it flows. Cirencester, or Ciceter, as it is called by the natives, claims a fuller notice. Its story commences before the time that modern English historians recognise. Monkish writers relate, and Polydore Vergil repeats after them, a tale that says much for the patient courage of its early inhabitants. Long before the Saxons came into England, in the days of King Brute, which is nobody knows how long ago, Cirencester was a famous town. Strong were its walls and stout the hearts of its citizens and little did it dread the visit of an enemy. But one came who was not disposed to lose his labour. Gormund was an African prince, - in what part of Africa his kingdom was situated, or how he found his way to England, is not stated, and does not matter, but certain it is (if Polydorus is to be depended on) that he laid siege to Cirencester. Seven long years he kept his army before it, but never a step the nearer was he to the inside of its gates; when one day a bright thought struck him. Houses were not tiled then, and Gormund judged that if he could only manage to set fire to the thatched roofs of those in the town, he should be likely, in the commotion that would arise, to gain an easy entrance. Resolved to put the stratagem he had conceived into speedy practice, he set all his soldiers to catch sparrows; and when as many were caught as he considered sufficient, he had certain combustibles fastened to their tails, and then let them loose. The poor birds flew straight to their nests under the thatches, which of course were quickly in a blaze; and while the unfortunate housekeepers were busy endeavoring to

> quench the flames, Gormund succeeded in entering the town - in memory whereof (says Giraldus Cambrensis) it was afterwards called the City of Sparrows. Whatever may be thought of this story, there is sufficient evidence in authentic history of the ancient greatness of the place. It was the metropolis of the Roman province of the Dobuni, and was named Corinium, or Duro-Cornovium. Three of the great Roman roads - the Fosse road, Akeman Street, and Ermin Street, met here. The last two were British roads, and there is good reason to believe that Cirencester was a British town. [Rambles by Rivers Thames by James Thorne (1849)]

The story hints at Gormund being a Muslim since the term mawmet is an archaic form of mammet - a name used in the Middle Ages for an idol, because in the Middle Ages Europeans incorrectly believed that Muslims worshipped images representing the prophet Mohammed (pbuh). Gormund constructed a tower (a minaret?). We are also told that he recruited vast numbers of youth from Babylonia, Macedonia, Turkey, Persia, Nubia, and Arabia.

The story of Cirencester is remarkably similar to the story of the conflict between the Abyssinians, under Abraha, and the Quraysh of Mecca. Surat al-Fil (Sura 105), or the verse of The Elephant, tells of the failed Abyssinian invasion of Mecca. According to Islamic sources, the Abyssinian viceroy who governed Yemen, Abraha, is said to have invaded Yemen with 100,000 troops. The massacre of Christians by the Jewish Himyarites of Najran led to the Abyssinian invasion, which resulted in the defeat of Himyar and the complete occupation of South Arabia in AD 532. The Abyssinians led by Abraha, defeated the Jewish Himyarites and then sent a military expedition to try and destroy Mecca around AD 570. This is referred to as the year of the Elephant.

Abraha built a cathedral in Sana; he wished to make it a center for pilgrimage. He aimed to destroy Mecca, so as to make Sana the only place for pilgrimage. The expedition of Abraha occurred in the year when prophet Muhammad (pbuh) was born. In A.D. 570, Abd al-Muttalib *(who was prophet Muhammad's (pbuh) paternal grandfather)* and the Quraysh tribesmen defended the Ka'bah against the Abyssinians. During this conflict, the Quraysh received support from an unexpected source.

Abraha and his Abyssinians troops reached the vicinity of the Ka'bah. He gave the order to destroy the Ka'bah and suddenly he was faced with an enormous mass of birds (*Ababil*) that filled the sky and completely encompassed the Abyssinians. Each bird carried three pebbles and launched them directly onto the Abyssinians and the elephants. The Abyssinian troops were defeated, and their leader was fatally wounded, and later died in Yemen.

Sura 105 describes these events:

> Have you not seen how your Lord dealt with the companions of the Elephant? Did He not make their treacherous plan go astray? And He sent against them birds in flocks, striking them with stones of baked clay, so He rendered them like straw eaten up. (Quran, 105)

Gormund's story is remarkably similar to the account given in the Quran surat 105 al-Fil. Several medieval sources confirm the siege of Cirencester. Brut Tysylio makes use of additional sources and adds to what we have from Geoffrey of Monmouth. Brut Tysylio is believed to have been the author of Brut y Brenhinedd (Chronicle of the Kings) based on old Welsh books and gives a Welsh version of Geoffrey of Monmouth's History of The Kings of Britain:

> The Welsh renderings are not straightforward translations in the modern sense, but by contemporary standards, they are generally close to their Latin source text, with only some commentary or additional material from bardic traditional lore (cyfarwydd) appended to the text.[3] Importantly, several manuscripts include a version of the tale known as Lludd and Llefelys inserted in the segment about Lludd Llaw Eraint; the presence or absence of this tale has been used to classify the early versions of the Brut. [Bromwich, Triads. p. 416.]

All the accounts agree that Cirencester was held under siege by the Africans and was eventually destroyed by using birds (sparrows) to set the city on fire. Timothy Darvill's article *'Grismond's Tower, Cirencester, and the Rise of Springhead Super-mounds in the Cotswolds and Beyond'* published in the Transactions Bristol & Gloucestershire Archaeological Society 132 (2014), 11–27, explored the large domed mound known as Grismond's Tower located inside the walls of Cirencester Park on the west side of the town. It is believed to originally been a round barrow, and measures 30 m in diameter and is 4 m in height. The earliest written mention of Grismond's Tower was by William of Worcester in around 1478. Written sources have several variants of the name, such as Grosmond and Grosmund.

Early traditions make the mound the location where King Arthur was crowned ruler of the Britons. The itinerary of John Leland, between 1535 and 1543, provides an insight to this ancient structure. William Camden (1551-1623) gives an account that clearly mentions Gormund in connection with this mound:

> The British Chronicles record that this City was burnt, being

> set on fire by sparrows through a stratagem devised by one Gurmund, I wot not what Tyrant of Africk, whereupon Giraldus called it 'Passerum urbem', that is, 'The 'Sparrowes City', and out of those Chronicles Necham writeth thus: This City felt for seven years space Thy forces, Gurmund. Who this Gurmund was I know not. The Inhabitants shew a mount beneath the City which they report Gurmund did cast up, and yet they call it Grismund's Toure. Marianus, an Historian of good antiquity and credit, reporteth that Ceaulin King of the West Saxons dispossessed the Britons of it, what time he had discomfited and put to flight their forces at Deoham and brought Gloucester to his subjection Many years after this it was subject to the West-Saxons. [William Camden's full account can be found at vision of Britain.org.uk/travelers/Camden/13]

This account helps place Gormund's invasion in the time of Ceaulin or Ceawlin who died around AD 593 and was the King of Wessex. He was the son of Cynric of Wessex, and the grandson of Cerdic of Wessex, and was the leader of the first wave of Saxons to arrive in south-west England (later to become Wessex). It was during the leadership of Ceawlin that the Britons (Cymry) were expelled from the region.

The various sources consulted indicate that Gormund was a real historical figure, who was involved in the destruction of Cirencester. The events are associated with the Battle of Dirham in 577 AD. This battle led to the capture of Cirencester, Gloucester, and Bath; driving the Cymry across the river Severn and into Cornwall.

The adventures of the Moors extended far and wide in Europe. They penetrated deep into the Alps, where they are known to have built lofty castles. Has the intervention of the African Moors in early Anglo-Saxon England been ignored by academics? Compare the records we have of the Moorish adventures in Italy; did Gormund the African also intervene in Anglo-Saxon England during the same period?

> **When Naples in 837 AD appealed for Arab aid, the Moslem war-cry echoed on the slopes of Vesuvius as it had before on those of its southern sister – "the mountain of fire". .... About the same time the victorious Moslems made an appearance before Venice. In 846 AD even Rome was threatened by Arab squadrons which landed at Ostia and, unable to penetrate the walls of the Eternal City, sacked the cathedral of St. Peter beside the Vatican**

> **........the hold of the Moslems over Italy remained so firm that Pope John VIII (872-82) deemed it prudent to pay tribute for two years...... The Aghlabids did not limit their operations to the Italian coast. In 869 AD they captured Malta. From Italy and Spain piratical raids in the tenth century extended through the Alpine passes into mid-Europe. In the Alps are a number of castles and walls which tourist guides attribute to the invasion of the Saracens. Certain Swiss placenames, such as Gaby and Algaby (al-jabi, tax collector) which appear in Baedeker's Switzerland, may possibly be of Arabic origin. [by Gabriele Crespi, The Arabs in Europe 1986]**

Ancestry DNA tests of villagers from Bledington, only 15 miles from Cirencester, revealed that the Cotswold villagers only have 42% Anglo-Saxon DNA. The official census identified the population of the village as being 94.5% 'White' - however, the ancestry DNA tests on 120 residents revealed 42.54% Anglo-Saxon, 20.61% Western Europe, Irish-Scots-Welsh 17.03%, while the remainder had DNA from distant places such as South Asia, West Asia, North Africa, Finland, Italy, and Greece. A fact that certainly challenges the current concept of Britishness.

8 SKIN COLOUR & PHENOTYPE IN FOLKLORE

There are so many characters in the ancient Irish and Welsh Annals who have black skin. Ignored by modern writers, these characters cannot be dismissed. Irish history starts with the arrival of Cesair from Meroe, the Formorians ruled from the beginning of time, and even the 'cruel-hearted' Danaans are described as brown.

The famous Hobbit film based on J. R. R. Tolkien's fantasy novels, was hit by controversy when a British woman of Pakistani descent, Naz Humphreys, was turned away from an audition because she was regarded as too dark by the producers. She was not allowed to play a mythical character because of the colour of her skin. Tolkien was inspired by the stories of African Formorians and Middle eastern Danaans; and yet actors who have 'melanin' have been excluded from acting in these movies. The message '*No brown goblins need apply?*' seems to have been applied in this case.

No Brown Goblins Need Apply? Hobbit Movie Controversy.
Modified by the author, (Attribute to LadyofHats, creative commons via Wikimedia Commons)

When Renako McDonald featured as Cu Chulainn in RTE's Live Concert 'Centenary 1916'; internet forums became busy with racists who were offended because he was a black African actor. Tolkien's entire work was inspired by Irish folklore that he encountered during a trip to the striking Burren of Sligo. Irish folklore includes abundant references to characters who are African. The Gaelic hero Cú Chulainn is often described as a 'black, sorrowful man with black cropped hair and black eyebrows. Obviously, the trolls on the internet were not aware of this fact.

Irish folk songs have an embedded remembrance of its African past. Anthony Roberts gives an account of the 'Island of the Bless,' situated to the west of Ireland. To reach this paradise, one had to travel along a long road where all the inhabitants were black. Next comes a land where all the people are tall and drive chariots. Old songs also mention that in those ancient days people could fly. This could be a reference to the Shamanic-like practice of using plants to induce a meditative state to facilitate astral travel during healing rituals. Peter Lamborn Wilson explored this in his book *'Ploughing the Clouds: The Search for Irish Soma'*. In an interview with Mordecai Watts *[June 25, 1995]*, Wilson had the following to say about this subject:

> "The ancient 'Celts' had some kind of soma ceremony, some kind of ritual psychedelic, which would conceivably also involve the indigenous, non-'Celtic' people, who we believe - we Atlanteans believe, are the same people as the Berbers and the Iberians. So, my work is going on ......but unfortunately has not emerged from the world of the unseen yet. "[Peter Lamborn Wilson telephone interview with Mordecai Watts, June 25, 1995]

Although some cultures have been known to use psychoactive substances to enter trances; the ancient Formorians and Coraniaid, and even 19th century Irish healers such as Biddy Early had the natural ability of second sight and did not need to use any substances to access these abilities. The great monument called Stonehenge was believed to be a place of healing. Geoffrey of Monmouth gives an enthralling account of *'African giants taking baths under the standing stones of Stonehenge; they would carefully pour water onto the stones and use it to take healing baths.'*

The Welsh Mabinogion are the earliest prose stories of the literature of Britain. In the tale Lady of The Fountain a black man sits waiting on top of a hill with his large iron club. Curly haired individuals are frequently mentioned. For example, Eiryn Wych, son of Peibyhn, had rough curly hair. Most blond characters are described as having curly hair. The Mabinogion describes the court of King Arthur at Caerleon, South Wales. This enigmatic King was visited by a curly haired lay whose face is described as black and her hands the blackest imaginable. Another story describes a black man, also known as the black oppressor, who fought against many warriors at Ysbidinongyl Castle.

Ancient Irish literature gives an incredibly detailed description of the racial characteristics of the ancient inhabitants. The ancient Irish are describes as having every hair type and colour imaginable. Today the bulk of the Irish people have dark hair. Interestingly, blond hair is completely absent in some areas. An obvious indication that the Irish are unlikely to be the descendants of mythical 'Aryan Celts' from Central Europe.

A brief glance at *Leabhar na Luidhre* helps build a picture of the variety of ancient Irish phenotypes. The following extracts illustrate the variation of skin colour amongst the inhabitants:

> There came three great black warriors.
>
> On the fourth day came the woman to them, Beautiful was she, with golden hair.
>
> Then the black cropped man overtook them.
>
> A great black woman with a large mouth.
>
> *Cormac Condlongas is described as having fair golden hair on him, with a ruddy face.
>
> * The Cruithne in Da Derg's hostel are described as three big brown men with three round scalps of hair.
>
> * The swine herders of Conaire are named Dub, Donn, and Dorcha (i.e., Black, Brown, and Dark) and have black scalps upon them.
>
> * The Saxons at Da Derga's hostel have nine yellow manes on them.
>
> * The three giants of Fer Falga are big brown men with black hair on them.
>
> * Da Derga has red hair.
>
> * Cu Chulaind is described as a black, sorrowful man with black cropped hair and black eyebrows. His charioteer has red

hair.

* The fairy promises Cindla the Red, that if he accompanies her to fairy land he will be rewarded with a yellow hair above his ruddy face.

* Dub, Dorcha, and Teimel (Black, Dark, and Darkness) are the three cup bearers of Brian, Luchra, and Lucharba – three deities of the Tuatha De Danaans.

* Fergus has bushy, twisted yellow-white hair.

* Mnae Mathremail has brown curly hair.

* Connad Mac Morna has brown eyes and very curly yellow hair.

* Eirrge Echbel is a warrior with a fat belly, fat lips, broad head, and brown curly hair.

* Fergna Mac Findchonna is a broad brown warrior, with black hair.

* The Tuatha De Danaans have ruddy brown, forked beards.

* Conall Anghlonnach is a wrathful brown warrior.

* Uman Mac Remanfissig, Errgi Echbel, and Celtchair Mac Uthechais have brown, rough hair.

* Roimid has a black pointed scalp and a smooth blue-black face.

Medieval writers try to introduce a colour bias; they want the most important characters in the literature to have yellow hair, and they try to reduce those with black hair to subordinate positions. However, the most influential settlers were the African Formorians, whom the medieval editors try to ignore , but the Formorians keep reappearing and establishing themselves as rulers of Ireland during every era. They fought the Nemedians, Firbolg, Tuatha de Danaans, and the Milesians.

The Irish used the term momg (mane) for yellow hair, while referring to black haired types as berrad (shaven). In the Welsh Mabinogion blond hair is nearly always curly. The hero Cú Chulainn (Cúailnge, Cú Chulaind, or Cúchulain) is a dark, cropped haired individual. He is sometimes called the 'little Setanta' – a name that is closely related to the Setanti tribe of north-west England.

Beddoe's Index of Nigrescence

John Beddoe (1826 – 1911) a Victorian ethnologist was extremely interested in measuring the variations in British phenotypes. He travelled across the country making note of eye colour, skin colour, hair colour, height and incorporated these into his index of Nigrescence.

D + 2N - R - F = INDEX

Class D includes many shades of brown; Class N includes jet black and hard, very coarse hair; R includes that approach red more than yellow or flaxen; Class F includes all fair, yellow, golden, light shades of brown and some pale auburns.

It should be remembered that the Irish and Cymry were regarded as inferior by the colonial English. Even though John Beddoe was the President of the Anthropological Institute (from 1889-1891), his prejudiced views were typical of Victorian England. However, his observation of the 'Africanoid' type is worth mentioning, especially in Yorkshire and the English Midlands; said to be the home of this type. Also, the index of Nigrescence clearly shows that the tall, blond 'Celts' cannot be found in the British Isles or Ireland.

Some of Beddoe's beliefs are highly questionable, to say the least. However, his observations of skin colour and phenotype confirm my own anthropological observations. His definition of Index of Nigrescence is:

> A ready means of comparing the colours of two peoples or localities. Is found in the Index of Nigrescence. The gross index if gotten by subtracting the number of red- and fair-haired persons from that of darked haired, together with twice the black haired. I double the black, in order to give it its proper value to the greater tendency to melanosity shown thereby; while brown, (chestnut) hair is regarded as neutral, though in truth most person placed in B are fair skinned, and approach more nearly in aspect the xanthous type than to melanous variety. [p5, Beddoe, Races of Britain]

Victorian anthropologists were obsessed with ascribing racial categories to various populations they encountered around the world. Beddoe is interesting because he applied these categories to his own Britons; he acknowledged the remnants of Africanoid, dark Iberian, 'Mongolian', and Ugrian phenotypes amongst the modern population of Britain:

> If our Paleolithic race were really the ancestors of the Eskimos, or at least their near relations, as Boyd Dawkins would have them to be, it is at least possible that they may have left descendants behind them to mingle their blood with the Neolithic races and their descendants of today. Now I think some reason can be shown for suspecting the existence of traces of some Mongoloid race in the modern population of Wales and the West of England. Their most notable indication is the oblique or Chinese eye, with its external angle in a horizontal plane a little higher than the internal one. This is usually accompanied by an almond-like form of the opening, and a peculiar thickness of the upper eyelid: these latter characters may occur without the obliquity of the opening, but with a physiognomy referable to the same type. I have notes of 34 persons with oblique eyes. Their heads include a wide range of relative breadth, from 72 to 86, and the average index of latitude is 78.9, which is not much greater than the average of England and Wales. But in other points the type stands out distinctly. The cheekbones are almost always broad; the brows oblique, in the same direction as the eyes; the chin, as a rule, narrow or angular; the nose is often concave or flat, seldom arched; and the mouth is rather inclined to be prominent. The forehead usually recedes a little....... The iris is usually hazel or brown, and the hair straight, dark brown, black, or reddish. This type seems to be common in Wales, in West Somerset, and especially in Cornwall. [Beddoe]

Beddoe places the frequency of prognathism (a heavy prominent mouth) in the population as 6% of the English, 8% of the Welsh, and 20% of the Irish. He then observed that the 'Mongoloid/Ugrian' and the 'prognathous' overlapped in some cases - with the later having longer and narrower heads. He gives a full description:

> The cheekbones are much narrower, but almost invariably prominent in the face. The usual form of the forehead is flat, narrow, and square; that of the chin, narrow and often receding; that of the nose, oftener concave than straight, oftener straight than sinuous or aquiline, usually prominent at the point, with the long slitty nostrils, which, whence so ever derived, are a characteristic of the modern Gaels. The flatness of the temporal region, which comes out in the narrowness of

> the diameter at the root of the zygoma, gives to the norma verticaolis that coffin- or pear-shape which Daniel Wilson ascribes to the Celts. The hair is generally very dark and often curly, but the eyes are more often blue or light- or dark-gray than of any shade of brown; they belong to the blue and violet scales of Broca rather than to the orange. [Beddoe]

Victorian ethnologists documented the phenotype variations across these islands. My own observations have confirmed some of these statements made by Beddoe. The 'Africanoid' certainly exists in Yorkshire and is quite easily distinguished from the pale Scandinavian looking population of Viking origin. The discovery of y-DNA haplogroup A in Yorkshire has confirmed the presence of sub-Saharan Africans.

There are some regions Beddoe did not cover, which are worth noting. Travelling through the South Wales Valley, I have encountered a 'sea' of darked haired, brachycephals (round-headed with cephalic index of 80 or more). The highest concentration of this type can be observed in Caerphilly, where they make up the majority of the population.

To find out more about the predominant phenotype of Caerphilly, I conducted an experiment, reminiscent of that described in G. M. Morant's paper. Travelling through Caerphilly on a busy Monday morning, one can quite easily observe that the overwhelming majority of the population are extremely round headed, with dark hair. It seems this type is distributed in an 'arc' shape across the South Wales Valley - occurring again at Blaenavon, continuing across Rhondda Cynon Taff, Merthyr Tydfil, and Torfaen.

The Black Mountains and Brecon Beacons appear to have been an effective barrier to Silurian expansion, keeping this type restricted to the South Wales Valleys. Overall, the coastal region is predominantly mesocephalic, with outcrops of brachycephals in the Valleys. The description that comes to mind is 'Australoid-Afalou' because of the hair type and robust-rugged features are very similar to both the Paleolithic North Africans and the Australian aborigines.

However, dispersed within the 'sea' of brachycephals are the strikingly different long headed population, with long arms, thin body, with a strong resemblance to Afro-Mediterranean populations.

An 'indigenous' person from the Welsh Valleys described how she was constantly bullied in school because of her long head. On further questioning, this person revealed some of her private beliefs she had about her ethnicity: She recalled how she would ask her mother, *'are we descended from Aborigines (from Australia) because grandmother has features which are identical to Aborigines.'*

I recall another story, someone confided in me of their anxiety that their sister may give birth to a 'black' baby; even though she was not in a mixed relationship. A vague memory of 'dark-skinned' ancestors still exists amongst people in certain regions. Concerns over having dark skinned children are reflected in the occurrence of the 'Mongolian Spot' - a congenital birth mark that occurs on the lower back of some babes. Midwives have reported high incidences of the 'Mongolian Spot' amongst new-born babies in Wales. The colour of these birthmarks tend to be black or blue-black. Erwin Bälz was the first European (c.1883) to document his observations of these dark-blue marks on Japanese infants while in Tokyo - hence, the origin of this inappropriate and outdated name. The correct medical terminology is slate gray nevus (congenital dermal melanocytosis).

These birthmarks mainly occur in people of African or Asian ethnic descent. These dark areas usually disappear during early childhood. The prevalence of the Mongolian Spot varies and occurs in only 10% of White infants, 50% in Hispanics and 90%-100% in Africans. *['How important are they?', World J Clin. Cases 2013; 1(8): 230-232]*

The occurrence of these birthmarks in children of mixed ancestry has led to parents being falsely accused of child abuse. In one case a mother from Basingstoke (England) came under suspicion because her doctor had failed to make a note of this natural birth--mark. She said, "When I told the midwife what I thought it was, she said she had never heard of them and said she wasn't happy with it and went to get someone else to have a look. The whole time she hung around my bed, as if she suspected me." The mum decided to raise awareness so that health professionals in the NHS and mum's to would be aware of the Mongolian Blue Spot. In contrast the high occurrence of these birthmarks amongst the Welsh has resulted in mid-wives being more aware of this congenial condition. *[Emily Roberts, Mum launches campaign after abuse suspicion at son's birth, Basingstoke Gazette 1st Aug 2020]*

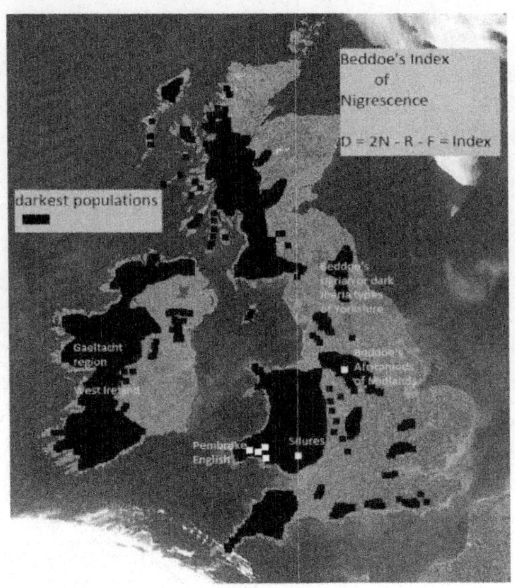

Map of Index of Beddoe's Nigrescence
showing distribution of the darkest populations.

The areas inhabited by the so-called 'Insular Celts' are also the areas inhabited by the darkest populations:

> In the south, Horsham and Ashford, by their darker colours, support the opinion that the Britons of Kent and Sussex, during the English conquest, found a refuge in the forest of the Weald, while the lighter colours of Hampshire, Berkshire, East Wilts and the Cotswolds, testify the strength of the invading population which is supposed to have landed about Portsmouth and Southampton Water. In South Devon, we know that the Cornish tongue survived into the Middle Ages; accordingly, the folk are dark in colour like the Welsh and Cornish, as Huxley himself noticed. But there are islands of Saxonry in Devon, especially near harbors, in some cases, I doubt not, of very early settlement, side by side with old British holdings, so that the two races must have lived peaceably within sight of each other. I do not believe the wars of those old days were always so sanguinary as we are led to suppose. {Beddoe]

Martin's book 'The Description of The Western Isles of Scotland' (1703) gives an interesting description of the complexion of the inhabitants. Below is the full extract from Martin's journal:

> The Inhabitants of this isle [Isle of Skye] are generally well proportioned, and their complexion is for the most part black. They are not obliged to art in forming their Bodies, for nature never fails to act her part bountifully to them; and perhaps there is no part of the habitable globe where, so few bodily Imperfections are to be seen, nor any Children that go more early. I have observed several of them walk alone before they were ten Months old. [p194]
>
> Here is another castle belonging to the Duke in the north-side of the Isle... there is a Harbour for Barks and Boats. The Isle of Arran is the Duke of Hamilton Property (a very small part excepted) ....and made part of the Diocese of Argyle. The inhabitants of this island are composed of several Tribes. The most ancient Family among them, is by the Natives reckoned to be Mack-Louis which in the ancient Language signifies the Son of Lewis: they own themselves to be descended of French Parentage, their surname in English is Fullerton.
>
> The Inhabitants of this Isle are well portioned, generally brown, and some of black Complexion; they enjoy a good state of Health and have a Genius for all Callings.......
>
> The Natives here are very well proportioned, being generally black of Complexion, and free from bodily Imperfections. They speak the Irish Language, and wear the Plad, Bonnet, &c, as other Islanders
>
> The Isle of JU lies to the Weft of Jurah, from which it is separated by a narrow channel: it is twenty-four Miles in length from South to North, and eighteen from East to West; there are same little Mountains about the middle on the East-side. [p239]
>
> The Isle Collonsay is four Miles in length from East to West; and above a Mile in breadth The mould is brown and sandy on the coast and affords but a very small Produce, through the plough their ground three times; the middle; is rocky and

> heathy, which in most places is prettily mingled with thick ever-greens of Juniper and Cats-Tail.
>
> The cattle bred here are Cows, Horses and Sheep, all of a low Size. The Inhabitants are generally well-proportioned and of a black Complexion; they speak only the Irish Tongue [p248]

The reader should note that Martin is very particular in his description of skin colour; some are Brown, some are Black; while others are compared to inhabitants of neighboring islanders and are White. The observations he made about skin colour in the Hebrides, well over 300 years ago, was before the mass migrations associated with the industrial revolution.

The same can be said regarding South Wales, where half a million English migrated into the area during the industrial development of the coal industry. Towns such as Fleur-de-lis in the South Wales Valleys was settled in the 17th century by Huguenots that had fled from France. While South Pembrokeshire, further west, is known as 'little England'. Henry I and Henry II planted large number of Flemish people into the area. Professor Harold Carter quoting the 'Brut y Tywysogyon' (Chronicle of the Welsh Princes) states that the original inhabitants were driven away by force. As a result, Flemish became the main language for some time until it was ousted by English.

Beddoe's observations were at the beginning of the industrialization of Britain. Martin's journal was based on his travels before people from different parts of the island started to move from their 'ancestral' areas, moving from the countryside to the towns. Internal migrations within these islands rapidly increased during the 1800's and early 1900's. This had a considerable effect on the distribution of various phenotypes, resulting in the movement of Africanoid and Ugrian types from rural regions to the main urban centers.

During the nineteenth century, there was a high rate of internal migration in Britain.

> The vast majority of moves took place over short distances, with people and families remaining rooted in particular localities over generations. However, while not making up the bulk of all internal migration, it was net movement from the countryside to Britain's fast-growing urban areas that was one of the most important demographic features of this period. Indeed, it has been estimated that 40 percent of the demographic growth of urban Britain during the nineteenth

century was due to this movement; there was also an absolute decline in the population of Britain's agricultural areas during the second half of the nineteenth century, losing more than four million people between 1841 and 1911 through internal migration. [Amy J. Lloyd, Emigration, Immigration and Migration in Nineteenth-Century Britain, , University of Cambridge, 2007]

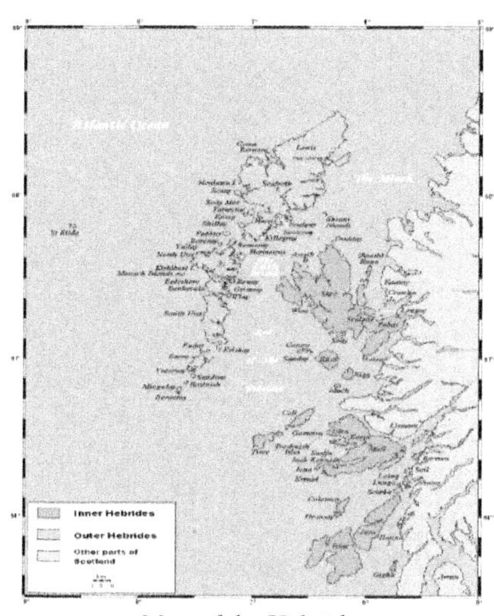

Map of the Hebrides
attributed to Kelisi creative commons via Wikimedia Commons.

9 THE ANCIENT ANNALS OF IRELAND

Ancient Irish manuscripts, dating from at least a thousand years ago, mention the arrival of various ancient tribes from different parts of the world. These manuscripts were transcribed by monks from the original sources. Much of the material was edited in such a way to create a bias in favor of the Milesians. Even with this editing, we still have a permanent record of the history of Africans arriving in Ireland. They appear throughout the ancient annals of Ireland; they fought with every tribe, and they were the original inhabitants of Ireland.

The Annals of Clonmacnoise, the Leabhar Gabhála (Book of Conquests) and the Annals of The Four Masters, all contain detailed accounts of African sea-pirates – The Formorians. The Irish Annals are not simply a collection of old folk tales. They give the location of ancient burial mounds and tumuli, the sites of battles, and other details which have been verified by archaeologists.

The opening chapter of The Annals of Ireland give an account of the Irish version of the great flood. These fascinating stories have been handed down through generations and are unique to Ireland. Modern books ignore the African Formorians and delete any reference to Africa. The Irish Formorians are the most important characters in Irish folklore. History begins with the Formorians, who are said to have always resided in Ireland from the beginning of history. They were the original inhabitants of Ireland, and all folktales start with them. Many modern books on Irish folklore delete references to these Africans.

The Annals of Ireland start with the discovery of Ireland by three fishermen from the Iberian Peninsula. This event is said to have occurred before the great flood. These fishermen were the first individuals to set foot in Ireland. They did not stay long in Ireland but returned to the Iberian

Peninsula. Ireland remained uninhabited until the arrival of Noah's granddaughter – Cesair (or Kesair). Fifty women and three men (Fintain, Bith and Ladhra) accompanied Cesair. The Leabhar Gabhála gives a full account of how Cesair left her homeland in northern Sudan, crossed into Egypt, and then sailed to Ireland.

The travels of Cesair are remembered in an ancient Irish song:

Forty days of the strenuous journey
Was Ireland found before the flood?
Cesair found it, fair of colour,
With people of her bright-skinned ships.
Cesair, wherefore came she, with fifty-three.
Persons well complexioned.
Tuesday, she set out, harsh the omen,
From Meroe Island.
Twenty days from the crooked Capsian Sea.
To the Cimmerian Sea of protection.
Twenty days from Asia Minor sailing
To the glorious Alps.
In eighteen days, she came hither,
To the lofty corner of Spain
Thence to noble Ireland,
In space of nine days from Spain.

Cesair's (Ceasair, Keasar, etc.) homeland is mentioned as being Meroe Island. This fact was not noticed until I publicized it in my first edition of the Black Celts. The Irish poem refers to Meroe Island, which is not actually an island - ancient writers describe Meroe (Nubia, Sudan) as an island because it is surrounded on three sides by the river Nile. The capital of the ancient kingdom of Nubia was initially located at Napata; later it was moved further south to Meroe.

These Irish legends suggest that the first people to settle in Ireland came from the Nile Valley. The improvements in DNA science have proved that there is some truth to these legends. The Neolithic settlers that introduced farming to Europe included people with the sub-Saharan y-DNA E1b1. The matriarch Cesair landed at a place called Dun na Mbrac, in either County Cork or County Wexford. The three men who accompanied Cesair settled in different places. Ladhra settled in Wexford, Bith moved to County Monaghan, while Fintain was buried near Lake Derg in western Ireland. Irish folklore locates Cesair's grave at *Cuil Cesair*, in the province of Connaught.

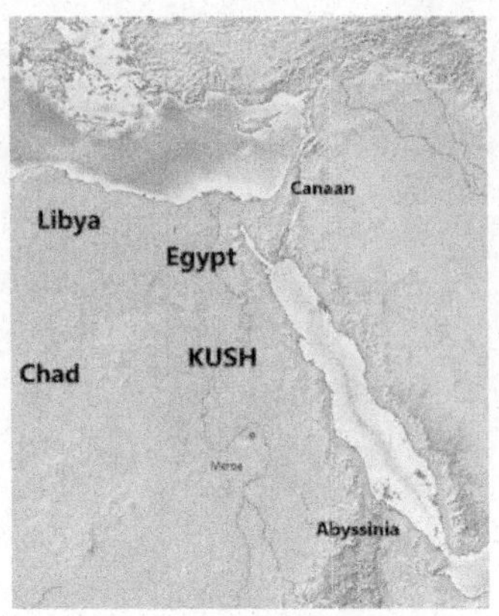

Location of Meroe, Kush (Modified by the author).
(Attributed to DMEROE EMIS Mapserver,
creative commons via Wikimedia, public domain.)

In the Leabhar Gabhála, O'Clerys places Carn- Ceasair on the bank of the River Boyle, and that Cuil-Ceasra was in the same neighborhood. Cuil-Ceasra is mentioned in the Annals of Kilronan, in 1571, as on the River Boyle.
The location of Bith's grave is believed to be known:

> Carn of Sliabh Beatha This carn still exists, and is situated on that part of the mountain of Slieve Beagh which extends across a portion of the parish of Clones belonging to the county of Fermanagh [Annals]

O'Donovan confirms the location of the landing place of Cesair and her followers:

> According to the Book of Lecan, fol. 272, a, the Leabhar-Gabhála of the O'Clerys, and Keating's History of Ireland, they put in at Dun-na-mbarc, in Corca-Duibhne, now Corca-guiny, a barony in the west of Kerry. There is no place in Corcaguiny at present known as having borne the name; and the Editor is of, opinion that " Corca Duibhne" is an error of transcribers for " Corca- Luighe," and that the place referred to is Dun-na-mbarc, in Corca- Luighe, now Dunamark, in the parish of Kilcommoge, barony of Bantry, and county of Cork. [O'Donovan]

Fintain's grave is believed to be located at a pace called Tultuine, it is described as in the territory of Aradh, over Loch Deirgdheirc, now Lough Derg, an expansion of the Shannon, between Killaloe and Portumna. According to a legend, preserved in Leabhar-na-h-Uidhri, Fintain survived the Deluge, and lived for many generations by undergoing various transmigrations. This tale has given rise to the well-known Irish proverb common across Ireland, *"If had lived Fintain's years, I could say much."*

The version of the deluge found in these Annals show that Ireland was a matriarchal society. Noah's granddaughter is associated with the island of Meroe, a region famous for its ancient queens. The people of this region are all known to have been matriarchal societies; the Nubians, Beja, Berbers, and Himyarites were all matriarchal in pre-Islamic times. This contrasts with Indo-European culture which has always been patriarchal. The Scythians, Germans, Indo-Iranians, and Hittites were exclusively patriarchal cultures.

Women played an important role in the cultures of the Sahara, the Nile Valley and southern Arabia; areas dominated by famous queens. In contrast, Herodotus has left us a description of the role of women in Scythian Indo-European culture. He observed that the Scythian women stayed behind in the horse drawn wagons and did not participate in warfare; they were only allowed to do domestic duties. According to Herodotus, 'the long-lived Ethiopians and the Libyans were ruled by powerful queens.' In Africa and the Arabian Peninsula, it is the custom for the groom to give a dowry to the bride or her family. Among the Indo-Europeans, the tradition has always been for the bride to pay a dowry to the groom or his family; with transfer of wealth occurring from the bride's family to the groom's family. The reverse happened in Irish society; wealth transference was to the bride and her bride's family - identical to African and Islamic culture.

Ireland was colonized by six successive tribes: Formorians, Parthalonians, Nemedians, Firbolgs, Tuatha De Danaans, and finally the Milesians or Goidels. The Formorians are the oldest inhabitants of Ireland, and we can presume that they represent the Neolithic settlers.

The Formorians or Fomoriag Afraic

The Formorians, Fomhóraigh, or Fomoraig Afraic are described, throughout the Irish Annals, as the sons of Dubh, son of Formore. The word dubh is Irish for the colour black. Some scholars have regarded the characters in Irish legends as purely mythical characters. However, both Welsh and Scottish folklore also mentions the arrival of Africans. They are intimately associated with the Megalithic monuments that are scattered across the landscape of these islands.

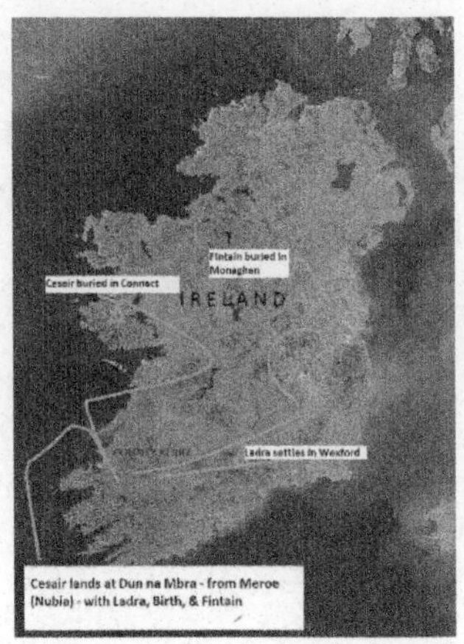

Map of Cesair's arrival in Ireland - first Queen of Ireland.

The Formorians appear at the beginning of Irish history. They reappear constantly throughout each era. The genealogy of the Formorians eventually becomes modified and merges with Milesian branches. In the 1st century AD, the Irish ruler Elim, a descendant of Dubh (Black), son of Formore, was also regarded as being of the royal line of Ir, a branch of the Milesians. The name Ir bears close similarity to the tribal name Ir-ir (Erer) found East Africa; the eponymous ancestor of the Dir tribe, who are regarded as oldest inhabitants of the Horn of Africa (the Dir are said to be as old as the grass).

The people called the Formor or Fomhóraigh were referred to in older Irish texts as Fomoriag Afraic. Fo muireaig or Fomhoraic translates as 'Sea Robbers' or 'Masters of the Sea' – the Leabhar Gabhála and the Annals of Four Masters give these pirates an African origin. In the Annals of Clonmacnoise, the Formorians are described as the descendants of Ham, son of Noah. They are always described in the most unflattering, exaggerated way. The very first battle believed to have taken place in Ireland was between the indigenous Formorians and the invading Parthalonians. Theses mysterious Formorians fought each of the invading tribes; they outlived the Firbolgs, who were banished to the land of Tir na nog; they outlived the Tuatha de Danaans who were crushed by the Milesians; and they re-appear among the Milesians as part of the royal line of Ir. They survived into the Christian era, and eventually merged with the other Irish clans; eventually evolving into the modern Gaels of Ireland.

The Parthalonians

Parthalon, the son of Sear, sailed with his people from the Mediterranean. They sailed from Greece to Sicily, then to Iberia, and eventually reached the west coast of Ireland. Parthalon came into Ireland, accompanied by his chieftains, they were Slainge, Laighlinne, and Rudhraidhe; and his four sons:

Dealgnat, Nerbha, Ciochbha, and Cerbnad, and their four wives.

The first battle to have taken place in Ireland was between the Formorians and the Parthalonians. From the account in the Leabhar Gabhála, it is clear that the Formorians were in Ireland before the arrival of the Parthalonians. O'Donovan clarifies this:

> It is stated in the Leabhar Gabhála of the O'Clerys, and in Keating's History of Ireland, that this Cical and his mother, Lot Luaimneach, had been in Ireland before Parthalon. [John O'Donovan, Annals of Ireland, 1856]

They were the earliest recorded people in Irish history. The poem refers to them as the 'manly' Formorians – because these African warriors dominated Irish history and commanded the sea routes connecting the Atlantic and the Mediterranean.

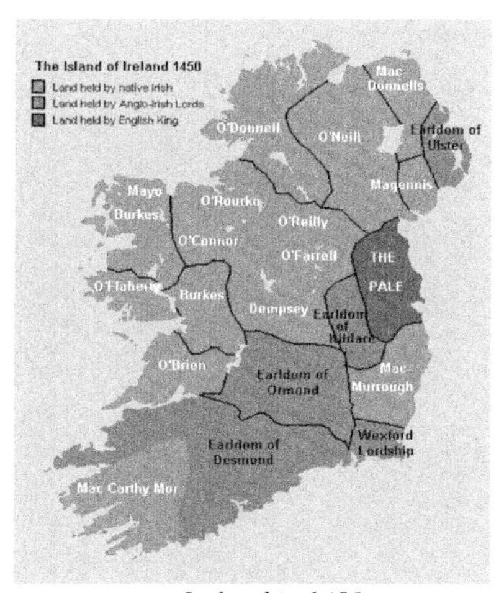

Ireland in 1450,
(attributed to Automated conversion at Wikipedia)
Public domain, via Wikimedia Commons.

These stories have been passed down to us through various hands; each time the stories have been edited. The Formorians are eventually described as semi-human monsters. These descriptions are obviously nonsense. Irish folklore begins with the Formorians. When Parthalon arrived, he was confronted by fleets of ships commanded by the Formorians. The epic battle between the Formorians and the Parthalon tribe is captured in the following poem:

After ten complete years,
After Parthalon's coming here.
Came a fleet on him, with great fury.
Of the manly tribe of the Formorians.
Two hundred years had they before that
Lived on fish, on birds of air.
So that thence they came hither,
With no use of other food,
Eight hundred was the size of the fleet.
As Inbher Domnann, Ciogul, son Gol,
Son of Garbh, son of fiery Tuathach,
Son of Umor, over the sea from the east,
From which the Formorians are named.
Lot the nimble was his stately mother,
From Caucasus holy and beautiful.

Ciogul, who ruled Ireland before the Parthalonians arrived, was descended from Umhor. The Sliabh Mountain, according to Keating, was named after Umhor. After a ten-year interval, a battle was fought between these two tribes at Muigh Ithe. This place has been identified as Sleamhnai Maighw Ithe, near Lough Swilly in County Donegal.

The Irish Annals have the following:

> In this year, the first battle was fought in Ireland, i.e., Cical Grigenchosach, son of Goll, son of Garbh, of the Formorians, and his mother, came into Ireland, eight hundred in number, so that a battle was fought between them [and Parthalon's people] at Sleamhnai-Maighe-Ithe

When the battle was won, Parthalon divided Ireland into four parts. Each of his sons was given a province to rule. Er, Orbha, Fearon, and Feargna was their names. Er took control of the territory north of Dublin; Orbha governed Leinster and Munster; while Fearon took Galway, and Feargna took the remaining territories.

The account given by Eochaidh O'Flinn is the form of a poem:

It was an honor to the aged monarch,
The dying Parthalon, that his sons,
Four valiant youths deserved the kingdom after him.
These princes equally the island shared.
They live in friendship and without ambition.
Their love in early infancy appeared,
And rose as childhood ripened into man,

Overrun with brambles and perplexed with thorns.
Until by the mutual pains and hard fatigue
Of these young heroes, it began to bear.
And yield a harvest suited to their hopes.
Er was the eldest, noble, wise, and brave,
He governed northwards from Oileach Neid
To Dublin; and from thence Barrymore,
A pleasant Isle, the bounds of his command,
Orbha possessed.
Fearon, from the grave of Nemedius,
Enjoyed the fruitful tract, with plenty stored,
To Galway and from thence to Oileach Neid,
These youths were, by the indulgent care of heaven,
Designed as blessings on their native Isle.

After thirty years in Ireland, Parthalon died. The entire island was then ravaged by a plague. Nine thousand people died in one week. They were buried at Taimhleacht Muintire Parthalon, now called Tallaght – near Dublin. Ancient burial mounds have also been found in this area. The entire tribe of Parthalon was wiped out, leaving the Formorians in control of the island. The reason the Formorians were able to survive the plague was their ability to cross the sea. The annals frequently mention large Formorian fleets sailing to Africa and Scotland. They were particularly associated with the islands off the western coast of Scotland. The Parthalonians did not leave any lasting impression in Ireland. The Welsh Annals associate them with the Basques. Geoffrey of Monmouth, the medieval Welsh historian, believed that they were driven from Ireland to the Orkney Islands, just off the Scottish coast.

The Nemedians

The plague that spread across Ireland, caused the extinction of the entire Parthalonian tribe. It was a combination of successive wars with the Formorians and the plague that resulted in the demise of Parthalon's people. The African Formorians grew immensely powerful, and eventually forced the newly arrived Nemedians into servitude.

Nemedius, the son of Adnamhain, set out from his homeland on the Black Sea with a large fleet. In the Annals of Clonmacnoise, the Nemedians originally came from Greece. The similarity between the name Nemedians and the African Numidians is far too close to be disregarded. The African Numidians were a Berber speaking tribe that inhabited the northern coastal region of Algeria. Both the Carthaginians and the Romans used this tribe as mercenaries.

Nemedius and his followers sailed from the Mediterranean and landed in the north-east of Ireland. The four sons of Nemedius were installed as chiefs. Starn, Jarbhainel Faidh, Ainnin, and Fergus Leathdheag were their names. The present county of Armagh was named after the wife of Nemedius, who was buried there. In the regions they occupied, forts were constructed:

> These were the forts that were erected, the plains that were cleared, and the lakes that sprang forth, in the time of Neimhidh, but the precise years^ are not found for them: Rath-Cinnech, in Ui-Niallain Rath-Cimbaeith', in Seimhne; Magh-Ceara, Magh n-Eabha, Magh-Cuile-Toladh, and Magh-Luirg, in Connaught; Magh-tochair, in Tir-Eoghain; Leagmhagh, in Munster; Magh m-Brensa, in Leinster; Magh-Lughadh', in Ui-Tuirtre; Magh-Sered', in Teffia; Magh-Seimhne, in Dalraidhe; Magh-Muirtheimhne, in Conaille; and Magh- Macha, in Oirghialla; Loch-Cal, in Ui-Niallain; Loch-Muinreamhair, in Luighne, in Sliabh Guaire. The battle of Murbholg, in Dal-Riada; the battle of Baghna; and the battle of Cnamh-Ross against the Fomorians. Neimhidh gained these [battles].

In county Armagh, a fort known as Cinnech was erected, while in county Antrim fort Cimbaeith was built. These forts were constructed by Bog, Robhog, and Rubhe – the three sons of Madain Muinreamhair, an African Formorian. After building these forts for the Nemedians, the four Formorians were murdered on the orders of Nemedius. They were executed at a place called Doire Lighe:

> The demolition of the tower of Conainn in this year, by the race of Neimhidh, against Conainn, son of Faebhar, and the Fomorians in general, in revenge for all the oppression they had inflicted upon them [the race of Neimhidh], as is evident from the chronicle which is called Leabhar-Gabhála; and they nearly all mutually fell by each other; thirty persons alone of the race of Neimhidh escaped to different quarters of the world, and they came to Ireland some time afterwards as Firbolgs. Two hundred and sixteen years' Neimhidh and his race remained in Ireland. After this Ireland was a wilderness for a period of two hundred years

The Four Masters mention the following battles: the battle of Murbholg in county Antrim, the battle of Baghna in county Roscommon, and the battle of Cnamh Ross or 'Wood of Bones' fought near Barry's Cross in county Carlow. The Nemedians were successful in all these battles. Two Formorian kings, Gann and Senghann, were killed in the battle of Baghna. Although the Nemedians were victorious, they endured heavy fatalities. Faebar, the son of Nemedius, was killed by an African general called Conain. This marked a turning point in the struggle between the Formorians and the Nemedians. Nemedius lost faith and died with 2000 of his subjects at a pace called Oilean arda Nemhid; identified as Barrymore in County Cork.

The entire island was taken over by the African Formorians. Their headquarters was situated on Tory Island, just off the coast of north-west Donegal. Those Nemedians that survived were subdued and then forced to pay tributes. The Formorian fleet was strengthened by Conain and Moor, the two main leaders among the Formorians. At Magh Cetne a collection point was set up. All Nemedians were ordered to bring tributes once a year, during the month of November. The Formorians demanded half of their cattle, children, milk, butter, and wheat. The taxes were collected each year by a Formorian woman. Every Nemedians had to bring tributes to the same field each year. One year the Nemedians had great difficulty in paying the taxes. They decided to unite and travel to Conain's castle on Tory Island. When they arrived, Alma was elected to plead with Conain. Alma asked for an interval of three years before paying the taxes. Conain refused outright. Alma returned to his people and told them of this. He was then instructed by his people to try again. On the second meeting, Alma asked if they could be given a year's grace; after which they would pay the taxes in full. Conain agreed to this request with one condition. This was that the Nemedians should during that year congregate in one single place. If the taxes were not paid in full, the Formorian prince vowed that he would kill them all.

The Nemedians decided to try to free themselves from the rule of the Formorians. They formed an army under the command of three generals: Beothach, Fathach, and Fergus. They organized the army and resolved to fight until they had either defeated the Africans or perished while trying. They managed to raise an army of 30,000 men. When the battle commenced many were killed on both sides. The African leader Conain was killed and his fort on Tory Island was captured by the Nemedians.

Moor, the other Formorian leader, was away with his fleet in Africa during this battle. He returned after the battle had finished but was unable to land on Tory Island due to the opposition of the Nemedians. The African leader eventually landed on Tory Island with his men on the beach. A fierce battle then took place with heavy casualties on both sides. The battle was so intense that the soldiers on both sides did not notice the incoming tide. As a result, a large number drowned. The African leader Moor returned to his ship with his followers at high tide. The Nemedians were without any ships, and as a result they drowned. According to the Irish Annals only 30 Nemedians survived, the remainder were either killed by the Formorians or had drowned. After this defeat those Nemedians that remained in Ireland decided to leave. They had to wait 7 years before an opportunity became available. The account given in the Leabhar Gabhála differs slightly. In this version the Greeks receive news of the plight of the Nemedians. In response they sent a large fleet to Ireland, and on reaching Tory Island they demanded that the Formorians release the Nemedians. As always, the Formorians were eager for battle and immediately refused. The Greek fleet waited patiently off the northern coast of Ireland. Next the Leabhar Gabhála gives an account of how the African druids and the Nemedian druids fought one another.

This was the first victory over the Formorians, Conain and his troops rushed out of their castle and engaged the enemy. A fierce battle was fought, which resulted in the death of Conain. He was killed by Fergus Red-side, son of Nemedius. After the death of Conain, two Formorian generals took over the leadership of the Africans. They were Giolcas, son of Faebhar, and Orcifanat. In the Leabhar Gabhála, the Nemedians looted the castle, and massacred all the Formorians.

The Greeks and the Nemedians rejoiced at their victory. The Leabhar Gabhála then proceeds to give an account of how Moor, son of Dele, arrived back from Africa and destroyed the Nemedian and Greek forces. Some Nemedians fled to Britain, while others fled back south towards the Mediterranean. The leaders of the surviving Nemedians were Beothach, Semeon, and Briotan.

It was Semeon Breac, son of Stairn, son of Nemedius, who fled to Greece with his followers. After arriving in Greece, these Nemedians were enslaved by the Greeks and forced to work in the mines. Generations later this group returned to Ireland and became known as the Firbolgs. In the Leabhar Gabhála, Briotan Maol settled in Mon Conain in Wales; while Keating places them in Scotland. When the Picts were expelled from Ireland, they settled in Scotland and eventually absorbed the Nemedians. The ancient annals also give Briotan Maol as the eponymous ancestor of the Britons. The Africans were left undisturbed in Ireland for a further 200 years. They ruled without any external or internal challenges, and they were the complete masters of Ireland.

The Firbolgs

After this tranquil period, the Nemedians returned to Ireland from Greece under the leadership of Semeon Breac. The annals refer to these people as the Firbolgs. This name is derived from the word Fir = people or men and Bolg = bag. Those Nemedians that sought refuge in Greece were enslaved and forced to carry bags filled with earth. While the Nemedians that dug the pits became as Firdomnannians, i.e., people of the deep. The Nemedians that use to guard their brothers were called Firgallians, i.e., people of the spear. These three groups are usually referred to in the annals as the Firbolgs.

Slainaghe, son of Dela, the King of the Firbolgs landed on the Irish coast near Wexford. He had four brothers – Gann, Genann, Seangan, and Rudhraigne. The province of Leinster was taken by Slainaghe; Gann ruled southern Munster; Genann moved to Connaught, while Ulster was placed under Rudhraigne. The people under Genann and Rudhraigne are frequently referred to as Firdomnannians. The rule of Slainaghe was very brief. He was on the throne for only one year and was buried at Dun Righ near Ballyknockan. Next to take the throne was Rughraighe, who ruled for two years, after which he died at Brugh near the river Boyne. Gann and Genann were joint rulers for four years; both were buried near Cork. Seangan ruled for five years. Fiacha Cenn Finnain ruled for five years. Rinnal, son of Genann, ruled for six years. Foidhbhgen ruled for four years. Eochaidh, son of Erc, ruled for ten years. Eochaidh married Taite, the daughter of Magh-moor King of Spain. In the tenth year of his rule, the Tuatha De Danaans invaded Ireland. The Firbolgs fought the invaders at Mugh Tuireadh in Connaught. A massive slaughter of the Firbolgs took place, and Eochaidh was killed in battle. One hundred thousand Firbolgs were killed the rest fled to the Aran islands, Eilie, Rachruin, and Inis Gall.

The leader of the Tuatha De Danaans, Nuadhat Airgeatleam or Nuadhat of the 'silver arm,' lost one of his arms in this battle. Many centuries later the Firbolgs were driven from their island sanctuaries by the Picts. They sought refuge under the King of Leinster. They were given land, but they soon found themselves oppressed. The Firbolgs moved from Leinster to Connaught and gained the protection of the queen of that province. She granted them land and they lived in peace. The Firbolgs are said to have survived into the Christian era - their descendants are said to be the Gabraidhe of Suca in Connaught, the Tairsigh of Leinster, and the Gaileoin of Leinster.

The Tuatha De Danaans

The Tuatha De Danaans were believed to have special powers. These powers were not natural powers, they were derived from the dark arts or as the Irish would say they were piseógs *(pronounced pi-shohg; meaning sorcery or witchcraft).* Their bitter rivals, the Formorians, were said to have the gift of second sight. In contrast, Danaans are remembered in Irish folklore as the 'cold-hearted' Danaans – they were feared because they would use curses and they had knowledge of black magic and spells.

They originally lived in a land located between Crete and Palestine (i.e., the land of the Philistines). During the wars between the Greeks and the Philistines, the Tuatha dé Danaans supported the former. The Philistines defeated the Greeks and then made war on the Tuatha de Danaans. As a result of these conflicts, the Danaans were driven out of Palestine and fled from the Mediterranean. They then sought refuge in a place called Dobar in northern Scotland. The Leabhar Gabhála states that Dobar was the first place the Danaans landed, and it was from this base in Scotland that they invaded Ireland.

In Keating's History of Ireland, the Danaans first landed in Scandinavia and settled among the people of Denmark; and subsequently founded 4 cities - Falias, Gorias, Finnias, and Murias. However, both accounts agree that the Danaans first landed in Scotland and then invaded Ireland. On landing in Ireland, the Danaans burnt their boats so that they did not fall into the hands of the fierce African Formorians.

The Formorians and Danaans are real historical characters that existed in pre-history:

> For some account of the monuments which anciently existed at Brugh-na-Boinne, see Petrie's Inquiry into the Origin and Uses of the Round Towers of Ireland, pp. 100, 101. The monuments ascribed by the ancient Irish writers to the Tuatha-De-Danaans colony still remain, and are principally situated in Meath, near the Boyne, as at Drogheda, Dowth, Knowth, and Newgrange. There are other monuments of them at Cnoc-Aine and Cnoc-Gréiné, in the county of Limerick, and on the Pap Mountains .... These monuments are of the most remote antiquity and prove that the Tuatha-De-Danaans were a real people, though their history is so much wrapped up in fable and obscurity. [John O'Donovan, Annals of Ireland, 1856]

In the battle of Magh Tuireadh, the King of the Tuatha dé Danaans lost his arm and had to have it replaced with an artificial arm. While recovering from his injuries, Breas, son of Eathlan, ruled over Ireland. Breas stepped down after 7 years and allowed Nuadhat to resume the throne. Nuadhat of the 'silver arm' reigned for a further 20 years. It was in this 20th year that the African Formorians returned to Ireland and killed him. This Tuatha de Danaan King was killed during the battle of Magh Tuireadh nab h-Fomorach in county Sligo by the African Formorian Balor of 'the mighty blows:

> Magh-Tuireadh na bh-Fomorach. — This name is still remembered in the country and is now applied to a townland in the parish of Kilmactranny, barony of Tirerrill, and county of Sligo. There are very curious sepulchral monuments still to be seen on this battlefield, of which a minute description has been given by Dr Petrie in a paper read before the Royal Irish

> Academy in 1836……. There was also a long account of this battle of the northern Magh-Tuireadh, as well as of that of the southern Magh-Tuireadh, or Magh-Tuireadh- Conga.

Balor is the most famous figure in Irish oral tradition. The story of Balor represents an Irish oral tradition reflecting a possible clash between Neolithic and Bronze Age cultures in Ireland.

Balor an African King of Ireland

There flourished in ancient times three brothers: Gavida, Mac Samhthian, and Mac Kineely. The first was a distinguished metalsmith, who had a forge at Drumnatinne, a place in the parish of Rath Finan. Mac Kineely was lord of that district and was in possession of a cow called Glas Gavlin. This cow was coveted by all his neighbors. Many attempts were made to steal her.

At this remote period, a famous African warrior called Balor ruled over Ireland and had his headquarters on Tory Island. His glance was enough to strike people dead:

> This Balor, the general of the Formorians, is still vividly remembered by tradition throughout Ireland, as dalop déimeann, and in some places they frighten children by his name; but he is more vividly remembered on Tory Island, — where he is believed to have chiefly resided, — and on the opposite coast of Donegal, than anywhere else, except, perhaps, at Cong, in Mayo.

One day he was informed by a druid that he could only be killed by his own grandchild. On hearing this advice, Balor took precautions against this and imprisoned his only daughter Ethnea. He locked her up in a tall tower, which his ancestors had built long ago on the summit of An Tor Mór, a lofty, inaccessible rock on the eastern part of Tory Island.

An Tor Mór, Tory Island – the site of Balor's Tower
Tory Island attributed to Colin Park, creative commons via Wikimedia Commons.

Balor instructed twelve matrons to guard Ethnea. They were given strict orders not to let any men near her. For many years Ethnea remained alone and imprisoned on Tory Island.

As the years rolled by, Balor grew more confident. His warlike activities increased. The whole of Ireland was at his mercy. He became the ruler of the Formorians by attacking their ships and forcing them to recognize him as king. However, one ambition eluded him. The one thing he desired was the beautiful cow called Glas Gavlin. This cow, on the opposite coast, was guarded day and night. One day Mac Kineely, the chief of the tract of land opposite Tory Island, went to his brother Mac Samhthian who was entrusted with her safe keeping. He also came to see the sword being made. Balor 'of the mighty blows' transformed himself into a little boy with red hair. He then proceeded to tell Mac Samhthian that his brothers, Gavida and Mac Kineely, were about to cheat him and make his sword out of iron, while making theirs from steel. Mac Samhthian immediately rushed to find his brothers, leaving his cow in the hands of the little boy. Balor changed back into his normal appearance and rushed off back to Tory Island.

Mac Kineely consulted a druid for advice on how to regain possession of his prized cow. The druid told him that Balor would have to be killed before the cow could be recovered. A spirit called Biroge assisted Mac Kineely in his efforts to regain his cow. She dressed him in lady's clothes and flew him to Balor's fort on Tory Island. Biroge knocked on the door of the castle and demanded to be let in. The matrons guarding Balor's daughter opened the door cautiously. Biroge, using her special powers, made all the matrons fall into a deep sleep. Mac Kineely, having left Balor's daughter pregnant, was carried back to the mainland by Biroge, Ethnea gave birth to three sons. Balor immediately placed the babies in a sheet and fastened it with a pin. He cast them into a whirlpool. The pin holding the sheet became undone; one baby fell out and landed in the sea. The others were not so fortunate and were carried up into the whirlpool. The spirit saved the child and carried him across the harbor to his father, Mac Kineely.

Balor was informed by a druid that Mac Kineely was the father of Ethnea's children. Angered by this, Balor immediately set out to gain revenge. Landing on the mainland, Balor seized Mac Kineely and cut off his head. He then installed himself as the ruler of the district opposite Tory Island. Mac Kineely's son, Balor grandson, grew up to become an excellent metalsmith. Balor grew very fond of him; not knowing his real identity. Mac Kineely's heir was well aware of the fate that befell his father.

One day Balor came to the forge to get a spear made. It happened that Gavida was away from home, so that the work had to be carried out from home by his foster son. During the day Balor happened to mention, with pride, his conquest of Mac Kineely, but to his own misfortune. The young smith which for the opportunity and taking a glowing rod from the furnace thrust it through Balor's head, slaying his grandfather. Some historians place this event at Knocknafola or 'bloody fore land'.

Other accounts state that Balor was killed by his grandson. Lughaidh Lamhfad or Lugh of the long arms, in the battle of Magh Tuireadh. This story clearly indicates that before the overthrow of Balor, the Danaans were a client tribe. This status meant that they had to paid tributes to the Formorians. After a period of time, these tribes mixed together; a tactic used by the Danaans to infiltrate the Formorian tribe. According to the Irish Annals, the Firbolgs survived into the Christian era, while the Tuatha De Danaans disappeared completely from the pages of the Annals. It is believed that they sought refuge in Britain and gave rise to the Brigantes tribe.

Gweedore area - Bloody Foreland
The place where Formorians clashed with the Tuatha de Danaans.
attributed to Joseph Mischyshyn, wiki common license public domain.

With the overthrow of Balor, Lugh of the long arms ruled in his place. He ruled for 40 years and was killed in the battle by Mac Cuillat Caendrum, near Ballymore in west Meath. The next ruler was Eochaidh Ollathar, who ruled for 80 years. He died from the wounds which Cethlenn inflicted in the battle of Magh Tuireadh. Cethlenn was the wife of Balor the African.

According to the Annals of Clonmacnoise, Enniskillen was named after her. Most monuments ascribed to the Danaans are located within the following areas: near the Boyne in County Meath, Drogheda, Doeth, Knowth, New Grange, Cnoc Greine in Limerick, and in around the Pap mountains in southeast Kerry.

The next ruler of Ireland was Dealbhaeth, son of Ogma, who ruled for ten years. He was killed in the tenth year of his reign by Eogon of Inbher. This tribe was overthrown by the Milesians from Iberia. The last person of this tribe was believed to have lived in the 3rd century A.D., somewhere in Connaught. The Milesians were the last of the ancient tribes to invade Ireland.

The Milesians

The Milesians, also known as the Goidels or Gadelians, are believed to have arrived in Ireland between 800 B.C. and 100 B.C. British historians invented the myth that they were Indo-European speaking 'Celts'. The Irish Gaels never called themselves Celts. This identity was fabricated; an invention which started in the late 1700's A.D. The description within the Annals clearly shows the Milesians were of mixed ancestry.

The story of the Milesians starts in the Urals in Russia. They then migrate to the Middle East, mix with the Egyptians, and then they travel westwards towards the Iberian Peninsula. Keating's says the Milesians were originally called Scythians in ancient times. Niul, son of Feniusa Farsa, is referred to in the Irish Annals as a Scythian. He was the second son of Feniusa Farsa and was sent abroad to Egypt. Gadelas, the eponymous ancestor of the Irish Gaels was born in Egypt; at the time when Moses led the Hebrews out of the land. In the Annals, Gadelas was the son of Niul, son of Feniusa Farsa, – the King of Scythia; his mother was Scota the daughter of Pharaoh. Some historians bring Gadelas from Greece; others derive the Gadel or Goidel from the Phoenician Gadal (i.e., great).

The Irish Annals recall that Feniusa Farsa, the King of Scythia, had two sons – Nenuall, who was the eldest, and Niul, who was born in Mesopotamia. Niul was a learned scholar. He travelled to Egypt, where he married Scota, the daughter of Pharaoh. Afterwards they settled in Crete. There is a tradition that Gadelas was bitten by a green snake, which gave Gadelas a green scar; from that moment onwards, he was given the nickname Gadelas Glas or Gadelas the Green.

When Moses led his people out of Egypt, the Gadelians assisted the Hebrews. In retaliation, the Egyptians invaded Crete and drove out the Irish Gadelians. The leader of the Gadelians, during this time, was Sru, son of

Easru, son of Gadelas. Other accounts say that the Gadelians did not sail directly to Spain but first entered Scythia. Dagha, son of Bratha, the 15th descendant from Sru, is reputed to have landed in Iberia. Sru was pushed out of Egypt and forced to take refuge in Crete. He became ruler of this island and sailed from there to Scythia. Gadelas is believed to have been contemporary with Moses (around 1000 B.C.). Heber Scott, son of Easru, son of Gadelas, was the 4th generation of Egyptian-Irish Gadelians. The time between the expulsion of the Irish Gadelians from Egypt, and their landing in Ireland is given as 400 years. Sru travelled from Egypt, sailed north into the Aegean Sea, and then passed into Asia Minor. He sailed up the river Tanis and marched, under Heber Scot, into Scythia. The Gadelians killed the Scythian King, and shortly after this event they were driven out of Scythia. Adoin and Heber were the two sons of Tait, Son of Agnamon, son of Beogaman, son of Heber Scot, son of Sru, son of Easru, son of Gadelas. The Gadelians stayed in Scythia for three generations, Adoin had three sons: Ealloid, Lamhfionn, and Lamfhglas. Heber had two sons – Carcer and Cing.

The Gadelians sailed westwards until they arrived on an island in the Pontic Sea, They stayed on this island for a year. It was on this island that Heber, son of Tait, died. The leaders of this expedition were Ealloid, Carcer, Cing, and Lamhfionn. After a year on this island, they passed into the land of the Goths. It was here that Lamhfionn had a son called Heber Glunfionn. They remained on this island for eight generations.

Bratha, the son of Deaghatha, the eight descendants from Glunfionn was the principal commander of the Gadelians from Gothland into Iberia. He sailed from Gothland, with Crete on his left, and steered towards south-western Europe. When they arrived in Spain, they fought the Iberians, and after a short period of time fused with them, giving rise to Celti-Iberians. Breogan the son of Bratha, was born in Iberia, shortly after the Gadelians had arrived there. This Breogan had ten sons: Breaghs, Fuad, Muirtheimhne, Sula, Cuailgne, Blath, Aibhlae, Nar, Ith, and Bile.

Milesius, the son of Bile, the eponymous ancestor of the Irish Milesians, became the ruler of Spain. He conquered large areas of the Iberian Peninsula. He then launched an expedition against the Scythians. After campaigning against the Scythians, Milesius sailed down the Tanis river, across the Black Sea, and eventually landed in Egypt.

The Irish Annals give an account of a war between the Egyptian and the Ethiopians, at the time when Milesius arrived in Egypt. The Gadelian troops were used by the Egyptians as mercenaries. During his stay in Egypt, the wife of Milesius died in Scythia. The Pharaoh of Egypt then decided to give his daughter Scota to Milesius for marriage. Scota shared the same name as the wife of Niul, who lived many generations before her. Milesius had two sons by the Egyptian Scota. They were Heber Fionn (Heber the White) and Aimhergin. The total length of their stay in Egypt was seven years. Milesius led his followers back to Iberia and clashed with the Goths. The following ancient verse describes the route Milesius took:

The valiant Gallamh, who was called Milesius,
And fought young princes of his royal blood.
Aireach Feabhruadh, and the noble Donn,
Both born in Scythia.
Near the river Nile, in Egypt, Heber Fionn
And Aimhergin drew their first breath.
The most courageous Ir, a hero,
Who in flight surpassed them all.
Colpa, a prince that well could wield a sword.
The prince Arranan and Heremon,
Born in the tower of Brigantia (in Iberia).

The Leabhar Gabhála mentions three battles fought by the Milesians in Iberia: a battle against the Toisiona, a battle against the Bachra, and another against the Lombards. A son was born to Brath in Iberia, his name was Breogan. He founded a city in Iberia and named it Brigantia. He constructed a large fort and named it Breogan's Tower. In Iberia, his wife gave birth to a son called Bile, who in turn had a son called Mil. The first Gadelian to set foot in Ireland was Ith, son of Breogan. Ith set out from northern Iberia with his son Lughaidh and sailed directly for Ireland.

The Gadelians landed in the northern part of Ireland, which at that time was ruled by the two Tuatha De Danaans kings- Cearmada and Miorbheoil, the son of Dagha. They ruled Ireland from the province of Ulster, at a place Muigh Ith. The Gadelians were defeated and returned to their ships along with Ith. They sailed back to the Iberian mainland. Lughaidh then sought the assistance of his people. The Milesian fleet immediately set sail for Ireland. They landed on the northern coast of Leinster, at Inbher Slainge, now called Wexford. They defeated the Tuatha De Danaans at Inbher Sceine in western Meath. They landed in this area and marched across the mountains called Sliabh. While travelling through this region they came upon a lady of the Tuatha de Danaans lady called Eire, who attacked them.

Ir was the bravest of princes and always was on the front of any engagement. He founded the Clana Rughraighe, who held court at Eamhain; a place in Ulster, which they held for 700 years. Heremon landed with his fleet at a place called Inbher Colp, now called Drogheda. The Tuatha De Danaans were eventually defeated, with heavy casualties on both sides. Donn, Ir, Aireach, Feabhruadh, Arranan, and Colp all died in the conflict.

Three days later Heber and his followers arrived ashore. They were attacked by Eire, the wife of Mac Greine, one of the Tuatha De Danaan rulers. Another casualty was Scota, the Egyptian wife of Milesius, who was killed in this battle. She was buried in a place called Sliabh Mis, near Annagh in County Kerry. The three Tuatha De Danaan Kings fought an intense battle against the Milesians at a place called Tailtinn or Teltown, in County Meath. The Milesian prince Fuad fell at Sliabh Cuailgne, near Carlingford in County Louth. (Note: The Milesian Prince Fuad has a Hamito-Semitic name). The Tuatha de Danaans were defeated, and retreated to isolated refuges:

> That there were very many places in Ireland where the Tuatha-De-Danaan were then supposed to live as sprites or fairies, with corporeal and material forms, but induced with immortality. The inference naturally to be drawn from these stories is, that the Tuatha-De-Danaan lingered in the country for many centuries after their subjugation by the Gaedhil, and that they lived in retired situations, where they practised abstruse arts, which induced the others to regard them as magicians. So late as the third century, Aine, the daughter of Eogabhal, a lady of this race, was believed to be resident at Cnoc-Aine, in the county of Limerick, where she was ravished by Oilioll Olum, king of Munster. Looks very strange that our genealogists trace the pedigree of no family living for the last thousand years to any of the kings or chieftains of the Tuatha-De-Danaan, while several families of Firbolgic descent are mentioned as in Hy-Many, and other parts of Connaught. — See Tribes and Customs of Hy-Many, p. 85-90, and O'Flaherty's Ogygia, part iii. c. 11. [John O'Donovan, Annals of Ireland, 1856]

The only surviving sons of Milesius was Heber, Heremon, and Amergin. Heber and his followers were successful against the Tuatha de Danaans. He marched into the Province of Leinster and joined Heremon. The fierce battle of Sliabh Mis was won by the Gadelians. After this victory, the island was divided by Heremon into two parts; the northern region, north of the Boyne, was administered by Heremon, while the southern portion was placed under Heber Fionn. Heremon built his palace called Rath Beothach, in Leinster. His brother settled in the province of Munster.
The descendants of Heremon inhabited Connaught and Leinster, the family of Heber, son of Milesius, remained for many generations in the province of Ulster. Heber and Heremon governed Ireland jointly for one year. After this period elapsed, a dispute arose over the possession of three valleys – one in Maine, one in Maonmuighe, and one in Munster.

This event is recorded in a poem:

The royal princes, Heber and Heremon
With mutual consent, and kind affection,
The Isle divided and reigned in peace.
Until the ambition of a woman's heart,
The wife of Heber urged them to war.
By pride overcome, she queen of the Three Vales.
The most delightful lands in all the Isle,
She vowed, raging passionately, swore,
That she would never sleep on Irish ground
Until she was mistress of those fruitful plains.
A battle followed on Geisol's fatal plains.
When Heber Fionn fell a sacrifice
To the ambition of a haughty wife.

Heremon became the sole ruler of Ireland, ruling for 14 years. He divided Ireland into five provinces. Leinster was placed under Er, Orbha, Fearon, and Feargna - the sons of Heber Fionn. Connaught was given to Un and Eadane. The province of Ulster was governed by Heber, son of Ir.

It is worth briefly mentioning that Heber (Eber of the Old Testament) is believed to be identified with prophet Hud (asw), a prophet mentioned in the Quran. He was sent to preach monotheism to the people of Ad, in Hadhramaut, Yemen. *[see Quran, sura 11 (Hud), ayah 50-57]*

During the reign of Heremon, the Picts entered Ireland. Keating maintains that the Milesians allowed the Picts to settle in Ireland because he required assistance against the Tuatha Fiodhga (the Britons) who had invaded the island. Later the Picts attempted to take over Ireland themselves. When the Milesians became aware of this, they quickly drove the Picts out of Ireland. The defeated Picts sought refuge in Scotland, taking their Milesian wives with them.

Heremon died at Airgiod Ross (Silver Wood) in Rath Beothaice, near Feior. During his reign, Heremon expelled the Brigantes, some Tuatha De Danaans, and the Picts. The Brigantes, that is the descendants of Breogan, settled in northern England. When Heremon died his three sons, Muimhe, Luighne, and Laighne reigned jointly for three years. Heremon's sons were killed by the sons of Heber Fionn; they were called Er, Orbha, Fearon, and Feargna. They ruled for one year and were slain by Irial, the son of Heremon. A year later Irial fought the battle of Ard Inmath, at Teabth, where Stirne, son of Dubh, son of Formore, was slain. Another battle was fought against the African Formorians. A third battle was fought against Lugrot, the son of Moghfeibhis.

Rudhraighe overthrew Criomhthan Crosgrach, of the line of Heremon. Rudhraighe was the son of Silthrighe, son of Dubh, son of Siorlamh, son of Fionn, of the line of Ir, son of Milesius. He was a descendant of Formore, of the royal line of Ir. He ruled Ireland for 11 years and was killed by Lughaidh, son of Jonadhmar. He was slain by Congall Claringneach, son of Rudhraighe. Next to take the throne was Duach Dalta Deaghadh, of the royal line of Heber Fionn.

In 54 A.D. Cairbre Cinncait took the throne. He was the son of Dubthaig, son of Rudhraighe, son of Luighre, son of Oiris, son of Earnduilbh, son of Rionoil, son of the King of Denmark. He was called Cairbre Cinncait because his ears were similar to the ears of a cat. He belonged to the Firbolg race. Keating has the following:

> Cairbre Cinncait (Cairbre the Cat-headed), Keating states, was so called because he had ears like those of a cat. In the Leabhar-Gabhala of the O'Clerys a more de tailed account of the murder of the Milesian nobility by the Firbolgic plebeians is given, of which the following is a literal translation:
>
> The Attacotti of Ireland obtained great sway over the nobility, so that the latter were all cut off, except those who escaped the slaughter in which the nobles were exterminated by the Attacotti. The Attacotti afterwards set up Cairbre Caitcheann, one of their own race, as their king.

Cairbre Cinncait was later overthrown by Elim, son of Conragh, son of Rudhraighe, son of Silthrighe, son of Dubh, son of Formore, of the royal line of Ir, whose mother was the Egyptian Scota. It is clear from these genealogies that the Milesians and the Formorians were closely related. The royal line of Ir, descendants of Dubh, son of Formore, became an important part of the Milesian clan. The Ir line produced the bravest of warriors and represent the descendants of Egyptian Scota:

> The Age of Christ, 665. The first year of Seachnasach, son of Blathmac, in the sovereignty of Ireland. Baeithin, Abbot of Beannchair [Bangor], died. Ailill Flaun Easa, son of Domhnall, son of Aedh, son of Ainmire, died. Maelcaeich, son of Scannal, chief of the Cruithne [of Dal-Araidhe] of the race of Ir, died; Eochaidh larlaidh, King of the Cruithne, also died. Maelduin, son of Scannal, chief of Cinel-Coirbre, died. Duibhinnreacht, son of Dunchadh, chief of Ui-Briuin^, died. Ceallach, son of Guaire died. The battle of Fearsat, between the Ulidians and the Cruithni, where Cathasach, son of Laircine, was slain. Faelan, son of Colman, King of Leinster, died. [John O'Donovan, Annals of Ireland, 1856]

A Summary of The Annals

The Annals of Ireland are quite clear and precise in locating the original homelands of the various ancient tribal groups that settled in ancient Ireland. The first settlers are associated with Meroe and the matriarch Cesair. It would be reasonable to presume that these migrations happened during the Neolithic era. The Formorians or Formore Afraic were the masters of the sea. They were the aboriginal population of Ireland and fought each of the incoming tribes. They possessed numerous ships and travelled back and forth to Africa. The Parthalonians, Nemedians, and the Firbolgs were dominated by the 'manly' Formorians.

The Parthalonians passed from Greece to Sicily and then Iberia before settling in Ireland. The Nemedians also sailed through the Mediterranean and landed in Armagh (north-eastern Ireland) The 'cold-hearted' Tuatha de Danaans came direct from the land of the Philistines - giving them a Middle Eastern origin. Lastly, the Egypto-Gaels, under Gadelas, bring the Milesians from Scythia to Egypt; they were chased out of Crete by the ancient Egyptians and forced to migrate to Iberia. Eventually they passed from Iberia to Ireland. Heber Fionn and Aimhergin were born on the Nile, while Aranan and Heremon were born in the Iberian towers of Brigantia.

It is worth revisiting the poems contained in the Irish Annals:

The valiant Gallamh, was called Milesius,
and fought a thousand battles with success.
Had eight young princes of his royal blood.
Aireach, Feabhruadh, and the noble Donn,
both born in Scythia.
Near the Nile in Egypt,
Heber Fionn and Aimhergin
drew their first breaths.
The most courageous Ir,
a hero who in fight surpassed them all;
born in Irene, near the Thracian shore.
Colpa a prince that well could wield a sword.
The prince Aranan and Heremon,
born in the tower of Brigantia (Iberia).

From these ancient poems, it would be reasonable to presume the Gaels migrated from Egypt and Crete before settling in Iberia; where they introduced towers called Briga. 'Celtic from The West' theory put forward by Professor Cunliffe and Professor Koch place the origin of the 'Celtic' languages in Iberia. The theory is based on the widely distributed 'Celtic' toponyms, such as briga, found across the southern and western regions of

Iberia. If academics were more open-minded, they would pay more attention to the information contained in the Irish Annals. These ancient written sources inform us that the people who introduced the toponym Briga migrated from Scythia to Egypt, were driven from Crete, and eventually landed in Iberia where they created the settlement Brigantia [tower]. The Irish Annals support the theory of Egypto-Gaels, with some Scythian ancestry, settling in Iberia before eventually landing in Ireland.

10 THE NEOLITHIC REVOLUTION

The agricultural revolution brought a wave of dynamic changes that would reshape Europe permanently. The dark-skinned Mesolithic hunter gatherers were faced with a new wave of human migrations from the south. Migrants from the Levant, the Natufians, would slowly expand their knowledge of farming. The Middle East Epipalaeolithic period (known as the Mesolithic in Europe) provides clear evidence that the Natufians were gradually developing a complex society based around the development of a sedentary farming lifestyle and a range of innovative cultural products. This period between 23,000 BC to 11,000 BC would see lifestyle changes from hunter-gathering and fishing communities to settled, well organized farming societies.

The spread of agriculture was slow and gradual, as Lisa A. Maher, et al., highlights below:

> Gordon Childe coined the term "Neolithic revolution" to refer to the development of human control over the reproduction and evolution of plants and animals, which arguably was the single most significant social, cultural, and biological transition since the origin of our species............many "revolutionary" features of the Natufian and subsequent Neolithic periods developed gradually over a long time in the Late Pleistocene. During more than 10,000 years, we see evidence of the very early systematic exploitation of plant and animal species, mobile art and ornamentation in a range of materials, evidence for specialized technologies (nets, cordage, wood construction),

> and refinement of older technologies [Lisa A. Maher, et al., Evolutionary Anthropology 21:69–81 (2012]

The diffusion of farming technology marked the beginning of a clash of cultures. The Mesolithic hunter-gatherers, who we now know were very dark skinned, faced a new challenge from a more dynamic people, who would start the Neolithic revolution. Evidence suggests that these newcomers spoke proto-Hamito-Semitic (Afro-asiatic) languages. Dark skinned Mesolithic tribes came face to face with equally dark skinned proto-Hamito-Semitic Neolithic tribes. Both the Mesolithic and Neolithic population have left a deep contribution to the European genetic pool:

> Some mitochondrial-DNA studies suggest that the contribution of Near Eastern farmers to the European gene pool is about 20% [15,16]. A similar percentage (22%) is suggested by a Y-chromosome study carried out by Semino et al. However, the data in were re-examined by Chikhi et al. [18], who found (through a different methodology) an average contribution of between 50% and 65% by Near Eastern farmers to the European gene pool. Estimations depend not only on the markers employed but also on the model used (and its inherent assumptions). A recent study that makes use of mitochondrial-DNA, Y-chromosome DNA, and other autosomal markers find that the Neolithic contribution is much higher than 20%, and decreases from east to west, as expected under the Near Eastern demic diffusion model. [Pinhasi R, Fort J, Ammerman AJ (2005) Tracing the origin and spread of agriculture in Europe. PLoS Biol 3(12)]

The introduction of the Neolithic into Europe is closely associated with the arrival of men with the African y-DNA E1b1:

> The Y-chromosomal analyses permitted confirmation of the existence in Spain approximately 7,000 years ago of two haplogroups previously associated with the Neolithic transition: G2a and E1b1b1a1b. These results are highly consistent with those previously found in Neolithic individuals from French Late Neolithic individuals, indicating a surprising temporal genetic homogeneity in these groups. The high frequency of G2a in Neolithic samples in western

> Europe could suggest, furthermore, that the role of men during Neolithic dispersal could be greater than currently estimated. [Marie Lacan, Ancient DNA suggests the leading role played by men in the Neolithic dissemination, Proceedings of the National Academy of Sciences · November 2011]

The haplogroup E1b1 can be traced back to East Africa and is believed to have originated 26,000 years ago. The earliest farming communities in ancient Palestine, the Natufians, were also mainly E1b1. The spread of agriculture from the Levant was mainly due to the people with this haplogroup. The subclade E-V13 emerged from E1b1 (E-M78) around 6000 BC; Fulvio Cruciani believed E-V13 developed from an Egyptian 'hub' before subsequently migrating into the Balkans, expanding into the European hinterland along the Danube river, and spreading along the southern Mediterranean coast eventually colonizing the entire Western European Atlantic fringe. DNA analysis has shown that the male population belong to specific haplogroups; namely E1b1 E-V13, G2a, T1a1, and J). The spread of Hamito-Semitic (Afro-asiatic) can be associated with this sub-Saharan haplogroup. Some have attempted to link the spread of E-V13 with the spread of proto-Indo-European; however, this is extremely unlikely since it is a sub-Saharan haplogroup. The reality of the situation is quite simple; a sub-Saharan African haplogroup was introduced directly into Greece and the Balkans along with the spread of agriculture.

The male haplogroup T1a1 occurs at exceedingly high frequency in areas associated with Phoenician settlement such as Cyprus, Cádiz, Ibiza, and northern Morocco. The distribution of this haplo group is widespread:

> Haplogroup T is one of the most widely dispersed paternal lineages in the world. In Europe, it makes up only 1% of the population on most of the continent, except in Greece, Macedonia and Italy where it exceeds 4%, and in Iberia where it reaches 2.5%, peaking at 10% in Cadiz and over 15% in Ibiza. The maximal worldwide frequency for haplogroup T is observed in East Africa (Eritrea, Ethiopia, Somalia, Kenya, Tanzania) and in the Middle East (especially the South Caucasus, southern Iraq, south-west Iran, Oman and southern Egypt), where it accounts for approximately 5 to 15% of the male lineages. Over 50% of haplogroup T has been reported

> in some tribes in northern Somalia and Djibouti. Another hotspot are the Fulani people of Cameroon (18%). Besides these regions and Europe, T is found in isolated pockets as far as Zambia, South Africa, India, Central Asia and Northeast Asia, including southern Siberia, Mongolia (2%) and northern China (1%). [see www.eupedia.com/europe/Haplogroup_T_Y-DNA.shtml]

Scientist have recently discovered remarkably high occurrence of this haplogroup in the Somali region of eastern Ethiopia, between Dire Dawa and Jijiga. It has also been discovered that this haplogroup could play a major role in the performance of marathon runners from the Horn of Africa. It is positively associated with individuals who have abilities in long distance running. It was found in 14% of 'elite' runners. Considering the Somali region of eastern Ethiopia has the highest frequency of haplogroup T1a1a recorded so far; it is a puzzle why Somalis from Ethiopia have not appeared in the Ethiopian National Team. Even though the majority of Arussi Oromo population tend to have haplogroup J - an astonishing 43% of Arussi elite runners were found to haplo T1a1 - a clear indication that this haplogroup can be positively associated with becoming a successful long distant runner. *[see Moran, Colin, et al. (2004). 'Y chromosome haplogroups of elite Ethiopian endurance runners.' Human Genetics.15 (6)]*

In 1942 Gordon Childe proposed that the large growth of these early farming communities led to their need to expand into new regions. Childe proposed that the expansion of agriculture was due to human migration and not due to adoption via commerce with incoming new communities. However, we know that the spread of agriculture can involve more than one mechanism. To understand the African Substratum Theory, and its association with the adoption of farming, we must appreciate that there are several ways in which the knowledge of farming spread.

Distribution of Haplogroup T y-DNA,
(modified earth image by Arek Socha from Pixabay.)
(For a detailed map of % haplo T, see Liseranius, creative commons via Wikimedia Commons.)

The late Marek Zvelebil's research approach has enriched our knowledge of Mesolithic-Neolithic interactions by applying Bioarcheology. His paper, *'The agricultural transition and the origins of Neolithic society in Europe,'* Marek Zvelebil has strengthened our understanding. Below are some mechanisms that need to be considered:

> Folk migration – direct population movement, with direct population replacement.
>
> Demic diffusion – non-direction, colonization of small areas by small households or groups with gradual population replacement.
>
> Elite dominance – arrival of a social elite, who impose themselves over an existing population, causing genetic continuity with genetic markers of new elite population being retained.
>
> Infiltration – small and gradual infiltration, sometimes of specialist groups with specific skills, e.g., craft-men/women. Sometimes not genetically detectable but there may leave behind small-scale genetic signature.
>
> Leapfrog colonization - this involves selective colonization of an area, forming an enclave settlement among native inhabitants and giving rise to a genetic island.

> Frontier mobility – involves small-scale movement of population within contact zones.
>
> Contact – involves trade and with no gene replacement. [Zvelebil, Marek. (2001). The agricultural transition and the origins of Neolithic society in Europe.]

The Mediterranean islands of Cyprus was settled by Near Eastern farmers around 8200 BP. For Crete, the next neighboring island, it took another 1000 years before farming would be adopted. This still poses a real puzzle for archaeologists. There is ample evidence for the wide-spread use of boats by ancient communities in southern Italy and Crete, and yet the slow spread (1000 years) of farming from Cyprus (a relatively short distance away) certainly needs further investigation.

One route involved maritime-based colonization of Cyprus, Central Anatolia, and Crete and Greece starting from a Levantine based. The second route was a land route from Central and Western Anatolia, into Thrace and spreading into south-east Europe. Pinhasi comments on this:

> In their analysis of craniometric affinities between populations, point to the homogeneity between Catal Hoyuk and early Neolithic Greek and south-eastern European groups. This homogeneity contrasts with the pronounced heterogeneity found among other Pre-Pottery Neolithic groups in the Near East. On the basis of these results, they hypothesize that a founder population from Central Anatolia (represented by specimens from Catal Hoyuk) spread into south-east and Central Europe…. At the present time, it is unclear whether farming reached south-east Europe by means of a secondary demic expansion from Anatolia or as a continuation of the initial dispersal involving Cyprus, Crete, and mainland south-east Greece. [Pinhasi R, Pluciennik M (2004) Curr Anthropol 45: S59–S82.]

The spread of farming across Europe involved non-linear successive waves of expansion. Farmers from the Levant and Anatolia pushed into Greece by the 8th Millennium before the present era (BP) [c.6000 BC], followed by a pause of several centuries, the push continued into Europe following two routes. One route followed the northern Mediterranean coast and reached the Iberian Peninsula by the 7th Millennium BP [c.5000 BC]. The second route involved pushing into the Rhine-Danube region up to the Paris basin by the early 7th millennium BP [c.5000 BC.] Again, a long pause occurred and finally the spread of farming moved into NW Europe by the early 6th millennium BP [c.4500 BC] finally reaching southern Scandinavia, Britain, and Ireland.

The investigation of fats preserved in Neolithic ceramic vessels has shown that early farmers practiced dairying from the onset of domestication in the Near East. It was not a later development in Europe but was an early adopted process. [see Antiquity. 79. 882-894.]

The earliest indication of domestic plants in the Nile Valley region is from Nubia (at R12) dating from the 8th millennium BP [c.6000 BC]. Knowledge of farming soon spread southwards from the Levant to Egypt. The adoption of agriculture in Egypt's fertile regions by the 8th Millennium BP [c.6000 BC], occurred at sites such as Merimde Beni Salama, and Sai. It later spread to Egypt's Fayum region at Kom K and Kon W at around mid-7th millennium cal BP [c.5500 BC].

Further west, in northern Morocco we have some earlier dates at Ifri Oudadane and at Kaf Taht el Ghar at around mid-8th millennium BP [c 6500 BC]. The early spread to Morocco was due to influences from Iberia, following the introduction animals and plants by Neolithic seafarers. However, the region between Morocco and Libya has not uncovered any adoption of farming during that period; however, the absence of farming may be due to the dominance of thriving pastoral communities. *[see Mulazzani, et al., The emergence of the Neolithic in North Africa Quaternary International.]*

These developments would have a deep impact on Europe; an agricultural revolution, with the newcomers introducing animals and plants, leaving behind a legacy of animal call-words in modern 'Celtic' languages. New cultural traditions were also introduced which resulted in the construction of giant Megalithic monuments like Stonehenge.

Domestication of Animals

The brief look at the mechanism behind the spread of farming leads us to look at the domestication of animals and how early African settlers brought their animals with them. This explains why the present day 'Celtic' speakers still use African Hamito-Semitic (Afro-asiatic) words, especially in connection with animal husbandry.

Researchers are not agreed on the dates for the earliest domesticated animals in Egypt. Some propose an introduction between the 8th and 9th millennium BC at Nabta Playa-Bir Kiseiba. An assessment of early stock keeping in ancient Egypt by Linseele, et al., (2014) has the following:

> The evidence from the Nabta Playa area remains isolated, with no contemporary remains recorded from neighbouring areas. Claims for very early domesticated cattle in northern Sudan,

> starting from 7200 BC, which would have provided independent support for early finds in the Western Desert, were revised, as the bones come from large wild bovids instead of domesticated cattle. If the 9th -8th millennium BC date for domesticated cattle at Nabta Playa-Bir Kiseiba is correct, cattle keeping in Africa is as old as or older than in the Near Eastern domestication centres. Therefore, the putative domestic cattle from Nabta Playa-Bir Kiseiba are of crucial importance in the discussion on the existence of a local domestication of cattle in Africa. However, based on a recent genetic study on over 1500 modern cattle individuals worldwide, it is hypothesized that extant African unhumped cattle are descendants of domesticated cattle from the Near East, but with a high level of admixture with local African aurochs. This hypothesis of admixture remains speculative in the absence of genomes from African aurochsen. Only from the Middle Neolithic onward (6100–5400 BC) do uncontroversial domestic cattle remains appear, now metrically distinct from aurochs, in the Nabta-Bir Kiseiba region. [Linseele V, et al. (2014) New Archaeozoological Data from the Fayum "Neolithic" with a Critical Assessment of the Evidence for Early Stock Keeping in Egypt. PLoS ONE 9(10)]

Animal Husbandry

The distribution of various animals across the British Isles would have been affected by the nature of the environment. Horses existed in significant numbers in Britain during the Mesolithic Period, as shown by excavations at Gough's Cave. The lack of evidence for the presence of horses in Ireland during the same period still remains a mystery; some presume the nature of the landscape might have been unfavorable in some way. Domesticated species such as cattle (Bos taurus) and sheep (Ovis aries) were established by the early Neolithic, while the horse (Equus caballus) arrives a little later c.4000 BP. The Irish Quaternary Fauna Project has shown that some Mesolithic communities had knowledge of domesticated animals. The domesticated dog (Canis familliaris) was present in Ireland during the Mesolithic era. Interestingly, the Irish Quaternary Fauna Project has shown that Kerry red deer were introduced by Neolithic settlers. Numerous red deer antler bones and artefact have been recovered from Neolithic burials (4700 BP) at Annagh, County Limerick. These antlers were made into mushroom headed pins and many have been found in passage tombs. The earliest date we have for the remains of red deer in Ireland is 4190 BP from Stonestown, County Longford *[see Quaternary Science Reviews, Vol. 16, pp. 129-159, 1997]*

The pioneering farmers entered the Balkans, and then spread slowly along the two routes described. These pioneers successfully adapted to different environments and were able to breed their animals. It is intriguing that these sub-Saharan Africans were able to fill their boats with their animals and navigate the dangerous Atlantic Ocean. They were highly skilled and mastered navigating the seas using the stars.

The application of DNA analysis has increased our knowledge of the origin of domesticated cattle and confirms the introduction of cattle from Africa via a maritime route:

> The modern and ancient mtDNA sequences we present here do not support the currently accepted hypothesis of a single Neolithic origin in the Near East....Breeds domesticated in the Near East and introduced in Europe during the Neolithic diffusion probably intermixed, at least in some regions, with local wild animals and with African cattle introduced by maritime routes. As a consequence, European breeds should represent a more diverse and important genetic resource than previously recognized, especially in the Southern regions. [Albano Beja-Pereiraa, et al., The origin of European cattle: Evidence from modern and ancient DNA]

Domestication of Cats

Cats have a special place in the culture of many African and Middle Eastern societies. They are treated with the utmost respect. Growing up in such as society, one was told, 'be nice to cats, otherwise they will curse you.' They are seen as clean animals, and obviously beneficial in keeping mice and rodents away. Evidence from early Egyptian tombs has revealed cats buried near humans at Hierakonpolis during Pre-dynastic times, indicating an awfully close relationship, and it is feasible that domestication of cats reaches as far back as 6000 years ago. *[see Journal of Archaeological Science 45 (2014)]*

Since the earliest domestication of cats might have occurred in Egypt, it is not surprising that the word for cat in ancient Egyptian is also the same in other Hamito-Semitic (Afro-asiatic) languages. The knowledge of domestication spread from ancient Egypt and the Natufian Levant. It subsequently spread to the Balkans and the rest of Europe. Studies have indicated that the domestication of cats in China may have been stimulated by the transport of these animals from Western Asia along the trade routes accompanied by other animals such as cattle, goats, and sheep. *[see PNAS,*

2014 Jan 7;111(1):116-20.]

Animal Call-words

The Welsh educator David Thomas, O.B.E., completed the only known study of linking animal call words with human migrations. David Thomas, O.B.E., was born in 1866 in Llanwnnen, near Lampeter, Cardiganshire, Wales. His pioneering work 'Animal Call Words a Study in Human Migration' was published in 1939. He left South Wales in 1889 to take up an educational post in North Wales. He was dedicated to recording oral tradition of Cardiganshire and was surprised to find such a large number of dialects spoken within the Principality. When he was promoted to Inspector of Schools, the number of districts he was responsible for increased to cover portions of ten counties, extending from Snowdon to Shrewsbury and Herefordshire. During his 33 years as inspector of schools, David Thomas was able to study the different dialects and subsequently pieced together the link between local animal call words and human migrations.

As a result of this study, Thomas came across an interesting discovery:

> It was in connection with this research work that, in South Cardiganshire, in the very part where I had expected an important dialectal discovery to be made, I came across a strange system of numeration which had not previously been recorded - a system which the best philologists of the Continent regard as belonging to an epoch earlier than that of the most ancient Irish manuscript and used by those Goidelic Celts who had reached South-west Wales from Ireland. [David Thomas]

The inhabitants of the English counties of Herefordshire and Cumbria currently only speak the English language; however, rural shepherds continued to count using Welsh numbers well into the 19th century. These shepherds did not know what language they were counting in, a clear example of the substratum theory. David Thomas observed the same phenomenon with animal call words. For example, the animal words *sac*, *bis*, *thur*, *quish*, etc., are all derived from Hamito-Semitic (Afro-asiatic) languages. Although many words in 'Celtic' are Indo-European, others have been inherited from languages spoken by people who inhabited these islands in antiquity.

The African call word for cats is found in many parts of the world. In Norway people say '*psp-psp*' for calling cats; Koreans use '*tst-tst*'; in Mayan we have 'miss'; Finnish '*kissa*'' while the Irish have '*pish-wish*' for calling cats.; and the East African Somali uses '*bis-bis*' for calling cats.

It must be stressed that these call-words are not onomatopoeic; that is, they are not derived from the sound that a particular animal makes. Whereas, for example, in China the word for cat is '*mao*' and in Vietnamese there is '*meow*' - both are onomatopoeic and are derived from the sound cats make [in English a cat is said to make the sound '*meow*']. However, the forms derived from the word '*bis*' are derived from the Hamito-Semitic (Afro-asiatic) name for a cat, i.e., *bis* or *bis-at.* This word was transferred to Europe by African Neolithic farmers that colonized these islands.

Thomas begins his work by saying:

> **'British civilization had its origin neither in the Celtic people nor Romans, but with those people who came over to our country when the Pharaohs were ruling over Egypt and when Mesopotamian kings were sending out prospectors and traders to the uttermost ends of the known world.'**

After years of research, Thomas came to the following conclusion:

> I have been forced to believe that still older words are found among the terms used to speaking to domestic animals. This is due to the fact that these terms are seldom or never taught, but simply used by parents in their everyday work and heard by their children, and thus handed down from generation to generation for thousands of years with but little or no change.

The distribution of these call-words were mapped by Thomas. He carefully followed the occurrence of these names and then followed the trail of each tribe. He was able to map the distribution across different countries.

The Hutch Tribe

A tribe that brought the Neolithic to South Wales from the Persian Gulf. They travelled through the Mediterranean and into the Atlantic. The call word *kutch* (also *hootch ootch*, *wtsh*, *hwtsh*, etc.) was introduced from Arabia, where it is used to call camels. This form is found in Glamorgan, Carmarthen, and Pembrokeshire.

The Derry Tribe

The word *dir'a dir'a* is used as a call to goats for milking in Arabic. In Wiltshire, Glamorgan, and Monmouth the form *derry*, *dara*, *dera* or *deri* is associated with calling goats, sheep, or cows for milking.

The Thurr Tribe

Another Arabic call words *tar*, *tarra*, *atarra*, *trr* and *trrr* has been inherited by the inhabitants of Munster and Connaught, Ireland (*dhur-shee*), Manx (Isle of Man), Wiltshire, and Northern Ireland. From the distribution of the *Derry* and *Thurr* tribes, Thomas believed they arrived in these islands at different times; with the Derry tribe arriving first.

The Quish Tribe

The term *qs qs* or *qsh qsh* is used in Oman. Various similar forms have been found in Devon (*kash*), Cork (*koosh*), Shetlands Isles (*kush*), Caithness (*kush*), and Cardiganshire (Welsh *cuhwshi-git*) - terms for driving away fowl and cats.

The Keck Tribe

A guttural sound from North Africa used to communicate with camels, horses, or goats. Camel-drivers from North Africa use *ikh*, *heik*, *khe*, etc. Similar forms are found used in Devon, Wiltshire, Somerset, Hereford, Worcester, Shropshire, Pembroke, Merioneth, Lanark, and Perth.

The Troosh Tribe

This tribe is thought to be derived directly from Egypt or from an Egyptian colony in the Mediterranean. The term *trs trs* is used as a call to donkeys in Egypt. It appears as *trws-en* or *troos-en*, a call to cows in Carmarthen, Pembroke, and Cardigan. There is a wide concurrence of this term in Scotland. It is found in the form *troosh*, *truis* a *mach*, *truis*, *druis*, *troos*, *trooshy*; mainly used for driving cattle.

The Sook People

The migration of the Sook people took place in the Neolithic. The name occurs in various forms: *saq* (Arabia) *sik* (Egypt), *zak* (Tunisia), *sigal* (Arabia), *suk-kalle* (Denmark), *zoeg* (Holland), *sik* (Germany), and in Britain we have various form including sick, *zug*, *sica sicky*, *zuck*. Thomas observed how the Sook people settled in considerable numbers in Ireland. This is evidenced by the presence of call-words for a calf in the form *suck suck*, *sook sook* and *suk*.

Thomas also mapped the spread of Goidelic (Irish) terms into Wales. He came to an interesting conclusion as to the origins of the Welsh:

> These anthropologists further believe that the Brythonic Celts settled in considerably large numbers in England than in Wales, with the result that England contains at present more Brythonic blood than Wales. …. The Welsh language is thus spoken not by people of Brythonic descent, but by the descendants of those people whom the Brythons had subjugated. [David Thomas, chapter xviii, The Brythonic Invasion of Britain]

The pioneering research of David Thomas has never been repeated. The link between the animal call-words of Scotland and Egypt are particularly fascinating. It adds further support to the legend of Scota, daughter of Pharaoh, as the eponymous ancestor of the Scottish people.

11 OUT OF NORTH AFRICA

During the Bronze Age, a new group of people reached the British Isles. The skulls of this era are differed from the earlier Neolithic people; brachycephalic skulls start to become the dominant type during the Bronze Age. They differ from the Alpine brachycephals from Central Europe in many aspects. They both have similar cephalic indices, but the early brachycephals that arrived during the 2nd millennium B.C. came from the southern Mediterranean and the Moroccan coast. Anthropologists have compared them to the Sámi (Lapp); an indigenous Finno-Ugric people inhabiting parts of Norway, Sweden, Finland, and the Kola Peninsula.

The spread of the Bronze Age is usually connected with the spread of a type of pottery commonly referred to as Bell Beakers. The people who used this pottery have become known as the "Beaker Folk" - these beakers or bell beakers are believed to have spread along the Atlantic Ocean from southeast Spain and northern Morocco.

The Western Atlantic fringe countries and northern Africa adopted Bell Beakers, a new type of ceramic with decorated geometric patterns. Different communities adopted this new ceramic style, its spread was mainly due to a transfer of ideas through trade, rather than a human migration.

The long-headed Neolithic people still continued to populate many parts of the British Isles. This is proven by the excavations of the Bronze Age barrow at Pentraeth, Anglesey. Two types of diametrically opposite skulls are found; type I is remarkably brachycephalic with a cephalic index of 87.5, while type II is extremely dolichocephalic with an index of 71.

The brachycephalic skull is describe as being 5ft 6 in. and with a skull length of 164.5 mm and breath 144 mm. The cephalic index was 87.5 and the limb bones are slender with muscular markings.

The dolichocephalic skull is described as belonging to an individual with an estimated age of 49, with a height of 5ft 9 ins. The skull measurements were 186 mm long and 131 mm wide. The superciliary ridges were prominent and fused together on the forehead. The cephalic index was 71.2 and the limb bones were slender, with no pronounced muscular markings.

Iberian Bell Beaker Vessel from Ciempozuelos,
second millennium BC, attributed to Schulmeister Guillén, Verónica (photo)
(National Archaeological Museum of Spain, Madrid)

Who were the Roundheads?

There have been many theories concerning the origin of the Bronze Age roundhead (brachycephalic) people. The Beaker Folk, as they are aptly named, did not originate in central Europe and there is no evidence for them speaking an Indo-European language. They seem to have migrated from the southern Mediterranean coast. The first Indo-Europeans speakers arrived in the British Isles around 8th century B.C.

The district of Caerphilly, in South Wales, has a high number of roundheads that are on par with the Hythe skulls, both have not been well researched. The elevated levels of blood group A in that region could provide us with a clue as to their origins. The round-headed population in these areas have raven-black hair; certainly not the blond-haired 'Celts' expected by Eurocentric anthropologists.

In Scotland, the skeletons found in the Barra graves all have robust, squat bodies. The coefficient of racial likeness (CRL) indicates a close relationship between the Scottish Bronze Age and the Sámi (Lapp). These ancient people were a seafaring race that settled in coastal areas of Wales, Scotland, Norway, Brittany, North Africa, and the island of Gomera (Malta). The Irish brachycephals closely resemble the broad faced brachycephals found in parts of Morocco, the Kabyle region of Algeria, and on the island of Gomera (Canary Islands). Red Hair is common amongst this type, especially amongst the Gomerians and Atlas Berbers. Close examination of the skulls from the Irish Bronze Age, strongly suggest a north-west African origin.

Recent genetic analysis of Bronze Age skeleton shows a distinct difference with the prior Neolithic population. Recent theories of population replacement have re-ignited the Eurocentric desire for the arrival of waves of Bronze Age Indo-Europeans. The arrival around 2400 BC of broad-headed Beaker-Folk, with the Y-chromosome R1b-M269, changed the population dynamics of the British Isles and Ireland. The Neolithic population was sharply reduced to small pockets in Britain and Ireland. However, the analysis of 37 Beaker skeletons in Spain and Portugal has very little Steppe-related ancestry. These Iberian Beaker-Folk adopted new cultural customs, but their DNA was the same as the preceding Neolithic population. This indicates that the spread of Beaker pottery and culture across Western Europe was not exclusively through human migration:

> This continuity of customs is not highlighted here to suggest that migration did or did not occur during this time frame. Cultural continuity cannot be equated with population stability. Similarly, migration in itself does not automatically result in cultural change. .... Nevertheless, it remains hard to understand how newcomers could have been so strongly influenced by the people of Neolithic Britain if they had been rapidly and almost completely replaced during the introduction of the Beaker phenomenon. [Neil Carlin, Haunted by the ghost of the Beaker folk?]

The recent Eurocentric Population Replacement Theory is far from proven:

> Currently, the exact timing of the genetic changes that have been identified is quite unclear. The Beaker aDNA samples come from inhumation burials, a practice that re-appears in Britain (after a considerable hiatus of at least 600 years) as part of the adoption of the Beaker phenomenon. However, this burial rite did not become widely practiced until after 2200 BC and hence, most of the aDNA samples in the study come from burials that post-date the earliest appearance of Beaker pottery on this island by at least 300 years. therefore, it has not yet been demonstrated that the arrival of people with Steppe genes in Britain occurred in tandem with the spread of Beaker-related material traits. These changes may not have happened at the same time or been closely interconnected. [Neil Carlin,

Haunted by the ghost of the Beaker folk?]

Neil Carlin, a lecturer in the School of Archaeology at University College Dublin, questions the Bronze Age population replacement theory. He concludes, 'there is insufficient evidence to indicate that population replacement occurred as profoundly or suddenly in Britain *c. 2450–2200 BC* as has been claimed.'

African Brachycephals

During the Pleistocene, North Africa was inhabited by the Afalou type (or Afalou-Mechta). A 'race' of tall, large headed, heavy boned people with rugged cranial facial features. This Afalou type bore with it a tendency to brachycephaly. Remnants of those Afalou people who remained in North Africa are found in two refuge areas: mainly Morocco and the Canary Islands.

Even the anthropologist Carlton Steven Coon (who held rather prejudice views) recognized the African origin of the 'Irish look.' In his description of a black skinned Riffian Berber from Gzennay, Carleton Coon admitted, *'this individual possesses morphological features in the region of the eyes, nose, mouth, and jaw, which are clearly of Afalou inspiration, and which give him an Irish look.'*

The Shluh Berbers, according to C.S. Coon, show exaggerated Irish facial features. Although red hair is common amongst this tribe, others have black 'frizzy' hair. The mixing of light and dark population has resulted in high incidences of freckling. Amongst the Moroccan Riffian, the frequency of red hair and freckling exceeds that found in Ireland and Scotland. The number of red headed individuals in Wales is estimated at only around 5%.

Carleton Steven Coon's work 'The Races of Europe' includes a chapter *'Pleistocene White Men'* in which his conclusion can be interpreted as racist:

> Although the Pleistocene men are long dead, and factory workers scurry to their labors where the Magdalenian hunters once impounded reindeer, the problems of human racial origins, and of human development during the Pleistocene, are still of great importance. On the foundations of our knowledge of Pleistocene man, in Europe, in Asia, and in Africa, must be built. The interpretation of later and more complicated racial movements, racial survivals, genetic continuities, and genetic changes. For this reason, it seems better advised to state without trepidation the reconstruction of Pleistocene racial events which the facts themselves suggest, than to defer to more cautious and perhaps wiser opinions.

The rather prejudiced views propagated by C. S. Coon can be described as rather odd, and can be summarized as follows:

> * Homo sapiens was fully evolved as early as the mid-Pleistocene, if not earlier.
>
> * The earliest Homo sapiens known, as represented by several examples from Europe and Africa, was an ancestral long-headed white man of short stature and moderately great brain size.
>
> * The negro group probably evolved parallel to this white strain.

The conspiracy behind C S. Coon's work, an Assistant Professor of Harvard University, is obvious. The Harvard publication of 'The Races of Europe' in 1939 was an attempt to overturn the pioneering work of Giuseppe Sergi (1841-1936), He was the Professor of Anthropology at the University of Rome and is regarded as the father of European Anthropology. Sergi's Eurafrican or Afro-Mediterranean theory was published in his book 'The Mediterranean Race' in 1901. Sergi placed the origin of 'long-headed' Europeans in East Africa, and more importantly states 'ancient Europeans such as ancient Greeks, Ligurians, Italians and Iberians were originally Black and spoke African languages before the arrival of Brachycephalic Indo-Europeans.'

Sergi's work is ignored by C. S. Coon and his Harvard Colleagues. However, Sergi's summary is of great value:

> A celebrated anthropologist, when measuring the heads of the mummies of the Pharaohs, preserved in the Pyramids, wrote that the Egyptians belonged to the white race. His statement meant nothing; we could construct a syllogism showing that the Egyptians are Germans, since the latter also are fair. De Quatrefages classified the Abyssinians among the white races; but if they are black, how can they be white? If I had followed the old and irrational method hitherto followed by anthropologists, I could not have ascertained the affinities among the various Mediterranean peoples which have enabled me to attempt a reconstruction which is the result of a systematic analysis in every direction.......But that original

> stock could not have its cradle in the basin of the Mediterranean, a basin more fitted for the confluence of peoples and for their active development; the cradle whence they dispersed in many directions was more probably in Africa. The study of the fauna and flora of the Mediterranean exhibits the same phenomenon and becomes another argument in favor of the African origin of the Mediterranean peoples. [G. Sergi Mediterranean Race, 1901]

Ramzi Rouighi, an associate professor of Middle East studies at the University of Southern California, points out how the 'French to racialise Algerian Muslims into two different peoples: Arabs and Berbers. The division reduced the threat of their partnership against the settlers.' His fascinating book, *'Inventing the Berbers: History and Ideology in the Maghrib'*, documents how the European colonial powers turned Arab and Berber into a race:

> Confusingly, Europeans held on to 'Moor' as a name for the people but called the land Barbary, a word they did not imagine had anything to do with Berbers. Over a few decades in the 19th century, the French began to try to sort all this out and to devise a new way of representing the locals, one that adapted native nomenclatures to the project of French colonialism in Algeria. In the process, Barbary gave way to North Africa (Afrique du Nord), Arabs became Oriental Semites, and Berbers became a white race – or at least a non-black one – and the true indigenous inhabitants (indigènes, autochtones) of North Africa. Today, the accepted name for all Berbers from eastern Egypt to the Atlantic is Imazighen (singular: Amazigh, pronounced /ʔa.maːˈziːʁ/), the name of a tribe in central Morocco. [Ramzi Rouighi]

In 1890's the anthropologist Giuseppe Sergi was not fooled by these absurd classifications. He said of the East Africans, 'but if they are black, how can they be white?' Sergi insisted that the Afro- Mediterranean civilizations were populated by dark skinned people, and that light skinned appeared much later.

Toubou Tribe, North Africa.
(attributed to Ga, CC a Wikimedia CommonsToubou_man_traveling)

Ramzi Rouighi points out that the North Africans called their country Maghrib; even the Ottomans, who ruled the area, called it the Maghrib. The term Berber was not used by the local population; they call themselves Imazighen. In the 1800's Europeans started to re-classify the people of North Africa as 'White' - even if most were 'Black.' The Moors were also reclassified as 'White.' It should be remembered that the people of North Africa or Arabia do not use the same 'ethnic' definitions as the Europeans. People have elaborate genealogies, marriage and kinship ties, and tribal re-affiliations. It is these ties that define your identity, not skin-shade. The people vary considerably in colour within the same clan, and even within the same family.

Tuareg rebels in Mali (2012)
Attributed to Magharebia, via Wikimedia Commons public domain.

In the Atlas Mountains dark skinned and exceptionally light skinned individuals can be found within the same tribe. The Kabyles are much lighter than the Mauritanians (who are very dark), the Tuaregs and the Iseḥrawiyen (Sahrawi). are very dark-skinned; the Tunisians vary considerably in skin-colour, while the Fezzan Libyans are black skinned and noticeably similar to the Tebu of Chad. However, northern Africans cannot define themselves by skin colour as Nations since they are a thoroughly mixed people. North Africa cannot be described as 'white Africa' since, regardless of the shade of skin colour, sub-Saharan DNA dominates, e.g., 85% of Moroccan males have sub-Saharan E1b1 y-DNA.

Mauretanian Youth protest in capital, Nouakchott,
attributed to Magharebia via Wikimedia Commons public domain.

The reason why Europeans are reluctant to acknowledge the dark skin colour of North African tribes has much to do with Europe's traumatic memory of the Barbary states of Sale, Tunis, Algiers, and Tripoli. From 1600 to the late 1800's, these powerful African pirate ships terrified the western European states, and even the United States of America. Charles Sumner's account of 'White' slavery in the Barbary States' shows just how powerful these Africans were:

> The expedition against Algiers was followed, in 1637, by another, under the command of Captain Rainsborough, against Sallee, in Morocco. At his approach, the Moors sold a thousand of their captives, British subjects, to Tunis and Algiers. Intestine feud aided the fleet, and the cause of emancipation speedily triumphed. Two hundred and ninety British captives were surrendered, and a promise was extorted from the government of Sallee to redeem the thousand captives who had been sold away to Tunis and Algiers. An ambassador from the king of Morocco shortly afterwards visited England, and on his way to his audience at court was attended through the streets of London by four Barbary horses led along in rich caparisons, and richer saddles, with bridles set with stones; also, some hawks; many of the captives whom he brought over going along afoot clad in white.'" [Charles Sumner, White slavery in the Barbary states, 1847]

Charles Sumner laments at the bondage of countless 'White' Europeans being sold in Algiers or Morocco; at the same time Africans were being sold in the USA:

> How frequently have I seen in the Southern States of our own country weeping mothers leading guiltless infants to the sales with as deep anguish as if they led them to the slaughter, and yet felt my bosom tranquil in the view of these aggressions upon defenseless humanity! But when I see the same enormities practiced upon beings whose complexion and blood claim kindred with my own, I curse the perpetrators and weep over the wretched victims of their rapacity. Indeed, truth and justice demand from me the confession, that the Christian slaves among the barbarians of Africa are treated with more humanity than the African slaves among the professing Christians of civilized America; and yet here sensibility bleeds at every pore for the wretches whom fate has doomed to slavery. [Charles Sumner]

The anthropologist Carleton S. Coon was obsessed with 'Whiteness' and even believed that humans were divided into five races. He believed that each race evolved separately into modern humans at different times.

Giuseppe Sergi in his research, a generation earlier, came to a completely different conclusion:

> These three- varieties are the three great branches of one species, which I call Eurafrican, because it occupied, and still occupies, a large portion of the two continents of Africa and Europe.......... (4.) These three human varieties have nothing in common with the so-called Aryan races; it is an error to maintain that the Germans and the Scandinavians, blond dolichocephals or long-heads (of the Reihengraber and Viking types), are Aryans; they are Eurafricans of the Nordic variety.
>
> (5.) The Aryans are of Asiatic origin and constitute a variety of the Eurasiatic species; the physical characters of their skeletons are different from those of the Eurafricans.
>
> (6.) The primitive civilization of the Eurafricans is Afro-Mediterranean, becoming eventually Afro- European.

> (7.) The Mycenaean civilization had its origin in Asia and was transformed by diffusion in the Mediterranean.
>
> (8.) The two classic civilizations, Greek and Latin, were not Aryan, but Mediterranean. The Aryans were savages when they invaded Europe: they destroyed in part the superior civilization of the Neolithic populations, and could not have created the Greco-Latin civilization. [G. Sergi]

Carleton S. Coon foolishly proposed that the so-called 'Caucasoid' race evolving 200,000 years before the Congoid ('so-called' Negroid). His views were challenged by others, especially Columbia's Department of Anthropology, which was particularly hostile to his theories:

> contrast anthropologists Milford Wolpoff and Rachel Caspari find Coon naive in thinking that he had no responsibility for his notions about race. They charge that Coon the world traveler was also Coon the upper class, New Englander who had no real idea that the "natives", that he claimed to understand so well, were also people. Coon's work was racist, they write, because of his "clear insensitivity to social issues, born of his attitude toward anthropology that was engendered by his social class and training.

On the origin of the Irish, J.P. Mallory concluded that it is unjustifiable to search for the first Indo-European speakers during the Bronze Age. The Irish Association of Professional Archaeologists held a seminar in 1948; they came to the following conclusion:

> The Irish assimilated the local population of Ireland gradually over the course of centuries. They did not impose their language on the aborigines, but rather induced them to adopt Irish. Such language change is invariably receded by a period of bilingualism where the native speaks both his own language but also learns that of the intruder. Consequently, in-order to resolve the problem of Irish origins it is necessary not only to demonstrate intrusion but also explain the reason for bilingualism.

No attempt was made at the conference to tackle the question of what language was spoken by the original population of Ireland. Old Irish deviates from the Indo-European model due to the influence of Hamito-Semitic or Afro-asiatic. Not only did the original population learn to speak Irish in a Hamito-Semitic manner, but they also retained many words that have passed into modern Gaelic and Cymric (Welsh).

12 IRON AGE TRIBES OF BRITAIN & IRELAND

The inhabitants of Iron Age Britain are somewhat of an enigma. Many tribes lived an isolated existence and were far from being homogeneous. European anthropologist have tried to create artificial racial categories. The mythical 'Celts' were supposed to be tall and blond with blue eyes - and yet the native population of the western parts of Britain and Ireland (the Atlantic fringe) are well known for their raven hair, and some have distinctly swarthy appearances.

The 'Celts' are associated with the Iron Age that began with the Hallstatt culture in central Europe. However, it is worth remembering the antiquity of Iron production across the other side of the Mediterranean, in Africa. The British Museum guide to the Bronze Age proposes a spread of Iron Age technology from Kordofan to central Europe:

> Evidence in favor of the extreme antiquity of Iron in Egypt has already been given, and it must not be forgotten that in Africa, which as a continent never had a Bronze Age, was possessed of abundant ores from which good malleable iron could be extracted by processes far simpler than those required for the manufacture of bronze. The district west of the Upper Nile is very rich in iron, and Professor Gowland has shown that the furnaces used in modern times in Kordofan has close analogies with one represented on a tomb bearing the name Thothmes III (about 1530 BC) and with those employed by the Etruscans and other people of southern Europe west of the Apennines. The metallurgy of iron in this part of Africa was evidently both an ancient and

> vigorous art, and its origin may be more remote than is usually suspected. [British Museum, A Guide To The Antiquities of Bronze Age, 1904]

Attempts to identify with the 'Celts' starts to emerge in the 16th Century, with George Buchanan:

> Buchanan, in his history of Scotland, published in 1589, dismissed as fabulous, that section of the Irish and British genealogies that purported to trace the origin of each people, generation by generation, from Japhet.......... established the inductive method of scientific proof than the clear and well-marshalled argument by which Buchanan proves from numerous Greek and Latin sources that the Gaels and the Britons were branches of the ancient 'Celtic' people of the Continent. *[see Eoin Mac Neill, Phases of Irish History, 1920]*

The myth of a 'Celtic' race was successfully propagated in the 18th century and was initially proposed by the Breton nationalist Abbe Paul Yves Pezron (1639-1706). He wanted to create an artificial identity and lift up the status of the marginalized Breton people in France. It should be remembered that Brittany was annexed by France under the Treaty of Plessix in 1532. By the early 1800's, the marginalized Breton became re-invented (just like Ireland) into 'Celts' - with the re-emergence of romantic folklore and tales of mythical King Arthur.

Pezron extended the name 'Celts' to his neighbors, the Irish and Cymry - even though no ancient writer ever referred to them by this name. Suddenly they were included under the label Gauls or 'Celts' - a continental European tribe. However, the Gaels and Cymry regarded the Gauls or 'Celts' as foreigners. They would only be allowed to become Britons after 9 generations, as long as they obeyed the customs and laws of the Cymry (Britons).

The irony is that the Breton people trace their ancestry back to Cymry speakers who migrated from south-western Britain (Cornwall) during the time the Anglo-Saxon settled in Britain ($5^{th}/6^{th}$ century AD). Pezron was not a Gaul or 'Celt' and yet he propagated a misleading false identity - he was essentially Cymry in origin since the Bretons came from Cornwall and adopting a 'Gaul' or 'Celtic 'identity can only be seen a cognitive dissonance.

The people of Iron Age Britain were different from the invading Anglo-Saxon tribes. When we examine Anglo-Saxon graves, the average height is estimated as 5 ft 6 inches for men. While for Iron Age males Britons, we find an average height of 5 feet 1. Obviously, many local variations existed across these islands. But how do we explain Strabo's observation that the Britons were darker haired compared to the Gauls; obviously, they were not 'Celts' or Gauls.

Even Eoin MacNeil could not ignore the 'elephant in the room' regarding the obvious physical difference between the indigenous Cymry and the Anglo-Saxons:

> So far as the Iberian theory is not mere vacuum-filling, it appears to rest on a single passage of Tacitus. He is describing the Silures, a British people whose territory was in the south of Wales, and who offered a very fierce resistance to the Romans. "The swarthy complexion of the Silures," he says, "the prevalence of curly hair among them, and their position over against Spain, argue that the ancient Iberians must have crossed over [from Spain] and occupied their territory." We have often heard the occurrence of similar physical traits in the west of Ireland ascribed to a more recent Spanish mixture. It all amounts to this, which Irish tradition bears out, and which nobody questions, that these western isles contain descendants of an ancient dark-complexioned population, probably already of mixed race, which existed in western Europe before the arrival of the fair-complexioned people, whose distinctive features appear by all indications to have originated in the lands forming the basin of the Baltic Sea. [p62, Eoin MacNeil]

Was the creation of this new 'Celtic' identity motivated by Anglo-Saxon racism? Annie Loring Peters in her thesis (April 1986), presented to the Department of History and the Faculty of the Graduate College University of Nebraska, quotes a Cambridge Professor who visited Ireland in the late 1800's; and gives a racist description of the Irish:

> I am haunted by the human chimpanzees I saw along that hundred miles of horrible country. I don't believe they are our fault. But to see white chimpanzees is dreadful; if they were black, one would not feel it so much, but their skins, except where tanned by exposure, areas white as ours. [p143, Annie Loring Peters, also see L.P. Curtis, Anglo-Saxons and Celts, p.84]

The reader must contemplate the question: Was the desire to convert the Irish and Welsh into tall blond 'Celts' motivated by the racist views that dominated the academic institutions, and society during that period?

Burial Practices in the Iron Age

If the Celts invaded Britain during the Iron Age, extensive changes in burial customs would be expected. The only way to throw light on this is to examine the archaeological records, to see if any changes ever took place. The beginning of the Bronze Age in Britain saw the continuation of inhumation burials - they followed the same method used by the previous Neolithic inhabitants. The Bronze Age people built impressive barrows, containing rich grave goods, and they were used for burying important members of the community.

The middle of the Bronze Age saw a significant change in burials; cremations become the dominant burial method. In his study of Iron Age burials, Niall Sharples has the following:

> This general absence of formal cemeteries continues through the 1st millennium BC until the emergence of regional traditions of burial practice in the Late Iron Age, probably beginning at the earliest around the end of 2nd century B.C. The exceptions to this pattern include a distinct regional tradition in East Yorkshire and an isolated cemetery in Oxfordshire. [N. Sharples, 2014 Problems and Opportunities; Iron Age Burial traditions in southern Britain, January 2016].

Examination of Iron Age burials from the 1st century BC shows three separate types in southern England: cremation in the southeast; inhumation in Dorset - with the body in a crouched position, abundant grave goods, usually located just outside of settlements; while in Cornwall inhumation using stone cist cemetery burials, generally without grave goods. The examination of Iron Age burials shows a significant difference between communities in England and those across the Channel. The study by Sharples concludes:

> There is clearly a major difference between the societies on either side of the Channel during the Iron Age. This resulted from the breakdown of exchange relationships in the Iron Age societies of southern Britain, due to the undermining of the value of bronze at the end of the Bronze Age. Societies in southern Britain responded to this crisis by withdrawing into a state of isolated paranoia which rejected external contact. This was, however, only one regional response, in other areas such as Yorkshire, there was a very different response, which resulted in the development of a vibrant burial record that

> placed considerable emphasis on the individual, and status was clearly demonstrated by the use of distinctive material culture. These developments were heavily influenced by contacts with the continent which influenced the choice of two wheeled chariots as grave furniture and the nature of the artistic styles used to decorate the high-status metalwork. However, again these influences were transformed and reflect an indigenous interpretation of a continental tradition.

The Cymry (Britons) maintain that the 'Celts' or Gaul were allowed to settle in Britain only a few centuries before the arrival of the Romans. The burial traditions, examined so far, indicate different methods were used which reflected a heterogeneous culture; indigenous communities adopted some continental traditions and interpreted them in their own way.

Welsh soil is mainly acidic and as a result bones tend to be poorly preserved. Some areas with a more alkaline soil have preserved ancient skeletal remains. Areas of Wales where alkaline soil tends to be found are the south-east, north-east, the Gower peninsula and on Anglesey island. So far, no Iron Age burials have been found in the Gower peninsula. The main source of Iron Age burial materials comes from southern England and Yorkshire. Unfortunately, our knowledge of Welsh Iron Age burials is still poorly understood. Some believe the lack of material could be due to the practice of invisible disposal method, e.g., the scattering of cremated remains; but this area requires more study. Sharples concludes, 'that the scarcity of Welsh Iron Age burials, when compared to other regions in Britain, is due to both poor preservation and a bias in archaeological research strategies, rather than the dominance of an invisible burial rite.'

Sharples in his study managed to identify 112 verified human remains found in Wales. Based on the material available, we do not have any knowledge as to where Iron Age tribes fit 'ethnically' with the rest of the island communities. The 'ethnic' affinities of the Silures remains elusive - this has more to do with the reluctance of scientists and archaeologist to pursue the subject; maybe the fear of unveiling an African connection. Informal interviews with individuals with a Silurian background surprisingly revealed a belief that there was 'black' ancestry somewhere in their past. One person, privately expressed his concern for his pregnant sister - he said, "she's frightened that she might have a black baby." I further questioned him and asked if the father was black - he answered, "of course not, we know that it happens all the time." Beddoe's index of Nigrescence, a measurement of skin, eye, and hair colour amongst the British population; placed South Wales as one of the darkest populations in the British Isles.

What we have learnt so far is the lack of continuity in burials during the

Iron Age. If we are to find out whether any invading 'Celts' arrived in the 1st century, we need to examine the remains of graves that are clearly associated with tribes such as the Durotriges tribe. The Welsh Triads clearly states that the tribes from Gauls had to ask for permission to settle in Britain. Welsh sources state that the Gauls or 'Celts' could only become Britons (Cymry) after 9 generations, as long as they kept to the customs of the land.

Tacitus describes the Britons as differing in appearance - the Caledonians of Scotland are described as fair with light hair, while the Silures of Wales are described as dark skinned with crinkly curly hair; he believed them to be of Iberian origin. If the indigenous inhabitants of Britain were Hamito-Semitic (Afro-asiatic) speakers; when and how did they adopt the language, they speak today?

The evidence does not support waves of 'Celts' or Gauls invading these islands. A long process of assimilation in some parts of the island must have occurred, while other areas were only superficially affected: the language was adopted without any significant human migration. For example, the Durotriges, who dominated the county of Dorset, practiced inhumation (burial) from the c.400 BC and continued throughout the Romano-British period (4th cent AD).

Rebecca Redfern's thesis explores the health analysis of Iron Age Dorset. Interestingly, she gives the following comments in her 2005 thesis 'A Gendered Analysis of Health From The Iron Age to The End of The Romano-British Period in Dorset':

> The archaeology of Iron Age and Romano-British Dorset is not wholly understood, and many areas remain poorly investigated....... Iron Age west Dorset is described as a "black hole" and coastal Dorset as "unsorted" (Haselgrove et al. 2001, 25). [p43]

A superficial look at the Iron Age burials quickly reveals that so much is not known. For example, intact Iron Age skeletons from Wales are limited; Cornwall, Devon, and Dorset all practiced inhumation, while only south-east England showed any clear similarity with continental Europe. Even in the Iron Age it is difficult to understand who and what the 'Celts' were: the indigenous tribes seem to have maintained their customs, with no evidence of 'Celts' arriving in waves and taking over the country. A small trickle of continental tribes start to appear around the 1st century BC - but there is no evidence of a massive 'Celtic' migration from Europe.

Dr Simon James, of the University of Leicester, admitted in a lecture that there seems to be a lack of evidence for a 'Celtic' presence in these islands:

> When digging Iron Age sites like Gussage All Saints, Dorset,

> archaeologist expected to find evidence of the 'Celtic' invasion. But the more they looked for the invaders, the more they weren't there. Instead of cultural discontinuity and settlement by intrusive warrior societies radiating from Europe in the Iron Age; what they found was something quite different. They found basic continuity from the preceding Bronze Age in many basic features of society - such as house design (round houses), pottery traditions, farming, and burial rites. *[Dr Simon James Exploring Culture lecture series from the Department of Culture, Arts & Leisure]*

Dr James comments on 'Celtic' Art and proclaims that they represent indigenous influence and are modified regionally. Even the East Yorkshire chariot burial was decorated in an indigenous style and the body was placed in the crouching position, totally dissimilar to the Gaulish burial rites in Europe. Britain was culturally diverse - overall the inhabitants were egalitarian farmers and there is no evidence of a warrior or druid class dominating society.

Recent excavations in Pembrokeshire in West Wales, have unearthed an Iron Age chariot grave; the first of its kind to be found in Wales. In 2018 metal detector enthusiast, Mike Smith, found the first Iron Age chariot grave in Wales. The objects unearthed included bronze horse fittings, bridle, and harness, fittings; all in the La Tene style. An iron sword was also recovered from the grave, but due to the acidic soil condition it has disintegrated. It is the first chariot grave to have been found in southern Britain.

There are two ancient burial sites that can help us understand the 'ethnic' affinities of the Iron Age people of Britain. Maiden Castle is a massive Iron Age war cemetery situated in Dorset, South England. It is also the site of Britain's largest hill fort, where the Romans are believed to have massacred the local inhabitants. Further east we have the Hythe skulls at St Leonard's Church, in Kent. It is the largest and best-preserved collection of ancient human skulls and bones in Britain. If the theory of a 'Celtic' invasion was true, then the skeletons from both these burial sites should reveal the presence of phenotypes similar to those found in Iron Age burials in France and Belgium. If my African Substratum Theory is correct, then these skulls would show a greater affinity with groups from Africa.

The Massacre at Maiden Castle

Maiden Castle is Europe's largest Iron Age hill fort. This impressive structure derives its name from '*mai dun*' which means great fort. The settlement towered over the local Dorset landscape. It occupied nearly 50 acres, the defensive banks reached at least 80 feet in height, and it was the primary population center for Dorset. The 52 or more skeletons unearthed all show horrific injuries due to blunt force trauma and sharp-force trauma, typical of frenzied attacks. Around ¾ of the skeletons found in the surrounding area died from injuries received due to violence, and interestingly, both men and women were victims of this violence. The fort was besieged by the Romans in 43 A.D under the rule of Vespasian. Recent studies by Miles Russell offers an alternative narrative to the mainstream historical interpretation:

> over 74% of individuals represented had died violently, with evidence for targeted blows to the head and upper torso (Redfern 2011, 131–3), specific episodes were many and extremely varied in date, suggesting that the population had lived through multiple periods of stress, competition, and conflict from the first century BC on until at least the mid first century. [Russell, Miles. (2019). Myth makers of Maiden Castle: Breaking the Siege Mentality of an Iron Age Hillfort. Oxford Journal of Archaeology. 38. 325-342.]

It seems that the inhabitants of the Dorset region, the Durotriges, were involved in bloody conflicts with their neighbors even before the arrival of the Romans. The Romano-Britons of Dorset managed to survive for at least 250 years after the Romans left Briton. It took the Saxons a long time to conquer Dorset. It was finally subdued in the mid-7th century AD. The Durotriges seem to have been as fierce as the swarthy Silures of South Wales. Were they related?

Eurocentric historians would have us believe that Iron Age Britain was dominated by waves of Aryan 'Celts' - a deeper look reveals a great deal of uncertainty and lack of clear evidence for this theory. Some Gallic or 'Celtic' tribes were invited, or more accurately, given permission, by the Cymry, to settle in Britain. The name Cymry translates as 'compatriots' or fellow countryman - a diverse group of people sharing a common identity. Tacitus noticed the variation in the appearance (phenotype) of the ancient Briton: from dark skinned, curly haired Silures to the flame-haired Queen of the Iceni (Boadicea).

Aerial photograph of Maiden Castle from the west, (1937 public domain)

The Coefficient of Racial Likeness (CRL)

Dr. Geoffrey Mckay Morant was a physical anthropologist. He was born in 1899 and was an exceptionally talented scientist. He studied as a student under Pearson and diligently measured skulls for 20 years, when craniometry was at its peak in Europe.

Elazar Barkan's study, *'The Retreat of Scientific Racism: Changing Concepts of Race in Britain and the United States between the World Wars,'* documented how scientific racism slowly began to decline in the world of academia:

> Craniometry which was at the heart of European racial taxonomy a generation earlier, could not by 1940 command any academic position in London. In advocating a readership appointment be given to Morant, Haldane wrote that "his field is rather narrow," yet on the "metrical side of human craniology" a "topic which is not wholly trivial," he had "a serious claim to know more than anyone else in the world." [p158, Elazar Barkan]

The development of the coefficient of racial likeness (CRL) by Pearson and G. M. Morant was an attempt to standardize the measurements used and it was to provide a single numerical expression designed to measure the resemblance between two racial groups - data was input without assigning any order of importance to various characters. The data collected by G. M.

Morant, especially his study of the Swat and Hunza Valley people led him to conclude that they were indistinguishable from some European races [e.g., homo Alpinus type]. It seems the data did not fit with the racist belief of European superiority of the time. Barkan concludes that *'G. M. Morant believed professionally in racial typology but was not a racist. Concurrently with his racial studies, he participated in the Race and Cultural Committee, and when World War II began, he lamented that anthropologists did not do more to combat racism.'*

One reason for the abrupt decline in the science of 'race' was the lack of epistemological foundations for racial classifications. Barkan's fascinating exploration of the retreat of the science of race has the following:

> The 'Aryan Myth' was Central at the turn of the century not only in Germany but also in Britain and the United States. It was seductive to the European mind because it posited a high-brow racism underwritten by an increasing reputable science. But if science legitimized racism, it also made it vulnerable to changes in scientific outlook. .... It led to questioning and later the disappearance of a primordial race of mythical ancestors and an inevitable decline in the appeal of race: the greater the popularity of science of race became, the more data were available and the more elusive turned the primordial ancestors. [p19, The Retreat of Scientific Racism: Changing Concepts of Race in Britain and the United States Between the World Wars by Elazar Barkan]

What is clear to me is that European craniometry began to decline due to the data collected could not prove the Aryan theory. G. M. Morant's work simply proved that Iron Age Britons had a stronger 'racial' connection with the African Guanches and African Copts; and there were no significant affinities with central Europeans. In the 1940's we see a decline in the pursuit of the scientific study of race; craniology was abandoned, not because it was racist but because the results it produced kept undermining the 'Aryan Theory.' Even the British Iron Age, thought to have been the golden age of the fictitious blond 'Celts', turned out to have strong links with NW Africans, Etruscan's, and other darked skinned people. This was the true reason why craniology was abandoned and forgotten quickly.

Biological distance in physical anthropology uses the above measurements to estimate the degree of divergence amongst population groups. This method can be applied to both ancient and living populations. The measured phenotypic data is said to be an effective tool for estimating biological distance. Even modern anthropologists such as Howells in his study, *('Cranial Variation in Man: A Study by Multivariate Analysis of Patterns of*

Difference among Recent Human Populations'), fervently believed it to be an effective tool - however, in reality these scientists only used it to measure the 'other' or 'exotic' natives from some far away island or deep in the interior of Africa or Asia. At least G. M. Morant compared the skulls in his Iron Age series with those from the African Canary Islands and Coptic Egypt. If he had consulted the work of Giuseppe Sergi instead of Ripley, he would have been able to make sense of his findings. His evidence seems to add support to Giuseppe Sergi's Eurafrican theory.

European Craniometry was Immoral!

How were the skulls held in Museums across Europe, Canada, USA, and Australia collected? The reader can be assured that they were not always collected from lonely, isolated cairns or burial chambers. The last Tasmanians, for example, were regarded as a prize for European *'head-hunters'* or anthropologists. The data we have inherited through journals such a Biometrika, were the direct result of colonialism, brutality, and genocide. These skulls are still housed in European museums and should be returned for burial. However, in this chapter we are using this data to show that even with their eager measurements of thousands of skulls, the 'Aryan' theory could not be proven. On close examination of the data, all evidence confirms a southern origin, which includes the continent of Africa, for the Gaels and Cymry.

It should be remembered that during World War II an attempt was made by the Nazis to create an anthropological collection of the 'Jewish race' - the aim was to prove the superiority of the 'Aryan' Germans over the '*Untermenschen'* (or 'sub-humans'). This collection was housed in the Anatomy Institute at the Reich University of Strasbourg.

The 1940's saw craniology swiftly abandoned. Eurocentrics now had a new toy. The new field of blood group analysis was born. But even this was also abandoned because it surprisingly revealed a connection between 'Celts' and Berbers and other non-European people. By the 1990's DNA technology became established.

William Lanne the last Tasmanian
(attributed to Anson Bros., Public domain, via Wikimedia Commons)

William Lanne, also known as King Billy, was born in 1835 and died on 3 March 1869. He was the last *'full-blooded'* Aboriginal Tasmanian man. The mutilation of his body is described by James Bonwick 1817-1906):

> Besides the Royal Society, it seems that there were others who desired to secure Billy Lanne's skeleton, and who were determined to have it in spite of the positive orders of the Colonial Secretary. The dead- house at the hospital was entered on Friday night, the head was skinned and the skull carried away.......On this mutilation being discovered, the members of the Council of the Royal Society were greatly annoyed, and feeling assured that the object of the party who had taken the skull was afterwards to take the body from the grave, and so possess himself of the perfect skeleton, it was resolved to take off the feet and hands and to lodge them in the Museum, an operation which was carefully done. [James Bonwick, The last of the Tasmanians; or, The black war of Van Diemen's Land, 1870]

Iron Age Craniology

The collection of skeletons from Maiden Castle and St Leonard's Hythe provides abundant material from the Iron Age. Analysis of these remains should provide clues to whether the 'Celts' actually settled in Britain.

European research into physical anthropology was based on the philosophy that different 'races' had different characteristics that could be measured through craniometric measurements. They tried to divide the human population into 17 groups: three from Europe, five from Africa, two from Asia, four from Oceania, two from North America and one from South America [see W. W. Howells]. All these attempts were in vain, since every attempt to find a 'pure' Aryan only unearthed remnants of dark-skinned 'aboriginal' populations that had affinities with groups in Africa and Asia. The cranial studies of the British Isles are particularly interesting since we find an Africanoid population even in the Iron Age. The measurements continuously lead us back to Africa and the Mediterranean: which explains why craniology was eventually abandoned.

Here we are only interested in the measurement and interpretation of that data relating to the ancient skulls found in the British Isles and how they related to skulls found in neighboring regions. G. M. Morant measured over 31 characteristics with an emphasis on objects representing the more important regions of the facial skeleton. The number of skulls in a series is important - since the mean for a particular series are not usually based on the same number of skulls. G. M. Morant published his detailed study, *'The Preliminary Classification of European Races Based on Cranial Measurements', in Biometrika December 1928 [pp.301-375]*. He reminds the reader that the coefficient of racial likeness is a measure of how far on the given data we can assert significant resemblance or divergence. From his study he suggested the following classifications:

> *Serbo-Croats, Greeks, Turks, Magyars, Slovenes, Romanians, Czechs, Russians, and Italians (Siena).
>
> *Bavarians (Altbayerised), Badensians, Wurtemberger and Alsatians. Tyrolese and British Bronze Age.
>
> *Etruscans, Pompeiians, Guanches, Copts, and Basques.
>
> *English (Farringdon St.), English (Whitechapel), British Iron Age, Anglo-Saxon, Reihengraber.
>
> *Ancient Egyptian (26th - 30th Dynasties)

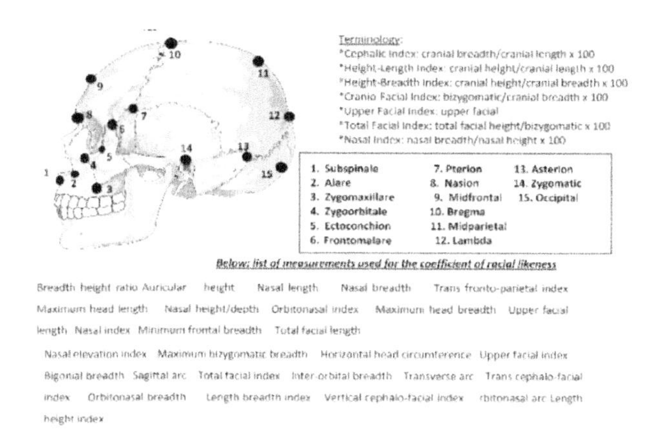

The above relationships were derived from coefficients of less than 7 with one or more of the series in the same group and one greater than 7 with every series in the other three groups. The relationship between these groups was found to be as follows - group D was widely removed from both group A and group B; the C group occupied an intermediate position and its bond with group D was more intimate than between any other pair of groups. The inter-relationships between G. M. Morant's groups are as follows:

> The D group as a whole is extremely unlike A and B groups, but there are several intimate connections between series C and D groups. The closest of those links are between the Etruscans, Pompeiians, Guanches and Basques of the C group and the British Iron Age and the two 17th century London series of the D group...........The bond between the C and D groups is very appreciably closer than those between the A and C. B and C. [p352].

The CRL data can be simplified as follows.

> The data gives some surprising results. Group C, which contains Guanches, Etruscans, Copts, Pompeiians, and Basques has a close affinity with the British Iron Age. Notice how the Iberian Bronze Age has no significant affinity with the British Iron Age (it shows only insignificant coefficient, p329). However, the Whitechapel medieval series has a group link with both the Etruscan and the Guanches [Whitechapel series cephalic index 74.3, Farringdon St series 75.4].

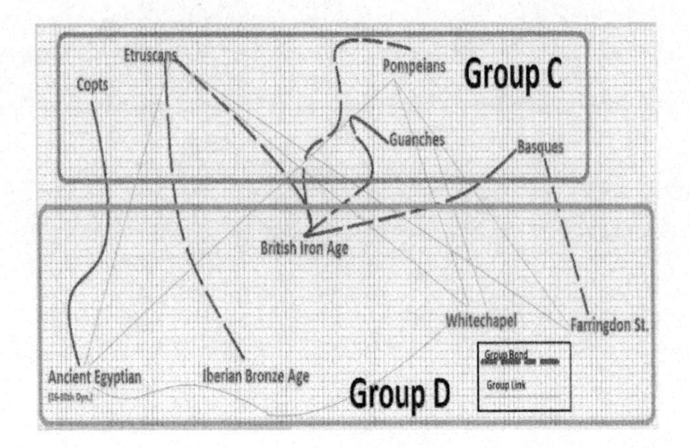

Coefficient of Racial Likeness: Group Bonds & Group Links, based on.

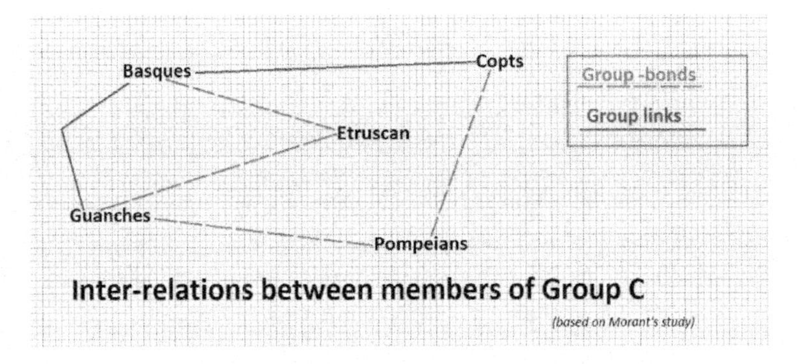

Inter-relations between Group C members

G. M. Morant reached the following conclusion:

> Several of the relations observed are not ones which would have anticipated, and a comparison with intermediate types will be needed to elucidate this somewhat anomalous state of affairs. These six series appear to be definitely bound to one another more closely than to any other of the series in the other groups, but the Etruscan, French and Pompeiians have some fairly close connections with some of the series in both A and B groups. The Copts, Guanches and Basques have no such connections, however. [p6, Morant]

Stoessiger and G. M. Morant's study of the Hythe crania produces an equally surprising set of results. These skulls were found to be quite different from most British types except the crania from Spitalfields Market, London, which it closely resembled. The Hythe skulls are extremely broad and have a cephalic index of 82.6 and 79.4, making it closer in index to the Bronze Age skulls (i.e., 80.9). The skulls are believed to be post-Roman, and the numbers exceed 1500. Many theories exist as to the identity of these people - some say they were the fallen from the battle between the Britons and the Saxons in 456 AD., others believed them to be slain Danes who were defeated by Gustavus, the governor of Kent in 853 AD., and another tale makes them slain Frenchmen who invaded Kent.

To find out if the present-day inhabitants of Kent were related to the Hythe skulls; a comparison of skulls of 49 boys from a local school was taken. The Hythe skulls are extremely broad and have a mean cephalic index 82 (corresponds to 84 on the living). The value found for the Hythe school children was 79.57; indicating that that only a small part of the present-day population of Hythe is descended from the medieval population.

The Hythe skulls do not fit with the general British Iron Age series, but they show an affinity with non-British series such as Etruscans, Finns and closest with the Spitalfields series (17th century AD). The Hythe skulls resemble closely the Spitalfields skulls, with a cephalic index of 82.6 and 79.4 respectively, and G. M. Morant comments *'they are quite different from the British Iron Age series.'* If we examine this more closely, we find that a direct comparison between the skulls from Maiden Castle, Dorset, and the Hythe skulls of Kent indicate that the populations are more heterogeneous than we have been led to believe.

Maiden Castle, the largest prehistoric fortified site in Europe, was first excavated by Mortimer Wheeler between 1934 and 1937. He documented 104 remains of individuals from the site. Over half of the skeleton showed evidence of violent trauma. C. N. Goodman and G. M. Morant completed a detailed analysis of the remnants of these Iron Age inhabitants in 1940. Dental anomalies were found in a high number of skulls. Many of the Maiden Castle skulls exhibited *Torus mandibularis*, a bony growth in the mandible usually present near the premolars. Goodman and G. M. Morant state, *"it occurs more frequently, and to a more marked extent in some modern races particularly the Eskimo [Inuit], but seldom found in European races. Dental anomalies appear to be exceptionally frequent in the short series of skulls from Maiden Castle."* The skeletal series would fit more comfortably within a series from the Bronze Age. The skulls appear to have a retreating frontal bone (comparable to the Farringdon Street skulls, of the medieval period); one particular female skull stands out - she was 4ft 9 ¼ and was taller than the other females, the nasal index was high (wide), and the nasal bridge was broad and depressed. Goodman and G. M. Morant commented on the facial bones having *'unusual premaxillary height, though it is not prognathous, are ambiguous.'* All he can say is *'that they are alien to Western Europe.'* In other words, they are foreign?

From the data we can develop a picture of what the Iron Age tribes looked like. The inhabitants of Maiden Castle were shorter than the Anglo-Saxons; their respective height being 5 ft. 6¼ inches for Anglo-Saxon males and 5 ft 5 inches for Iron Age males; and 5 feet 1 5¼ from Anglo-Saxon women and 5 ft 0¼ inches for Iron Age women.

The interpretation by G. M. Morant is highly questionable - the female skull, known as P36 is shown in Biometrika (plate II page 30) and identically matches the facial features of the Aurignacian Grimaldi skulls from Upper Paleolithic Italy, which are believed to be 'Africanoid.' The only real difference is the Grimaldi skull has a cephalic index of 70.9 [long headed] - the facial features of the Maiden skull (P36) and the Grimaldi are identical.

Men of the old stone age, their environment, life, and art
Osborn, Henry Fairfield, 1857-1935

The description given by Boule and Vallois of Grimaldi man [a skull found in Italy] and Asselar man [a skull found in Cercle de Kidal, Mali] in *Nature vol. 20, 1932* is a useful comparison for the Maiden Castle (*P36*) Female skull:

> The skull is high and the cranial capacity approximately 1520 c.c. There is distinct sub-nasal prognathism, though this character is not specially marked when the face is taken as a whole. When compared with other types of early and recent man in Africa, Asselar man is seen to resemble most closely types found in South Africa, especially the Hottentot and Bantu, more particularly in the features .... It is suggested, therefore, that Asselar man and Grimaldi man are

> derivatives, perhaps to be associated with the Capsian industry, from an earlier less specialized type, which divided, one branch going north and evolving in the direction of Cro-Magnon man, while the other, going south, became the ancestral type of the Bushmen and the less specialized Hottentot. [Boule and Vallois]

If the Maiden Castle skulls were found in Africa, they would have certainly been identified as having affinities with Khoisan or similar sub-Saharan phenotypes. *[Note: the terms Bushmen and Hottentot are offensive Eurocentric names, the appropriate term to use is Khoisan]*. Also, if these skulls were found in Asia, then they would have been assigned an Inuit or Mongolian origin. What is clear is that the measurements might be accurate, but the interpretations are clouded by Eurocentric cultural bias.

On close observation both female skulls from Maiden Castle [labelled *P20* & *P36*] show signs of slight alveolar prognathism, the upper face is rather flat, and both resemble either African Khoisan or Afalou-Mechta, or they could even be compared to an 'Asiatic' phenotype. The third female skull [*T21*] has a graceful, rounded forehead, with a distinctive flat, high check-bones and wide lower face. Again, the teeth are very prominent and have a wide appearance. One cannot help but assume an African or south-east Asian origin for the females. Good scientific research should not eliminate a possible match because of geographical distance or ethnicity. As with any forensic investigation - all data should be evaluated in a non-bias manner. At this stage of the investigation, we cannot rule out the possibility of these Iron Age warriors having African or south-east Asian wives. An African ancestry is more likely since we know that there was considerable contact between N.W. Africa and the British Isles in prehistoric times.

It is worth bearing in mind that Sergi challenged Testut, who believed that the ancient Chancelade skull had Inuit (Eskimo) affinities. *'On close inspection,'* Sergi found, *'the Chancelade skulls appear to me as Pelasgisus steguides of the Ellipsoid class, still found today in East Africa.' [Sergi,1900]*

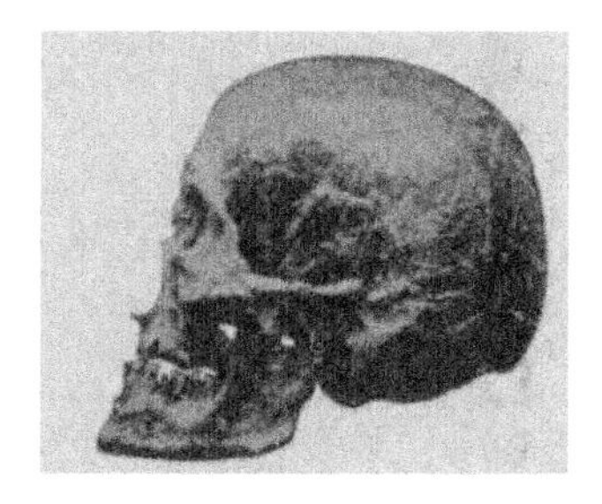

Chancelade skull, classified as Ellipsoide by Sergi [Sergi, 1900]

The male skull [labelled P30] illustrated in Biometrika has a robust appearance with a broad face, high wide check-bones, and a very wide chin. The males differ considerably from the females in phenotype - the closest skull I have found similar to the male Maiden Castle skull is one from Italy which has almost identical features. The modern Italian skull show many common features with the male skulls from Maiden Castle. We can see that the ethnicity of both the Durotriges massacred at Maiden Castle and the Hythe skulls from a similar period cannot be easily assigned to a northern or central European type at all – G. M. Morant admits outside influence but does not investigate further.

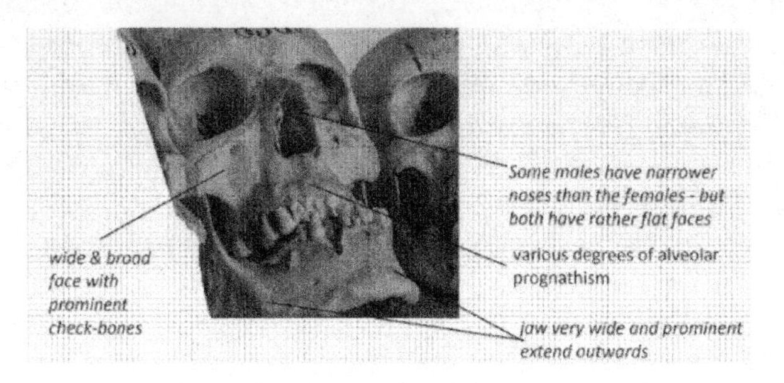

Modern male Italic skull with similar characteristics as the Maiden Castle skulls. (Modified image v2osk at Unsplash, public domain)

A study of the Romano-British skulls showed that they had the shortest nasal height, when compared to other periods. The evidence points to links with the African Guanches, African Copts, Etruscans from the Italian peninsula, and Pompeiians - and intriguingly a link with the Sami (or Lapp). The data is pointing towards a very multicultural ancient Britain. Sergi had also something to say about the possible connections between the 'Celtic' and the Mongolian (Turanian) phenotype:

> But I do not wish to close this article without referring to the fact that Pritchard observed in the 'Celtic' cranium of Great Britain, which is identical with that of other regions, the Mongol or the Turanian characters; that Nicolucci described in the Piedmont cranium, foolishly believed by him to be Ligurian, an error which is to-day repeated by the French anthropologists, the same Mongol or Turanian features, and that I myself in studying the skulls of Piedmont recognized these features many years ago. Finally, there is Herve who recognized the mongoloids in France, which he obstinately denominates Celto-Ligurians, while the Ligurians whom we

> Italians have in our country are Mediterranean Eurafrican, as the remains of Riviera, Genoa, and of Mentone evidently show. [G. Sergi, 'The Primitive Inhabitants of Europe' The Monist, Vol. 9, 1899]

Even the famous chariot graves of East Riding, Yorkshire; a collection of tumuli know as 'Danes Graves' or 'Danesdale' which formed part of the Arras Culture of inhumation dating back to the middle Iron Age, do not fit with the equivalent graves in Belgium or France. These tumuli are originally believed to have been 500 in number. J.R. Mortimer account gives a total 197. *[Proceedings of the Yorkshire Geological and Polytechnic Society, 13, 286-298, 1 January 1897]*. This area was home of the Parisi tribe and G. M. Morant gives the following description of these skeletons:

> The 'Danes Graves' skulls have lower cephalic indices than the English and Scottish Iron Age, so there is not the slightest suggestion of their bearing any close blood relationship to the brachycephalic peoples associated with the 'Late 'Celtic'' culture on the continent. [p73, G.M Morant]

The Aryan 'Celts' are nowhere to be found. The Iron Age inhabitants were extremely diverse and do not constitute a homogeneous group at all. European anthropologists tend to ignore anything that deviates from their 'norm' - as a result, they do not investigate further, even though the data is leading to a deep connection with southern lands and not continental Europe.

Jacqueline Wilson in her Doctor of Philosophy (PhD) dissertation, 'Becoming Irish' [2010], sums up the situation:

> In Ireland, the evidence for Hallstatt type material is slim, and material of La Tene design is patchy and separated geographically, and it is all but absent from the eastern, south-eastern, and southern counties. This lack of material becomes even more pronounced ....with only a few examples of decorated La Terse style metalwork from the whole of Ireland (Raftery 1994). If we were to continue to follow Megaw and Megaw's logic, then the lack of material evidence completely contradicts their description of the people of late Iron Age Ireland as "Celtic". [p41, Becoming 'Irish': The materiality of transcultural identities in the Later Irish Iron Age]

The 'Celts' are very illusive and seem to be difficult to find in the British Isles and Ireland. So let us turn to South Wales, the homeland of the Silures. It is worth mentioning John Beddoe's observation back in 1885:

> This one character of prognathism, taken separately, may be objected to as being of small value; but there is, as I have shown, a very great similarity in other respects among the individuals who present it. …….. my material is taken mostly from the laboring classes, yet in the prognathous list appears one of the ablest and most distinguished clergymen in Wales. I have also noticed it in the portraits of some well-known Welsh bards; in fact, eloquence, or at least readiness of speech, seems to be a general characteristic of the type. While Ireland is apparently its present center, most of its lineaments are such as lead us to think of Africa as its possible birthplace; and it may be well, provisionally, to call it Africanoid, applying the name Atlantean, which has been suggested, to the widely-diffused Ibero- Berber race type, of which it is probably a subdivision, in spite of the wide difference in the form of the jaws between it and the Basque type of Zaraus, the best accredited Iberian standard. Though I believe this Africanoid type to have been of very high antiquity ………… the best authenticated ancient skulls from Ireland may have belonged to it; for example, the three from the Phoenix Park tumuli ………These show the inclination to prognathism to be of remote date in Ireland, as well as the peculiar form of low, straight brow that still prevails there, and which is connected with low, square, horizontal orbits. [John Beddoe, The races of Britain; a contribution to the anthropology of Western Europe]

The evidence points to Africa and the Mediterranean as the homeland of the Gaels and Cymry (Britons). The Folklore of Ireland is quite precise; Cesair came from Meroe, the Formorians were African sea pirates and were the aboriginal population, the Tuatha de Danaans came from a land near the Philistines, and lastly the Milesians [Goidels] came from Scythia, settled in Egypt, and mixed with the Egyptians. The Mediterranean islands play a central role in the migrations story of the Gaels and Cymry (Britons). The skeletal data seems to match the folklore. The data reveals a remarkably close affinity between the Canary Islands, Maltese, Pompeiians, and the Copts. They appear to have played a large part in the peopling of the British Isles.

Mr. N Bradley spent time in Malta and noticed the close similarity between the people who inhabited the Maltese countryside and the Irish people.

Bradley's Maltese men, whom he compared to the Irish.

In his book *'Malta and The Mediterranean Race' [1912]*, he described his observations in detail:

> The reader is invited to compare the three 'excavators' in Gozo, in the foreground .... When the people were gathered round the work at Santa Verna an English observer, probably totally unacquainted with Mediterranean Race theories, remarked that they looked just like Irish. The man in the background of the picture represents the more ordinary dark type .... two peasant girls of Imtahleb, (below) a very isolated spot in Malta. They have blue eyes, and their features seem to form a link between Africa and Ireland. The " Finnish " Formorians of Donegal have traditional African origins. They are extremely dolichocephalic. In West Kerry also grey eyes and dark hair are met with. [N. Bradley]

Map of the Mediterranean Sea showing Malta, Tunisia, and Sicily. (AntikeGriechen1 Transferred from de.wikipedia to Commons by Maksim)

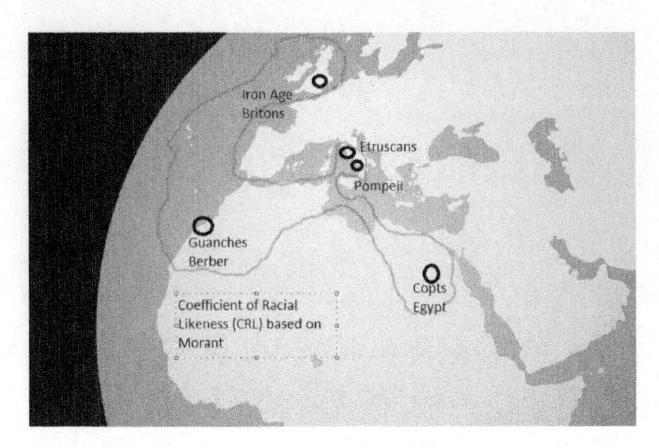

Coefficient of racial likeness based on G M Morant
(image modified by author, attributed to midifies HAns Braxmeier Pixabay).

Who were the Silures?

There has been surprisingly extraordinarily little written about the Silures, even though they are certainly the most interesting of all the Iron Age tribes of Britain. We have the detail description given by Roman Historian Tacitus:

> Ceterum Britanniam qui mortales initio coluerint, indigenae an advecti, ut inter barbaros parum compertum. Habitus corporum varii, atque ex eo arguraenta. Namque rutilae Caledoniam habitantium comae, magni artus Germanicam originem adseverant; Silurum colourati vultus, torti plerumque crines et posita contra Hispania- Hiberos veteres traiecisse easque sedes occupasse fidem faciunt. Proximi Gallis et similes sunt, seu durante originis vi, seu procurrentibus in diversa terris positio caeli corporibus habitum dedit [Latin]

The Silures as described by Tacitus. [A Complete Translation]

> Who were the original inhabitants of Britain, whether they were indigenous or foreign, is, as usual among barbarians, little known? Their physical characteristics are various, and from

> these conclusions may be drawn. The red hair and large limbs of the inhabitants of Caledonia point clearly to a German origin. The dark complexion of the Silures, their usually curly hair, (torti = twisted) and the fact that Spain is the opposite shore to them, are an evidence that Iberians of a former date crossed over and occupied these parts. Those who are nearest to the Gauls are also like them, either from the permanent influence of original descent, or, because in countries which run out so far to meet each other, climate has produced similar physical qualities. But a general survey inclines me to believe that the Gauls established themselves in an island so near to them. Their religious belief may be traced in the strongly marked British superstition. The language differs but little; there is the same boldness in challenging danger, and, when it is near, the same timidity in shrinking from it. The Britons, however, exhibit more spirit, as being a people whom a long peace has not yet enervated. Indeed, we have understood that even the Gauls were once renowned in war; but, after a while, sloth following on ease crept over them, and they lost their courage along with their freedom. This too has happened to the long-conquered tribes of Britain; the rest are still what the Gauls once were. [The Complete Works of Tacitus, translated by Alfred John Church and William Jackson Brodrbb, 1942]

The Silures are described as dark skinned and having twisted, curly hair; traits that Tacitus compares to the Iberians. They do not look like Gauls ('Celts') and he informs us that the center of druid culture was North Wales (Anglesey). Also, the culture and religion of the Gauls was inspired by the Britons. The original source of druid faith was from the Gaels and Cymry. The culture of the Gauls deviated from that of the Irish and Britons since it had absorbed many foreign, Germanic elements. The Welsh sources identify the Caledonians (living in the Highland of Scotland) and the Galadin (who arrived in south-east England), as non-Britons; they could only become Britons (Cymry) after 9 generations and had no rights to the land.

It is plausible to suspect that the Silures may have southern Iberian connections. One ancient map locates 'mons Silurum' in Andalusia, southern Spain. This needs further investigation; maybe looking at the skeletal remains may throw some light on the matter. One thing that we can agree upon is the dark skin-colour of this tribe.

Silurian Man is described in detail by F. W. Rudler:

> There can be little doubt that this ancient dark-coloured element still survives in the population of Britain and is especially abundant in parts of Wales. It is popularly believed that the ancient Britons were in large measure Melanochroi [Black].
>
> Witness the words which Mr. Tennyson puts into the mouth of Queen Bellicent:
>
> Dark my mother was in eyes and hair,
>
> And dark in hair and eyes I, and dark
>
> Was Gorlois; yea, and dark was Uther, too,
>
> Well-nigh to blackness.

Rudler continues further:

> When the writer of this article examined the physical characteristics of the Welsh students in the University College of Wales, for the Anthropometric Committee of the British Association, he found that at least 75%, were extremely dark. The dark colour in the modern Welsh is in all probability the effect of the old Silurian or Iberian blood which has lingered in the system from the distant days of the long-barrow builders....... And according to the late Dr. Nicholas, such an explanation would also explain the present Melanochroic element among the English; but of course, the swart blood is much less marked in England than it is in the Principality. It is evident from what has been advanced in this paper, that when we meet a Welshman of short stature, oval face and long skull, with mild features and swarthy complexion, with raven hair and flashing eyes, we are justified by the teachings of anthropology in believing that we have got "the genuine article" - a surviving representative of the Neolithic barrow-builder - a veritable vestige of Silurian Man. [p49-44, F. W.Rudler The University College of Wales Magazine, volume II, Dec 1879, No.2]

The Silures seem to exhibit some cultural differences too. Silver money was not used by the Silures, even though it was used by their neighbors the Dobuni. The Silures valued gold, however, they refused to adopt the silver currency used by neighboring tribes such as the Dobuni and Durotriges of Gloucester and Dorset. *[see Jerrad Lancaster, A Model of De-Centralised Political Structure among the Silures, Studia Celtica XLVIII (2014)]*

Archaeologist have noticed another difference between the Silures and their immediate neighbors. The hill forts in Gloucester and Herefordshire tend to be larger than those found in Gwent (South Wales) - only 4% of hillforts in Gwent are of the size 6 ha or over, and only one has an 'entrance-guard-chamber' in the whole of Gwent. [Jerrad Lancaster, South Wales in the Iron Age and Roman Periods, thesis 2012]

The Silures at Cardiff Castle

Visitors to Cardiff Castle are frequently unaware of the colourful golden mural on display beneath the Castle's south-east tower. The display is directly opposite the 3rd century AD remains of sections of the original Roman walls. The mural depicts village life, with men, women, and children displayed in their natural environment. Roman soldiers and rugged Silurian warriors make an impressive exhibition. This impressive mural was sculpted by Frank Abraham, a local artist, and was commissioned by Cardiff Council. The artist finally completed the mural in 1983; it took three years to complete. Frank Abraham captures the striking phenotypes that is frequently encountered amongst the Valleys population of South Wales. The theories encountered in this book hint at a possible 'Australoid' type in this region - F. Abraham's depiction of the Silures simply adds weight to my theory.

Silurian Warriors close-up; photo taken by © Ibrahim Ali.

Examination of the following photographs I took of the Silurian mural certainly adds to our 'forensic' investigation. It lends support to the data obtained from G. M. Morant's coefficient of racial likeness which links the people of Iron Age Britons with the African Guanches and Copts. Frank Abraham has captured some of the unique phenotypes that are still found today in the region. The broad check-bones and rugged features have been accurately captured by the artist and must been based on close examination of the local population over the 3 years it took to complete.

Silurian Warrior on the attack, photo taken by © Ibrahim Ali.

Silurian Leader, close-up, photo taken by © Ibrahim Ali.

Silurian Village, photo taken by © Ibrahim Ali.

13 ISOTOPE ANALYIS & MIGRATIONS

The use of isotope ratios within archaeology has proven to be an incredibly useful tool. The ratio between different isotopes varies considerably around the world. The main isotope ratios used in archaeology are as follows: Carbon ($^{13}C/12C$), Nitrogen ($^{15}N/^{14}N$), Oxygen ($^{18}O/^{16}O$), and Strontium ($^{87}Sr/86Sr$). Isotope ratios are measured using an isotope-ratio-mass–spectrometer.

There are four Strontium Isotopes ^{84}Sr (0.56%), ^{86}Sr (9.86%), ^{87}Sr (7.0%), and ^{88}Sr (82.58%). Strontium isotopes enter the human body through the plants ingested. It becomes absorbed by the body and replaces calcium in teeth and bone during infancy and childhood. This analysis allows us to figure out if a person has moved from one geographical region to another during their life. The amount of ^{87}Sr varies in rocks depending on the age. J. E. Ericson was the first to establish the link between the $^{87}Sr/^{86}Sr$ ratio in bones and teeth being directly related to the levels found in the geographical area a person grew up in. The composition of the enamel does not change after childhood. Analysis of the Strontium ratios can help determine human migration and mobility. The levels of Sr from a particular region can be compared to the Sr levels in ancient human bones. Different Sr levels in the enamel compared to the bone can indicate evidence of migration during childhood. The comparison between local and non-local $^{87}Sr/^{86}Sr$ range can give an indication of migration. However, this technique does have limitations:

Different regions must have a different Sr level so they can be compared - if people migrate from one area to another with similar Sr ranges, it will be difficult to use this technique. Consumption of a diet rich in marine food will results in that population having a Sr value close to that of sea water. Eating a lot of imported foods will also affect the Sr value.

Africans in Britain - Isotope Analysis

The use of isotope analysis is an exciting development which involves the examination of dental enamel and bones from ancient graves. In the chapter on the Iron Age, the coefficient of racial likeness and the striking appearance of the female skulls discovered at the Maiden Castle mass graves, led me to propose an African origin for these Iron Age wives. Can isotope analysis lend support to my new theory?

Location of graves examined using Isotope Analysis.
(Author modified original image of Jeff Schmaltz, MODIS in public domain.)

Mulder *[2013]* employed the use of carbon and nitrogen isotope analysis to identify the origins of individual migrants from the Romano-British period. Examination of various skeletons in York, northern England, revealed a possible exotic homeland for some individuals:

> Befitting this, the unusually high δ13C and δ15N recorded in their tooth dentine, which reflect diet around the same age or slightly later than the oxygen signal from the enamel, would normally be interpreted in terms of a diet rich in marine foods; although, such values could also be the result of consumption of C4-plants (or of animals with C4–plants in their diet), especially in arid regions (Dupras & Schwarcz 2001). Compared to available palaeo-dietary data from different regions of the Roman empire, they currently fit best with the population from Leptiminus, coastal Tunisia (Figure 5; Keenleyside et al. 2009), although this should not be taken as a secure attribution. The comparison with a North African assemblage nevertheless gives us an indication of how exotic the homelands of these two incomers may have been. [[Muldner, G. (2013) Stable isotopes and diet: their contribution to Romano-British research. Antiquity, 87 (335). pp. 137-149.]

The skeleton *TDC516* and *RE02*, were from a high-status background, and was buried in a stone sarcophagus covered by a stone slab cist. Long distant migrants have been identified as a significant portion of York's urban society.

Further south in Dorset, the examination of skeletal remains from the Roman cemetery at Lankhills, Winchester, have produced some interesting results. The town of Winchester was known as Venta Belgarum and formed part of the territory controlled by the Belgae tribe. The cemetery was in use during the 4th century AD. Strontium and Oxygen isotope analysis was carried out on 40 individuals from the Roman cemetery, with at least 11 being identified as possibly being 'foreign'. Paul Boot, et al., asserts that 'most of the foreigners were of unspecific but broadly western European origin, but three may have come from the Mediterranean area, possibly even from North Africa.'

My examination of the data from the Maiden Castle skeletons led me to conclude a possible African contribution to the Durotriges tribe. The female *P36* appeared to have a very similar phenotype to the Grimaldi Africanoids from the Upper Paleolithic. The coefficient of racial likeness data compiled by G. M. Morant points to Africa and the Mediterranean. Interestingly, my theory has been confirmed by the 2000/5 excavations at Lankhills, Winchester:

> Skulls, or parts of skulls were present in a total of 246 graves. Of that number there were 90 male and 89 female skulls. Many were fragmented and could not be reconstructed as part of this analysis. It was possible, therefore, to calculate indices for only 55 adult skulls without undertaking extensive reconstruction. .... Tentative observations have already been made on the basis of some cranial indices, including the identification of three individuals with a particularly broad nasal aperture, a feature which can be characteristic of skulls of Negroid populations (Bass 1987, 87). The isotope analysis has demonstrated that at least one of these individuals is likely to have originated in western or northern Britain. These findings underline the desirability of much further work on isotope analysis of this assemblage. Results of work recently made available as part of the Diaspora project hosted by the University of Reading have demonstrated that a high-status burial of the second half of the 4th century from York was that of an adult female of African origin. This clearly counters the assumption that all Blacks in Roman Britain were low-status male slaves. [The late Roman cemetery at Lankhills, Winchester: Excavations 2000-2005, Booth, Paul, et al., (2010) The late Roman cemetery at Lankhills, Winchester: Excavations 2000-2005. Project Report. Oxford Archaeology.]

If Paul Booth were acquainted with the work of G.M Morant, which we have discussed earlier, he would have been aware that the British Iron Age tribes examined were closely relate to the African Copts and Guanches. It would appear that the 'local' British population had African affinities and some of the incoming 'foreign' settlers had a more recent African origin; their childhood was spent in a warmer country, possibly Tunisia. The excavations at Lankhills produced some interesting results:

> The group of 'warmer' people did include three, however, all females, whose isotopic signature is significantly warmer than is typical for Britain, suggesting origins in an area with a hot and/or arid environment, consistent with many areas of the Mediterranean, and perhaps even North Africa. These are characterized as 'hot' in the abbreviated terminology

> employed in table 7.6. Remarkably, one of these, the young adult 119 in Grave 99, has cranial characteristics which suggest a possible origin in Egypt. Paul Booth, et al.,2010

This recent analysis lends support to the African Substratum Theory; and indicates that the settlers had African origins. Lankhills in Winchester is only a few miles away from Maiden Castle. The former was controlled by the Belgae, who are supposed to have been 'Celts' - the data suggests otherwise. Some of the settlers are believed to have come from '*Pannonian*' - a province of the Roman Empire, inhabited by the Illyrians. Today it corresponds to parts of Hungary, Slovenia, Croatia, and Bosnia

Further evidence supporting the presence of African settlers is the discovery of artefacts of African origin:

> In terms of artefact provision, the most striking of the 'warmer' burials is that of the adult woman in Grave 82, the deepest of the four stepped graves found in the OA excavation. This grave contained the two ceramic unguent flasks of probable North African origin, the only imported pottery vessels in the entire Lankhills cemetery assemblage, along with the comparable vessel from Clarke's grave 45, that of a prime adult female. [Booth, et al., 2010]

The city of Gloucester plays an important role in the battle between the Cymry (Britons) and the Anglo-Saxons. A study a 2nd century mass burial provides more evidence of settlers from Africa. Two individuals, *GLR1546* and *1561*, had values of *0.7109* and *0.7135*, respectively. These values indicate a childhood spent in warm coastal climates such as southern Iberia, the coast of Algeria and Morocco, and possibly Turkey. The analysis has shown that at least *7* out of *28* individuals tested had come from regions with a warmer climate. The town had a high number of settlers from other countries - making it a remarkably diverse town.

In Wales, the use of isotope analysis has also indicated the settlement of people from warmer climates. Katie A. Hemer, et al., conducted the first investigation of the early population *(c.500 AD to 1000 AD)* of Wales and the Isle of Man.

The cemeteries at Brownslade, Porthclew, and Llandough have produced some interesting results.

Porthclew is located in the county Pembrokeshire, West Wales, only a few miles from Pembroke. Llandough is a village in the Vale of Glamorgan, near Cardiff in South Wales. The three cemeteries located in these locations contained individuals who had $\delta^{18}O$ values that were consistent with consuming water with values above 4%, a value consistent with growing up in North Africa. This confirms the settlement of people from North Africa and suggests long-distance travel between Britain and North Africa was commonplace in the 2nd century A.D. *[see Katie A. Hemer, et al., A multi-isotope investigation of diet and subsistence amongst island and mainland populations from early medieval western Britain, American Journal of Physical Anthropology November 2016]* and *[Dr Caitlin Green Blog, 24/10/2015, Some oxygen isotope evidence for long-distance migration to Britain from North Africa & southern Iberia, c.1100 BC–AD 800]*

Further north, *91* male and female skeletons from the Bowl Hole cemetery in Northumberland (north England) were analyzed. The Isotope ratios of strontium ($^{87}Sr/^{86}Sr$) and oxygen ($\delta^{18}O$) were determined:

> Over 50% of those buried at Bamburgh were non-local. All ages and both sexes produced "non-local" signatures, some suggested childhood origins in Scandinavia, the southern Mediterranean or North Africa. Stature and other indicators of health status indicated differences in quality of life between local and migrant groups. These differences did not extend to burial practices. [Am J Phys Anthropology 151:462–476.]

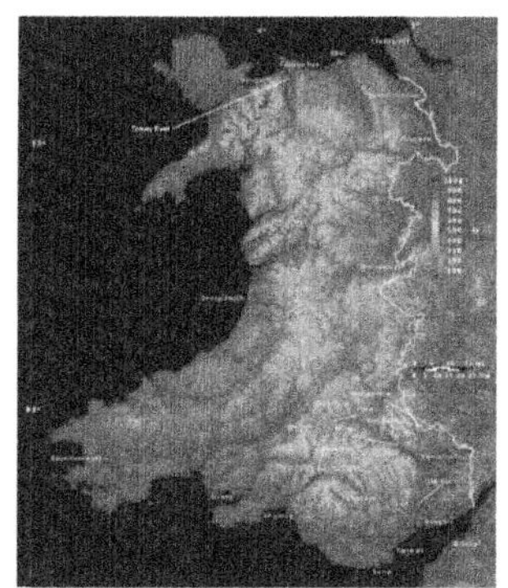

Location of Brownslade, Porthclew, and Llandough
(Image modified by author) original Wales_SRTM by PawelS creative commons via Wikimedia Commons.

The isotope analysis results from each location (south-west Wales, southern Dorset, Gloucestershire, and Northumberland) overwhelmingly confirmed the settlement of people from Africa during the Roman occupation of Britain. Also, the coefficient of racial likeness of Iron Age tribes has also revealed a close relationship with the African Guanches and

Copts.

The Romano-Briton graves excavated in Southwark (London), unearthed *22* individuals buried between the 2nd and 4th century AD. The cemetery at Lant Street, excavated in 2020, produced *84* inhumation that have added to our knowledge of migration patterns. From the examination of the skeletons and observable traits, the archaeologists classified the remains as follows: *28%* closest to the European sample, *24%* classified closest to the African sample, and 16% classified closest to the Asian sample. Again, the results show a cosmopolitan population with significant numbers of African and Asian people (constituting *40%* of samples):

> The population at Lant Street show isotopic patterns at variance with those found in other populations from Roman Britain. The carbon and nitrogen isotopes point towards a settled life in northern Europe with limited consumption of marine foods. On the other hand, the oxygen isotopes suggest that a significant proportion of the population, in particular burial *2, 15, 33, 44* and *45*, were immigrants to Britain who had spent their childhood in a climate like that of the Mediterranean. Likewise, study of population affiliation suggests that a significant proportion of the population, notably burials *3, 18, 27, 29, 33* and *64* are likely to have had African or Asian ancestry [Rebecca C Redfern, et al., Going south of the river: a multidisciplinary analysis of ancestry, mobility, and diet in a population from Roman Southwark, London, Journal of Archaeological Science, 74, p11-22, 2016]

Tribes of Britain
(Attributed to myself, CC creativecommons. Wikimedia Commons.)

Africans in Yorkshire & Kent

The English counties of Yorkshire and Kent are separated by 204 miles. Recent excavations have given a clearer idea of what life was like for the Romano-Britons. Multicultural communities flourished in ancient Britain. They have left behind graves of Africans buried with elaborate grave goods. The Ivory Bangle Lady of York and the Beachy Head Lady from Eastbourne are two examples of skeletons believed to be that of African settlers with a high social status.

Excavations of a Roman cemetery in 1891 in the village of East Dean, on the west side of Beachy Head unearthed three skeletons. One skeleton had several bangles around her arm, indicating that she was a high-status individual. Eastbourne Museums Heritage Officer Jo Seaman gives an in-depth account of the 2014 quest for the identity of Beachy Head Lady on the museum's website. The facial reconstruction of the skull was completed by Caroline Wilkinson of Dundee University, one of Britain's leading experts in this field. She has made regular contributions to the BBC TV series *'Meet the Ancestors'* and has also featured in the forensic documentary program *'History Cold Case'*.

Although facial reconstruction is a fascinating skill, it is susceptible to 'cultural bias.' The detailed analysis of the Iron Age British tribes by G M. Morant, who was the leading expert in skeletal analysis, led him to place the ancient Britons with the African Guanches and Copts. This was based on the coefficient of racial likeness that used over 31 measurements, with an emphasis on the more important regions of the facial skeleton. The coefficient of racial likeness is a measure of 'how far on the given data we can assert significant resemblance or divergence.' Modern day reconstructions do not used the coefficient of racial likeness, which is a helpful tool in comparing different populations.

Beachy Head Lady Reproduced with the kind permission of the copyright holder © Heritage Eastbourne, Eastbourne Borough Council

The Beachy Head skeleton had a height of 5ft and was that of a young female. Although the Beachy Head Lady was unearthed In 1891, nothing was known about her until the team at Eastbourne Museum, headed by Jo Seaman, started to investigate her origins; and decided to send the skull to Caroline Wilkinson for facial reconstruction. Caroline immediately suspected that the skull was sub-Saharan. From the radio-carbon dating, the Beachy Head Lady lived around 250 AD. This was during the Roman occupation of Britain.

The phenotype of this young lady led Caroline to place her origins somewhere in sub-Saharan Africa. Although this has not been confirmed, the use DNA and isotope analysis will help to locate her original homeland. However, we can presume she was from a high social class and had origins in Africa. An account of Jo Seaman's quest to find the identity of Beachy Head Lady can be found on the website; 'The mystery of Beachy Head Lady: A Roman African from Eastbourne' by Jo Seaman. *(See https://museumcrush.org/the-mystery-of-beachy-head-lady-a-roman-african-from-eastbourne)*

Jo Seaman's dedication and passion led to an amazing discovery. Driven by curiosity, he believed 'most archaeological museum collections hold these things but never do anything with them. It's all about telling these stories.'

York Ivory Bangle Lady

The largest town in northern Britain, Eboracum, became a provincial capital within Roman Britain. It developed into the modern town of York and was founded in 71 A.D. It became a major urban center with over 5000 Roman troops stationed within its walls. The Brigantes tribe dominated much of northern Britain; they were the largest tribal grouping within the region.

The large presence of the Roman military allowed Eboracum to become a thriving port and busy cosmopolitan urban town. Thomas Baines gives a glimpse of how important this town was:

> The country districts around the city were no doubt peopled by Roman colonists, and all the arts of life are very likely to have been as fully developed at York as in other provincial capitals. Alcuin speaks of Eboracum as a second Rome, the Palatium and Preetorium, that is, the seat of justice and of dominion, in Britain. He also describes it as a great emporium, and place of trade, by sea and land. For many ages it was the principal, if not the only place of trade in the north of Britain, and it was to this circumstance that it owed its early greatness, quite as much as to its military strength and importance. No port in Britain, except London, was better situated than Eboracum for the trade in copper, lead, corn, wool, hides, cattle, and slaves, the chief articles of export sought by the Romans. [Thomas Baines, Yorkshire, past and present: a history and a description of the three Ridings of the great county of York, from the earliest ages to the year 1870]

The paper 'A Lady of York: migration, ethnicity and identity in Roman Britain' by S. Leach, et al., *[Antiquity 84, 2010, p131–145]*, applied a series of techniques to analyze a grave of a single individual from the Roman occupation of York. The multidisciplinary team used a combination of scientific techniques to identify the origins of the 'Ivory bangle lady' discovered in 1901. The analysis involved a study of the grave goods, skeletal measurements, craniometric studies for ancestry assessment *(Mahalanobis Distance)*, and Strontium and oxygen isotopes.

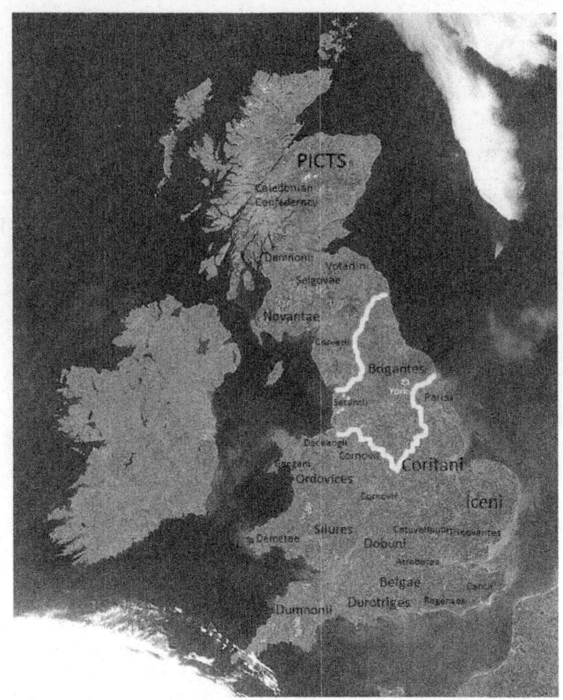

Location of the Brigantes tribe and York (Eboracum)
(Modified by the author, based on map Great Britain and Ireland by Jeff Schmaltz, MODIS Land Rapid Response Team, NASA GSFC (Goddard Space Flight Center) - Public Domain)

The Ivory Bangle Lady was unearthed in 1901 in Bootham, York. The coffin was undisturbed and contained rich grave goods that including jet, elephant ivory bracelets, earrings, pendants, beads, blue glass jug, cosmetics, perfumes, and a glass mirror. The skeleton was 5 feet 1 inches and did not show any signs of trauma. The cranial analysis performed on the Ivory Bangle Lady was not of the same standard as that pioneered by Geoffrey M. Morant. The terminology used is 'unscientific' and shows 'cultural bias.' The description used in the paper published in Antiquity uses the term 'White' traits and 'Black' traits – a Eurocentric assumption that has no foundation:

> Ancestry assessment methods that evaluate cranial and facial morphology (Bass 1995) traditionally use simplified categories such as 'mixed race', 'black' and 'white', but it is understood that skeletal assessment does not give information about skin colour, and that discretely defined racial groups do not exist (Brace 1995; AAPA 1996). Instead, morphological, and metrical assessments of the skull tell us about phenotypical variation of humans over geographic areas (Brace 1995;

> AAPA 1996). The remains of the 'Ivory Bangle Lady' were analyzed using standard methods for the assessment of ancestry in forensic anthropology (see Bass 1995; Byers 2005). During the osteological analysis it was noted that the facial characteristics of this female exhibited a mix of 'black' and 'white' ancestral traits (Figure 3). The skull exhibited a low, wide and broad nasal ridge and wide inter-orbital breadth suggestive of 'black' ancestry, while the nasal spine and nasal border demonstrated 'white' characteristics. [ANTIQUITY 84 (2010): 131–145]

The statement in the above text, 'a mix of black and white traits', has no real meaning. As we have seen, the cranial measurements of Iron Age Britons exhibited cranial features remarkably similar to the African Guanches and Copts. The phrase, *'White ancestral traits',* has no meaning; head lengths, nasal index, and other measurements do not belong exclusively to either 'White' or 'Black'. populations. The decision by these scientists to allocate certain traits to an ambiguous category - has no scientific value.

Facial reconstructions tend to presume that all excavated bodies must have had a skin colour that was 'White', simply because they were unearthed in Britain or Ireland. Today, the coefficient of racial likeness is not used correctly. The standards used by Geoffrey M. Morant are not matched by current scientists. Researchers tend to have a narrow field of thought when it comes to comparing populations. Looking further south, beyond the Straits of Gibraltar, for answers does not occur to modern Eurocentrics who wish to preserve the idea of a 'pure' Europe.

The paper starts with the discussion on ancestry:

> While some early craniometric studies were tainted by racism, ancestry assessment is today an established method in forensic anthropology and offers valuable additional information on the identity of an individual.

It is worth mentioning that 'unconscious' bias is an important factor that can limit the value of an anthropological study. The study of ancient Egyptian skulls is a typical example of such bias. Racial categories and sub-groups are invented out of thin air:

> Studies using the discredited Coefficient of Racial Likeness (C.R.L.), placed all of the Naqada crania with the "Upper Egyptian type" (Morant 1925; Batrawi 1946). The D' values of Mahalanobis showed a combined series (Naqada I/II and other non-specific Naqada period remains) to be more similar

to Tigrayan and Nubian groups than to those from northern late dynastic Egypt (Mukherjee et al. 1955). A multiple discriminant function analysis designed to ascertain African "Negro" influence found Naqada crania to have a greater similarity to the dynastic northern (Gizeh) and a southern, artificially constructed, Abydos series when compared to a Kenyan series, although Naqada crania show definite "Negroid" tendencies (Crichton 1966). Crichton suggested that he may use the wrong "Negro" group, and that a "Nubian" series would have been more appropriate, thus disavowing a typological notion of African. The race paradigm is non-evolutionary and comes from a biased anthropology. A Naqada I cranial series, called "Negroid", was found to be nearly identical to one from Badari, using the Penrose statistic (Nutter 1958). Group mean values for the combined Naqada series in recent work suggest that its greatest affinities collectively are with southern Egyptians and Nubians, and other more southerly Africans (Hillson 1978). Hillson discovered that Egyptian series divide into northern and southern trends using more acceptable methods. Criticisms of these studies include use of the C.R.L. (Morant 1925; Batrawi 1946), inadequate or inappropriate comparison groups (Crichton 1966) and the use of too many variables (Crichton 1966). Multiple cluster analyses using the Penrose distance statistic show a combined Naqada series to group with Nubians and more southerly Africans before linking with the late dynastic northern Gizeh series. [Shomarka O. Y. Keita, Analysis of Naqada Pre-dynastic crania: a brief report,1996]

The use of cranial analysis in determining the relationship between populations is hindered by inadequate or inappropriate comparison group:

The skull exhibited a low, wide and broad nasal ridge and wide inter-orbital breadth suggestive of 'black' ancestry, while the nasal spine and nasal border demonstrated 'white' characteristics. The shape of the nasal aperture was inconclusive. Although some post-mortem damage had occurred, the cranium was complete enough to perform a craniometric analysis, which quantifies the characteristics on an objective scale in an attempt to further defines the ancestral identity of an individual. Standard craniometric measurements were taken and were compared to Howells' worldwide

> reference populations and the forensic data bank, using FORDISC 3.0 discriminant functions software (Jantz & Owsley 2005). When using these multivariate analyses, similarity to a reference population does not indicate a specific identity, but rather a physical affinity of the unknown cranium to the closest population within the reference collection. It should be noted that this reference collection comprises only early modern populations, and that the recording of craniometric data of Roman-period skeletons from Britain and the Mediterranean is clearly a research priority. [ANTIQUITY 84 (2010)]

Leach's paper on the Ivory Bangle Lady from York goes on to suggest a mixed ancestry for the skeleton (*ST60*), because they believed it had 'both 'White' and 'Black' traits and no affinity to any of the 'White' populations in Howell's database. The author then states, 'Roman North Africa is well known for its mixed populations reflecting Phoenician, Berber and generally Mediterranean influence, and individuals from Roman North Africa are therefore more likely to display mixed rather than strongly Sub-Saharan features.' This conclusion was based on the measurement of the Mahalanobis Distance (*D2*), which gave the following results which indicated a similarity to 'Black American female' (*BF19*) because the MD is under 10 at 8.3 and the calculated probability is high at *0.6* - the following MD results were compared:

> Black American female 19th century (BF19) MD = 8.3
>
> Black American female 20th century (BF20) MD = 12.7
>
> White American female 19th century (WF19) MD = 14.5

It is worth repeating again that the work of Dr G. M. Morant established a clear link between the Iron Age Britons, African Guanches, Copts, Etruscans, and the Pompeiians. His work is regarded as the 'gold standard' for ancient cranial assessment using the coefficient of racial likeness (CRL):

> The CRL was critiqued because (1) it could not account for inter-measurement correlation. (2) only single standard deviation was used for all groups, and (3) the variable number has an effect on the calculation of the coefficient. Fisher (1936a) critique the CRL, as an unreliable test of significance that could not account for correlation or covariation, and instead offered an alliterative measure useful in the comparisons of two populations. Mahalanobis also reacted to

> these criticisms, creating a measure of group distances with Pearson on the proper solutions to problems identified in the CRL. Mahalanobis (1936) published his seminal paper on the "generalized distance," now termed the Mahalanobis distance statistic or D2. [Biological Distance Analysis: Forensic and Bioarchaeological Perspectives edited by Marin A. Pilloud, Joseph T. Hefner, 2016]

It seems that scientist have the habit of changing the rules; especially when the results do not fit with their deeply ingrained belief in the 'Aryan' race theory. G. M. Morant's work was pioneering - he was not afraid to compare populations from different geographical regions. Not all scientists had this outlook; some supported the racist concept of Eugenics. Karl Pearson was a dedicated supporter of Eugenics; he even praised Hitler and his '*racial hygiene'* policies. It is ironic that he should have supported such racist views; especially since his colleague, G. M. Morant, had unearthed a deep link between Africa and the British Iron Age tribes.

Iron Age British skulls are very heterogeneous - the Maiden Castle and Hythe Skulls are extremely broad (*C.I of 80 or more*); the Yorkshire Iron Age skulls are long with very distinctive features.

A look at the St. Helen's cemetery, the first of the medieval cemeteries of York, reveal the following:

> The skull type was largely brachycephalic with an average cranial index of *80.3* (men *79.4,* women *81.2*). Overall vault height was fairly low. About a quarter of all skulls were visually short and broad; a third were broad also but with the widest point near the back of the skull, thus forming a beloid shape when viewed from above. The remainder were largely oval. Several skulls showed a tendency to brachycephaly. The short skulls usually had a short back to the vault when viewed from the side. Some vaults were stretched in the middle parietal region giving an apparently longer skull. The average face was fairly broad and low and there were few instances of noticeable prognathism. Most faces had moderately prominent and high cheek- bones although in both sexes there was a noticeable difference in the two sides of the face with the left cheekbone frequently higher and more prominent than the right. The nasal bones were often missing or

> fragmentary, but both narrow and wide nasal roots were found, in straight, bulbous, and upturned forms. [Jean D. Dawes and J.R. Magilton, The Cemetery of St Helen-on-the-Walls, Aldwark, 1980]

The above description of the skeletons from the first medieval cemeteries in York, mentions both narrow and wide nasal roots - the author does not say 'White' and 'Black' traits. The presence of prognathism in some of the skulls does not induce the author to label the skull 'Black' or 'Negroid - it seems these terms are selectively used. If these skeletons were unearthed in a different geographical region - they would be defined differently. The phenotype of the York's medieval skulls is very reminiscence of the Silurian phenotype. The strontium isotope analysis is consistent with areas that include western France, the Iberian Peninsula, and the Mediterranean coast including North Africa. An exact location for her childhood homeland was not ascertained. We know that the Ivory Bangle Lady did not grow up in York - the analysis suggested various possible places of origin, namely western Britain, western France, Iberia, or the coastal region of North Africa. The archaeological evidence presented in the paper revealed information about the status, gender, and religious belief of the Ivory Bangle Lady of York.

Isotope analysis is a very useful tool and has provided overwhelming evidence of a cosmopolitan and 'multi-racial' British society, which included high-social status Africans and Asian.

14 SEARCHING FOR THE GAELS IN AFRICA

The similarities between the people of Morocco and Ireland have been noticed for a long time. The last 200 years has seen a great deal of writers exploring the obvious links that exist. As early as 1856. Francis M. Jennings observed the close connections between the Berbers of southern Morocco and the Gaelic speaking people of Ireland. He was also surprised to find brooches worn by the Berbers were identical to those used in ancient Ireland. Jennings examined a large number of brooches, necklaces, and rings. All the objects brought from Morocco were compared with objects found by archaeologists in Ireland. Two silver brooches, one found in Galway and another near Tralee (County Kerry), were identical to those made in Morocco.

In ancient times, North-west Africa was the home of diverse populations. These ancient people migrated along the Atlantic coast and settled in many parts of Europe. The differences between the various types of ancient, fossilized human remains should be regarded as superficial, they are all very closely related to each other. The invention of racial classifications by Europeans, from the 18th century onwards, was foolish. They were motivated by the desire to create an 'Aryan' race. However, there are no Caucasian races, no Hamitic races, no Semitic races, no Negro races, and no Mongoloid races. There is only one human race. The evidence presented in this book reminds us that these islands were populated by multicultural communities.

Theodore W. Allen's fascinating book, *'The Invention of the White 'Race,'* perfectly documents how 'white' identity is actually a recent invention.

Some readers of the first edition of 'The Invention of the White Race' were probably shocked by Allen's bold assertion on the back cover that, *'when the first Africans arrived in Virginia in 1619, there were no 'white' people there; nor, according to the colonial records, would there be for another sixty years.'*

That statement, based on twenty-plus years of research in Virginia's colonial records, reflected the fact that Allen found 'no instance of the official use of the word 'white' as a token of social status prior to its appearance in a Virginia law passed in 1691'. As he later explained, 'others living in the colony at that time were English; they had been English when they left England, and naturally they and their Virginia-born children were English, they were not 'white.' White identity had to be carefully taught, and it would be only after the passage of some six crucial decades that the word would appear as a synonym for European-American.'

It was during this time that the English and Spanish turned their attention to West Africa as an alternative source of free labor. This was mainly due to the dwindling supply of 'White' slaves; Cromwell had already shipped off thousands of Irish people to the Caribbean and America. Robert W. Emmet gives an incredibly detailed account:

> Emmet asserts that during this time, more than "100,000 young children [Irish] who were orphans or had been taken from their Catholic parents, were sent abroad into slavery in the West Indies, Virginia and New England, that they might lose their faith and all knowledge of their nationality, for in most instances even their names were changed... Moreover, the contemporary writers assert between 20,000 and 30,000 men and women who were taken prisoner were sold in the American colonies as slaves, with no respect to their former station in life." [Robert E. West, England's Irish Slaves, The CATHOLIC Weekly 1995]

For hundreds of years the powerful Barbary states left the Guanches in peace. Even though the Barbary Pirates of Sallée (Morocco), Algiers, Tripoli and Tunis were capable of raiding as far as Iceland; the Canary Islands were left in peace by these powerful North African pirates.

The pirates of northern Africa did not confine their ravages to the Mediterranean:

> They penetrated the ocean and pressed even to the Straits of Dover and St. George's Channel. From the chalky cliffs of England, and even from the distant western coasts of Ireland, unsuspecting inhabitants were swept into cruel captivity. The English government was aroused to efforts to check these atrocities. In 1620, a fleet of eighteen ships, under the command of Sir Robert Mansel, Vice Admiral of England, was dispatched against Algiers. It returned without being able, in

> the language of the times," to destroy those hellish pirates," though it obtained the liberation of forty " poor captives, which they pretended was all they had in the town.

Captain Walter Crocker gives the following account:

> Mr. Macgill saw about two thousand Sicilian slaves at Tunis who were likely to remain there for life, no less than a hundred of which had been captured from under British passports............ These Pirates do, what it has already been observed the Algerines never do, exchange their captives; but, with their usual capricious in- justice, they claim five Moors for two Christians. They have a regular rate of ransom for different nations, the lowest of which is the British, amounting to 1500 piastres per individual. Mr. Macgill relates a piece of politic humanity on the part of Napoleon which might be imitated by those who have deposed him: that is, wherever he acquired dominions in Italy, he immediately ransomed such of his new subjects as were in Moorish slavery. [Captain W. Crocker, 1815]

Captain Walter Crocker, English slaves, and other Europeans, at Algiers and Tunis, published 1815, public domain.

Peter Lamborn Wilson diligently covers the history of the independent Pirate Republic of Sale in Morocco in his book 'Pirate Utopias: Moorish Corsairs & European Renegadoes' *[2nd revised edition 2003]*. Many of the pirates were Europeans who had converted to Islam. The relationship between these pirate states was volatile:

> Around 1614, when the coastal city of Mamora fell to the Spaniards, a large number of international pirates fled to Sale

> and were welcomed by the Hornacheros and Andalusians. They formed the nucleus of the Renegado community and settled in Rabat – so actually the "Sallee Rovers" were Rabat rovers, although both settlements were commonly called Sale, and all three republics were involved in the corsair trade. Perhaps one might think of them as resembling three clans of Scottish Border Raiders, feuding incessantly with each other but teaming up for razzias on England. Sniping, quarrelling, dissention, slurs on honour and other pastimes gave way to open civil war from time to time, especially between 1627 and 1641, but nothing was allowed to get in the way of business or impede the flow of booty. [p81, Peter Lamborn Wilson, Pirate Utopias Moorish Corsairs & European Renegadoes, 2003]

The first casualty of the European expansion was the annihilation of the inhabitants of the Canary Islands, the Guanches. Tragically, from 1492 onwards, the Guanches were targeted by the Spanish. The Berbers traded peacefully with the Guanches and did not attempt to convert them to Islam; the Guanches retained their ancient monotheistic religion and lived undisturbed until 1492.

The Spanish set out to completely annihilate every male Guanches, while the remaining women were raped and enslaved. This Atlantean civilization was destroyed in a very short time. Eurocentrics have added insult to injury! Eurocentric writers, from the 1800's onwards, started to describe the ancient Guanches as descendants of a highly advanced 'White' Atlantis race. If this was the case, why did the Spaniards kill every male Guanches, and raped the women? After their destruction, the Guanches became the 'noble savage' – a fate that would befall the Native Americans a century later.

There are three easily recognizable phenotypes within the Canary population. The easiest to recognize is the Afalou type. A robust, strongly built people that dominated Paleolithic northern Africa. The facial features include a broad face with a broad chin, and a high flat forehead. These ancient 'fossil-men' are described as having exaggerated Irish features. Carlton Steven Coon uses these exact words to describe the Shluh Berbers of the Atlas Mountains. A brown skinned Berber was described by him as having the same facial features as the Irish. Carlton Steven Coon's academic career was sadly haunted by racial bias and prejudice; typical of 1950's America.

Pre-history of the Canary Islands

In addition to the robust Mechta-Afalou type, the Canaries was populated by Neolithic groups from the Nile Valley. The cultural influence and the spread of Neolithic people from the Nile Valley into northern Africa was marked by the spread of grooved axes and incised ware, attributed to a Nubian origin (Khartoum region) rather than an Egyptian origin. Pottery pieces found in Morocco with chevron like wavy lines have direct counterparts with pieces found in the Nile Valley, dating from the Mesolithic era. In Oran, northern Algeria, pottery with triangle designs and horizontal lines are similar to those discovered in the Nubian Pan Graves. The connection between the pottery from the ancient settlements in Morocco, Algeria, the Sahara, and the Nile Valley are very strong. The only explanation for these similarities is that ancient migrations from what is present day Sudan into Libya took place. These migrations then continued westwards into Morocco and the Canary Islands. Ancient people followed different migration routes. One migration route involved the Libyan-Chadian land route: as shown by the discovery of Nubian pottery. This area was not barren; its fertile grasslands sustained a densely populated civilization.

Another, more fascinating route involved the Mediterranean islands. African migrations from the Nile Valley reached the shores of Turkey and every island in the Mediterranean. The westward expansion eventually led to the peopling of the Iberian Peninsula. Africans certainly spread across the sea routes; however, one must also remember that south-eastern Europe and southern Russia was the home of cultures of African origin. The spread of these cultures involved a land migration across Europe, thousands of years before the arrival of Indo-European speakers.

The plain ware of the Almerian Culture, and the impressed-incised ware of the Cave Culture found in Spain have direct parallels in pre-dynastic Egypt – namely the Amratian and Badarian Cultures. The spread of plain ware into Iberia did not involve a north-west African route since there is a lack of this pottery in north-west Africa. The close relationship between Egypt and the Almerian Culture of Iberia, indicate a spread from Egypt through the Mediterranean islands.

The Oranian pottery (Algeria) spread into Iberia and continued to develop further. The Bell Beakers, found in Western Europe, are of African origin. Some archaeologist regard them as the progenitors of the Afro-Iberians of south-eastern Iberia. The incised and impressed ware found in Malta and the Sahara had its origins in Nubia. The spread of Neolithic African cultures was from east to west; the Neolithic cultures of the Sahara are older than the north-west African Neolithic.

The Mysterious Iberians

From the beginning of the 1800's western European historians started to propose the theory of dark-skinned Iberians, with long heads, migrating from Africa into the Iberian peninsula. It was believed that they eventually settled in the British Isles. These Neolithic migrations were attributed to Iberians because the Iberian Peninsula was seen as the ancestral home of the Megalithic people that spread across Europe.

The Iberian Peninsula (modern Spain and Portugal) was the home of a tribe whom the Greeks referred to as the *Iberi*. Hyde Clarke, et al., in the paper The Picts and Pre-Celtic Britain, recognized the Iberians as the original inhabitants of the British Isles:

> An important conclusion was that the Picts were in all probability non-Celtic, and Professor Rhys in his 'Celtic Britain' comes to the opinion that the Scots, too, were not Celtic, but Picts (p. 241) and non-Aryans (p. 258). If not Celtic, who were the Picts? They are excluded from the Celtic class by the labors of men who brought special Celtic learning to bear on the subject. My part of the task is to apply such knowledge as I have acquired with regard to the possibility of the Picts coming within the Iberian class. [Transactions of the Royal Historical Society, Vol. 3 (1886), pp. 243-280]

In the early Victorian period, historians constantly made references to the dark-skinned, long-headed Iberian race that inhabited the British Isles during the Neolithic period. The supporters of the Iberian theories of the 1800's generally accepted a link with the Hamito-Semitic (Afro-asiatic) languages of Africa. Most of the focus was on Phoenician and later Berber. When the ancient Iberian language is compared with Berber, the results showed a significant correlation. On comparing compare 100 Iberian words with an equivalent 100 Berber words, a 13% correlation was discovered, which proves there is a significant relationship.

The Iberian Irish

In Ulster, Connaught, and Munster travelers have frequently commented on the remnants of an ancient race; believed to be 'Iberian' in origin. Irish folklore gives detailed descriptions of the phenotypes of ancient peoples.

The Claddagh of Galway have, according to Stephen Gwynn, retained the racial characteristics of the ancient Firbolgs. In his book, 'Holiday in Connemara' published in 1909, he made an interesting observation:

> My own opinion is that we have here the descendants not of Spain but of the older Irish race who built the great dun at Aran, the Firbolg, whom the taller Milesians drove back into to outlying mountains and islands.

Hector Maclean believed the Milesians were a brown skinned, round headed race with weaker beards than the 'Celts'. The mysterious Tuatha de Danaans are frequently described as having broad faces and large thickset bodies. Boyd Dawkins believed that the Afro-Iberian population spread over the whole of Britain and Ireland during the Neolithic Age. The Firbolgs passed through the straits of Gibraltar and landed on the western coast of Ireland. Under the five sons of Dela, they divided the island into five regions: Ulster, Connaught, Leinster, Meath, and Munster.

O'Flaherty says of the sons of Dela came from southern Britain. Other writers such as O'Kearney and O'Brian associated them the Attacotti, the ancient race of Glasgow. O'Donovan discovered Attacotti or Aithech-tuatha was a term applied by the old Irish writers to describe the enslaved descendants of the Firbolgs. It was also applied to all those who were not of the royal line of the Milesians.

The Formorian Irish

The Formorians, Fomhóraigh, or Fomhoraigh are unpopular with Irish bards. They are frequently referred to as sea-pirates. Some have regarded them as the sons of giants; while others have confused them with the Phoenicians who left traces of their language in old Irish.

It is very odd that all O'Flaherty had to say of then was, 'the Formorians whether they were the aborigines of Ireland or not, were not the descendants of Phut, son of Ham.' What was O'Flaherty trying to hide? And why does he single out Phut, the least known of Ham's children?

We know that Phut is the brother of Egypt (Mizraim), Cush (Nubia), and Canaan (Phoenicians). The links between Ireland and the sons of Ham have been explored by numerous historians over the past 200 years.

The Old Testament gives detailed genealogies for all of Ham's sons except for Put/Phut, his third son. The most obvious choice for the identity of Phut is the ancient Land of Punt, regarded as 'God's Land' (*Ta netjer*) by the ancient Egyptians. Josephus attributes the founding of Libya to the Phutites; Ptolemy places the river Phut in Morocco (ancient Mauretania); while the Old Testaments refers to the recruitment of mercenaries from Phut by the ancient Egypt and Tyrians (Phoenicians).

As the Biblical verse in Nahum 3:9 has 'Cush and Egypt had limitless strength; Put and the Libyans were among her allies' - it can be assumed that Phut or Put is more likely to be the same as the ancient Egyptian Punt or 'God's Land' - located in the Horn of Africa, famous for its frankincense and myrrh. It is possible that the people of Punt settled in Morocco (Mauretania) in antiquity. The name Juba is found only in three countries; Juba is the capital and largest city of South Sudan; Juba river is the main river in Somalia; and Juba I was the King of Numidia and Mauretania, (reigned 60–46 BC).

Charles Vallancey identifies the Formorians with Put and the shepherds of Trogodytica. Flavius Josephus associates these nomadic tribes as the offspring of prophet Abraham and Keturah:

> **(Prophet) Abraham after this married Keturah, by whom had six sons were born to him, men of courage and sagacious minds. Zambran and Jazar, and Madan, and Madian, and Josobak and Sous. Now the sons of Sous were, Sabathan, and Dadan. The sons of Dadan were Latusim, and Afur, and Luom. The sons of Madan were, Ephas, and Ophren, and Anoch, and Ebidas, and Eldas. Now for all these sons and grandsons, Abraham contrived to settle them in colonies; and they took possession of Troglodytes, and the country of Arabia the Happy as far as it reaches to the Red Sea.**

Annals of Clonmacnoise confirm that the Formorians were descendants from Ham, son of Noah. Stories handed down through the ages have associated them with the Lochlan Naibh, the builders of the Irish Cyclopean forts. We know that the Phoenicians belong to the first Millennia B.C. The Formorians pre-date the Phoenicians by thousands of years. The European Neolithic period (c.5000 B.C.) marked the introduction of farming into Europe; a time when male sub-Saharan Africans with E1b1 DNA settled in Europe.

It now seems clear that O'Flaherty intended for the reader to ignore Phut or Put. However, the most striking similarities are found between Irish and Phoenicians. Sir William Betham believed the Phoenicians created a colony in Ireland, and he believed that the language spoken by the Phoenicians was related to Hiberno-'Celtic'. The example given by William Betham (and others too) certainly raises the question - is Irish really an Indo-European language?

The following example illustrates the amazing similarity between Punic and Irish:

> Punic: Gan ebel Bal-sameni ar san!
>
> Irish: Guna bil Bal-samen ar a son!
>
> English: O may the good Bal-samhen (Baal) favour thee!

D. Baldwin's fascinating book 'Prehistoric Nations' (1869) confidently proposed the belief that the Cushites colonized Europe and Asia. The events he described are thousands of years prior to the existence of the Phoenicians. However, he confuses the Cushites and the Canaanites (Phoenicians). Baldwin suggest that Stonehenge was the center of Baal worship. However, the ancient Africans, according to Geoffrey of Monmouth, built Stonehenge as a place of healing. These African giants, he says, would take baths under these stones and would be healed as a result. The Irish Tuatha de Danaans, however, appear closer to the Phoenicians in culture - 'the cold-hearted' Danaans were well known for their dark spells and could only defeat the African Formorians by using black-magic.

Stonehenge is not the only monument associated with the Africans. The mysterious *Lia-Fail* or Stone of Destiny (also known as The Coronation Stone, Jacob's Pillow Stone, or the Tanist Stone) was originally used for the crowning ceremonies of the early Scots kings of Dalriada. The 36th King of Dalriada, Kenneth I, united the Scottish and Pictish tribes into a single kingdom. The capital was moved to Moot Hill at Scone Palace in Perthshire - where all future kings would be crowned. The stone was originally brought from Syria to Egypt by King Gadelas. The Gadelians brought the stone to Ireland, and since then it was used to crown the Kings of Ireland at Tara. Later the stones were moved from Ireland to Argyll around 841 AD.

In 1296 AD the invading army of King Edward I forcibly removed the stone and carried it away to Westminster Abbey (London). It was placed in a wooden chair and was renamed King Edward's chair. It was used as a coronation chair for English Kings; starting with the coronation of Edward II; and subsequently used for the coronation of every monarch since:

> The legend which records the settlement of the monument at Stonehenge after it had been miraculously transported in succession from Africa, Spain, and Kildare in Ireland to its present situation may conceal an allegory — not improbably a fact — viz. that the form of such fanes was preserved by the Celtic nations which passed through these countries ; and when they rested for a sufficient time, erected such durable monuments that, where man has not accomplished their destruction, thousands of years of natural decay have made but slight impression on the rude pillars and ponderous altars which are the characteristics of these primitive remains. The tradition of a Spanish origin to certain British and Irish tribes may be reckoned in some degree confirmatory of a Celtic migration through Spain, and the legendary history of the lia-Fail, "the Stone of Destiny" in the coronation-chair at Westminster, points to migrations from Africa, through Spain and Ireland, to Scotland. [Leslie, Forbes, The early races of Scotland and their monuments, 1866]

The Leabhar Gabhála or the Book of conquests of Ireland has a colourful account of the origin of the Lia Fail:

> **Esras in Gorias, Usicias in Finnias, and Semias who was in Muirias. From Failias was brought the Lia Fail, which Lugh had in Temair; this is what used to scream under every king who took the sovereignty of Ireland, from the time of Lugh Lamhfad to the time of the birth of Christ, and it has never screamed thereafter under any king from that out; for it was a demon that had entrance into it, and the powers of every idol ceased in the time of the birth of the Lord, who was born of the Virgin Mary. From that [Lia] Fail is called Inis Fail, as Cinaeth O Hartacain proves, having said - 'The stone on which my heels stand, from it is named Inis Fail; between two strands of a mighty flood, Ireland altogether is called the Plain of Fal.**

The Lia Fail or Fal Stone is closely associated with the Tuatha de Danaans. They are described as a wicked and cruel people that used 'black magic' against their enemies. The term '*Lia*' refers to a magical stone, and *Fail* has been interpreted as *'the stone which protects sacred knowledge' [see Ali Isaac, The Lia Fail - Ancient Ireland's Sacred Stone of Knowledge, May 18, 2020]*

The Tuatha de Danaans fled from the land of the Philistines:

> After they completed their learning, they went between the Athenians and the Philistines, so that they dwelt between them. Then the Tuatha De join in friendship with the Athenians, so that they formed through druidry demon-spirits in the bodies of the soldiers of the Athenians who were slain, so that they were fit for battle; so that they used to encounter them [the Philistines] again. The Philistines thought it immensely astonishing to see the men they used to slay fighting with them the day after. They related that to their druid. Their elder gave them advice, saying, "Take," said he, "pegs of hazel and of quicken to the battle on the morrow; and if yours be the victory, thrust the pins in the backs of the necks of the men who shall be slain tomorrow; and if they be demons, heaps of worms will be made of them." They do so. The Philistines are victorious, and they thrust the pegs in the backs of the necks of the warriors they slew, and they were worms on the morrow. Thence the strength of the Athenians

> is humbled, and the Philistines were powerful. Then they remember their hostility and unfriendliness against the Tuatha De Danaans, in the matter of the confederacy they had made with the Athenians against them; so that this is what they resolved to assemble to attack them to revenge their spite against them. When the Tuatha De Danaans knew that, they went in flight before the Philistines till they received patrimony and land in Dobar and lardobar in the north of Scotland. Seven years were they in that place. Nuadhat being prince over them. This was the counsel decided by them at the end of that time, to attack Ireland against the Fir Bolg, as they were populous; for to reach there was theirs by heredity. [p146-147, Ó Cléirigh, Micheá, Leabhar Gabhála, the Book of conquests of Ireland, 1916]

The story mentions the use of demonic spirits by the Tuatha de Danaans. The story of the Irish Fal-Stone is very similar to the mysterious 'fal' stone in northern Somalia. The word 'fal' (فأل) in Arabic and Cushitic means 'omen', e.g., fal khayr 'Good omen!' (!فأل خير).

Surat Al-Falaq (The Daybreak - Arabic: اَلْفَلَق, al-falaq) was revealed by Archangel Gabriel to Prophet Muhammed (pbuh) as a protection against witchcraft:

> In the name of Allah, the Most Beneficent, the Most Merciful.
> Say: "I seek refuge in the Lord of Daybreak
> From the evil of that which He created.
> From the evil of the darkness when it is intense,
> And from the evil of malignant witchcraft,
> And from the evil of the envier when he envieth. [The Holy Quran, Surat Al-Falaq]

In Cushitic (Somali) there is specific meaning for 'fal'; it means incantation, charm, spell, e.g., '*wah fal*' = incantation, magician, sorcerer. In Somali folklore the '*fal-stone*' (located just north of Hargeisa) was a stone used by a Babylonian magician from the Yiberi tribe. It was used to make women fall under his influence. This stone is said to have dark magical properties because it had been layered with 'Babylonian' incantations. The power of the 'Yiberi' Babylonians was broken by sheikh aw Barkhadle from the King Dir tribe *(from the Madaxweyna Dir tribe)*, Awfat Sultanate (Harar province, Ethiopia). The battle between the powerful Sufi Sultanates of Awfat and the 'Yiberi' magicians seems to have many parallels with the struggle between the Formorians and the Tuatha De Danaans. It is reasonable to presume that this

Irish stone, that now resides in Westminster, was used in connection with Babylonian magic, since everything connected with the Tuatha de Danaans was based on 'dark' occult ceremonies, while the Formorians had natural second sight.

THE BLUE MEN AND THE IRISH

The Danes exercised a very important influence upon Ireland. The conquest and settlement of Irish ports eventually led to Ireland becoming exposed to more external influences. The Danes made Dublin, Wexford, Cork, and Waterford into commercial ports. In the Irish manuscript, Cogadh Gaedhil re Gallaibh – The War of The Gall with the Gael, we read:

> There was an astonishing and awful great oppression over all of Erin (Ireland).
>
> Throughout its breath, by powerful azure gentiles, and the fierce, hard-hearted Danars.

The Book of Leinster, believed to have been written in the 12th century AD, gives a full description of these Galls or strangers. The word Gall is Hamito-Semitic (Afro-asiatic) in origin. The name Donegal translates as the fort of the strangers. The East African tribe, the Oromo, are known to their neighbors as Galla (strangers/foreigners). The Highland Scots later applied this name to the Lowland Scots and the English.

The Gall-Gaedhill were a mixture of Danes and Irish. Old Irish manuscripts mention the Lochlanns, who were elsewhere called Gael-Gaedhil or *Dano-Irish*. They established themselves in Ireland and made alliances with the native Irish and adopted Christianity. When the Danes began to colonize Ireland, it is said that the *Lochlanns* gave up Christianity and joined with the Danes. It is these Lochlanns who are said to have been associated with the *Blue-men* or Black-men. Some believe that these Blue-men were recruited by the Lochlanns from Morocco. According to one story, the Lochlanns recruited the Blue-men from Morocco and used them to drive the Danes out of Ireland.

The Annals of Ireland indicate that the Blue-men came to Ireland between the 6th and 10th century A.D.; the text says, '*long indeed were these Blue-men in Erin.*' This Irish story seems to have many similarities to Geoffrey of Monmouth's account. In his account 160,00 Africans came to southern Britain. This was at the time when the Angles and Saxons were starting to colonize the southern British coast, between the 6th and 7th century AD. Gormund is said to have first settled in Ireland with his massive African army. The story takes an interesting twist. Some scholars believe Gormund was from Denmark. The constant reference to Black Danes and Black Vikings could be a reference to the African or Arabia settlement of Scandinavia during the Iron Age. It is obvious from the Bronze Age statutes unearthed in Denmark, that they have affinities with Africa and the Middle East. The exciting discovery of skeletons belonging to individuals with an Arabian mtDNA haplogroup provides the concrete evidence for the settlement of Afro-Arabians in Scandinavia during the Iron Age.

The Finns and The Cushites

The Sámi of Finland are regarded as one of the oldest 'ethnic'-tribal people of Europe. Today they are found scattered across Finland, Norway, and Sweden. The relationship between the Cushites and the Sámi (Lapp) might seem unlikely at first glance, but during the last Ice Age these two groups were neighbors and as a result they share the same maternal ancestry (mtDNA). Excavations of ancient graves in the Orkney Islands (lying off the northern coast of Scotland), have revealed short skulls that are identical to the modern Sámi (Lapp) and Inuit peoples. Dr Beddoe in his racial survey of the British Isles, concluded that an aboriginal type existed in the Shetland Isles. He found on a visit there, 'a few black-haired people of low stature, with facial features approaching the Inuit or Sámi type.' In Scottish short cist graves, numerous Bronze Age artefacts have been found. The bodies found in these ancient graves are usually in a flexed position. They contained the remains of both the earlier dolichocephalic (long-headed) population and the new brachycephalic (broad-headed) Bronze Age invaders.

The Cymry Iberians

The first reliable historical notice of the Welsh (Cymry) is from Tacitus, who recorded the existence of a dark, small race called the Silures. He observed, 'the dark complexion and crinkly-curly hair of the Silures.' He believed this indicated that they were a colony of Iberians that had settled in Britain.

Thurman declared the earliest Britons were a dolichocephalic race derived from the Iberian Peninsula. Professor Huxley detected Australoid affinities with the people of the Stone Age. Broca, the French ethnologists, believed the Iberians of Spain to have come from Africa. The antiquity of the Welsh is due to the Iberian element rather than the recent Brythonic element attributed to the Iron Age. The old inhabitants of Wales are located in the eastern and south-eastern hills; it is here that the ancient Iberian element can be detected.

Some ethnologists relate the Silures to the small, thick-set inhabitants of Brittany. The Irish, Bretons, Atlas Berbers, and the Guanches of the Canary

Islands all show physical features inherited from the ancient Afalou from Africa. The Silures inhabited the whole of South Wales, from Hereford to Dyfed. Pliny places the Silures just 30 miles from Ireland. The name Silures also appears on ancient maps of the Iberian Peninsula. The present-day Granada region was in ancient times referred to as mons Silurum. This certainly proves beyond doubt that the Silures had migrated from the most southern region of Iberia and were connected to the rugged, broad-faced tribes that spread knowledge of bronze between 2000 BC and 1200 BC.

The name Cymru is believed to be derived from the word for compatriot (*Kymer*), whereas the name Wealh or Welsh was the name given to the aboriginal tribes of southern Britain by the Anglo-Saxons. This name was used for any person with dark skin colour and can be translated as meaning foreigner.

The People of The Nile Valley

In 1911 the German entomologist Wilhelm Kattwinkel found fossils in the Serengeti Plains which contained vast numbers of fossils. In 1913 Reck inspired by Kattwinkel's journey into the Serengeti and discovered a skull which was named Oldoway Man. *[The Quest for the Origins of Human Life by Martin Meredith]*. The father of European Anthropology, the Italian anthropologist Giuseppe Sergi, was opposed to the theory of Aryans founding Europe. He believed that black, dolichocephalic people from the Nile Valley were the progenitors of the 'Mediterranean Race' and that the Europeans were the descendants of Eurafricans, black people from Africa. According to Sergi, this branch of mankind, the Eurafricans, were originally black skinned and were instrumental in developing the ancient civilizations of the Mediterranean. Fossil men from East Africa, such as Oldoway Man spread out into western Asian and Europe. The fossil records of East Africa have revealed that the inhabitants of this region have remained unchanged for over 100,000 years. Ancient Oldoway Man was tall (5ft 10) with a long narrow oval skull (cephalic index 66), prominent chin, mesorrhinian nose, and with slight alveolar prognathism. The fossil records of East Africa have revealed that the inhabitants of this region have remained unchanged for over 100,000 years. The expansion of people from East Africa into south-western Asia, and eventually into Europe cannot be denied.

Nubia

The Kingdom of Nubia, which had its ancient capital at Napata, has a long history. Later the capital was moved to Meroe, further south. The Napatans and Meroites were probably the progenitors of Nilo-Saharan and Nilotic tribes that inhabit southern Sudan and Chad. Many of the customs practiced by the people of Kush are still practiced by the tall Nilotic tribes of southern Sudan. The real identity of the people of Kush is very complicated. There are many things we still do not know about the people of Kush.

Firstly, there was not only one Kush – those familiar with the Bible will know that Kush was also in the Arabian Peninsula; Iraq is closely associated with Kush. In Islamic traditions, Nimrod (son of Kush) is remembered as a tyrant who was disobedient and refused to accept Monotheism. In Homer's Iliad, the opening chapter starts with the description of Zeus being absent from Mount Olympus because he and all the Greek deities were banqueting with the 'worthy Ethiopians' (Kush). During the Trojan War, the hero Memnon the Ethiopian (Kush) came to the assistance of the Trojans. Interestingly, Memnon the Ethiopian came from Susa, southern Iraq (the other Kush).

The exact relationship between Meroe Kush, Iraq Kush, and the Arabian Kush is obscure – we know that the relationship between ancient Egyptians and the Kushites was not friendly. In the conflict between Egypt and the Sea Peoples, the Kushites took sides with the Asiatic invaders. Also, the close and friendly relations between Carthage and the Kushites is indicated by the story of Candace, Queen of Nubia, seeking refuge in Carthage.

The Nubian civilization was influenced by its powerful Egyptian neighbor. The Egyptians referred to Nubia as the land of the bows. The archery skills for which they were famous even continued into Islamic era. During the Egyptian Old Kingdom, there flourished in Nubia a culture known as the A-Group. The pottery produced by these people was of high quality and very distinctive. Their graves consisted of circular pits with the body placed in a contracted position with the head usually pointed in a westward direction. This group came to an end around 2700 BC. The land became abandoned, and the people disappeared from the pages of history.

The decline of the Egyptian Old Kingdom saw the rise of a new Nubian group – commonly referred to as the C-Group. They flourished from 2200 BC to 1500 BC and were primarily cattle herders. Considerable interchange occurred between the ancient Egyptians and the C-Group people. During the 18th and 19th Dynasties, the C-Group population decreased. These people migrated to the South and West. It is generally accepted that they pushed southwards, since they appear centuries later at Napata. However, their north-western migrations have been largely ignored by historians. A possible route to the north-west to Libya would have been via the Kufra Oasis, near the Libyan-Egyptian border.

The people of the Nile conducted many military campaigns against the Libyans. The presence of the C-Group in Libya is a matter of great controversy. Excavations on the island of Crete, a few hundred miles north of the Libyan coast, clearly indicates the settlement of the C-Group Nubians. Large stone structures, constructed in a bee-hive shape have been found in the southern portion of the island. These sepulchers are identical to those of the Nubian C-Group graves. Further connections between the Nile Valley and Crete are indicated by the similarity of the Nubian bows with the 'plain' Cretan types. Also, a series of ancient Cretan stones sculptures, found in such sepulchers, is identical to their counterparts found in pre-Dynastic tombs at Naqada, Egypt. Archaeologist have failed to find any C-Group graves in Nubia from 19th and 20th Dynasties. It is during the Napatans Empire that C-Group graves reappeared.

Crete and Egypt played a Central role in Irish folklore. The Irish Milesians fled Egypt, sought refuge in Crete before sailing westwards to Iberia. The ancient African migrations to Britain and Ireland was through two routes. One route from the Nile Valley to the Libyan coast, across Malta and then leap-frogging from island to island across the Mediterranean – finally landing in the British Isles. The second route taken by the Neolithic Africans was via Anatolia (Turkey) and the Balkans (Greece), followed by migrations into the Danube Valley.

Racial Analysis

First, there is only one race – the Human Race. The different phenotypes (facial features) found across the globe does not indicate different races. All these foolish definitions were invented by Eurocentric academics who have dominated the educational system.

In 1924 the British School of Archaeology in Egypt carried out a series of excavation in the district of Badari. These skulls were dolichocephalic, smooth, fragile, and very feminine in type. Although the extreme narrowness of the jaws can be compared with the Somalis and Tigrayans, the Badarians were slightly more prognathous, while the Somalis and Tigrayans are orthognathous. Excavations of Nubian graves at Kerma have provide a great deal of information about the ancient population. The examinations of skulls, 141 male and 114 females, has shown that the closest relationship of the Kerma Nubians is with the Pre-dynastic Egyptians. The skulls found at Kerma date from the 12th and 13th Dynasties. When compared with the Tigrayan and Somalis series, the coefficient of racial likeness indicates a close relationship; however, the closest relationship is between the ancient Egyptians and Kerma Nubians. The skulls from the Egyptian 9th Dynasty are remarkably close to the Cretan type. G. M Morant's examination of Cretan skulls led him to the following conclusion:

> **These relationships suggest that we are dealing with a sample from a population of Egyptian origin, and they may be taken to indicate that at some unknown period**

there was a direct or indirect link between the native Egyptians of Sediment and the Cretan people.

The Ancient People of Canary Islands

The Canary Islands are only a few miles off the African coast. They are a volcanic archipelago consisting of seven islands: Hierro, La Palma, Tenerife, Gomera, Grand Canary, Lanzarote, and Fuerteventura (only 67 miles off the west African coast). During the 800 years of Muslim rule in Spain, the Moors did not interfere with the indigenous Canary Islanders. The powerful Moorish Empire, only few miles away, did not try to convert the Canary Islanders; the Guanche kept their ancient culture and language until the brutal conquest by the Spanish in the 16th century. The Spaniards killed the male inhabitants and enslaved the female population, wiping out an entire civilization in only a few years.

The Spanish invasion of the Canary Islands began in the 15th century. The first island to fall was Lanzarote. It would take another 94 years before the Spanish were managed to finally take the island of Tenerife, in 1492. All the islands suffered from Spanish violence; even Lanzarote and Gomera, which did not confront the Spanish at first, eventually revolted against the inhumane treatment they received.

The following is based on an early manuscript that gives an accurate description of the inhabitants before their destruction. It is a translation of a Spanish manuscript written In the year 1632. It was found in the island of Palma, *by Juan de Abreu de Galineo*, a Franciscan friar from Andalusia. *[see Abreu de Galindo, Juan de; Glas, George, published 1764, The history of the discovery and conquest of the Canary Islands: tr. from a Spanish manuscript lately found in the island of Palma. With an enquiry into the origin of the ancient inhabitants. To which is added, A description of the Canary Islands, including the modern history of the inhabitants, and an account of their manners, customs, trade, &c.]*

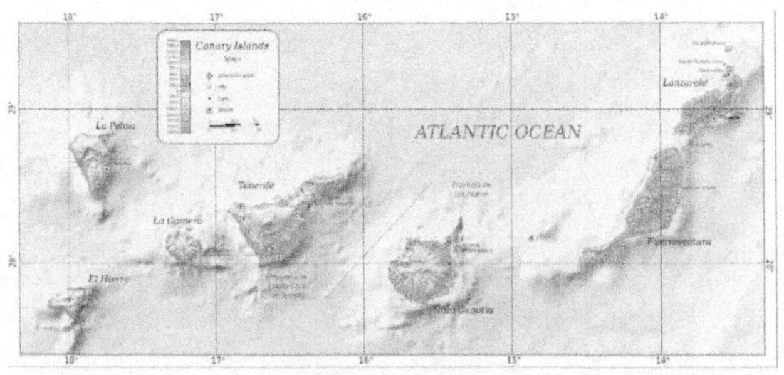

Map of The Canary Islands,
(Attributed to Mysidderivative work Augusta 89,

Public domain creative commons via Wikimedia Commons.)

The description given in this early manuscript is important. It shows that the Eurocentric attempt to include the Canary Islanders into a mythical 'Aryan' race is complete nonsense. All the evidence available indicates that they were closely related to the people of north-west Africa.

According to Pliny, this island was named Canaria on account of its abounding with dogs of a large size, two of which were presented to Juba, the king of Mauretania. This opinion, however, seems to want foundation since when the Europeans came to Grand Canary, they did not find any dogs on the island.

Another theory attributes the name to an African tribe called Canarius, that dwelt near mount Atlas (Morocco), and crossed over, calling the island after their own name. Pliny mentions a tribe called Canaria, who dwelt beyond Mount Atlas and bordered upon the country of the Ethiopians. Ptolemy called Cape Blanco, in Africa, Gannaria Extrema. The inhabitants who live along the river Senegal called the country between this river and Mount Atlas, Gannar.

Lanzarote and Fuerteventura

These two islands were divided into portions by walls of loose stones; each portion being ruled by a chief who was held in great esteem. The ancient inhabitants of Lanzarote and Fuerteventura are described by ancient manuscripts as cheerful, and very fond of singing and dancing. Their music was vocal, accompanied by a noise they made by clapping their hands and beating their feet. They were very nimble, and took great delight in leaping and jumping, which were their principal pastime. Two men would take a wooden pole, held above their heads, keeping it parallel, all the men would then take it in turns to leap over it. Some of them were experts in this sport; they could leap over three poles placed in this manner. This custom still survives among some East African tribes, such as the Nilotic tribes. The inhabitants of these two islands were of a large size, and generally taller than the other islanders.

At the foot of a mountain in Lanzarote, called the Mountain of Thorns, an ancient sepulcher exists, 19 feet high, where a person called Mahan is believed to be buried. The people of this island frequently fought among themselves. In combat they used a stick, 3 feet long, which they called Tezzezes. Regarding quarrels, they had a law or a custom, that if a man entered by the front door of his enemy's house, and harmed or killed him, he was not punished; but if he came upon him unaware by leaping over a wall, and killed him, then the chief of the tribe would order that the attacker be put to death. The manner of executing criminals was this:

> They carried the person to the seashore and then placed his head upon a flat stone, and then with another stone they dashed out his brains; his children were afterwards held as infamous.

They were excellent swimmers; and killed the fish on their seacoast with sticks. Their houses were built of stone, without cement, lime, or mortar: doors were narrow that only one person could go in at a time. They also had houses of worship they called Efeguen. In these temples they offered to their God, they only worshipped one. Milk and butter they sacrificed to him on mountains, pouring milk, and adoring him at same time by lifting their hands towards the heavens.

The clothes of the people of Lanzarote were made of goat skin, sewed together, and fashioned like a cloak, with a hood. The seams were closed in a very neat manner which they cut and prepared these thin things of leather. They cut and prepared these thongs with sharp flint instead of knives. They also wore bonnets made of goat skins, having three large feathers stuck in front. The women wore the same, with a fillet of shrubs. The cloak was called Tamarco and the hood Guapil in their language.

Whenever they fell sick, they cured themselves with herbs that grew in the country; and when they had acute pain, they scarified the part affected with sharp stones or burnt it with fire, and then anointed with goat's butter.

The Ancient Gomerians

The island of Gomer was inhabited by people of middle stature. They were famous for their skills in slinging stones and darts, which they were trained in from infancy. The clothing of the Gomerians was a cloak made of goat's skin. The women wore a petticoat called Tahuyan, and a head-covering that reached down to their shoulder, which as well as the petticoat were dyed red. When the men had a quarrel, they laid aside their cloaks, tied a bandage around their waist, and bound their foreheads with a painted turban.

The Inhabitants of Hierro

The people were of middle stature, and of a melancholy turn of mind; for all their songs were on grave subjects to which they all danced in a ring, joining hands together, and jumping in pairs. They dwelt in large circular enclosures, the wall of which were of dry stone, each containing twenty families. They lived under one King and were not warlike. Each man had one wife; they had no rules in their marriages (except that a man should not marry his mother or sister). Each man married the woman he liked best, without regard to rank or nobility. It was customary for the man, when choosing a wife, to make a present of cattle to her father according to his ability, as an acknowledgement of goodwill in letting him have his daughter. A custom which is identical to that practiced by the tribes who speak Hamito-Semitic languages. The King received no stipulated tribute from his subjects, but everyone made him a present of a sheep, according to his wealth or pleasure, for they were not obliged to give him anything.

When anyone fell ill, they rubbed the patient body all over with sheep's marrow; or they burned the affected part and then anointed it with butter.

They adored two deities, one male and the other female. The male deity was named Eraoranzan, and the female deity was called Moneyba. They had no images or representatives of these deities, nor did they sacrifice to them. They only prayed to them when they wanted rain. When the Heirrians were forced, to accept Christianity, they invoked Jesus and Mary by the names Eraoranzan and Moneyba.

Ancient Inhabitants of Grand Canaria

When the Europeans first came to Grand Canaria, the island contained 14,000 fighting men. They were dark in complexion, like the people of Lanzarote and Fuerteventura. They were warlike, good natured, and faithful to their promises.

In their wars they never injured or harmed the women or children of their enemy. Neither did they damage the houses of worship during hostilities. The weapons used by the Canarians in war were clubs called Modagas, and a sharp pointed pole called Amodagas. Certain public places were set aside for duels. When a challenge was given and accepted, the parties went to the Sabor (council) in-order to obtain a license to fight. Then they went to the Faycag to have the license confirmed. They would gather relatives and friends to observe as spectators. The challenge took place within a raised platform, three feet in diameter. Each had to stand without moving their feet, until each had thrown three stones at each other.

Ancient Inhabitants of Tenerife

The islands were named Tenerife, or white Mountain, by the inhabitants of Palma. The name is derived from Tener (mountain) and Ife (white). The people are described as being of middle stature, and dark skinned. The people who dwelt in the northern part of the island tended to have lighter hair and were said to be fairer than those that lived in the southern portion of the island. Many European anthropologists have tried to desperately look for a European origin for these people, based on the presence of individuals with light hair. However, the Moroccan highlands, only a few miles away, have the highest recorded occurrence of red hair. This hair colour originated in Africa and is closely associated with the Paleolithic Afalou -Mechta.

The ruling family seem to have practiced a strange custom which could have been derived from the ancient Egyptians. The King of the island was obliged to marry a person who was his equal. However, if an equal could not be found, he would marry his own sister; this custom was restricted to the royal family.

They believed in one God, whom they called by the name Achguarergenan, Achoran, and Achaman - which signified in their tongue 'the sustainer of the Heaven and Earth.'

They had a custom among them, that when a man by chance met a woman alone on the road, or in a solitary place, he would not look at, or speak to her, unless she spoke to him first. If he behaved in an unbecoming manner, he was severely punished. The men wore cloaks of goat skin, smeared with butter. The women wore long cloaks that reached down to their feet. Both men and women anointed their bodies with sheep oil, because they were particularly lean, and their skins were very dry. Their language differed entirely from those of the other islands; it sounded more guttural. They often had disputes among themselves about their flock and pastures. Their offensive weapons were darts, sharpened and hardened by fire. They also had a weapon like a spear that they called Anepa. The inhabitants of Tenerife were divided into three classes, nobles, gentleman, and peasants. The first were called Achimeniey (belonging to the King's house); second, there were the Cilhiciquico; and third were the Achicarnay.

Physical Character of the Population

The African population of the Canary Islands has been shown to have strong racial connections with the ancient population of the British Isles. The work of G. M. Morant, published in Biometrika, has revealed a deep connection between the Iron Age tribes of Britain and the Guanches, Egyptian Copts, Etruscans, and the people of Pompeii,

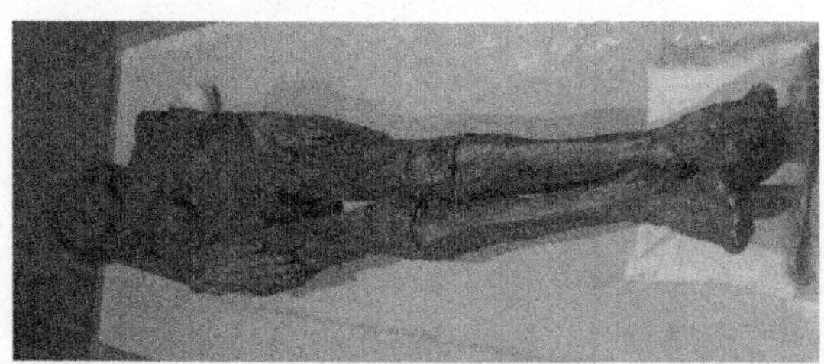

Guanches mummy, found in Barranco de Herques, in the south of Tenerife. (attributed to Momia guanche MNA Outisnn creative commons via Wikimedia Commons.)

Childe's investigation of 169 skulls from Grand Canary, Tenerife, Gomera, and Ferros found only 8 brachycephalic skulls. The average cephalic index for the whole group was 76.3. Childe concluded that the 'race' that inhabited the Canary Islands were dolichocephalic and closely related to the Cro-Magnon type, the Berbers, and the ancient Egyptians. He believed that the real 'aboriginal type' lived in Grand Canary; while the more rugged type found in Tenerife were descended from the north-west African Afalou-Mechta.

On the island of Grand Canary, the number of brachycephalic skulls were only 5%., the overwhelming majority of the population were long headed. The largest number of brachycephalic skulls were found on the island of Gomera, especially among the women. No brachycephalic skulls were found in either Palma or Ferro.

Verneau considered the Guanches as of part of the Cro-Magnon, and the at Tenerife they presented its character in stature, skull, and face; mingled with a Semitic element. He added a third type with a short head and broad nose. Thus, taking the islands all together, he founds; Guanches, Semitic type, across between the two types, short head type with a broad nose, and a Berber type.

Island	% Dolichocephalic (long-headed)	% Mesocephalic (medium head proportions)	% Brachycephalic (broad headed)
Tenerife Island			
Male Skulls %	37.00	44.70	22.30
Female Skulls %	16.67	58.33	25.00
Gomer Island			
Male Skulls %	15.39	45.15	38.46
Female %	-	25.00	75.00
Male Skulls %	15.39	45.15	38.46

Verneau's analysis of Guanches head/breath ratio, Sergi 1990

Meyer and von Luschan believed that there were three physical types found in the Canary Islands. The first type, the Guanches were tall with a stature of between 1.70m and 1.90m. They had robust bodies and large dolichocephalic heads. They had well developed foreheads, the occipital was strong and low, the face low and broad, the eyes large and the jaws were very wide. The nose was relatively short and the teeth slightly prominent. Overall, the skulls resemble the prehistoric Afalou-Mechta type found in northern Africa. This prehistoric Afalou-Mechta type was instrumental in giving the Irish and Scots certain characteristic; the most well-known being red hair.

The Guanches type was diffused throughout all the islands but was strongest in Tenerife. This type came originally from the Moroccan Atlas Mountains, where it is the dominant type. Old Spanish manuscripts describe the language spoken by the people of Tenerife as being different to the language spoken by the other islanders. We have no doubt that the Canary islanders spoke languages belonging to the Hamito-Semitic (Afro-asiatic) language family. The Tenerife people spoke a guttural language which indicates a connection with the Semitic languages such as Ethiopic, South Arabian, Arabic, Phoenician, etc. The rugged and robust Afalou type may have spoken a proto-language that was common in northern Africa before the spread of the Berber and Chadic languages.

Verneau's second type had a stature of 1,65m, slender body, and had a delicate Mesocephalic skull. The face was long and narrow, skin black and hair black. A Nile Valley origin for this type is likely. It was found in strength in Grand Canary, Palma, and Ferro, but not found in Gomera.

The third type was of short stature. The face long and narrow. The cephalic index was 84, extremely brachycephalic. This cranial shape has been compared to the Armeniod, pre-Semitic type of Western Asia. Sergi strongly believed that this type was not Armeniod at all.

Sergi argued that although the skull was brachycephalic, its form was different. Generally, the occipital sloped vertically or a little obliquely so as to approach the vertical; the summit of the cranial height is much behind the bregma, and from the summit there is an oblique descent towards the forehead. Meyer's third type cannot with any probability be described as Armeniod. Sergi renamed it *Canariense* because he had never seen a similar form elsewhere. Sergi concluded that the population of the Canaries was essentially similar to the population of the Nile Valley.

The Afalou/Cro-Magnon, and a third type the Canariense, both came out of Africa. Carleton S. Coon makes an interesting observation:

> **The Afalou type survived in the Canary Islands. The early Alpine like strain found in the Canaries, especially Gomera, may be attributed to a re-emergence of the brachycephalic element in the Afalou people, in a somewhat reduced form. This type is comparable to minor brachycephalic element found in other parts of North Africa, as in Gomera and among the Kabyles, and it may conceivably be connected with the brachycephalic of Jerba. [Carleton Steven Coon, Races of Europe]**

Both the long headed and short headed types migrated from Africa to Britain and Ireland. The long-headed type migrated from Africa and crossed into Europe during the Neolithic period. The round headed or brachycephalic element in the British Isles has been traditionally regarded as Central/Eastern European in origin. However, closer examination of this type has revealed that this ancient broad-headed type, that arrived in the Bronze Age, came from Northwest Africa, and the Mediterranean.

The Ancient Afalou Type of North Africa

The Algerian cave of Afalou-bou-Rummel is an important archaeological site where numerous ancient skeletons have been unearthed. They were assigned to the Aterian level and were equivalent to the Upper Paleolithic period in Europe. The Mechta skeleton excavated at Qustantinah, Algeria, also belonged to the same era. These ancient Paleolithic people, commonly referred to as the Mechta-Afalou, hold the key to the origin of the ancient Irish and Britons. Mechta-Afalou inhabited large parts of north-west Africa during the late Paleolithic and Mesolithic era. This type has been associated with the Iberomaurusian culture, which appeared during the Last Glacial Maximum, between *c.25,000 and 23,00 B.P.*

The average height of the skeletons were 5 feet 6 inches, some however reached 5 feet 11inches. They had broad shoulders and long forearms. The cranium was large, pentagonal shape, and the cephalic index varied from dolichocephalic to mesocephalic. The eyebrows were well developed and joined at the glabella, and the root of the nose was depressed. The face was short and broad, disharmonic with the cranium, and the lower jaw projected forward.

The introduction of the Neolithic, from the Nile-Valley, resulted in the Mechta-Afalou being absorbed. This has resulted in the diverse appearance of the Berbers. Today, the Berbers stretch from the Siwa Oasis (Egypt) to the Atlantic coast of Northwest Africa. The Berbers vary in their skin colour and phenotypes; every shade of skin colour can be found ranging from bright white to dark blue-black. From a genetic perspective, it is remarkable that male Berbers share the same DNA haplogroup - E1b1. For example, genetic analysis of Moroccans revealed that over 80% of male Moroccans have sub-Saharan E1b1 y-DNA.

Mechta-Afalou Type in the British Isles

The Irish and Cymry (ancient Britons) have strong similarities with tribes of north-western Africa. Mechta-Afalou inhabited large parts of North Africa during the late Paleolithic and Mesolithic era. This type has been associated with the Iberomaurusian culture. Mechta-Afalou flourished across northern

Africa, from Morocco to southern Libya and extended into the neighboring islands. Genetic testing of their skeletal remains from Afalou and Taforalt have shown that the majority had male y DNA E1b1, and also had a significant relationship to West Africans and Hadza hunter-gathers of Tanzania.

The female skeletons were found to have mtDNA haplogroup U6 and M1, while all the males belonged to haplogroup E1b1. indicating that they could have been the earliest group to spread Hamito-Semitic (Afro-asiatic) languages. The results indicate that the skeletons found at Taforalt had an ancestry that contained a clear affinity with South, East, and Central African tribal groups. [*see Marieke van de Loosdrecht1, Pleistocene North African genomes link Near Eastern and sub-Saharan African human populations, Vol. 360, Issue 6388, pp. 548-552*]

Berber Tribe	Phenotype / Description
Siwa Berbers (NW Egypt)	Hair black, 25% have fuzzy curly hair - strong variation in skin colour from light skin to black. Dark skin with grey eyes is frequent.
Awjila Berbers (NE Libya)	Hair brown or black, nasion depression, chin receding.
Libyan (Central)	Thickset type, large hands, square face, retreating forehead, heavy eyebrow ridge, nasion depression.
Libyans (Fezzan)	Long and oval faces; black hair hair, slender body, narrow jaws.
Tuaregs (Mali & Niger)	Long and narrow skulls, slender bodies, dark skinned.
Jerba Berbers (Jerba Island)	Medium stature, round headed, flat occipital bone, brunet hair.
Kabyle Berbers (Northern Algeria)	Short stature, wide forehead, 85% brown or black hair, red hair 4%, freckled complexion, wide Afalou jaw.
Riffian Berbers (Morocco)	90 % brown or black hair, red hair 10%, hair form varies fro frizzy to straight, appearance described as "exaggerated Irish type" - prominent eye folds,and chin, with strong jaw. Features inherited from ancient Afalou race. Individuals from the Beni Urriaghel tribe are described having exaggerated Irish features; freckled skin, square jaws, and broad faces.
Shluh Berbers (Morocco)	Mainly black hair, 5% brown hair, smaller face than Riffian tribes, narrow jaws and chins, and mainly dark in colour.

Phenotype descriptions of different Berber Tribes

Most of the E1b1 DNA found in Europe belongs to the *E-M78 lineage*, with the subclade *E-V13* being the main male DNA type in Greece, Albania, and the Balkans. 85% of Moroccan males belong to E-M78. Fulvio Cruciani, et al., proposed *'that Egypt was the 'hub' for the distribution the E-V13 subclade into the Balkans.'* Skeletons from Catalonia (Avellaner Cave) dating to over 5000 years ago have been found to be E1b1 (E-V13). The male specimens examined belonged to the paternal haplogroup *E1b1b1a1(M78)*, with one skeleton bearing the *E1b1b1a1b1* parent lineage to *E-V13*, one male specimen belonged to *E1b1b (M215*)*.

The typical Irish and Cymry phenotypes have been inherited from the ancient Africa Mechta-Afalou 'type' that lived in northern and western Africa during the Late Paleolithic and Mesolithic era. The Last Glacial Maximum saw the spread of icesheets across Europe and a general drop in temperature. This influenced human migrations with people taking refuge in more sheltered environments. This led to an increase mixing between different groups. Geneticists have discovered that Europe's most northerly group the Sámi (indigenous inhabitants of Finland) and the Saharan Tuaregs are closely related. Alessandra Achilli, et al., concluded in his 2005 paper, that both groups shared the same female ancestry:

> It is suggested that European haplogroup U5 and the more prevalent U6 "Berber cluster" diverged from a common ancestor in the Near East and spread along the north and south coasts, respectively, of the Mediterranean, as far as Iberia to the north and Cyrenaica to the south. It is very plausible that descendants of the Mesolithic hunter-gatherers carried U5b1b1 and sister lineages across the Straits of Gibraltar into North Africa [59], but there is no indication of when this migration may have happened. [Alessandro Achilli et al., The American Journal of Human Genetics 76(5)]

The facial features of John F Kennedy (former USA President), Piers Brosnan (actor James Bond), Patrick Duffy (actor, Dallas), to name a few, have inherited features from the ancient African Mechta-Afalou people that dominated Morocco and the Maghreb countries and were responsible for spreading the Iberomaurusian or Oranian stone-age industry. This culture stretched from NW Africa to Spain. The oldest radiocarbon dates for the Iberomaurusian are 21,900 ±400 BP from Taforalt, in the Beni Snassen mountains of eastern Morocco (Garcea, Elena. 2010).

Even the anthropologist Carlton Steve Coon, who held prejudiced beliefs, described the Shluh Berbers as having exaggerated Irish features, inspired by the ancient Afalou race of northern Africa. It seems that from these observations, the origin of red hair in Ireland and Britain seems to have been inspired by these ancient Mechta-Afalou. Even red hair, it seems, has an 'Out of Africa' origin. It is reasonable to conclude that Late Paleolithic-Mesolithic Africans, known as the Mechta-Afalou, contributed significantly to the phenotype of the modern people of Ireland and Briton.

The Atlas Berbers tend to have 90 % brown or black hair. The occurrence of red hair has been found to be around 10% of the population - varying from frizzy 'afro' hair to straight. The description given is 'exaggerated Irish type with prominent eye folds, and chin, with strong jaw.' Carleton Steven Coon (a very Eurocentric anthropologist) admitted that these facial features were inherited from ancient Afalou race. Individuals from the Beni Urriaghel tribe are described having exaggerated Irish features, freckled skin, square jaws, and broad faces. He did not seem to understand that the people he observed displayed every skin colour imaginable, varying from black, brown, olive, and pale white.

Unfortunately, C. S. Coon held some prejudice beliefs. He believed that humans were divided into five races and that they evolved into modern humans at different times. John P. Jackson Jr. examined the controversy surrounding this anthropologist and concluded:

> 'Carlton Steven Coon actively aided the segregationist cause in violation of his own standards for scientific objectivity.' [see John P. Jackson Jr., "In Ways Unacademical": The Reception of Carleton S. Coon's "The Origin of Races" - Journal of the History of Biology, Vol. 34, No. 2 (Summer, 2001), pp. 247-285]

Examples of Mechta-Afalou inspired features.
wide forehead, epicanthic eye-folds are common, prominent jaw, & tendency to freckle. Skin-colour varies from black, brown, olive, and white.
[Patrick_Duffy_at_PaleyFest_2013 attributed to iDominick wiki common license.jpg
Pierce-Brosnan- attribute to Petr Kratochvil public domain
Marrakesh Moroccan attributed toDavid6303 pixabay]

(above) Moroccan Woman
(Attributed to Emily Hasson, Pixabay public domain.)

(above)
Irish Woman
(Attributed to Pixabay public domain.)

The Harvard publication 'The Races of Europe' was an attempt to replace the theories put forward by Giuseppe Sergi. The Eurafrican or Afro-Mediterranean theory proposed by Sergi held the belief that dark-skinned, long-headed humans migrated from Africa and populated ancient Europe. Sergi attributed the founding of Greece, Egypt, and other civilizations to these Eurafricans; he was deeply opposed to the Aryan theory. For Sergi, the Aryans were uncivilized and did not contribute to ancient Greece. Sergi believed that the original Neolithic settlers from Africa were dark-skinned.

The change in skin colour occurred very recently in Europe. It was during the Bronze Age (c.3000 BC to c.1000 BC) that migrants from the Russian Steppes introduced genes responsible for lighter skin colour; one of the key pigmentation genes in humans is SLC24A5:

> in Europe and demonstrate that skin lightening happened as late as 5000 years ago through immigration of lighter pigmented populations from western Anatolia and the Russian steppe but not primarily via evolutionary pressure for vitamin D3 synthesis [Andrea Hanel and Carsten Carlberg, Skin Colour and Vitamin D: An Update, Experimental Dermatology, June 2020].

Notice that skin colour changes were not due to evolutionary processes, the dark-skinned Mesolithic and Neolithic populations inhabited Europe for thousands of years. The Atlantic fringe countries were the last to undergo skin colour changes; this would have started c.1000 BC:

> The Atlantic Bronze Age is a cultural complex of the Bronze Age period of approximately 1300–700 BC that includes different cultures in Portugal, Andalusia, Galicia, France, Britain, and Ireland and is marked by economic and cultural exchange that led to the high degree of cultural similarity exhibited by coastal communities, including the frequent use

> of stones as chevaux-de-frise, the establishment of cliff castles, or the domestic architecture sometimes characterized by the round houses.

This explains why dark-skinned tribes continued to populate the British Isles in large numbers.

15 NEOLITHIC POPULATION OF IRELAND & BRITAIN

The transition from the Mesolithic to the Neolithic Age was initiated by the arrival of a new dynamic people who entered Europe via the Balkans and southern Mediterranean coastal regions. Tribes from the Near East, with the haplogroup E1b1, T, and G2a, introduced farming to Europe. These people transformed Europe and built giant stone structures known as Megaliths.

These Africans are still remembered in Irish and British folklore. The oldest Irish texts refer to the Formorians as the Fomoraig Affric. They are remembered as a 'race' of sea pirates that dominated the northern Atlantic Ocean. The people that introduced the Neolithic Age have left a deep impression on both Ireland and Britain. These African pioneers introduced many plants and animals. Otto Jacob Max Hilzheimer, who was an expert on the domestication of animals in antiquity, credits Africa as the source of the long horn cattle, the greyhound, the Black Cattle of Wales, the Red Cattle of Devon, the Hereford, and Highland Cattle. The introduction of these animals was by both land and sea. Neolithic people braved the Atlantic Ocean, loaded their boats with livestock, and even reached isolated locations such as the Hebrides and Orkney islands off the northern Scottish coast.

The Neolithic Age is famous for the giant stone monuments and circles scattered across much of Europe. Geoffrey of Monmouth collected early manuscripts from which he composed his History of 'The Kings of Britain'. According to this 12th century document, the famous stone circles of Stonehenge were built by giants from Africa. DNA analysis carried out on the bones found within the Neolithic tumuli has confirmed this story - scientists have now confirmed that the Neolithic Age involved people who carried the African male DNA haplogroup E1b1. Local traditions from the

Isle of Lewis, in the Hebrides, associate the large standing stones with black men who wore robes decorated with feathers.

Highland Cattle
(Attributed to Frank Winkler from Pixabay)

The River-bed People

In 1862 T.H. Huxley described the human remains from the Trent Valley. This type, which he labelled Iberian, had very long skulls with high slightly retreating foreheads, protruding occipital, no metopic suture, frontal bone grooved by the super-orbital nerve, and was of medium stature (5 feet 5 inches).

The name Riverbed 'race' was applied to skeletons from this period since they were often found near major rivers and along the coast. These Riverbed people traded in purpura shells, from which purple dyes are obtained.

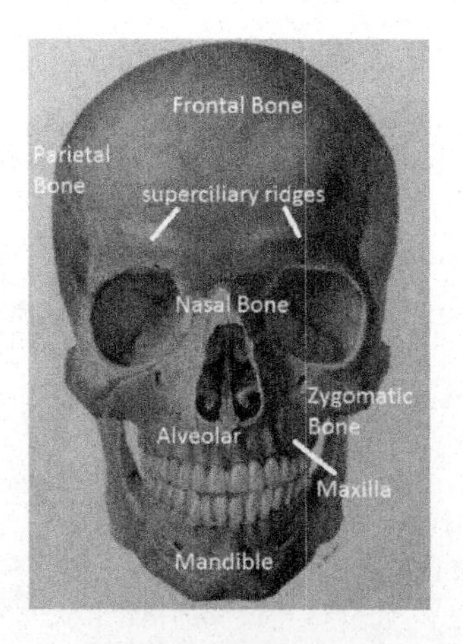

Facial bones modified by the author,
(Original from Werner Spalteholz, Hand-Atlas of Human Anatomy 1861)

The Whitepark Bay skeleton was found inside a circular stone hut in County Antrim. The skull was long and narrow, the forehead receding, frontal bone grooved by the superciliary ridges, which were large, metopic suture absent, the jaw wide, and estimated height was around 5 feet 5 inches. Although the skull is long, the facial features show a close similarity to the robust African Afalou-Mechta. The side profile shows clear signs of prognathism. In many ways the Whitepark Bay skeleton is related to the Riverbed people. The main difference is the former is more robust and has a more strongly developed lower face and jaw.

The Ringabella skeleton was found in County Cork. It differs from the Whitepark Bay skeleton in many ways. Even though both have long skulls, the Ringabella skull shows a clear tendency towards alveolar prognathism. The lower jaw is missing, but was probably narrow, while the forehead was high and rounded.

The Balbriggan skeleton was found in county Dublin in 1840. Again, it belongs to the long and narrow category and in general is very similar to the Ringabella skull. The profile of the skull was straight (orthognathous) and closely resembles the dynastic Egyptian skulls. The face is narrow with prominent check-bones and a protruding occipital bone.

The Kilgreany B skull was discovered during an exploration of Kilgreany Cave in county Waterford in 1928. The profile of the skull is very similar to the East African Elementia skull. The forehead is slightly retreating, no metopic suture, frontal bone is not grooved by the supra-orbital nerve, slight alveolar prognathism, while the facial height is short and the skull long and narrow. It is believed to belonged either to the 3rd millennium or 4th millennium B.C.

Bronze Age Skeletons

During the Bronze Age, a new group of people reached the British Isles. The skulls belonging to this era differ from the earlier Neolithic type. Brachycephalic skulls start to become the dominant type during the Bronze Age. However, they differ from the Alpine brachycephals from central Europe in many aspects. They both have similar cephalic indices, but the early brachycephals that arrived during the 2nd millennium B.C. arrived by sea from the Mediterranean. Anthropologists have compared them to the Sami (Lapp) people of Finland and Sweden.

The spread of the Bronze Age is usually connected with the spread of a type of pottery commonly referred to as Beakers. The people who used this pottery have become known as the 'Beaker Folk' - these beaker or bell beakers are believed to have spread along the Atlantic Ocean from southeast Spain and northern Morocco.

The long-headed Neolithic people continued to populate many parts of the British Isles. This is proven by the excavations of the Bronze Age barrow at Pentraeth, Anglesey. Two types of diametrically opposite skulls are found; type I is remarkably brachycephalic with a cephalic index of 87.5, while type II is extremely dolichocephalic with an index of 71.

The brachycephalic skeleton is described as around 50 years old, height 5 feet 6 inches, skull length 164.5 mm, skull breath 144 mm., cephalic index 87.5 - the limb bones are slender with muscular markings.

The dolichocephalic skull is estimated as being 49yrs old, height 5 feet 9 inches, skull length 186 mm., skull width 131 mm., superciliary ridges prominent and fused together on the forehead, cephalic index 71.2, limb bones slender and muscular markings not pronounced.

The skeletal remains from the Neolithic period are generally regarded as belonging to people that originally migrated from Africa and the Mediterranean. The Neolithic tribes arrived in a land that was already inhabited by Mesolithic hunter-gather tribes. The previous inhabitants, the Mesolithic hunter-gathers, had a completely different lifestyle. The intrusion of the new Neolithic farmers resulted in fierce conflict, and also resulted in the permanent re-shaping of the British and Irish landscape

16 BLOOD GROUP ANALYSIS

The ABO blood group system is defined by two antigens on the red blood cells, A and B. These are governed by the presence or absence of three alleles A, B, and O. An individual's blood type is defined by the red blood cell antigens A and B. People with blood group A have the antigen A, those with blood group B have antigen B, while those with blood group AB have both antigens A and B, while blood group O will have neither antigen. These blood groups are governed by Mendelian inheritance; the genes that control the ABO type in humans is located on chromosome 9 (9q34.1) and is called ABO glycosyltransferase. The combination of these alleles determines a person's blood group. In addition to the ABO system, an individual can be Rhesus positive Rh (+) or Rhesus negative Rh (-). If an individual has the protein RhD antigen, their blood will be classified as Rhesus positive. If this antigen is absent, they will be classified as Rhesus negative. The Rh system is complex and involves several antigens, the most important are D, C, c, E, and e. Various antigens combinations occurs at different frequencies - the combinations cDe occurs in high frequencies in Africa and is regarded as an African genetic marker.

How these blood groups evolved is not known. One theory proposes that all blood groups evolved from O and certain ethnic groups with this type were assumed to be the most ancient (e.g., Inuit, Native American, etc.). An alternate hypothesis favors AB as the oldest type which mutated to give rise to all other types. However, the origins and evolution of blood groups are still unclear.

Rh positive is very widespread, while Rh negativity varies considerably; amongst the Basques people it is as high as 35%, while in Asian populations (Chinese, Japanese, & Native Americans) it is rare and occurs in only 2% or less of the population.

Anthropologist were very quick to assign new racial theories connecting 'race' with blood group type. Supporters of 'Celticism' were eager to prove the 'out of Central Europe' theory and researchers began eagerly collecting samples from various groups.

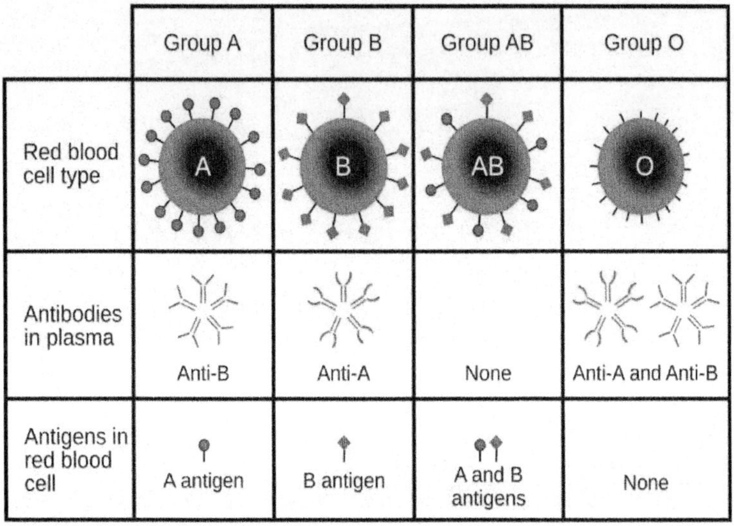

	Group A	Group B	Group AB	Group O
Red blood cell type	A	B	AB	O
Antibodies in plasma	Anti-B	Anti-A	None	Anti-A and Anti-B
Antigens in red blood cell	A antigen	B antigen	A and B antigens	None

ABO_blood type
Attributed to InvictaHOG, Public domain,
CC via Wikimedia Commons

Arthur Ernest Mourant was recognized as the world's leading pioneer in the study of human blood groups. [Not to be confused with G. M. Morant]. Arthur Ernest Mourant was the first hematologist to map the distribution of blood groups around the world. In 1946 he founded the Blood Group Reference Laboratory in London, and in 1954 he published *'The Distribution of Human Blood Groups'* - later an expanded second edition was published in 1976 *(The Distribution of Human Blood Groups and Other Polymorphism)*. Western scientists began to explore the link between diverse populations and the frequency of the ABO blood groups. To their surprise they discovered that the Irish, Welsh, and Scots did not share the same ABO blood group patterns of their European neighbors. Instead, they exhibited the same ABO frequencies as the people of the Sahara, northern Africa, parts of East Africa, and parts of the Caucasus region. All these groups carry a high percentage of the O gene, and relatively low levels of the A and B gene.

Arthur Ernest Mourant was not afraid to suggest a connection between the British Isles and North Africa:

> A search of the 'Celtic' languages for the presence of non-Indo-European words is not, therefore, likely to meet with any great success except in the names of places, of rivers, of mountains, and of valleys, which have a much greater tendency towards permanence......The famous Welsh mountain which is similar in shape to a mighty chair and bears the name Cader Idris (Idris' Chair) seems to suggest that Idris was an important personage. When one considers that a line of Berber kings also bore the name of Idris the coincidence seems noteworthy. It would appear then that long before the invasions of 'Celtic'-speaking tribes much of Europe and also perhaps North Africa was inhabited by a people speaking a common non-Indo-European tongue. [p27, Mourant, Blood Groups, Anthropology and Language in Wales and The Western Counties, P27]

What made Arthur Ernest Mourant different from other scientists of his day was his deep interest in geology and prehistory. He even excavated caves such as Cotte de St Brelade and Neolithic tombs. Because he was an open-minded scientist with diverse interests, he was able to apply his expertise in blood groups and discover the connection between the people of the British Isles, the population of the western Atlantic 'fringe' and specific African groups.

> A. E. Mourant's paper set out to demonstrate that, *'the available data as to the ABO and Rh blood group frequencies of the peoples of Western Europe, especially Wales, and of North Africa, suggest certain correlations between the distribution of the blood groups and the findings of historians, pre-historians and philologists.'* The study of blood group patterns in Wales revealed a clear divide between North Wales and South Wales. The coalfields and the principal cities of South Wales were excluded from the study since the present-day inhabitants do not represents the original populations - the county of Glamorgan (between 1861 and 1911) received more than 400,000 immigrants from outside - while Monmouth received even more numbers of English settlers.

In most populations the number of individuals with blood group AB is typically low. The level of B varies from one population to another; for example, the Basques have a B gene frequency of 0 to 3%. While in many parts of Asia there are high frequency of the B gene. For example, the Manchu have 33.7% and the Mongolians have 33.3% type B phenotype. *[see Jue Liu, et al., Frequencies and ethnic distribution of ABO and RhD blood groups in China]*.

Scientists were surprised to find several tribes living in Africa had the same ABO gene frequency as the so called 'Celts' of Ireland and Britain. They found that the O gene always exceeds 70%, the A gene varies between 15% to 20%, and the B gene ranges from 4% to 7%. This so-called 'Celtic' blood group pattern was completely different to that observed amongst the Iberians and central Europeans. The studies discovered that the inhabitants of South Wales (descendants of the Silures) do not have the same ABO pattern as the other 'Celtic' speakers. The inhabitants of South Wales and Cornwall have much lower levels of type O. The Silures (South Wales) and the Cornii (Cornwall) represent ancient tribes that differed considerably from the Ordovices and Deceangli of North Wales.

ABO FREQUENCIES IN WALES

South Wales and the Forest of Dean (Gloucestershire) remained culturally isolated. These areas are believed to be the refuge of what the early anthropologist referred to as the Iberian race. Unfortunately, the label Iberian does not help us unveil the true identity of these tribes. The people of South Wales did not have the same origin as their fellow Cymry of North Wales. The population of North Wales have retained the ABO blood group pattern of their dark-skinned Neolithic ancestors. The analysis of the population of South Wales has revealed a very different pattern. There is a sharp drop in the level of the O blood group in the South Wales Valley. In this respect the people of South Wales have more affinity with the inhabitants of Cornwall.

In North Wales from Bala to Towyn the level of the A blood group is higher. The increase can be attributed to the migration of a thick set, broad faced type with heavy eyebrow ridges and epicanthic eye-folds. Interestingly the features associated with this type was labelled by early anthologists as Mongolian/Ugrian, while Beddoe classified them as Africanoid.

The Silures represents a bit of a mystery. They were culturally and economically isolated. The coinage of the neighboring tribes, the Dobuni and the Belgae, did not circulate amongst the Silures. Their culture was dominated by stock raising. The Romans regarded the Silures as the most warlike of the British tribes. Tacitus remarked on their similarity to the Iberians and mentioned their swarthy skins and twisted curly hair. There is no evidence at all to suggest that the Silures were 'Celts' - the first 'Celtic' speakers or more accurately Gaulish speakers in this region were the Belgae tribe, who had just crossed over from France during the 1st century BC. The physical features of the Silures and Cornish type is often described as rather rugged. Fluere noted that this broad faced, rugged type is mainly found in the coastal areas of Brittany, Ardudwy coast (Wales), around Gibraltar and on the African coast of Morocco. This group of coastal people have pronounced features which indicate connections to the ancient African Afalou-Mechta type that dominated many regions of Morocco and Algeria.

The Black Mountains and the Eppynt Mountains (Brecon Beacons) represents the northern boundary of the Silures. As a result, mid Wales has a higher level of blood group O type, and the people tend to be more dolichocephalic. The frequency of the A blood group tends to be around 19%, while in South Wales it never falls below 25%.

The most interesting aspect of the blood group analysis of this region is the extreme high levels of blood group B. The level reaches as high as 17% in some places and is very reminiscent of the Chadic and northern Egyptian ABO patterns. The ancient inhabitants of the Black Mountains were once widespread. They were driven into the less productive lands such as the moorlands and the mountainous areas. In 1903 Professor E. Anwyl had the following to say about the early settlers of Mid Wales:

> "There is sufficient indication that Neolithic Man of the polished Stone Age inhabited Breconshire, and he, too, doubtless conformed to the general dolichocephalic type..........within the large dolichocephalic area a dark complexion prevails."

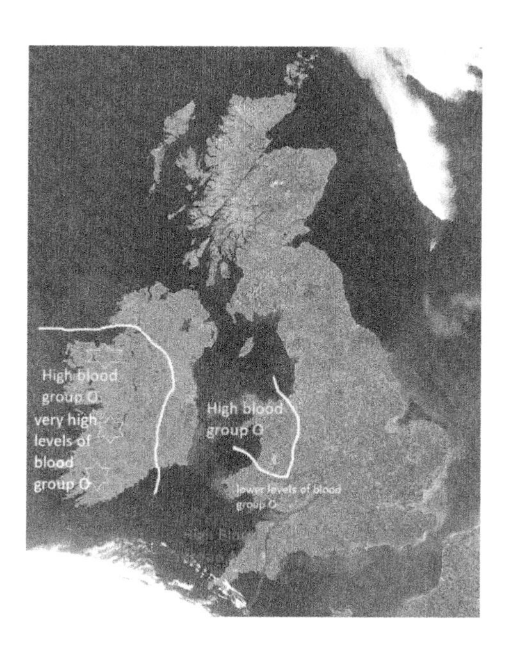

Map of ABO Blood Type Frequencies in Wales, modified by the author.

The Neolithic traces on the Breconshire side of the Wye may perhaps be represented by two carnau on the mountain called Carn Gafallt (or Carn Cabal) and Saith maen. Within this zone, the apparently pre-'Celtic' names that stand out are Chwerfri (a small stream), Cymrum in Nant Cymrun, and Gynowyn in Blaen Ganolwyn. There are several river names in this district that elude derivation on sound phonological principles from any Indo-European roots.

This is not an isolated phenomenon. It is noticeable that there are many pre-'Celtic' names that are associated with rivers; examples of which are: the *Bidan, the Onneu, the Gwdi, the Honddu, the Senni, the Cilieni, the Yscir, and the* Sgio.

Blood Groups in Ireland

The ABO blood group frequencies for most areas of Ireland are closely related to the patterns found in the Sahara. The areas of highest O frequencies are those which have retained their Gaelic language. The areas which deviate from this pattern are mainly found in the south-eastern coastal areas of Ireland, regions that were settled by the Anglo-Normans and Scandinavians. These areas have elevated levels of the A blood group. The Blood group O type is generally regarded as a marker for the Gaels, while the eastern counties of Wicklow, Wexford, Dublin, and Waterford show double the frequency of blood group A compared to western Ireland.

The blood group distribution across the island indicate that the Irish are essentially pre-'Celtic' and have remained unaffected by the migration of small groups from mainland Europe such as the Belgae tribe. The Gaels believe that they migrated to Ireland directly from Iberia. The Annals give the Milesians an Egypto-Scythian origin. The oldest population of Ireland, the Formorians, probably introduced the high level of blood group O. The entire island was originally populated by people of African origin; most likely to have spoken Hamito-Semitic (Afro-asiatic) languages (or related proto languages).

The provinces of Connaught, Munster and Kerry have extremely high levels of blood group O. In county Kerry, blood group O frequency reaches a level over 80%. In all the counties in the west of Ireland, the frequency of the O blood group never falls below 75%. A study of the Rhesus Gene Complex in western Ireland suggests the presence of a large African component. The Rhesus complex, *cDe* (or *Ro*), has been found to be 7%. This value is higher than that found in Spain, which has an average *cDe* level of 5%. European scientists attribute the 5% *cDe* level in the Spanish population to the Moorish occupation of Spain. The same scientists remain very silent on the higher levels of *cDe* (an African marker) found in Ireland. Galicia also has high levels of this African genetic marker. Since this region of Spain was not occupied by the Moors, it must have been inherited from the Megalithic tomb builders that settled along the Atlantic fringe region of western Europe.

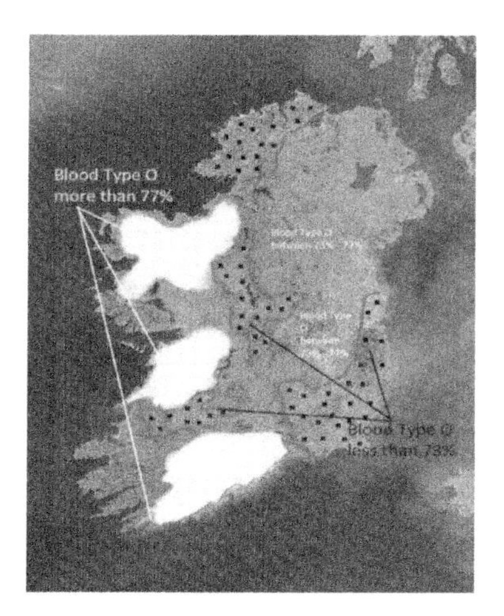

Map of Distribution of Blood Group O in Ireland

(modified by the author.)

ABO Blood Group Frequencies in Africa

During the Neolithic period both Ireland and Britain became the home to a dolichocephalic type. This group entered from the south; both the Cymry and Gaels Welsh claim to have wandered through North Africa and Egypt before sailing from the Mediterranean and across the Atlantic. To fully understand the relationship between the British Isles and northern Africa, it is important to become familiar with the different tribal groupings that live in Africa.

Northwest Africa

Most tribes in Mauretania have become Arabised, and no longer speak Berber. Some have also changed their genealogies, tracing themselves back to fictional eponymous ancestors from Iraq. Herodotus (5th century BC) noted that the north-west African Nasamones were the only tribe to bury their dead in the sitting position. Travelers have noticed that this custom was still practiced by Mauritanian tribes before their conversion to Islam (around 800 years ago). In contrast, the Tuareg Berbers of Mali and Niger have retained their language and culture; they have fiercely maintained their culture and independence.

Tuareg folklore states that they are descended from Mazigh, the son of Canaan (son of Ham). Legend has it that the original inhabitants of the Hoggar were Chadic speakers such as the Hausa. The Tuareg advanced from the Nile region and pushed the Hausa and other Chadic tribes further west and southwards. The linguistic comparison of Berber dialects indicates that they have recently developed separate identities within the last 2000 years. The Berber dialects spoken in Egypt (Siwa Oasis) differs very little from that spoken a thousand miles away in the Moroccan Atlas.

It should be noted that the coastal Berber tribes have some ABO traits that are not found among the Berbers of the interior. The sickle cell trait among the coastal Berbers, especially the Kabyle, indicates a close connection with Bantu tribes further south. The occurrence of sickle-cell anemia (HbS) amongst some of the coastal tribes certainly proves a previous Bantu presence, maybe dating back to the Aurignacian period. It is worth recalling that there was an old connection between Nubia and Carthage represented by the folk-story of Queen Candace of Nubia migrating to Sbeitla (northern Tunisia).

The Tuaregs also have a similar blood group pattern to the Atlas Berbers, with the A gene being slightly lower amongst them. In contrast the Tebu of the Tibesti mountains in Chad have very low A and very high B blood group frequencies. In this respect they resemble the coastal Egyptians. While the Haratin tribes scattered across this region have a much higher B blood group than their dominant neighboring Berber tribes.

The Atlas Berbers of Morocco have extremely high O and very low A and B frequencies. The Ait Haddidu Berbers from the Atlas Mountains have the following pattern: 89% O, 6.5% A, and 4.5% B. Amongst the Moroccan Berbers the pattern does not vary greatly.

The Libyan and Egypt coastal populations deviate from these patterns. In Egypt, the level of B increases to 20%, while the A gene frequency varies between 25% to 30%. Maybe this explains why the South Wales and North Wales have different frequencies. The Silures show similar patterns to coastal Libyans and northern Egyptians, who have elevated levels of type A blood.

Studies performed on a total of 40,591 healthy blood donors in Egypt revealed the following results: blood group A 35.12%, blood group O 31.94%, blood group B 23.12%, blood group AB 9.74%. The study shows A> O > B > AB, with 91.78% Rh positive. This contrasted with the southern Egyptian tribes *[e.g., Aswan, Luxor, etc.]* who have high O frequency of around 70%. *[Abdelmonem, Mohamed, et al (2019). Distribution of Blood Types and ABO Gene Frequencies in Egypt. American Journal of Clinical Pathology. 152.]*

The Canary Islands - the Guanches

The 15th century expansion of Europeans resulted in the first contact with several islands off the coast of Northwest Africa. European contact with north-west African islands such as the Azores, Canary Islands, Madeira, and Cape Verde, resulted in the destruction of the indigenous inhabitants. In 1449 the Kingdom of Portugal officially ordered the large-scale colonization of the Azores. Proof that the island was already inhabited has come from the analysis of pollen and fungal spores found in the sediments. This research has shown that there were settlements around Lake Azul dating to around 1300 AD. Farming and livestock husbandry was practiced on the Azores before the arrival of the Portuguese. *[see Rull, V., et al. (2017), Vegetation and landscape dynamics under natural and anthropogenic forcing on the Azores Islands, Quaternary Science Reviews, 159, 155-168].*

The impact of the Spanish invasion of the Canary Islands is well documented. The islands were densely populated by the African Guanches. Contact with Europeans resulted in genocide; with the genetic pool of the islands irreversibly altered. The male population was virtually eradicated, while the remaining female population were raped and enslaved by the invading Spaniards.

The study by Rosa Fregel, et al. used DNA-based techniques which allowed the analysis of the ABO gene. A total of 643 teeth, belonging to 493 different aboriginal individuals, were involved in the study using material collected from several burials across the seven Canary Islands. The individual breakdown of where the teeth was collected is as follows: Fuerteventura 10 skeletons, Gran Canaria 115 skeletons, Tenerife 39 skeletons, La Gomera 52 skeletons, El Hierro 44 skeletons, and La Palma from 38 skeletons.

Studies carried out on mummified remains revealed extremely high levels of blood group O at 97% on Gran Canaria and 91% on Tenerife. These frequencies are remarkably similar to levels found amongst the Ait Haddidu Berbers, from the Atlas Mountains, who have O blood group frequencies at 89%. The study by Rosa Fregel, et al., has shown that the indigenous Canary Islanders were closely related to their African neighbors:

> The Canarian aboriginal sample is not significantly different from any of the North African populations, from the historical sample of La Concepción, or from La Gomera, the island that better has retained the prehispanic gene pool. On the contrary, it is significantly different from the Iberian Peninsula and the rest of the present-day Canary Islands populations that have received a stronger European genetic input than La Gomera. At ABO level, North African populations are differentiated from the Iberian Peninsula

> because they have higher frequencies for B101 allele, lower frequencies for A101 allele, and 1:1 ratio between O01 and O02 alleles……However, for the ABO gene, it seems that the Canarian colonization process has exacerbated the parental Berber allele frequency peculiarities in the Guanches. The Canarian aborigines are related to Northwest African samples and show the farthest distances from the Iberian Peninsula and modern Canary Islands populations……In addition, they also show the highest frequency for O03 allele that has been consistently detected in North Africa but only sporadically in the Iberian Peninsula. [Rosa Fregel et al., Temporal evolution of the ABO allele frequencies in the Canary Islands: the impact of the European colonization Immunogenetics (2009) 61:603–610].

A.E. Mourant further explains:

> **The Sardinians, the Cretans, the peoples of the Western Caucasus, and certain Berber tribes of North Africa show ABO frequencies almost identical with those found in the peripheral north-western regions of Europe—Iceland, Scotland, Ireland, and parts of Wales**.

The north-western European populations on the Atlantic fringe are neighbored by nationalities that have low B frequencies. In contrast, the Berber tribes and the tribes of the Caucasus region are surrounded by populations with very high B frequencies. This indicates a lack of mixing with high B neighbors. Some Berbers have mixed with Arab populations and have elevated levels of type A. People of the Atlantic fringe all share similar blood group patterns with North African tribes and some Nile Valley tribes.

The Nile Valley

In southern Egypt, the frequency of the blood group A drops to 19% and the B frequency is around 10%; while the O gene frequency always exceeds 70%; very similar to the people of the Western European 'Atlantic fringe' population.

Further south, amongst the Somalis and Afar the O frequency sharply increases up to 75% or more, while the frequency of B drops to around 8%. For most Cushitic speaking tribes in this region, the A gene is relatively constant, usually between 15% and 19%.

The ABO blood group patterns across Africa vary considerably. Studies of Ethiopian soldiers serving in the Korean war found the following ABO blood group frequencies:

> A = 28.5, B = 24.0, O = 41.2, and AB = 6.3%.

Ethiopia is composed of various distinct nationalities, and further research has unveiled some interesting differences. The Nilotic speaking Anuak and Nuer from the south-west Ethiopian province of Gambelle had 71.0% O blood group, while the Amhara and Tigre 'highlanders' had a frequency of 55.49% O blood group. A study of ethnic group-based ABO distribution across Ethiopia has shown that O type is dominant amongst the Nilotes and reached 100% amongst some isolated populations. *[see Lemu Golassa, et al., High rhesus (Rh(D)) negative frequency an ethnic group-based ABO blood group distribution In Ethiopia]*.

It is very important to remember that ABO and Rh blood group data is only valid for the specific population where that data was collected. For example, studies of Yoruba blood groups found different frequencies for Ibadan Yoruba compared to Yoruba from Ogbomosho, only 100 km apart. Blood group patterns can only be of anthropological value if the exact geographical, ethnic, and cultural background is noted. Unfortunately, many Eurocentrics do not collect enough data on the specific origins of the people from whom samples were collected.

ABO Blood Type Frequencies of Other Europeans

If we look at various blood group patterns from different parts of Europe for comparison, the evidence proves that the Irish and Britons are not closely related to the people of Central Europe. The data suggests a southern origin for the Irish, Cymry, and Scots. A brief look at various European populations shows just how different the people of the Atlantic fringe are:

> Greece: 38.44% for blood group A, 13.06% for blood group B, 4.77% for blood group AB, and 43.73% for blood group O. The northern Greek region of Thrace has a significantly higher level of blood group B than the rest of Greece. [Theodore Lialiaris, et al., Distribution of ABO and Rh blood groups in Greece: An update]

> Switzerland: The frequency of blood group A (47.2% and 45.2%), B (8.4% and 9.8%), and AB (3.0 and 4.1), 41.4 and 40.9 for blood group O. [Thomas Volkena, et al., Blood Group Distribution in Switzerland – a Historical Comparison, Transfus Med Hemother 2017;44:210–216]. Notice how different the patterns are from the so called 'Celtic' patterns

of Ireland and Britain.

> South-West Germany: ABO allele frequencies were blood group O (64%), blood group A (27.9%), blood group B (8.1%), - Rhesus haplotype frequencies were as follows cde: 0.394, *CDe*: 0.431, *cDE*: 0.136, *cDe*: 0.021, and *Cde*: 0.011. D category VI represented 7% of all weak D (formerly *Du*) *[see Wagner, et al., Frequencies of the Blood Groups ABO, Rhesus, D Category VI, Kell, and of Clinically Relevant High-Frequency Antigens in South-Western Germany. Infusions therapie und Transfusionsmedizin. 22. 285-90.]*

> Jewish: The Jewish pattern closely agrees with the Polish and Ukrainian pasterns. The B level is rather high and the *cDe* frequency much higher than other European groups, with exception of Galicia (NW Spain) – Regarding the *cDe* value, A. E. Mourant comments 'this can hardly be other than the result of a 'negro' component, probably received through Egypt.' The commonest Rhesus gene combinations in Europe are *CDe*, *cde* and *cDE*. The combination cDe is common in Africa - a raised cDe frequency suggests a sub-Saharan influence. *[see A.E. Mourant, The Blood Groups of The Mediterranean Area]*.

A brief look at ABO blood group distributions has revealed that even Galicia (NW Spain) has a considerable genetic contribution from Africa. Blood group analysis is a useful tool that shows clearly that the ancient Britons and Gales could not have originated in central Europe - the high O gene frequency connects them with the African Berbers, Guanches of the Canary Island, Crete, Sardinia, and southern Egypt.

The evidence indicates that the populations living around the Mediterranean are heterogeneous – A. E. Mourant concludes:

> Three populations living in or near the Mediterranean area have been found to possess relatively high cDe(R,) frequencies; the Egyptians, the Arabs of Iraq and the Galicians of north-west Spain. The Egyptian Rh distribution can be derived from that of the Sardinians together with a 'negro' admixture. This hypothesis is strongly supported, at least with regard to the 'negro' contribution, by work now in progress

> which shows an almost continuous change along the Nile Valley from Egyptian to Negro. Moreover, the relatively high B frequency of Egyptians may have some connection with even higher B frequencies found in Central Africa. The Rh constitution of the Arabs of Iraq lies between that of the Egyptians and that of the Latvians of east Central Europe. [p226, A.E. Mourant, The Blood Groups of The Peoples of The Mediterranean Area]

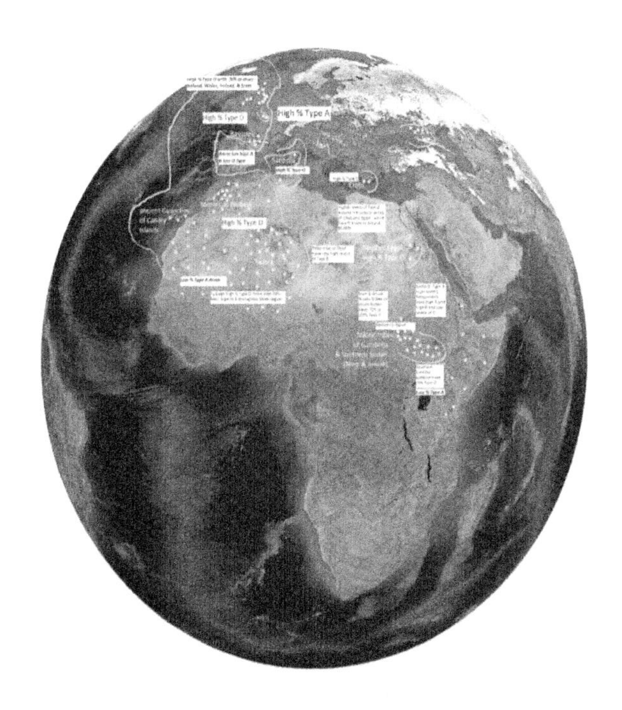

Map showing High Blood Type O in Western Europe and Africa

The evidence indicates that the populations living around the Mediterranean are heterogeneous – A. E. Mourant concludes:

> Three populations living in or near the Mediterranean area have been found to possess relatively high cDe(R,) frequencies; the Egyptians, the Arabs of Iraq and the Galicians of north-west Spain. The Egyptian Rh distribution can be

derived from that of the Sardinians together with a 'negro' admixture. This hypothesis is strongly supported, at least with regard to the 'negro' contribution, by work now in progress which shows an almost continuous change along the Nile Valley from Egyptian to Negro. Moreover, the relatively high B frequency of Egyptians may have some connection with even higher B frequencies found in Central Africa. The Rh constitution of the Arabs of Iraq lies between that of the Egyptians and that of the Latvians of east Central Europe. [p226, A.E. Mourant, The Blood Groups of The Peoples of The Mediterranean Area]

17 FOOT SHAPE & ETHNICITY

Phyllis Jackson was a humble podiatrist from Gloucestershire. She spent 50 years of her life working in remote areas of the Cotswolds (south-western England). Her amazing and pioneering work helped to establish a new branch of ethnoarchaeology, which aimed to unravel the connection between foot shape and ethnicity. Her theories were first published in Current Archaeology (Vol 12, pp. 466-470), which inspired me to undertake some of my own research to find out more about the foot shape of South Wales. Armed with a pencil and paper, I eagerly collected foot shapes from a very diverse range of ethnicities, ranging from Georgians (Russia) to Ugandans. I was fortunate enough to received assistance from Phyllis who helped me interpret various foot outlines in my collection.

Looking back at my correspondences from 20 years ago, I had tried to explore whether there was a link between foot shape, ABO blood groups, and the cranial index. Phyllis wrote back and informed me:

> I have just been re-reading them (data you sent) and the A's and O's do seem to tally with what my research work indicates. There is a cross-marriage between an A and an O, which will be dominant? I am of the B Rh neg group but where that, from I wouldn't know. Mothers was Scots, French, and English. My father English and a smattering of Welsh; my nephew inherited the B Rh negative, but I don't know about the nephews or the other side of the family.

This was the beginning of my collaboration with Jackson on this new branch of ethnoarchaeology. The analysis of foot shapes was able to throw more light on the differences between the people of North and South Wales. My aim was to find out if foot shape could prove a relationship between the Insular 'Celtic' speakers (Irish, Scots, Welsh, and Cornish) and the Guanches, Egyptians, Berbers, and other African tribes. Was there a link between foot shape, craniology, and ABO blood group type?

Phyllis Jackson's insight into various foot shapes I had sent her was very insightful and made an impact on me; encouraging me to explore this new area of ethnoarchaeology. Jackson's comments indicated my own outline was similar to the Egyptian type:

> With your outlines, this toe-line slopes steeply ending with a very short 5th toe. I am interested too, in the available space between the toes. Most people find extreme difficulty in pushing the marker down to the base of their toes. This makes This make me wonder if the toes are capable of movement such as grasping an object……. In my article in No. 156 of Current Archaeology, you will have seen my selection of ethnic foot outlines going East across Eurasia and then west from Egyptian along to Spanish (Basque feet are not like Spanish) and up to Germany, England & the Scots/Irish, Welsh (not South Wales), Cornish & Breton. It is with these latter, already mentioned, you will see a similarity of main structures. It can be seen too, on the Russian/Polish foot, but again, the toe-line is rather level, not sloping as are yours

Jackson observed the statutes of Rome, Greece, and ancient Egypt, and made some useful addition analysis:

> I hope the foregoing will be of interest to you. If ever you have the opportunity to see the Greek and Roman statutes in the British Museum, you will notice they all have a very small mal-aligned 5th toe. This prevails today with Italian and Swiss people. Recently a stone oil-lamp carved to this shape of a foot was discovered on a Roman site in London; it, too, has the tiny 5th toe or this wick-hole was where the 1st (Great) toenail should have been! [Phyllis Jackson, personal communication]

Ethnoarchaeology and Foot Shape

Phyllis Jackson noticed that inter-marriage within the Cotswold and

Herefordshire region had created a particular foot shape. However, an even more astonishing discovery was made by her; the entire foot structure of the local people was completely different from the typical English foot shape. On close examination she discovered that the shape of the cuboid bone varied considerably. With the indigenous inhabitants she noticed that the cuboid bone was actually cuboid in shape, whereas with the Saxons this bone was quadrilateral in shape with very short outer borders.

Phyllis Jackson's work also revealed that there was a difference in foot structure between the Insular 'Celts' and the Anglo-Saxon foot. Jackson wanted to find out if the indigenous Britons had an established foot shape before the Anglo-Saxons tribes established themselves in these islands.

Phyllis Jackson had spent decades as a podiatrist in Herefordshire and the Cotswolds. She first noticed regional foot shapes and then, more importantly, made an astonishing discovery - the Anglo-Saxon foot shape could be easily distinguished from the local (British) foot shape.

Feet tend to be hidden away in European cultures. Even within the home shoes are still worn by Europeans. This is totally different to what we find in other cultures: Muslims, Koreans, Chinese, and Japanese cultures (to name a few), do not wear shoes in the home - feet are always on display. Jackson's study was so ahead of its time, and her standards have never been reproduced. The beauty of Phyllis Jackson's research is the meticulous details recorded with regards to ancestry. This is the only way to understand population movements and how they relate to foot shape. She recorded where people were born and their ancestral origins, i.e., both paternal and maternal grandparents were recorded.

With the help of the museum of Gloucester and Cirencester, Phyllis Jacksons investigated the feet of monks from the Saxon Priory of St Oswald's in Gloucester and compared them to those of the Saxon period at Abbey, Cirencester. She also investigated the feet of lay people in Gloucester City cemetery.

The aim of Jackson's study was to find out, if possible, how many had the 'local British' type and how many were incoming Saxons. Her examinations commenced with St Oswald's, a very early Priory - in possession of relics of King Oswald of Northumbria. Phyllis started out with the belief that as Oswald was a follower of the original 'Celtic' religion. She presumed that, 'it would be unlikely, at first, to have Christianized Saxon monks.'

In her own words, Phyllis described what she found:

> 'What I did discover, as well as the fact that "local British"

men and some women - were in the majority, together with several (see CA 146 Nutbane illustration). was the very high incidence of deformity either congenital or acquired through injury or caused by disturbed balance in the upper part of the body. These foot conditions were rarely seen amongst the lay people. It was the situation which caused me to turn to Cirencester Abbey. Here again, the local British bone structure predominate in the early years, but Saxonisation began to predominate in post-medieval times. However, throughout the numbers of feet examined, this incidence of deformity etc., was even greater than St Oswald's! I have come to the conclusion that men entering into monastic life because with such a crippling deformities or injuries, they could not have survived the intensity of land labor in the everyday world. Another interesting thing I have discovered is a repetitive type of pressure-wear on the head of the metatarsal, together with evidence of an abnormal tension on the posterior tale-calcaneal ligament. I think this might, in modern terminology be called an "occupational hazard" caused by this shocking numbers of hours kneeling to pray - apparently, this could be as much as seven hours - once again, this fact wear does not occur with lay people's feet.' [Phyllis Jackson, Personal Communications with the Author].

Differences in Foot Shape

Foot shape can be used in ethnoarchaeology to track the migrations patterns of newly arrived groups. It helps us to understand whether displacement or expulsion has occurred. Phyllis Jackson collected a large number of foot outlines. The Irish-Scot foot is described as long and narrow foot, with the toe alignment in a straight line; the Anglo-Saxon foot is broader and wider, with the toes sloping down sharply. She discovered the absence of Anglo-Saxon foot bones in excavations to the west of Offa's Dyke on the Welsh boarder, but to the east of the boarder she found a variety of different 'ethnic' foot-shape. *[see p48-53, Walter Ellis, Foot Note to History, Sunday Times, 1996]*

Jackson examined various skeletons from the cemetery from different periods, ranging from the Neolithic to the Saxon era (4000 BC to 600 AD). Jackson mentions numerous sources from where she obtained samples - Butlers Field, Lechlade cemetery, Gloucestershire Museum where she was able to access skeletons from the Cirencester (Roman Corinium), Devizes museum, Wiltshire Bronze Age barrow at Wilsford South, cemeteries at Mildenhall, Collingbourne Ducis and Pewsey Nutbane Neolithic long barrow, Iron Age Hillfort at Danebury, and Pewsey

The local inhabitants of the region, before the arrival of the Saxons, had cuboid bones that were actually cuboid in shape, whereas the Saxon foot has a quadrilateral shaped cuboid bone. There were differences in some other characteristics, but the cuboid bone was the most useful to her studies.

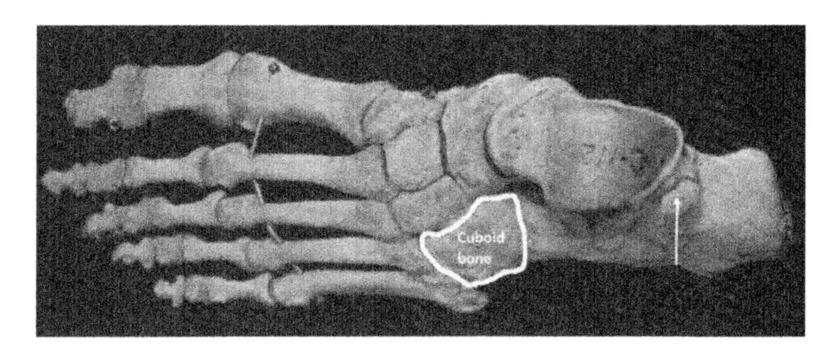

Location of the Cuboid Bone in the foot

The Irish-Scot (and northern Welsh) foot shape differs considerably from the Anglo-Saxon shape; and can be a useful tool to trace the migration patterns of ancient people. The narrow ancient Egyptian type of foot has persisted in some area; surprisingly, the Picts had foot shape that was similar to the Ancient Egyptians. With the modern Irish-Scots and North Welsh foot we find a narrow foot with the toes more aligned in parallel. The Picts have a narrow foot with the toes sloping downwards and is identical to the ancient Egyptian and Neolithic type in general.

Wherever possible, Phyllis Jackson collected the outlines of both feet because they sometimes differed from one another. 'This appears to be the case', Phyllis noted, 'if there is mixed ancestry or hereditary anomaly somewhere within the structure, it will manifest itself. The maternal influence tends to show itself in the left foot.' [Phyllis Jackson, personal communication with the Author, 2001]

Jackson was able to collect a number of foot outlines from different European countries. The Basque outline was taken from a lady whose parents were both Basque and had strong Basque ancestry. The Spanish and Basque foot are very different. Not surprisingly the Basque foot resembles the long and narrow ancient Egyptian foot.

I have attempted to fill in the gaps in the present knowledge by collecting foot shapes from South Wales, in an attempt to throw more light on the origins of the Silures. Also, since ancient Iberia shared its name with the

Caucasus region (the other Iberia), I collected Georgian outlines for comparison.

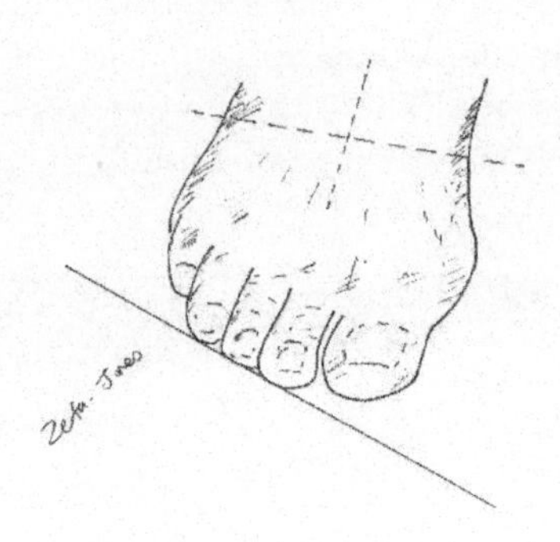

South Wales foot

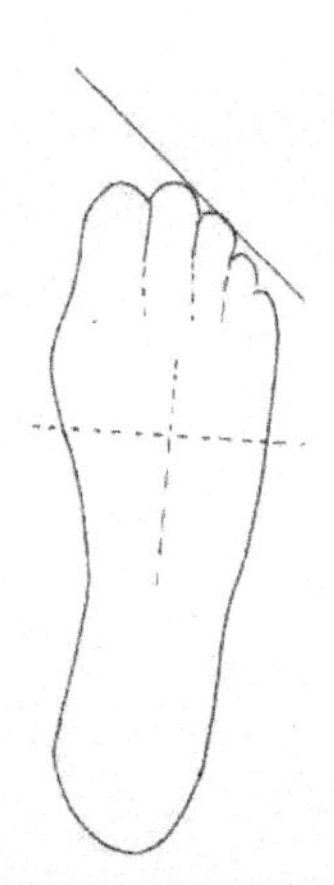

South Wales foot, Abergavenny.

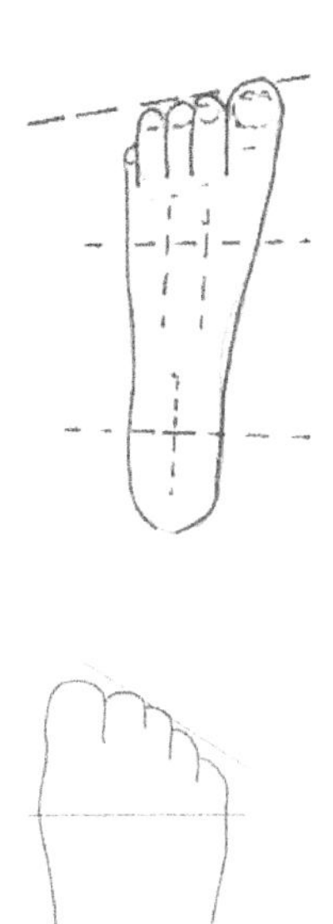

Typical English foot - with wide cuboid bone, sample from male, Nottinghamshire by author © Ibrahim Ali

The foot outline from the Llŷn Peninsula is typical of the Irish-Scots foot. The population of North Wales has the same high blood group O frequency as the Irish. The ancient Gangani tribe occupied the coastal region around Llŷn, while the more powerful tribe known as the Ordovices dominated most Mid and North Wales. The Deceangli tribe, a smaller tribe than the Ordovices, inhabited the area between Abergele and Wrexham (near the English boarder). The market town of Abergele, 50 km from the Llŷn Peninsula, has the highest concentration of sub-Saharan E1b1 y-DNA (EV13) male haplogroup gene discovered in Britain. Some have speculated that this phenomenon is due to a heavy Roman presence in the area. No evidence for this proposal exists; North Wales has the highest frequency of blood O group in Britain. If the inhabitants of Abergele were descendants of a 'lost' Roman legion (as some have suggested), there would be elevated levels of Blood Group A amongst the male population. It is useful here to refer back to A. E. Mourant for some clarity:

> There is no single zone of high O frequency in the Mediterranean area, but a number of isolated populations

> show a combination of high O and low B, similar to that of the Scots, the Irish and the Icelanders. Such are the Basques, the Sardinians, the Cretans, a few Berber tribes in north Africa and, rather to the east of the region, the peoples of the western Caucasus. The Basques differ from the other high O peoples, both of the Mediterranean region and of north-western Europe, in their extremely low B frequency which is the lowest in Europe. [p2, A.E. Mourant, The Blood Groups of The Peoples of The Mediterranean Area]

A few foot outlines from Abergele would answer this question and would confirm whether the population represents people with Neolithic ancestry (with ancient Egyptian foot shapes) or represents a Roman legion that decided to stay behind. However, the blood group analysis, which shows very high levels of blood group O, places the Abergele population with the Berbers, Guanches, and other southern people.

Foot shapes from South Wales are very different from those of North Wales. However, there is a gap in our knowledge since we do not have, at the moment, outlines from Powys and inland areas of North Wales. I suspect the ancient Egyptian type is found in many areas such as the Preseli Hills, Brecon Beacons, Builth Wells, and other areas with significant occurrence of non-Indo-European placenames.

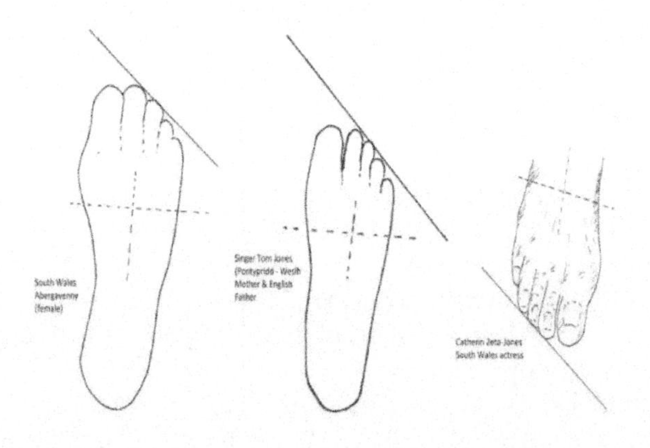

Three Examples of South Wales Foot Shape (Siluria), center Tom Jones, right Catherine Zeta Jones

Foot-shape in Southwest England

Phyllis Jackson received many foot-outlines from members of the public after the broadcast of her interview on the Natural History programme. One outline she received from a member of the public who had ancestry from the West Country (i.e., Somerset, Devon, Cornwall, & Gloucestershire) is particularly useful for the African Substratum Theory. She received a letter from one member of the public who thought his ancestors might have been linked to the Phoenicians:

> There is a joke in my family about our 'Phoenician toes'. I think this may have come about from my father seeing a Phoenician statue with similar feet. As for our family origins, all I know is West Country and Wales, but there is a certain darkness of hair and complexion which seems quite strongly through the generations – this also is sometimes commented upon! [West Country resident]

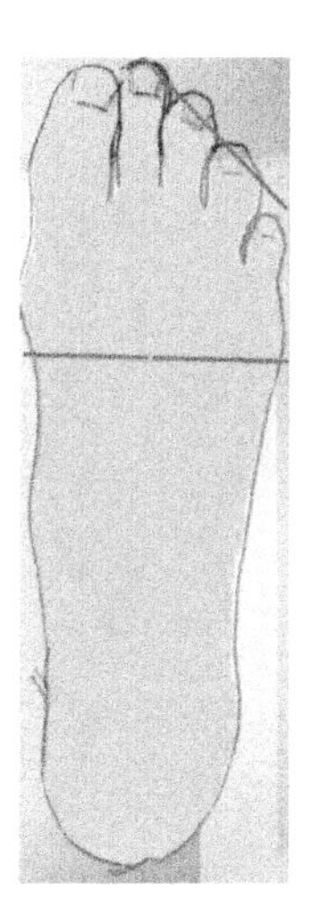

Foot Shape from Other Countries

On comparing the foot shapes of the so-called Insular 'Celts' with the continental Europeans, clear differences can be observed. The first thing that becomes apparent is the difference between the Basques and the Spanish foot. The Basque foot resembles those of ancient Egypt. The Spanish foot is broad like the Anglo-Saxon foot, with toes that slope downwards. The theory that the ancient Iberians were related to the ancient Egyptians is supported by the foot outlines.

I managed to collect foot outlines from Georgians (Russia). This was useful since ancient writers referred to the Caucasus region as 'the other Iberia.' This was the foreign name for the Georgian kingdom of Karti. It is worth noting that Its direct neighbor was Colchis. The land famous for Jason and the Golden Fleece, Herodotus' description of the Colchians is worth including here. The statement by Herodotus confirms the similarity between the Colchians and the ancient Egyptians:

> [104.] For it is plain to see that the Colchians are Egyptians; and this that I say I myself noted before I heard it from others. When I began to think on this matter, I inquired of both peoples; and the Colchians remembered the Egyptians better than the Egyptians remembered the Colchians; the Egyptians said that they held the Colchians to be part of Sesostris' army. I myself guessed it to be. so, partly because they are dark-skinned and woolly- haired; though that indeed goes for nothing, seeing that other peoples, too, are such; but my better proof was that the Colchians and Egyptians and Ethiopians are the only nations that have from the first practiced circumcision. The Phoenicians and the Syrians of Palestine acknowledge of themselves that they learnt the custom from the Egyptians, and the Syrians of the valleys of the Thermodon and the Parthenius, as well as their neighbors the Macrones, say that they learnt it lately from the Colchians. These are the only nations that circumcise, and it is seen that they do even as the Egyptians. But as to the Egyptians and Ethiopians themselves, I cannot say which nation learnt it from the other; for it is manifestly a very ancient custom. That the others learnt it from intercourse with Egypt I hold to be clearly proved by this that Phoenicians who hold intercourse with Hellas cease to imitate the Egyptians in this matter and do not circumcise their children.
>
> 105. Nay and let me speak of another matter in which the Colchians are like to the Egyptians: they and the Egyptians alone work linen, and have the same way, a way peculiar to themselves, of working it; and they are alike in all their manner of life, and in their speech. Linen has two names: the Colchian kind is called by the Greeks Sardonian; l that which comes from Egypt is called Egyptian. [Herodotus, Histories, P391, Alfred Denis]

The foot-shape from the Caucasus region resembles the Neolithic Egyptians, Saharan tribes, other parts of Africa: the toes slope downwards, and the foot is long. The Silurian type has a closer resemblance to the Basque and Egyptian but is not an exact fit; it is not a slender and has a shorter appearance. The alignment of the toes is not as dramatic, and the slope is not identical to the ancient Egyptian type. However, the cuboid bone shape has more in common with the Neolithic types, and is very different from the modern Spanish foot shape. The Basque foot is very easily distinguished from the Spanish foot shape. It should be remembered that the Basques are the descendants, on the maternal side, of Mesolithic hunter-gatherers. They are a product of the union between Mesolithic females and newly arrived Bronze Age R1b males.

(above) Basque foot based on Phyllis Jackson, (personal communication with the Author.)

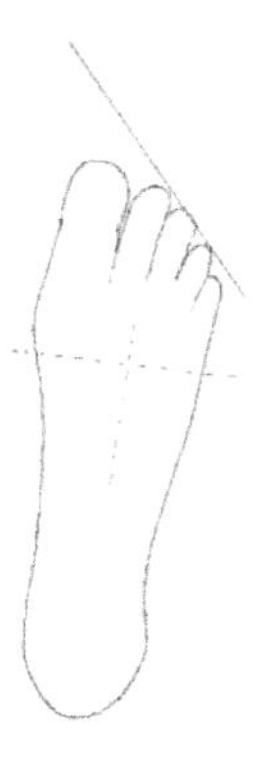

Georgian (Russia) foot (the other Iberia) © Ibrahim Ali

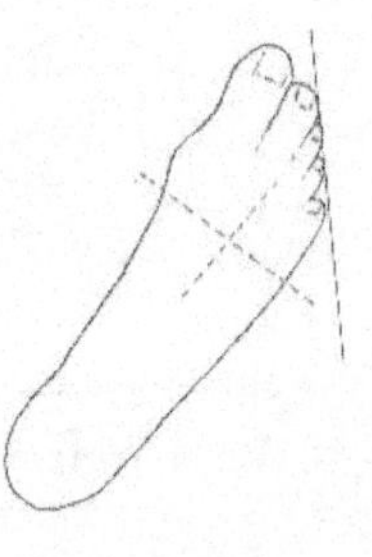

African Ugandan outline© Ibrahim Ali

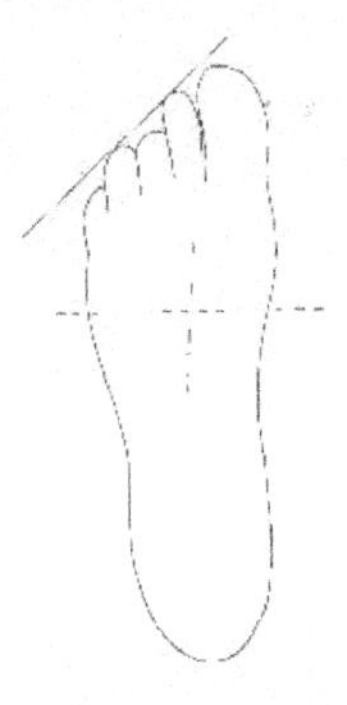

East African outline (author) © Ibrahim Ali

Roman foot showing a 2nd and 3rd toes with unusually similar lengths.
Roman foot - Ara Pacis - Friezes of Entrance Walls.JPG

The shape of the cuboid bone can certainly assist in tracking the migration patterns of ancient populations. Jackson made observations of ancient statutes and noticed that they accurately portrayed the 'ethnic' foot shape. The Romans left behind an abundant number of statues, which contribute to our understanding of foot shape variations.

The Roman foot is easily recognizable because the 2nd and 3rd toes tend to be long and are of similar lengths. The Etruscans, who inhabited the Italian peninsula before the Romans also had a similar long 2nd and 3rd toe, which are of similar lengths.

Etruscan statute - long 2nd and 3rd toe (Monumenti Etruschi o di Etrusco nome by Franceso Inghirami published 1821)

As we have seen the earliest inhabitants of Ireland are believed to have been from Meroe. (Kush) The Irish Annals start with Cesair, the granddaughter of Noah, landing in Ireland with her followers. The Kerma (Kush) statutes show foot shapes that are identical to the Neolithic settlers of Europe, who introduced agriculture. The Bronze Age Beaker folk had a very different foot shape. The Beaker folk had a cuboid bone that was quadrilateral in shape with very short outer borders. The foot was broad and very different from the so-called 'Insular Celts' of Ireland and Britain. Population replace is believed to have occurred during the Bronze Age. Skin colour changes started to take place during the Bronze Age, around 2200 BC, with the introduction of new technology and weapons which resulted in the Neolithic populations being overwhelmed. Mixing between the two populations did take place, and pockets of Neolithic tribes continued to flourish.

There are many questions that need to be answered before we can fully understand how the population changed from 'Black' to 'White' - a process which started only during the Bronze Age. Some tribes remained 'Black', the Silures and the inhabitants of the Western Isles are good examples.

Even Victorian anthropologists commented on the dark skin colour of the inhabitants of some regions: the Isle of Jura and the Africanoids of central England and Ireland, have already been discussed. As for the Calendonii of Scotland with their ruddy complexions and light hair, they were Germanic tribes who were adopted by the Cymry; they were allowed to settle in Britain on the condition that they obeyed the Cymry law for 9 generations - only then would they become Cymry (or Britons). We can conclude that British and Irish society was 'multi-cultural' and was composed of diverse communities for millennia.

SUMMARY OF FOOT OUTLINES					
British Mesolithic & Neolithic	Basque (Iberian)	Roman	Modern Irish-Scot	Southern Welsh & Cornish	Georgia (Caucasus region)
Long narrow feet dominated Western Europe from 12,000 BC to 2,000 BC - very similar to Ancient Egyptian feet shapes.		Very unusual 2nd and 3rd toes - long and similar lengths.	Irish-Scots toes are parallel and not inclined. This is not the only Irish foot shape - Neolithic Egyptian type feet are common & in some districts the broader Bronze Age type feet dominate.	The Southern Welsh have distinct foot shapes. More than one type exists - long Neolithic feet occur in some areas, while pockets of Bronze Age broad feet can be found in the Valleys. Pockets of brachycephalic populations occurs in Caerphilly, Blaenavon, and other towns.	The Basques and the Georgians were both referred to by the name Iberians - interestingly, their foot shapes are similar. Both are long and narrow with sloping toes - just like the ancient Egyptians.

Comparison of different 'ethnic' foot shapes, © Ibrahim Ali

The maternal influence shows itself in the left foot, and the paternal influence is reflected in the right foot *[reference, Phyllis Jackson, personal communications with the author]*. The illustrations show the comparison of the outline of an individual who had an English Yorkshire mother and a father of Somali/Sudanese ancestry - the resulting foot has sloping toe and an overall wider foot shape - that resembles the Anglo-Saxon foot more than the paternal East African outline.

(Left) mixed ancestry English Yorkshire + Somali/Sudan.
(Right) English Anglo-Saxon. © Ibrahim Ali.

The inheritance of foot shape is very complicated - why the cuboid bone varies so much within populations is not known. The variation can be used as an ethnoarchaeological tool to assist in tracking ancient migrations. More data is required from diverse population s so that a more complete picture can be reconstructed.

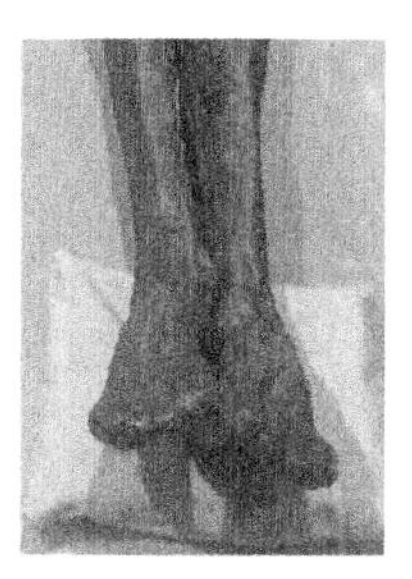

African Guanches (Canary Islands) feet showing similarity to Irish-Scots feet.
Attributed to Momia guanche MNA Outisnn, creative commons via Wikimedia Commons.

The foot outline of the African Guanches provide the missing link between the British Isles, Ireland, and Africa. The alignment of the Guanches toes are identical to the Irish-Scots foot; they are long and narrow foot, with the toe alignment in a straight line. The Irish-Scots foot is totally different to the Neolithic, Bronze Age, Spanish, Italian, English, German, and other European foot outlines. The Irish-Scots cuboid bone shape is identical to the African Guanches; the cuboid bone is actually cuboid in shape: again, more evidence pointing to Africa as the homeland of the Iron Age people of Ireland and Britain.

18 PRE- CELTIC LANGUAGES

The so-called 'Celtic' languages spoken in Britain, Ireland and Brittany are commonly referred to as Insular 'Celtic'. The extinct languages of mainland Europe are referred to as Continental 'Celtic' (Gaulish, etc.). It is important to remember that the Irish, Cymry (Welsh) and Scottish people never referred to themselves as 'Celts'. Continental 'Celtic' cannot be fully reconstructed, with respect to syntax, since only fragments are available. Research into 'Celtic' languages has involved Insular 'Celtic.' The Irish language is the oldest 'Celtic' language of which we have records. Although the date this language arrived in Ireland and Britain is uncertain, it is quite likely that the Irish people arrived before the Gaelic language.

What language did the Gaels and Cymry speak originally?

Irish folklore is an excellent starting point. According to the ancient books of Ireland, the first people to settle in Ireland were from the Nile region. After this there was successive waves of invaders, the Formorians, Parthalonians, Firbolgs, Tuatha de Danaans, and then the Milesians.

Goidel or Gadelas, believed by some to be the eponymous ancestor of the modern Irish, was born in Egypt around 1200 B.C. He was the son of Niul, son of Feniusa Farsa - the king of Scythia. About 600 years later Bratha led the Milesians to Iberia. Four generations later, Milesius led the Gaels from Iberia to Ireland. The genealogy of the characters in the Annals clearly illustrates the multiracial ancestry of the Gaels.

Milesius had an Egyptian wife called Scota. Their children were Heber Fionn, Heremon, Ir, Aimhergin, Colpa, and Aranan, they were all Egypto-Gaels. The second wife of Milesius was Seang the Scythian. She had two sons, Don and Airach. It was the Egyptian sons of Milesius that took over Ireland from the Tuatha de Danaans. Heber Fionn and Heremon conquered Ireland between 600 B.C and 500 B.C. - this estimation is based on placing Gadelas in Egypt around 1200 B.C. - there were twenty generations before Bratha reached Iberia. This would give a date of around 600 B.C. for the arrival of the Milesians in the Iberian peninsula. Three generations later (c. 550 B.C.), the Milesians conquered Ireland. Heremon took the portion of Ireland that lay north of the Boyne, while Heber Fionn administered southern Ireland. The following verse found in the Annals shows how multicultural the ancient Irish were:

> The valiant Gallamh, was called Milesius,
>
> and fought a thousand battles with success.
>
> Had eight young princes of his royal blood.
>
> Aireach, Feabhruadh, and the noble Donn,
>
> both born in Scythia.
>
> Near the Nile in Egypt, Heber Fionn and Aimhergin
>
> drew their first breaths.
>
> The most courageous Ir, a hero who in fight surpassed them all.
>
> born in Irene, near the Thracian shore.
>
> Colpa a prince that well could wield a sword.
>
> The prince Aranan and Heremon, born in the tower of Brigantia (Iberia).

The Irish Annals are a valid source that can be used to explain the links between the Gaels and other nations. From these sources we can summarize as follows:

> The eponymous ancestors of the Gaels originally came from Scythia, i.e., present day southern Russia. Niul, the son of Feniusa the King of Scythia married an Egyptian woman called Scota (I); while Niul's brother was born in Iraq. The initial tribal movements occurred just before the Israelites were expelled from Egypt. The Gaels stayed in Egypt for four generations.

The Egyptians expelled the Gaels, who then sought refuge in Crete. The Egyptians forced them to leave Crete. Under pressure, the Gaels fled to Scythia, where they were subsequently expelled. After wandering across the Mediterranean, they finally reached Gothland.

The Gaels stayed in Gothland for four hundred years; fifteen generations in total, probably from 900 B.C. to 600 B.C. Bratha leads the Gaels from Gothland to Iberia, probably from 600 B.C. and 500 B.C. Milesius, leader of the Gaels in Iberia, travels to Egypt and marries an Egyptian woman called Scota (II) - the daughter of Pharaoh.

After seven years Milesius returns to Spain and his uncle Ith is killed by the Tuatha de Danaans in Ireland. This results in Milesius gathering his forces in Iberia and launching an invasion of Ireland.

From this summary we can see that the Gaels believe that their ancestors originally came from Scythia and then spent many generations in the Middle East and Egypt; before finally travelling to Spain and then Ireland. Interestingly the Irish language shows strong influences from both Africa and the Urals.

The references to Egypt in the Irish Annals have been inherited from the pre-Gaelic inhabitants of Ireland. The first known inhabitants of Ireland were the Formorians; also known as the children of Ham, the Formor Afraic of early Irish manuscripts. According to the Leabhar Gabhála, Ireland was uninhabited until the arrival of Cesair. She set sail from her homeland (Meroe) and was first to settle Ireland with her companions.

The connection between Insular 'Celtic' and African languages has been suspected by scholars for many centuries. The linguistic evidence reveals a connection between 'Celtic' and many African languages. To fully understand the connections, it is essential to remember that the African languages are much older than the present-day European languages. Proto-Indo-European can be traced back to around 3000/4000 B.C.; whilst proto-Hamito-Semitic certainly dates back to at least 16,000 B.C. [see Ehret]. When we look at other African languages such as the proto-Kir languages, a sub-branch of Nilo-Saharan, it was already spoken by 500 B.C. While we have evidence of Ancient Egyptian existing long before 3400 B.C. When we look at Akkadian, spoken in Mesopotamia, we know that it was already in use by 3000 B.C - whilst further south, South Arabian and Ethiopic had already separated from each other by 3000 B.C.

The internal differences within Cushitic are of great antiquity. The Beja language, spoken by the nomadic inhabitants of the Red Sea province of Sudan, only have 1% common vocabulary with Lowland Cushitic (Afar, Oromo, Somali, Rendille, etc.). This indicates that the Cushitic languages had already become distinctly separate languages at an early date, long before 3000 BC. The Beja are mentioned in the accounts of the ancient Egyptians and referred to as the 'troublesome nomads of the eastern desert.' These examples show how these individual African languages were spoken in antiquity, before the development of Indo-European languages (which are obviously younger).

Beja Tribesman, 12th dynasty (c. 1985-1773 BC)
(C. G. Seligman, Public domain, via Wikimedia Commons

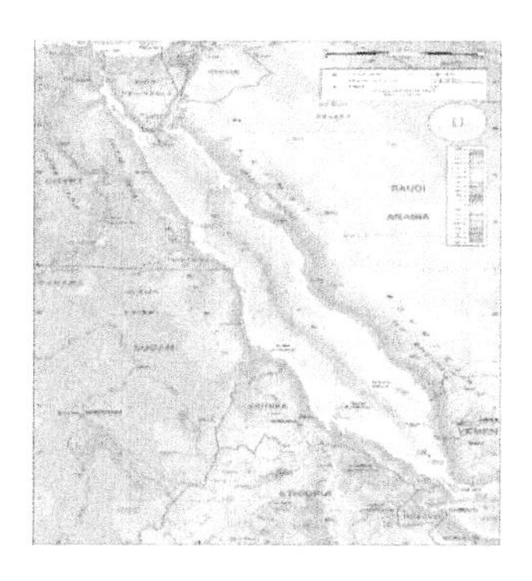

Red_Sea_topographic_map
Attributed to Eric Gaba (Sting - fr:Sting),
CC creativecommons.org via Wikimedia Commons

African Substratum in 'Celtic' Languages

Before exploring the possibility of a linguistic connection between 'Celtic' and various African languages; the place of linguistics in academia should be considered:

> The place of the field of linguistics in academia has been debated since its inception. When we look at universities, we may find a linguistics department in either the social sciences or the humanities. …….. So where does linguistics belong? The answer is not in where linguistics is placed administratively, but rather in how linguists think. Here the

> answer is quite clear: linguists by and large view themselves as scientists and they view their field as a science, the scientific study of language. This has been true since the nineteenth century, when Max Mueller would entitle a book published in 1869 'The Science of Language' and the first chapter of that book "The science of language one of the physical sciences." The fact that linguistics is today defined as the scientific study of language carries with it the implicit claim that a science of language is possible, and this alone takes many by surprise. For surely, they say, language, like all human activity, is beyond the scope of true science. Linguists believe that their field is a science because they share the goals of scientific inquiry, which is objective (or more properly inter-subjectively accessible) understanding. [Mark Aronoff And Janie Rees-Miller, The Handbook of Linguistics The Handbook of Linguistics, 2002]

Simply reading this chapter, will convince you that the study of languages is certainly not a science. Scholars have divided themselves into two factions - the pros and cons. If the study of languages was a science, the rules used should be enough to decide if a relationship exists between different language groups.

The following discussion on Nostratic illustrates the enormous confusions within language classification:

> IS's (Illi™-Svity™) original proposal included Indo-European (IE), Uralic, Altaic, Kartvelian, Dravidian, and Hamito-Semitic (later called Afro-Asiatic). Dolgopolsky's included most of these but excluded Dravidian, while he was sympathetic in his early writings to the possibility of Chuckchi-Kamchatkan also being included. Starostin (1989:43, 44) wants to exclude Afro-Asiatic, believing Nostratic and Afro-Asiatic to be related at a deeper level, but to include Eskimo-Aleut. Bomhard's version of Nostratic holds Indo-European, Afro-asiatic, Uralic Yukaghir, Elamo-Dravidian, Altaic, and possibly Sumerian, to be genetically related (Bomhard & Kerns 1994:2, 34). Other proposals would expand Nostratic to include, or at least be related with in higher-order genetic units, also Eskimo Aleut, various American Indian groups, Yeniseian, Gilyak (Nivkh), Sumerian, Elamite (with

> Dravidian), Sino-Tibetan, North-Caucasian, and others, thus connecting Nostratic with major segments of the world, including Africa, the Americas, and Asia. [p107-152., Lyle Campbell, Nostratic: A Personal Assessment]

The Thirteenth International Congress of 'Celtic' Studies, July 2007, was organized by Sprachwissenschaftliches Institute. The papers presented at the workshop included a contribution by Gearóid Mac Eoin titled *'What Language was Spoken in Ireland before Irish?'* Since this congress was held in Bonn, Germany, one would have expected Theo Vennemann (professor of linguistics at Ludwig Maximilian University, Munich, from 1974 to 2005) to have been invited - especially since he has written the most papers on this subject; and he is the leading academic expert on the Semitic (Punic) substratum in German.

The paper presented by Mac Eoin is uncomfortable; he is an Irish scholar (from Galway University) who appears to be at ease with 'Celticism' and openly hostile to the African Substratum Theory. He is obviously unaware that Irish history starts with the African Formorians., a fact that many modern academics are still not acquainted with.

The 'fantasy' of a Nostratic super-language family has some followers - mainly because it is based on Eurasian building blocks. The African Substratum Theory supports Giuseppe Sergi's Eurafrican theory which attempted to overthrow the racist 'Aryan' theory. In the 1930's Mussolini, under pressure from his German Nazi allies, announced that the Italian people were now 'Aryans' (and no longer Mediterranean).

The 'Aryan' identity was rejected by many academics. Giuseppe Sergi was the most adamant opponent of 'Aryan' identity – instead, he supported the Eurafrican identity for Italians. Pressure from Nazi Germany and the defeat in Africa at the hands of the Ethiopians, had a lasting impression on the Italian psyche:

> The defeat of Italian attempts to conquer Ethiopia at the Battle of Adowa in 1896 seemed to seal Italy's fate as a second-class power. Some Northern Europeans attributed this failure of Italy's ambitions to racial degeneracy. So pervasive were racial explanations for national cultural traits in late nineteenth-century Europe that many Italian intellectuals themselves thought it imperative to understand Italy's racial composition in order to understand the reasons for its apparent inability to rival its northern neighbors. As Alan Cassels has written, "nearly all of Italy's troubles have stemmed from the inferiority complex of its people." Two

> solutions to this crisis presented themselves to Italian intellectuals seeking a racial foundation for Italian culture. One could identify with the dominant ethnic identity of Northern Europe, i.e., assume Italians were "Aryans." The heroic and intellectual virtues of the Aryans, as had been elaborated on by (mainly) German and French scholars for much of the nineteenth century, would then explain Italy's past greatness or future potential. In this interpretation, Southerners were usually assumed to suffer from racial "pollution" of some type and therefore not to be capable of the same level of civilization as Northerners. [p22-23, Racial Theories in Fascist Italy Aaron Gillette]

Early Pioneers of The Substratum Theory

When Welsh scholars started to translate the Bible into their own language, they quickly noticed many similarities between Welsh and Semitic Hebrew. Dr John Davies of Mallwyd (c. 1567 – 1644 AD), a great Welsh scholar, produced his famous Welsh edition of the Bible in 1620 AD. He then went on to produce his book on Welsh grammar in 1621 AD - *Antiquae Linguae Britannicae Rudimenta* [see Rhiannon Francis Roberts, 1959]. He derived many Welsh words from Semitic Hebrew. Other scholars soon followed, and by the early 1800's many historians and linguists were openly exploring and accepting these connections.

The early 1900's saw an explosion of supporters for the African substratum theory; Giuseppe Sergi (published 1901 & 1936), Morris (published 1900) and Pokorny's article were published between 1927 and 1930. During this early period, it looked as if the African Substratum Theory was winning. The tide began to reverse from the 1930's onwards with the rise of fascism across Europe. Educational institutions were encouraged to promote the 'Aryan' theory and as a result the African Substratum Theory was slowly being replaced with the racist 'Aryan' Indo-European model. 'Celtic' scholars began to completely ignore the pioneering work of Morris-Jones, et. al. It was not until Wagner (1969) and Quinn (1984 Atlantean), that we see the confident re-emergence of support for the connections between 'Celtic' and Africa/Arabia. Quinn's Atlantean was the single most important attempt at exploring the subject - an Irishman's viewpoint, ahead of its time - Quinn completely rejects 'Celtic' - he challenges the Eurocentric concept of the 'Celts' and developed a four-part documentary on the subject.

'Celtic' Languages & the African Substratum

The so called 'Celtic' languages deviate from the other Indo-European languages. Did they inherit their speaking patterns (syntax) from an ancient African language spoken throughout Western Europe?

The extend of the African influence is equal with regards to Goidelic and Brythonic. Did the initial encounter with Neolithic Africans occur in central Europe or in the Iberian Peninsula?

The spread of the Neolithic from Orkney islands, in the north, and later to southern Britain, resulting in the building of Stonehenge, has been proposed by some archaeologists. The new theory suggests that the Orkney islands were the driving force for the stone-age builders. The radio-carbon date of 3512 BC (Ness of Brodgar) - indicates the possible diffusion of ideas from the north to the south of Britain. *[see BBC2 Britain's Ancient Capital: Secret of Orkney 1/3 Neil Oliver, etc.]*

African Language Family

There are four language families in Africa: Hamito-Semitic (also called Afro-asiatic, Afrasian, or Erythraic), Nilo-Saharan, Bantu, and Khoisan. The latter is the smallest group in Africa. Once widespread, Khoisan is now restricted to Southwest Africa. The East Africa Khoisan speakers have now adopted either Cushitic or Nilotic languages. They once extended across North Africa - before being absorbed by bigger, and more powerful groups. Khoisan is a very ancient and archaic language family. Gerald Massey explored the links between the Ancient Egyptians and the Khoisan. The connection between Khoisan and China, Tibet, and Mongolia, however, is speculative and requires more research. They certainly resemble each other physically; but many other people have the same phenotype. The portraits of the ancient Egyptians in conflict with the Hittites in Syria shows many people with south-east Asian features (Korean, Mongolian, etc.). Some are very dark and the same colour as the Nubians and Egyptians, while others are shown having yellowish skin colour. Ancient Syria was a melting pot - where every type of phenotype was on display.

The Nilo-Saharan super family is mainly composed of mid-central African languages. The western branches have affinities with Berber and Bantu; while the eastern Nilotic branches have come under the influenced of lowland Cushitic. With regards to the classification of Nilo-Saharan, linguists are completely divided. Greenberg classified Ik (Teuso), spoken in Uganda, as Eastern Sudanic [Nilo-Saharan], while Tucker concluded that Ik has certain common features with Ancient Egyptian and Berber, not found in 'Orthodox' Cushitic.

The word order with 'Celtic' has certainly been influenced by ancient

Egyptian, Berber, and Semitic. The general pattern in all four of these language families are Verb-Subject-Object [VSO], while the Cushitic and Chadic languages tend to follow Subject-Object-Verb [SOV] sentence pattern. However, the 'Celtic' verbal forms are related to the Cushitic and ancient Egyptian. Periphrastic constructions, as described by Morris-Jones, in Welsh and Irish are derived from Cushitic and ancient Egyptian. With Cushitic, the verbs are of two types - Class I verbs are conjugated primarily by means of prefixes; while Class II verbs are conjugated by means of suffixes - these suffixes are composed of a conjugated Class I auxiliary verb. This type of conjugation is also found in sub-Saharan languages such as Tebu and Zaghawa. Class I verbs are found frequently in Beja, Afar, Saho, and less frequently in Somali and Agaw. Class III are characteristic of both Ancient Egyptian and Cushitic.

Dolgopolsky discovered that 'Common Cushitic is the dialect of Hamito-Semitic that best preserves the original phonological system.' The Beja of eastern Sudan [Northern Cushitic] and the Ethiopian Agaw [Central Cushitic] share certain similarities with Ancient Egyptian, that are not commonly found in other Cushitic languages. The Beja, who inhabit the Red Sea Province of Sudan, also share a vocabulary with the inland Nubian and the Zaghawa [Nilo-Saharan] found further west on the Chad-Sudan boarder.

Somali and Afar (Lowland Cushitic) have retained the proto-Hamito-Semitic verbal system. Bender and Cooper noticed that Somali and Afar-Saho have been least influenced by other languages. For some unknown reason Somali, Afar-Saho, and Beja have remained remarkably close to Old Hamito-Semitic (Afro-asiatic): that is, they have preserved Archaic Cushitic patterns. The internal differences within Cushitic are far greater than those found in Berber, Semitic, Chadic, or Ancient Egyptian. This is an indication of the antiquity of Cushitic. In contrast the Berber dialects are all mutually intelligible (from Morocco to the Siwa Oasis in Egypt). When we look at the neighbouring Cushitic languages such as Oromo and Afar, we find that they share only 3% similarity of vocabulary. This proves that the Cushitic languages became differentiated at an incredibly early date.

Omotic, a 'fringe' Cushitic language, found in south-west Ethiopia, lacks some features found in all the other Hamito-Semitic languages. For example, the same word for cow/cattle occurs in all the Hamito-Semitic languages: from Berber in the north to Southern Cushitic spoken in Tanzania. Omotic, meanwhile, has retained many archaic forms.

Sir John Rhys and Sir John Morris-Jones

The great Welsh philologist Sir John Rhys proposed that the first 'Celtic' inhabitants of Britain were the Irish Gaels. Rhys has the following:

> Before the Brythonic came the Goidels (Gaels) had presumably occupied the island [by 500 B.C]..... the Goidels have already been represented as a mixed race, and when later this mixed Goidelic population became one people with the Brythonic, the result was still more composite; one may see Welsh people of the present day is made up of three elements: the Aboriginal, the Goidelic, and the Brythonic. It would be unsafe to assume that the later predominates for the 'Celtic' invaders, both Goidelic and Brythonic, may have come in comparatively small numbers, not to mention that the Aboriginal race, having been here possibly for thousands of years before the first Indo-Europeans arrived, may have had such an advantage in the matter of acclimatization, that it alone survives in force. [Rhys]

It is natural to assume that the Irish Gaels arrived before the Brythonic tribes. Many Gaelic place names have, over a period of time, changed into Brythonic. Anthropologists such as Beddoe observed the so-called 'Irish type' in the rural districts of England.

Beddoe made the following observations:

> If I am correct in my belief, based on observation, that persons of thoroughly Gaelic aspect are common in the Mendips and Exmoor [SW England], while we know of no Irish immigration into the Mendips during historical period, and while these are precisely the districts into which a conquered race might flee for refuge.

Peate, the assistant Keeper of the National Museum of Wales (1932), completely rejected the idea of the Gaels being the first people to settle Britain:

> It remains, however, reasonably certain that there are no Goidelic [Irish] elements of pre-Brythonic [Welsh] date in Britain; there is no evidence of any traces of Goidelic placenames of prehistoric dates in this country.

According to Peate [quoting Hubert], 'the least controversial element [in 'Celtic'] is the linguistic one.'

Early Welsh scholars, from Edward Lhuyd (1707) to Rhys (1900), accepted the antiquity of the Gaels in Britain. *"I am of the opinion,"* wrote Anwyl *[1909], "that Irish was carried into Ireland through Britain, and that on its way thither it spread to Wales."*

The population of South Wales were neither Gaelic nor Brythonic but belonged to an 'aboriginal' population, direct descendants of Ibero-African tribes. The Roman Tacitus described the Silures as a dark-skinned race with twisted curly hair. Early Irish settlers probably dominated northern Wales, but in the southern half of the country the population remained isolated from their neighbors - the Silures did not extend into central Wales (Powys); the Black Mountains seem to have been an effective barrier.

If, as Peate suggests, the Irish did not settle in Wales before the Brythonic tribes, the question of who the Silures were remains unanswered by him. He suggests that 'the least controversial [in 'Celtic'] is the linguistic one' - does not actually hold true.

In 1909 Anwyl made the following observation:

> There are several river names in the district [Mid Wales], which elude derivation on sound phonological principles from any known Indo-European roots...... there are many river names in Wales........ it is noticeable to that many of the pre 'Celtic' names fall into two types of according to suffix with which they end. Many examples end in -wy, which by the way, nowhere occurs in Welsh as a separate word meaning 'water,' as some have supposed. Then again many of these river name's end in ly suffix quite distinct from wy another suffix of this guide is ach we have also search suffixes as i o n a n it is the existence of these various suffix forms that confirm the suspicion that these words if we only had the key to them and not meaningless.

So, we have a number of river names in Wales that cannot be derived from 'Celtic'; these include the following: Conwy, Mynwy, Usk, Bidan, and Onneu.

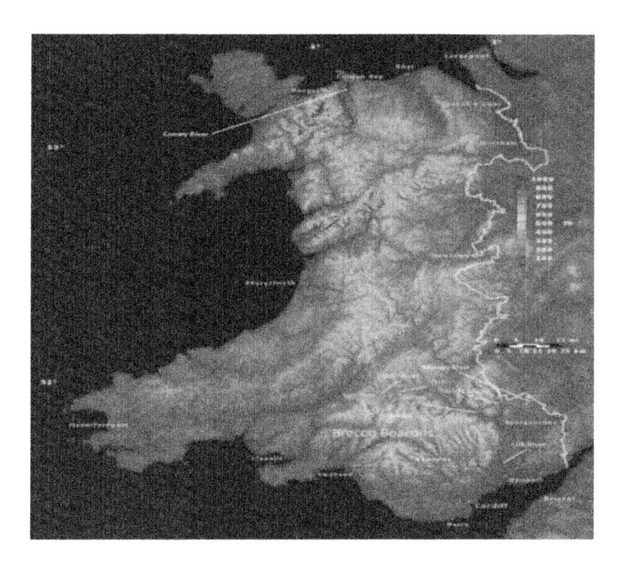

Non-'Celtic' River names, Wales
Modified image of Wales attributed SRTM by PawelS, creative commons via Wikimedia Commons.

Sir John Morris-Jones (17 October 1864 – 1929), public domain.

Rhys suggested to Morris-Jones that the reason why Welsh and Irish were very different to other Indo-European languages was due to a 'pre-Aryan' language (i.e., a non-Indo-European language). Morris-Jones had communicated the theory of an ancient Egyptian substratum within Insular 'Celtic' to John Rhys as early as 1891.

Morris-Jones was born Jones, at Trefor in the parish of Llandrygarn, Anglesey. In 1868 the family moved to Llanfairpwllgwyngyll where he received elementary education. In 1876 he entered Friars School, Bangor. In

1879 the headmaster of Friars School, Daniel Lewis Lloyd, was appointed to Christ College, Brecon, and Morris-Jones accompanied him there. In 1883 he attended Jesus College, Oxford, where he graduated with honors in mathematics in 1887.

While at Oxford, Morris-Jones studied Welsh books and manuscripts in the Bodleian Library, and attended lectures by Sir John Rhys (1840–1915), the Professor of 'Celtic'. Morris-Jones and Rhys prepared an edition of The Elucidarium and other tracts in Welsh from Llyvyr agkyr Llandewivrevi A.D. 1346 (The Book of the Anchorite of Llanddewi Brefi), a collection of Medieval Welsh manuscripts in Jesus College Library, which they published in 1894. Morris-Jones was one of the original members of Cymdeithas Dafydd ap Gwilym[cy] (the Dafydd ap Gwilym Society), which was founded in 1886 and is still a students' society.

In 1889 Morris-Jones was appointed as a lecturer in Welsh at the University College of North Wales, Bangor (now Bangor University) where he was promoted to professor in 1895. His works included Welsh Orthography (1893) and A Welsh Grammar, Historical and Comparative: phonology and accidence (1913). He established and edited the literary journal, Y Beirniad [cy], published between 1911 and 1919. In 1918 he was knighted.

The following extract summaries his theories:

> It might be suggested as an explanation, that the earlier Celts mixed with a non-Indo-European race, whose language had this syntactic peculiarity of Neo-'Celtic' [Hamito-Semitic] as regards the position of the verb, and that they thus evolved the Goidelic language [Irish, Scottish & Manx]. The next stage might similarly be supposed to be a mixing of the Brythonic with the Goidels of the description just suggested, when it became the turn of the latter to be conquered, the result being that Brythonic emerged, having indirectly acquired some of the linguistic peculiarities of the Aboriginal inhabitants of Gaul, Britain, or both. Whatever the real explanation may prove to be, it is needless to say, to postulate a pre-'Celtic' race whose language was characterized by the chief peculiarities distinguishing Neo-'Celtic' from Gaulish.

Rhys believed that the Goidelic [Irish] and the Aboriginal elements were strongest in North and South Wales, while mid-Wales, according to his observations, was marked out by the Gaulish affinities of the Powys dialect.

The study conducted by Morris-Jones was completed in 1898. It is rather lengthy and would be of interest to those who have a deep knowledge of grammar. The paper is reproduced in the Appendix, located at the end of this edition.

The syntax of 'Celtic' languages has puzzled linguists ever since the Bible was translated into Welsh. The story of how this unfolded is worth retelling here.

The Problem of 'Celtic' Syntax

Discussions about the connection between 'Celtic' and Semitic, particularly Hebrew, start to appear during the 1600's AD, when the Bible was translated into Welsh. The early scholars concentrated on the strong similarities between Semitic and 'Celtic'. John-Morris (1898) deviated from this tradition by concentrating his efforts towards the so-called 'Hamitic' African languages [Egyptian and Berber] rather than Semitic. He reached the conclusion that, 'Neo-'Celtic' was related to the languages spoken in Africa's northern and eastern regions.' It must be remembered that he was the first chair of Celtic Studies at Oxford University and was the highest authority on 'Celtic' in the entire country.

It should be note that the idea of a connection between the 'Celts' and Africa did not begin with Rhys or John-Morris.

In 1843 the reverend R. Garnett made the following criticism:

> One of the latest writers on the subject ['Celtic' language], Mr. Johnes, though he regards Asia as the cradle of the race, thinks it probable that the Celts did not, as is commonly supposed pass by the Euxine and the Danube in their progress westwards, but by Syria and Africa into Spain, and afterwards into Gaul. The serious objections to this hypothesis are: There is no mention whatever in ancient history of Celts either in Syria, Egypt, or Mauretania. Ancient writers uniformly represent the Celts as intruders from eastwards upon the Iberians. There is no positive traces of 'Celticism' in any known African language: while every Indo-European dialect, from Hindustan to Portugal shows unequivocal proofs either of admixture with "Celtic" elements or of a community of origin, and not infrequently both.

Let us examine the above argument carefully. The first point he makes is -

"no mention of Celts in Syria, Egypt, or Mauretania" - however, this is somewhat incorrect, since we have seen that every ancient book, both Irish and Welsh sources, mention those countries. The Cymry (Welsh) claim to have wandered in Mauretania before migrating northwards to Iberia, and eventually landing in Cornwall. The Cymry boldly state that they came from the land of Haf or the Land of Summer.

The second point made is true, the 'Celts' of south-west Europe expanded from the areas east of the Iberian tribes; slowly moving southwards and reaching the furthest southern corners of the Iberian peninsula. But these expansions were relatively recent in history; the first migrations taking place between 800 BC and 500 BC.

With regards the third point is true, 'there are no traces of Celticism in Africa', as stated by Reverend Garnett is correct. However, there are traces of the Gaels and Cymry in Africa; it must be remembered that they did not call themselves 'Celts' or Keltoi. They may have shared a linguistic connection with the 'Celts' or Gauls but they were not the same people.

In 1857 Pritchard, noted the large number of Semitic words found in some Indo-European languages:

> It must be allowed, that the Semitic dialects constitute a very distinct department of languages, which can by no means be associated or brought into the same class with Indo-European languages, some features have been pointed out which display a remarkable analogy to the well-known characters of Hebrew and its dialects; I shall only instance the system of pronominal suffixes. This point in which the 'Celtic', at the same time that it appears to be the least artificial and grammatically cultivated of the Indo-European languages, forms an intermediate link between them and Semitic; or perhaps indicates a state of transition from the characters of one of these classes of languages to those of the other.

Professor Kuno Meyer [Professor of Celtic, Berlin University] explored the affinity between Welsh and Coptic. Professor Meyer (1858-1919) founded the School of Irish Learning (1903) in Dublin, founded and edited the Ériu Journal, and in 1911 he became Professor of 'Celtic' Studies at the Friedrich Wilhelm University (Berlin) in 1911 - he was an important supporter of the revival of modern Irish.

The reverend John Davies, in his work, 'The Connection of Keltic With The Teutonic', made some interesting comments on the subject:

> The Goidels and Irish are, however, still more closely connected with the Semitic family, and there is therefore an element of truth in the theory proposed by Sir W. Betham and others, of the Phoenician origin of the Irish language; but the truth which they were able to discover was so exaggerated and distorted by them as to become practicality false. There is here a very interesting field of research, containing many important truths connected with the early history of both Semitic and Indo-European."

Another scholar, Louis Albert Necker, promoted the idea that the Gaels had an Eastern origin in 1822:

> The examination which we are about to make of the manners of the Gaels will furnish us with some interesting peculiarities of their connection with certain customs of the ancient people of the East; without pretending that such coincidences are sufficient multiplied to authorize us to consider them as proofs, these resemblances are striking enough to deserve consideration by those who, from henceforth, undertake the laborious and difficult task of elucidating the origin of the Gaels. Considering then the ancient tractions of the first inhabitants of this country having arrived from the East, and of the analogy of the Gaelic language to the Hebrew. [p84, L.A. Necker, A Voyage to The Hebrides, or Western Isles of Scotland, 1822]

Many early writers were aware of the affinity between 'Celtic' and Semitic; the research by Rhys, the head of 'Celtic' Studies at Oxford University, and Professor John Morris-Jones promoted the connection with the Hamitic languages; most of his academic peers warmly supported his theories.

There was one exception, Professor H. H. Johnson criticized Professor Morris-Jones for making a connection between 'Celtic' and Hamito-Semitic languages. Johnson believed, *'that this was an old evil dream.'* Professor Morris-Jones dealt with Johnson's criticism with far superior intellect and dignity. A summary of that debate appeared in the 'Celtic' Review [1904].

In 1904 Johnson submitted his views opposing the substratum theory titled *'The Heresy of Connecting Welsh with Semitic, etc.'* In the same issue of The 'Celtic' Review, Sir William Preece submitted his article supporting the substratum theory with his paper 'Egyptians and Celts.' He begins:

> A recent enforced visit of long duration in Egypt has supplied me with sufficient wisdom of ancient Egypt to enable me, I hope, to excite some new consideration." .... the worship of Isis (Ceridwen?) was brought into Egypt by a tribe called 'Pharaoh'. They came into Wales from Cornwall, and they introduced the worship of the eagle and wolf.

The title of Johnson's article, *'The Heresy of Connecting Welsh with Semitic, [1904],* can be regarded as an openly prejudiced, and racist response. He knew nothing about ethnology, and his understanding of syntax was zero. Johnson's article begins:

> Welsh has neither part nor lot in Shem and Ham. One had thought that this had been an article of creed for a century or more. And yet in these latter days come. The Welsh People, y Brynmor Jones, with its appendix by Professor Morris-Jones of Bangor; Sir W. Preece of Caernarvon on Welsh and Egyptian languages, obiter dicta of Principal Rhys of Oxford. These all, directly or indirectly, seem to find a connection between Cymric and Semitic (and Hamitic). But one had hoped, and in part believed, that all this was an old evil dream that had passed.

In response to Sir William Preece's connection between Welsh and Coptic, Johnson says:

> 'surely as good Welshmen, little cause to connect ourselves with illiterate beggars, the Copts, or the Nubians (or Berbers), pure Negroes, as black as those of Senegal or Congo, with woolly hair.'

In defense of his views, Johnson suggested that both professor Kuno Meyer and Anwyl rejected Morris-Jones's theory. According to Johnson, Anwyl said the following:

> "these derivations of Welsh make one ashamed for the honour

> of the country."

This statement was proven to be untrue: and was challenged by Professor Morris-Jones.

Professor Morris-Jones replied:

> "Since Professor Johnson speaks of professor Anwyl and Professor Meyer, as sharing his views, that both have dissociated themselves from him, the former publicly in The Welsh Leader, the latter in a letter to me."

The debate between the two schools of thought makes fascinating reading, especially considering it was more than a century ago. Johnson's main criticisms of the African substratum theory proposed are as follows:

> [Johnson] "One may, of course say at once that there are an extraordinary resemblance between Cymric, on the one hand, and Arabic, Hebrew, and Hamitic (e.g., Berber) on the other. These resemblances pervade accident and syntax, as well as vocabulary."
>
> [Johnson] "The similarity of pronominal suffixes, I consider as accidental...........Indo-European is Indo-European, and must not be mixed, however slightly, except as regards loan-words, with other great divisions of human speech.
>
> [Johnson] "Now for the rationale. In every language the verb is the soul of the sentence, and it is naturally and rightly put first. Especially is this true when the subject is secondary. Even in English poetry we find such a strong statement as - 'Spake full well in language quaint and olden a bard who dwelleth on the castle Rhine' and in French or Italian any subject followed by adjectives, relative phrase, etc., must regularly follow its verb. Nature itself points to this system."

Professor Morris-Jones responded to Johnson's attack in an article published in The 'Celtic' Review:

> [Morris-Jones] "Professor H. H. Johnson's attack upon me in the October number of The 'Celtic' Review makes it necessary that I should say a few words in reply. I say attack upon me,

for that is, in the main, what it is, ...The title of my paper is 'Pre-Aryan Syntax in Insular 'Celtic'; it deals with syntax only, indeed, it is expressly stated in it that 'I confined myself strictly to syntax and have not ventured to suggest any phonetic equations'."

[Morris-Jones]

"He has apparently never seen 'The Welsh People'; he speaks of it as the work of Brynmor-Jones, without mentioning Professor Rhys; all he knows of my paper apparently is a reference or two at the 'Celtic' Congress, the rest of his description he supplied his own imagination."

[Morris-Jones]

"I found that the ancient Egyptians formed his sentence in exactly the same way as the modern Welshman forms his. I compare 'Celtic' with Hamitic syntax, not with Arabic at all, ...I have distinctly stated 'Celtic' syntax agrees with Hamitic."

[In response to Johnson's statement, that Indo-European has not mixed with other languages, Morris-Jones gave the following reply]

[Morris-Jones]

"There are many Welsh and Irish words which cannot be explained from Indo-European roots, and some of them may possibly be derived from a pre-'Celtic' tongue. With regards to syntax, however, the case is different; the structure of the old language may very well, and frequently does, persist in the new. An extreme example is Pigeon English, The peculiar construction of Welsh and Irish, which have always puzzled our grammarians, are therefore exactly the non-Indo-European element which we should expect to find. Some years ago, philologists denied the possibility of mixture in language, in the very teeth of the fact that mixed languages do actually exist."

Johnson's statement on the position of the verb, is to say the least, ridiculous. In Indo-European languages the word order is Subject-Object-Verb (SOV) In the African (Hamitic) languages the general pattern is Verb-Subject-Object (VSO); Irish and Welsh follow the African pattern and not the Indo-European pattern.

[Morris-Jones]

> on the position of the verb - "In Neo-'Celtic' tongues [Hamitic] the verb comes first in every simple sentence without exception; if a noun comes first the sentence is a mixed one. This is true of Hamitic also. But in Indo-European the verb naturally comes last. Professor Johnson's answer is that it may come first in Indo-European - 'Spake full well .... a bard.' He does not see that there is all the difference in the world between language in which it must be put first, and one in which it may in artificial diction, be put first. He might as well argue that there is no difference between a man and a dog because the dog may stand on its hind legs."

The reverend M. Maclennan gave his view on the subject:

> "In neither can Professor Johnson's criticism be said to be in the least degree successful. He tells us, for example, that 'in every language' the verb is naturally and rightly put first. We rub our eyes and read this over again to make sure that the mistake is not ours. One is astonished to find the words in cold print. Can this be the true order? A careful survey of his own article shows that scarcely a single sentence begins in this way. One of three things must follow - English is not a language, or Professor Johnson does not know to write it, or this statement is sadly mistaken."

Maclennan rejects Johnson's view on the position of the verb. He says:

> "the reverse of what Professor Johnson maintains is the natural order. If he could manage to stumble so in matter in which we are all more or less competent to form an opinion,

> what guarantee can he give us that he is not doing the same in regions into which we need not pretend to follow him?"

Modern 'Celtic' scholars tend, in general, to remain silent on this subject. The German philologist, H. Wagner, was an exception. He supported the African substratum theory [1969]:

> "...........most of the many features of insular 'Celtic' have analogies in Basque, Berber, ancient Egyptian, Semitic, and even in Bantu African languages." [H. Wagner]

Wagner's belief that the Lewys Atlantic type languages of Europe belonged to a larger Eurafrican type is also supported by ethnological data. The Atlantic type languages corresponds to the Dolmen regions of Western Europe. The Megalithic monuments of Europe were constructed by settlers from Africa and the Mediterranean region while the Indo-European speakers [proto-Indo-European] were still living somewhere in Russia. The Dolmen builders spread a culture that has left traces in many parts of the world. These ancient structures were designed to be a link with the 'unseen world' - a tribute to the ancestors. The practice of building these monuments continued in other parts of the world, long after they ceased to be built in Western Europe. The building of dolmens continued in Madagascar and Ethiopia long after construction ceased in Europe.

The African substratum in Insular 'Celtic' cannot be attributed to a single source. I believe it would be more realistic, considering the antiquity of Hamito-Semitic (Afro-asiatic), to imagine a multi linguistic contribution from Africa. The reader should remember that the Berber language family is the least differentiated Afro-asiatic language. Hence, it represents a fairly recent expansion across North Africa from an original homeland on the Nile. The Berber dialect spoken in Siwa [Egypt] is mutually intelligible to the Berber speakers in Mauritania; separated by a distance of 4271km. These Berber dialects became differentiated around 100 BC; the rapid expansion of the Berbers was due to the introduction of the camel from East Africa.

Poulnabrone *Dolmen, County Clare, Ireland*

(attributed to Kglavin, creative commons via Wikimedia Commons)

The southern region of Algeria, now inhabited by the Tuaregs, was once the home of the Chadic speaking Hausa. The expansion of the Berber language resulted in Chadic speakers being pushed out by the Tuaregs. The Hausa migrated southwards into Mali, Niger, and Nigeria. The 'extinct' languages of North Africa have yet to be researched. The ancient migrations within Africa reveal a complicated interaction between different language groups, something worthy of further research.

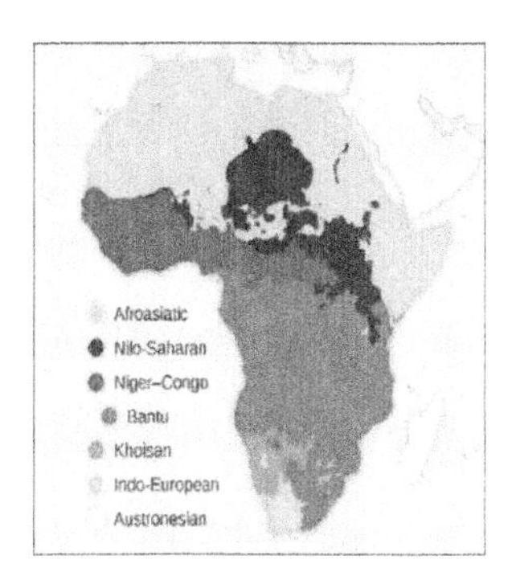

Map of Languages of Africa,
(attributed to SUMI creative commons via Wikimedia Commons.)

Antiquity of African Languages

Proto-Indo-European, the ancestral 'parent' language of most European languages, was spoken around 3000 B.C. somewhere in southern Russia. This relatively young date for proto-Indo-European contrast sharply with the great antiquity of the individual members of Hamito-Semitic (Afro-asiatic) and Nilo-Saharan.

If we compare the relationship of Ethiopic to South Arabian languages, and Greek to Hittite; we find that the latter became separate languages around 2000 B.C. Compare this with a comparison between small subsection within Semitic, Tigrayan, and Modern South Arabian, Mahra, which became separated from each other between 3300 B.C. and 2600 B.C. This illustrates the obvious greater antiquity of Hamito-Semitic (Afro-asiatic).

The antiquity of the Cushitic languages is illustrated by comparing the separation dates within the members of this language family. The differences within Cushitic are greater than those within Semitic. The lexical resemblance between Oromo of Ethiopia and Beja of northern Sudan, is less than 1%. The internal differences within Cushitic are greater than any other members of Hamito-Semitic (Afro-asiatic).

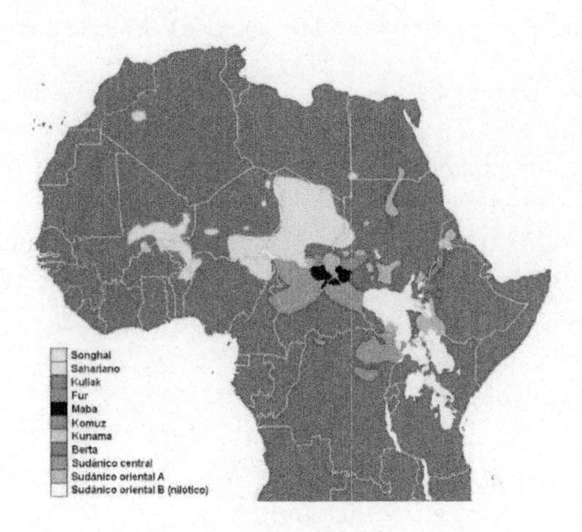

Distribution of Nilo-Saharan Languages
attributed to Maulucioni, creative commons via Wikimedia Commons.

The Nilo-Saharan language super family goes back to an ancestral language spoken around 8000 B.C. or earlier. This language family extends from the Chad to Tanzania. The possible influence of this language family on 'Celtic', Basque, and ancient languages in Mesopotamia deserves further consideration.

The connection between Nubian and Basque has been investigated by several linguists *[see H. Schuchardt 'Nubisch und Baskisch' and Leo Reinisch 'Die Sprachliche Stellung des Nubia]*. On comparing a word list of 100, Basque was shown to have a 15% common vocabulary with Berber, and a 5% common vocabulary with Caucasus [Georgian] languages. Although there are some features that 'Celtic' and Basque have in common, the relationship is not remarkably close. The ancient inhabitants of the Caucasus mountains were, according to Herodotus, possibly related to the ancient Egyptians. The Sumerian and the Elamite languages share many similarities with the Caucasus languages; both are agglutinative.

The Nilotic languages are separated by at least 1000 miles from lowland Cushitic. And yet, *"Shilluk, Dinka, Nuer, Acholi, Lango and Luo"*, Fleming proclaimed, *"all have specifically Somali forms in the form of loan words in Nilotic."* The Cushitic loan words found in Nandi, Suk, Turkana, and Masai, are derived from Rendille and Somali. This clearly shows that the migrations patterns and interactions between different African tribes needs to be revised and seen from an African perspective [rather than a Eurocentric viewpoint].

Distribution of Nilotic languages
attributed to Davius, creative commons via Wikimedia Commons.

For example, the ancestors of the Masai migrated from a place called Endikir-e-Kerio [possibly Afarland or Djibouti]; a place believed to be far north of their present location in the Masai Mara. The substratal relationship between Somali and southern Sudanese Nilotic deserves further research.

C. Cardale Luck in his 1926 publication, The Origin of the Maasai and Kindred African tribes and of Bornean Tribes, suggested a connection between the Nilotic tribes, such as the Turkana and Maasai, with the Canaanites:

> Maasai-this name written more phonetically according to Hollis is Maasae and comes very near to the Hebrew Manasay, meaning "one who causes to forget." We have thus the Ma-a-sae the first clan of which tribe is that of L' Aiser the first family of which clan is called Gidon. The exact equivalent and sequence is found in the Biblical records of the half tribe of Manasseh that would have gone into exile into Egypt. The name of this tribe is as seen Ma-na-say the first clan of which was Abi-ezer or Je-ezer the great hero of which clan was the judge, Gideon, so famous in the history of the Israelites. The 0l oibonok, i.e .. the elders of the Maasai all claim that they come of the family of Gidon, and according to their ancient traditions the founder of this family, to whom they trace their pedigree, was one Kidonoi. (The rest of the evidence to be drawn from this very interesting tradition concerning their elders will be dealt with in another chapter). The other three clans of the Maasai are Il Mengana, Il Mokesen, and Il Molelyan. They would appear to sub-divide and translate as follows: - Il Me-'ngana=The people of Canaan, 'ngana

> probably an abbreviation for Canaan. Il Mo-kesen=The people appointed, from the Hebrew kese meaning, "appointed." Notice the similarity to the well-known term "The chosen people." Il-Mo-'l-elyan=The people of the Most High, from the Hebrew elyon = "Most High,"

He compared the Maasai language with Canaanite:

> Maasai: Amala river /Canaanite: Amala
>
> Maasai: Moleyan /Canaanite: elyon = most high
>
> Maasai: Kisongo /Canaanite: Kishon,waters of Megiddo

He further suggests:

> Esubat 'n olon means thus in present day Maasai good day," but Esubat is so like the Hebrew Shabbath that one cannot doubt that these words are derived from the same source. And more especially so when one considers the olon, which is also the Maasai for Sun. We believe this word to be derived from the Hebrew elyon, meaning "most high," which is equally applicable to olon as sun (Eng-golon=the power, authority), and to Esubat 'n olon which would thus come to have had the original meaning of "The Sabbath of the Most High," which is exactly the sense in which it stood to the anoint Israelites, and stands to the Jew of to-day. This is an extremely interesting example of how words can have come to acquire an entirely altered meaning in course of time. [Cardale, 1926]

The flow of people from Africa to Asia in ancient times is now largely ignored. The old theories of Hommel [1897] and Petrie helped shine a light on ancient migrations that took place across the Red Sea. They proposed an Elamite migration into East Africa and Egypt. Glaser argued that from the 12th Dynasty onwards a new people made an appearance along the Nile, the Kashi in Nubia. Interestingly, a name originally applied to Elam, in Mesopotamia. The Kassites conquered Elam between 2000 BC, and 1800 BC. On this subject Ripley noticed the remnants of black-skinned Persians:

> "finally, our third subtype of the Persian occurs among the Suzians [Elam]. Look at our portrait [see W.Z. Ripley 'Races of Europe'p.448] of one of these - is not the strain of 'negroid'

> blood at once apparent! Notice the flattened and open nose, the thick lips and black hair and eyes. We have reached the confines of India, Here we meet the first traces of the aboriginal population underlying the Hindoos [Dravidians]. It includes all the native Indian Hill tribes and extends away off overseas into Melanesia." [W.Z. Ripley 'Races of Europe]

According to Wagner [1980], *"Chadic, Nubian, and Cushitic provide a very old link between Asia and Africa."* Hommel proposed the theory of a migration of Elamites from Iraq into Nubia and the Horn of Africa. While Petrie believed, *"the Falcon tribe migrated from Mesopotamia, settled in Somalia, and then moved along the Nile before finally conquering Egypt."* I believe the opposite is true - Nilo-Saharan (Nubian, etc.) and Cushitic speakers spread out of Africa and settled in Arabia, passing into the Caucasus region, and eventually settling in Western Europe. Herodotus, writing in the 5th century B.C., confirms the theory of an African colonization of the Caucasus region:

> "Still the Egyptians said that they believe the Colchians to be descended from the army of Sesostris [1971 BC. - 1928 BC.]. My own conjectures were founded first on the fact that they are both black-skinned and have woolly hair...........they also, in their mode of life and in their language resemble one another." [Herodotus Book II]

Heinrich Wagner (b.1923) was a major supporter of the African Substratum Theory. He was an accomplished scholar. He was the chair of Germanic Philology at the University of Utrecht by the age of twenty-eight. Later he became Professor of Germanic at the University of Basil., and by 1958 was appointed Chair of 'Celtic' and Comparative Philology at Queen's University, Belfast. In 1979, he accepted a Professorship at School of 'Celtic' Studies, Dublin. He mastered the Irish language, including regional dialects of Kerry and Donegal.

The connection between Irish Gaelic and Cushitic was explored in detail by Wagner [1969]. He concluded that 'chain-alliteration, typical of Archaic Irish verse and rhythmical prose, is also found in Somali and Meroitic [Ancient Kush] and Ancient Egyptian.' Wagner passionately believed that chain-alliteration of the early Irish type was introduced by Africans.

Byrne [1885] noticed that the lilting type of intonation found in Ireland and Wales was the same in the languages of North Africa. Sean nós, the old Irish singing style, is derived from an African source. - probably a legacy of the ancient African Formorians. T. Gwyn Jones [1912] compared the Welsh Hwyl, a chant-like singing style, with the Muezzin call to pray in Islam. Sean nós is identical to the signing styles found across Africa - from Guinea to

Ethiopia. Quinn [1984] was inspired to explore the connections between the Gaels, North Africa, and even the Tartars of Russia in his four-part documentary Atlantean. The connection between Ural Altaic singing style with both Gaelic and Hamito-Semitic (Afro-asiatic) singing styles recalls the old stories of the Finns and Cushites as the 'aboriginal' inhabitants of Ireland. The oldest African element in 'Insular Celtic' probably belongs to Nilo-Saharan, Chadic, Cushitic, and Ancient Egyptian. One can speculate that the affinities between 'Insular Celtic', Berber, and Semitic could belong to a much later era. However, having said this, it has to be admitted that there appears to be a special relationship between the Gaels, Berber, Punic and Chadic people (add to this the R1b-V88 tribes of West Africa). The role of Chadic and Nilo-Saharan still needs further attention. 'Celtic' has retained many archaic elements - that can only be explained by the African Substratum Theory.

Séamus Mac Mathúna University of Ulster gives the following summary of Wagner's work:

> **Research into Irish dialects reinforced his interest and belief in linguistic typology. He had come to the conclusion at an early stage in his career that important aspects of 'Celtic' grammar could not be adequately explained within a strict Neo-Grammarian framework of Indo-European. Under the influence of Pokorny, and following Morris Jones, he became convinced that there was a relationship between the Hamito-Semitic languages and Insular 'Celtic'. An introductory course in Arabic in 1943/44 — the same year in which he started the study of Old Irish with Pokorny — confirmed him in this view. His position on the nature of the relationship tended to fluctuate, ranging from an acceptance of a** Hamito-Semitic substratum in Insular 'Celtic' to the more moderate view that there existed in the British Isles, prior to the arrival of the Celts, a population which spoke languages or dialects typologically, though not necessarily genealogically, related to Hamito-Semitic. [Etudes Celtiques, vol. 26, 1989. pp. 215-217]

Julius Pokorny (b.1887) was the chair of 'Celtic' Philology at Berlin University in 1920. He was a leading scholar in 'Celtic' studies and produced two volumes of 'Indo-European Etymological Dictionary' in 1959.

Professor Kuno Meyer (b. 1858) was another accomplished scholar who supported the African Substratum Theory. He was appointed as Professor of

'Celtic' studies at the Friedrich-Wilhelms-Universität, Berlin, in 1911. Kuno Meyer was the most talented translator of Gaelic poetry into the English language. He founded the School of Irish Learning in Dublin (1903), but sadly his name was removed from the Roll of Honour in Dublin City Hall in 1915 because England had gone to war with Germany. Unfortunately, he died in 1919 before this was rectified once Ireland became independent from the British.

Denis Fahey lists Kuno Meyer's academic achievements:

> Before the war, he had been a respected academic in the United Kingdom, recognized by his peers as the greatest living authority on Old Irish language and literature, the founder of the school of Irish learning and its journal Ériu, a professor of Teutonic languages and, later, honorary professor of 'Celtic' studies at Liverpool, a visiting professor of 'Celtic' studies at the Royal Irish Academy, a Freeman of Dublin and Cork and a doctor of the Universities of Oxford, Wales and St Andrews.......At a meeting of Clan-na-Gael, in Brooklyn on December 6th, he hinted that an Irish Brigade was being formed by Casement from among prisoners of war to fight for Germany and he promised that "when Germany obtains the great objects for which she fights, the nations that now bear the yoke of England will not be forgotten". Not surprisingly, he was excoriated by former colleagues for his ingratitude to the country that had given him a livelihood for 27 years, while the Corporations of Dublin and Cork rescinded the honours, they had given him..........in 1920, the two Corporations posthumously restored his name to their rolls of Freemen. [Denis Fahey, Digitisation could turn Meyer's dream for ancient Irish poetry and prose into reality, The Irish Times, July 1, 2019]

Professor Kuno Meyer, Professor of Celtic Friedrich-Wilhelms-Universität, Berlin

(attributed to Public domain, via Wikimedia Commons.)

Ranko Matasović's very comprehensive paper *'The substratum in Insular 'Celtic'* offers some intriguing new avenues to investigate. Matasović's insight is incredibly important because he expands the search for the substratum to include other African languages beyond Hamito-Semitic (Afro-asiatic):

> Orin Gensler, in his dissertation (1993) applied refined statistical methods showing that the syntactic parallels between Insular 'Celtic' and Afro-Asiatic cannot be attributed to chance. The crucial point is that these parallels include features that are otherwise rare cross-linguistically but co-occur precisely in those two groups of languages. This more or less amounts to a proof that there was some connection between Insular 'Celtic' and Afro-Asiatic at some stage in prehistory, but the exact nature of that connection is still open to speculation. Namely, it is not necessary to assume that the British Isles had been populated by speakers of Afro-Asiatic languages prior to the arrival of the Celts: they could also have been populated by speakers of unidentifiable, extinct languages which shared a number of typological characteristics with Afro-Asiatic due to their being spoken in the same macro-area encompassing prehistoric Western Europe and North-western Africa. [Matasović]

The comparison between 'Celtic' and Afro-Asiatic by Graham R. Isaac (National University of Ireland, Galway) presents a substantial lengthy argument and concludes (surprisingly) against any substratum contact:

> The position I have taken in this paper is certainly not that the AA/IC [i.e., Afro-asiatic & Insular 'Celtic'] contact theory is unproven and unprovable, therefore, to be rejected. On the contrary: it has been my intention to demonstrate as clearly as possible that it is simply wrong. But perhaps I am being too rigorous. Perhaps, in my insistence on details of argumentative logic and objective testing of the theory against real-world data, I am making unreasonable demands of a 'probabilistic' theory, by its nature unprovable, but no less valid for that. In case that is so, I may myself be allowed to end with an unprovable argument of plausibility. I can hardly be criticized for doing so by those who insist that their own theories are of the same nature. The central empirical postulate of the AA/IC contact theory is that ancient and early medieval Europe, whether as a whole or in the west alone, was permeated by a language or group of languages, which, throughout a period of significantly more than 3000 years, much of it in the full light of extant linguistic history and geography, remained completely invisible and typologically, unwaveringly stable. How rigorous a 'proof' do we need of the implausibility of that? [Graham R. Isaac]

It seems that this Galway academic has decided that the theory is implausible; or to be more accurate set out to prove that it was implausible; while we have seen that, Matasović convincingly states *'there is proof that there was some connection between Insular 'Celtic' and Afro-Asiatic at some stage in prehistory'*; which academic is correct?

Matasović makes clear points of comparison, that can be useful in identifying the source of the substratum in 'Celtic':

> The inter-dental fricative /þ/, is found very frequently in languages of Western Europe (including Insular 'Celtic' languages) .... but also, in many varieties of Berber (e.g., in Kabyle) and in several Atlantic languages of the Niger-Congo family in NW Africa (e.g., Balanta). The initial consonant mutations, or regular alternations of initial consonants caused by the grammatical category of the preceding word, or the grammatical construction of the word in question, are extremely rare cross-linguistically. All Insular 'Celtic' languages have this feature, Interestingly, the same phenomenon is found in a number of Atlantic languages in NW Africa, including Fulbe. Proposed independent definite articles

> characterize most languages of Western Europe, including Insular 'Celtic' languages - this type of definite article is also found in many Atlantic languages (Wolof, Balanta) and also some Mande languages of NW Africa (e.g., Bambara). This illustrates that areally [i.e., not comparable] significant features of Insular 'Celtic' go beyond Afro-Asiatic [Matasović]

The Wodaabe are a subgroup of the Fulani. They are found over a vast territory extending across much of western and central Africa. The Fulani are one of the biggest tribal groups in Africa. They are found in most West African countries and the Sahel, across central Africa, and eastwards in Sudan, and Eritrea.

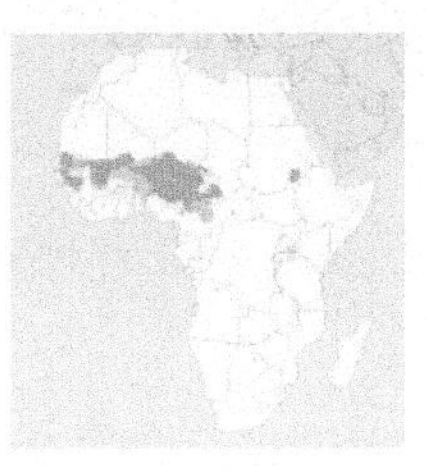

Map of Fula language
attributed to Noahedits, creative commons via Wikimedia Commons.

It is quite likely that they once dominated the northern coast of Africa and the islands in the Mediterranean Sea. They could have been part of the Sea People coalition that attempted to invade ancient Egypt.

Wodaabe performing a Yaake dance. Niger 1997,
Attributed to Dan Lundberg, creative commons via Wikimedia Commons.

Tatyana A. Mikhailova in her paper, *'Macc, Cailinand Ceile - an Altaic Element in Celtic'* shows hostility to the African Substratum Theory. She starts her paper with the following statement which clearly reveals the authors hostility to the subject:

> The substratum theory has been so compromised by numerous fantastic speculations (Basque, Uralic, Altaic, Kartvelian, Hamito-Semitic, etc.), that the problem itself become a perpetum mobile of 'Celtic' and Germanic studies. (Tatyana A. Mikhailova]

The author speculates on various 'Celtic' connections between Altaic and other Asian languages; however, she regards the connection with Hamito-Semitic (Afro-asiatic) as simply fantastic speculation.

Why?

Tatyana A. Mikhailova quotes Pokorny, when it fits with her views, and speculates that *'there is no doubt that there exists very old connection between the British Isles and the eastern Baltic countries.......an Upper-Paleolithic substratum of an unknown Arctic race which may have been of Uralic origin.'*

Mikhailova explored *'the problematic etymology of the famous Old Irish macc'*, which she begins by 'attempting to render the meaning of this term.'

She proceeds to explains that *'Goidelic and Brythonic form data gives a proto-'Celtic' form *maqw qw -os which has no sure Indo-European etymology.'*

She gives three suggestions for this word; a connection with Germanic **maghu* - son; a specific etymology connection with the idea of growth, or a term that is a loanword from an unknown non-Indo-European language.

Mikhailova obviously does not want to look to Africa as a source, but her conclusion is worth inspecting:

> We now propose the possible presence in central and northern Europe of another branch of Nostratic super family which did not leave direct daughter-language, but which left vague traces in 'Celtic' and Germanic. We suppose that a new approach to the old problem of a Pre- IE substratum in Europe would represent a useful way forward for future investigation. [p20 Tatyana A. Mikhailova, 'Macc, Cailinand Ceile - an Altaic Element in 'Celtic'?]

The belief that *mac* (son of) is of Berber origin has had many supporters for centuries. In 1912, R. N. Bradley described in his book, *'The Maltese Race and The Mediterranean'*, all the similarities he noticed between the Irish and the Berber tribes. He quotes a letter in his possession from Colonel W.G. Macpherson, who remarks on the remarkably close similarity between 'Celtic' and some languages in Africa:

> When I was in Morocco City in 1896, I met a Gaelic-speaking missionary doctor who had come out there and went into the Sus country (Trans-atlas), where Shluh is the language spoken, just as it is the language of the Berber tribes in the Cis-atlas country. He told me that the words seemed familiar to him, and, after listening to the natives speaking among themselves, found they were speaking a Gaelic dialect, much of which he could follow. This confirmed my own observation regarding the names of the Berber tribes I myself had come across, namely the Bini M'Tir, the Bini M'Touga, and the Bini M'Ghil. The Bini is simply the Arabic for Children of and is tacked on by the Arabs to the 'M' of the Berbers, which means 'sons of' and is exactly the same as the Irish 'M' or Gaelic 'Mac' Hence Hamitic language traces the M'Tir, M'Touga, and M'Ghil become in our country the MacTiers, the MacDougalls, and the MacGills. I prepared a paper on this subject, which was read by my friend, Dr. George Mackay of Edinburgh, at the Pan-'Celtic' Congress there in 1907, I think, or it may have been 1908. It caused a leading article to be written in the Scotsman., I believe, but otherwise does not appear to have received much attention. ..... I honestly think that philologists will in time see that I am right and that it is geographically and historically very natural to find a 'Celtic' language amongst the mountain tribes of Morocco, just as we find Celts in Brittany, Cornwall, Wales, Ireland, and Scotland, driven into the mountains and islands. Why not also across the Straits into Morocco and the Atlas?" [p242-243, R. N. Bradley, 1912]

In 1919 Harold Bayley noticed the similar meaning of the Berber and Irish mac:

> In 'Celtic' mako or maga means "I feed" - in Welsh magu means breed, and to nurse; in Welsh magad is' broad. It is to this root that obviously may be assigned the Gaelic Mac or Mc, which means "breed of" or "children of" - In the Isle of

> Man, the inhabitants claimed to be descended from the fairies, whence perhaps the MacAuliffes of Albany originally claimed to be children of the Elf. Among the Berbers of Africa Mac has precisely the same meaning as among the Gaels, and among the Tudas of India mag also means children of, "Surely after this," says a commentator, "the McPhersons and McGregors our England need not hesitate to claim, as Scotch cousins the inhabitants of the Indian peninsula."

Notice how Tatyana A. Mikhailova statement, *'the substratum theory has been so compromised by numerous fantastic speculations,'* does not make sense. She does not show any hostility to the hypothesis of Nostratic super Family, a very wild and speculative idea (to say the least).

The obvious similarities between 'Celtic' and Hamito-Semitic (Afro-asiatic) has been supported by some of the most prominent experts in 'Celtic' studies; however, today it is not given the respect it deserves. The African languages are of greater antiquity and existed several millennia before the birth of Indo-European languages. It is quite strange that linguists cannot agree on language classifications.

The concept of Nostratic language family was conceived by Holger Pedersen and it has found its supporters (mainly in Russia) - namely Merritt Ruhlen, Allan Bomhard, Vladislav Illich-Svitych and Aharon Dolgopolsky. Some supporters of the Nostratic hypothesis refuse to include Hamito-Semitic (Afro-asiatic) - while the concept of Euro-asiatic, proposed by Joseph Greenberg, has been central in the search for a Euro-asiatic super language family - a concept still unproven. One cannot but wonder if this search for an expanded Euro-asiatic proto-family was motivated by a desire to counter Sergi's earlier theory [1900] of Eurafricans colonizing Europe in antiquity.

The Hoax of The Indo-European Language Family

Angela Marcantonio

Before launching into the diverse opinions held by linguists, it is worth giving some time to view-points that are rarely taught in academia. Angela Marcantonio is an associate professor of Linguistics at the University of Rome 'La Sapienza'. She has conducted research between the linguistic connections between proto-languages, and specialized in Finnish, Hungarian, and Ob-Ugric languages.

Professor Marcantonio's refreshing outlook is desperately needed. She brings attention to the Eurocentric bias and flaws that haunt the classification of the Indo-European language family; she questions its validity:

> Chapter X The main thesis of Angela Marcantonio's chapter: Evidence that most Indo-European lexical reconstructions are artefacts of the linguistic method of analysis, is that the methods of historical linguistics, including the comparative method, can be so flexible – by their very nature – that they can be stretched to account for almost any data. This means that the explanatory system runs the risk of becoming dangerously circular, and, therefore, of yielding misleading results – in this case within the field of IE studies. Over the course of about two hundred years of everyday practice of reconstruction within IE the encountered counter-evidence has been typically 'explained away' through all sorts of (often ad-hoc) justifications, so that today one can find hardly any evidence counter to the model. [Angela Marcantonio, associate professor of Linguistics at the University of Rome La Sapienza]

Marcantonio suggests that Eurocentric linguistics have 'fitted the Indo-European data to the model or have made it so flexible that it can fit any data, including potential counter evidence?'

The points raised by professor Marcantonio make sense:

> The leaders and rulers could have been of one ethno-linguistic group, the military base and its economy of another ethno-linguistic group, the Indo-Aryan Levites of a third group, farmers, and their economy of a fourth group, and artisans still of another group.

Professor Marcantonio introduces her paper in the Journal of Eurasian Studies and gives the following conclusion:

> One of the founding principles of the traditional version of the theory was the assumption that morphological paradigms cannot be borrowed, and therefore it is possible to trace genetic inheritance through them. However, we have seen evidence of wholesale paradigm borrowing, based on studies of languages in contact. In any case, some scholars now hold that morphology is less relevant than other factors – but it is

> at present unclear whether, or how, these other factors may be verified or falsified. It has been the purpose of this book to bring to the fore these contradictions and open questions associated with the theory. It is for the reader and the linguistic community to decide the way forward. [Angela Marcantonio (ed). The Indo-European Language Family: Questions about its Status, Journal of Indo-European Studies. Washington DC: Institute of Man (2009)]

Different Opinions Explored

Prominent linguists from late 1800's and early 1900's supported the African Substratum Theory. Vallancey, Wagner, and Pokorny have provided abundant and detailed examples which are difficult to dismiss. Ranko Matasović's investigation into the features in Insular 'Celtic' finds clear parallels in the Hamito-Semitic (Afro-asiatic) language family. However, his conclusion warns us of presuming Hamito-Semitic (Afro-asiatic) as the only source for the substratum - instead, he settles for the possibility of 'the existence of a number of typologically similar languages in Western Europe and North-Western Africa prior to the arrival of the Celts (and other speakers of IE dialects) in no way implies that they all belonged to a single linguistic stock, including Afro-Asiatic'; Matasović's conclusion is worth evaluating:

> Finally, the fact that there appear to be only a few words of non-IE origin shared by Goidelic and Brythonic, but not by other 'Celtic' or Indo-European languages, points to the conclusion that Proto-Insular 'Celtic' was not the language spoken by the Celts who first came into contact with the pre-Indo-European inhabitants of the British Isles. As far as the evidence of these loanwords is concerned, Proto-Insular 'Celtic' never existed.

Can this linguistic scene be comparable to a 'murder mystery thriller? How do we solve the puzzle? We must ask which theory is true, or which aspects proposed by these learned scholars should the 'jury' believe?

<u>Can these views be challenged?</u>

There appears to be abundant Hamito-Semitic (Afro-asiatic) words in Insular 'Celtic' (as illustrated by Vallancey). It is reasonable to assume that there could be more than one source for the Substratum in 'Celtic' languages.

Matasović's replying to Tatyana Mikhailova is concise; *'the exact number of substratum words in Insular 'Celtic' is uncertain, and I am quite convinced that it is indeed larger than the number indicated in my Etymological Dictionary of Proto-'Celtic' (Matasović 2009)*

We can see that modern linguists seem to be very 'conservative' and tend to be too quick in rejecting the significant Hamito-Semitic (Afro-asiatic) influence on Insular 'Celtic'. This will be explored later after considering some other experts, to see if any agreement can be reach between them.

Of all the subjects covered in this book, it is the area of language that seems to have produced the most diverse and contradicting opinions. It is important to offer a balance view and consider diverse opinions.

Raymond Hickey explored the language change in early Britain and comments on Wagner's work:

> Wagner's methodology consists of repeatedly pointing out typological parallels between the languages of the British Isles and those in north Africa (Wagner 1982) which together form his 'Eurafrican' type which contrasts with a 'Ural-Altaic' type which he sees as having influenced Proto-Germanic (1959: 148). There are strengths and weaknesses in Wagner's approach. His forte lies in the broad typological perspective which he brings to his subject matter, the inherent weakness of his investigation is that it is almost ideologically in favour of typologically similarity through contact. There is no consideration of language-internal arguments so that the other side is never given a hearing.

Without going into too much detail, Raymond Hickey's article is refreshingly balanced and in his *Note 1* he offers a very helpful observation that could explain the true source of the substratum:

> [Note 1] Vennemann rightly remarks on the reticence of scholars to accept contact explanations in the Indo-European context who otherwise have no such reservations when dealing with language outside this group. He furthermore postulates that the reasons may lie in the vested institutional interest of scholars to preserve the largely contact-free status of Indo-European in order not to undermine the subject. [Raymond Hickey, Language change in early Britain: The convergence account (Berlin: Mouton-de Gruyter, 2002, pp.

185-203)

The substratum theory begins with the translation of the Bible into Welsh in the 1600's. Can Karl Jongeling's comparison of Welsh and Hebrew, in 2000, offer us any clarity on the subject?

His lengthy discussion on the subject concludes with:

> In short, this scenario would mean that we should consider Western Europe and North Africa as an old coherent area of VSO-character. The influence on the three northern Afro-asiatic groups, Semitic, Egyptian and Berber is comparable to the influence on the Celtic sub-grouping of Indo-European. There is, in that case, a great difference in time between the period of influence on Semitic and Egyptian on the one hand and Celtic on the other. As the VSO-character of a language may be kept intact over several thousands of years, as proven by the known historic development of Semitic and Egyptian, this does not seem to constitute a real problem. Another problem may be found in the supposed relation of the substratum influencing several Afro-asiatic languages and Celtic. As the study of Gensler proves the relationship of both are beyond doubt, one might suppose that Western Europe and North Africa once formed one great contiguous VSO area. This area was split by the incoming Indo-Europeans. The proportion of Indo-Europeans on the continent was so great that any influence of a pre-existing language was blotted out, while the number of pre-Indo-European inhabitants on the British Isles was such that their influence was felt long after they were gone from memory. [p163, Karl Jongeling, Comparison of Welsh, and Hebrew, 2000]

As the list of academic theories grows, it becomes more apparent that the study of linguistics cannot be regarded as a science - classifications are 'culturally' sensitive - it is worth repeating Vennemann's opinion that '<u>the reasons may lie in the vested institutional interest of scholars to preserve the largely contact-free status of Indo-European in order not to undermine the subject</u>'.

However, there is an interesting trend appearing which may actually lead to a break-throw in understanding the complexity of the substratum in

Insular 'Celtic' languages. Before exploring this, it is worth consulting two more academics, Stephen Hewitt and Theo Vennemann, who have different opinions.

Stephen Hewitt's paper, *'The Question of a Hamito-Semitic Substratum in Insular Celtic and Celtic from the West'* [2104], revisits the substratum theory in light of Cunliffe's proposed Iberian origin of 'Celtic' languages.

Stephen Hewitt has produced several valuable papers and is fluent in French, Russian, Arabic, German, Swedish, Breton, and Welsh. His revised conclusion is worth adding to the analysis:

> The existence of striking structural similarities between the Insular Celtic and the Hamito-Semitic languages is beyond question. However, the matter of whether this is to be attributed to substratal influence through prehistoric contact or to typological tendencies and correlations remains unresolved. Gensler's statistical approach (the low likelihood of such clustering of "exotic" features in two genetically unrelated families) is in itself skewed: by focusing on the shared features, he loses sight of the bigger picture, including all the features that are not shared by the two families. …….. Surprisingly, Gensler's scores suggest that it is the Insular Celtic languages which are most typical of the "Celtic/Hamito-Semitic type" rather than the Hamito-Semitic languages, and this is borne out by our table of shared features by author and language, where the various features are more consistently present in Insular Celtic than in Hamito-Semitic. This is the reverse of what one would expect if the shared features really had their origin in Hamito-Semitic. Rather than positing some Berber Urvolk, or Phoenician settler ghosts (who have somehow managed to leave no archaeological traces), substratalists (and it should by now be clear that I am skeptical) might take a cue from Jongeling (2000), who moots a single prehistoric substratum to both Hamito-Semitic and Insular Celtic. Such a substratum might have been centred on north-western Europe or even the British Isles, where it might have affected the incoming Celtic languages strongly, but the more distant Hamito-Semitic and North African languages less so. The identity of such a substratum would, however, perforce be so shrouded in the mists of prehistory as to be quite unknowable. Clearly, more work is needed on both the substratal and the typological approaches to this fascinating question. [Steven Hewitt, 'The Question of a Hamito-Semitic

Substratum in Insular Celtic and Celtic from the West' 2014]

Hewitt's conclusion once again reminds us of the difficulty of pre-historic language reconstruction in identifying substrata languages.

Although Berber is a good candidate for the substratum language; it must be acknowledged that the Berber expansion across the Maghreb is relatively recent:

> The Berber languages at the earliest stage of their so far traceable history were most likely spoken in central North Africa. Two different eras of major Berber expansion can be discerned from the linguistic record (Ehret 1999a, b). The earliest stage spread the ancestors of the Znaga to the western Sahara and of the Kabyle to northern Algeria, with the ancestral speech community of the remainder of the Berbers, which we might call the proto-Tibu (i.e., Libyans), taking shape in some other part of central and western North Africa. An eastern outlier of this period of Berber expansion is likely to be reflected in the Middle Kingdom Egyptian records of warfare with peoples who attacked from the west around the close of the third millennium BC. The second period of Berber expansion, involving peoples of the Libyan grouping of Berbers, lay probably in around the late second millennium and the early first millennium BC, when renewed attacks on Egypt from the west are recorded. Only after this period, and possibly not until the coming of camels to the region around 2000 years ago, did the Tuareg spread into the central Sahara. [Christopher Ehret, Linguistic Stratigraphies and Holocene history in North-eastern Africa]

This leaves us with a significant challenge. The Hausa (Chadic speakers) provide us with some evidence, through their folklore, that they once inhabited the Hoggar region of central Algeria, and subsequently migrated further south due to pressure from the Tuaregs.

Christopher Ehret attempts to reconstruct the linguistic relationships within Hamito-Semitic (Ehret uses the term Afrasian) helps us with the chronological construction:

> These stages of history, in this scholar's view, most likely

> belong to successive eras in the period between the last glacial maximum and 8000 BCE. I reach this conclusion partly on the basis of what I see as strongly plausible archaeological correlations for the initial breakup and expansions of the proto-Chado-Berber, stratum 4b in the linguistic stratigraphy, as argued in the next paragraph. If correct, these correlations would place the close of stage 4b in the ninth millennium BCE. The context of the prior divergence of the proto-Erythraic group, brought about by a spread of North Erythraic communities, stratum 3, northward toward Egypt, remains an issue. Possibly the proto-North Erythraic group followed the Nile corridor north; possibly they followed a Red Sea hills route. In either case their original northward spread needs to be dated well before the ninth millennium BCE.

Proto-Chadic and Proto-Berber probably hold the key to the identity of the substratum influence within Insular 'Celtic' and further research is required in this area. The Chadic speakers once dominated the Mediterranean and extended further north into the Italian Peninsula.

The most exciting of all the modern substrata academics is Theo Vennemann, a retired professor of linguistics, Ludwig Maximilian University, Munich from 1974 to 2005. I regard him as 'the Charles Vallancey of the 21st Century.' Vennemann has produced an impressive list of publications - including Europa Vasconica - Europa Semitica (2003), The Semitic Component of Early Germanic: Language and Culture by Robert Mailhammer & Theo Vennemann, and The Carthaginian North: Semitic Influence on Early Germanic: A Linguistic and Cultural Study by Robert Mailhammer, Theo Vennemann (published October 2019) are just a small example of his prolific output on the subject.

Vennemann covers many intriguing topics. His concept is based on the theory of Atlantic language expansion of Hamito-Semitic (Afro-asiatic) into Europe during the Neolithic, resulting in substratal influences in German, 'Celtic' and other western European languages. His work has emphasized the Semitic connection, with the Phoenician Punic being regarded as the prime source of the substratum. He also places Pictish within this Atlantic group.

Vennemann's theory attempts to answer some difficult questions. Regarding Proto-Germanic a total of <u>one third</u> of the vocabulary has non-Indo-European etymology. *[see Etymologische Beziehungen im Alten Europa, chapter 7, Reprinted in Europa Vasconica]*

Vennemann gives the following outline:

> The Old European languages belonging to the Vasconic

> family, the only surviving member of which is Basque; and the Atlantic languages belonging to the Hamito-Semitic family of which many members survive in North Africa and the Middle East……. For the British Isles it has long been known that whatever went before, their languages were Hamito-Semitic at the time when the Celtic languages intruded from the Continent; the substratal influence is seen in the structural transformation of Insular Celtic into a syntactic type resembling that of Hamito-Semitic more than typical Indo-European. Reference is made to two British toponyms that had shortly before been interpreted as Semitic in origin, Uist and The Solent. Superstrates primarily affect the lexicon of their substrates, less so their structure. Hamito-Semitic languages are assumed to have been superstrata to very early Germanic, and it is shown with reference to a sizeable number of appellative loan-words that the assumption may be true. [Europa Vasconica]

Vennemann is bold and confident in his theories, a highly admirable stand.

Dr. Caitlin Green in her fascinating 'long distance contact' blog draws attention to Semitic placenames in pre-Roman Britain. Caitlin's blog *'Thanet, Tanit and the Phoenicians: Place-Names, Archaeology and Pre-Roman Trading Settlements in Eastern Kent?'* - is a refreshing viewpoint for a current archaeologist. Although these ideas are certainly not new, modern archaeologist tend to be unaware of the substratum theory; academia does not encourage research into this area. Dr. Caitlin makes the following observation:

> Moreover, recent work on British placenames suggests that Thanet may not, in fact, stand alone, and is instead one of a small number of obscure and difficult names from Britain that could potentially have Proto-Semitic/Punic roots. So, for example, Rame Head in Cornwall is an Iron Age promontory fort ………This name Rame in 1086 and thereafter—is, according to Oliver Padel, 'completely obscure' and 'unexplained', with no convincing explanation possible in either Cornish or English; however, it has been pointed out that there may well be such a potential and appropriate explanation available in Proto-Semitic, via the Semitic height-word rām, as found in the modern place-names Ramat Gan……. and Ramallah, Palestine (Proto-Semitic root *rwm),

> which would fit this imposing, conical headland well. [Dr. Caitlin's blog]

Dr. Caitlin refreshingly indulges in Vallancey style speculation on the origin of some British placenames such as Sark (an island) = sarq Arabic for east, and Scilly (an island) = sela Hebrew for rock. This approach is something that modern students will be completely unfamiliar with. Bob Quinn's documentary exposed how lecturers at a Dublin University instructed Irish students to avoid John Rhys and John Morris-Jones publication - 'The Welsh People' - because connecting Hamito-Semitic (Afro-asiatic) with Irish/Welsh was regarded as unacceptable.

Dr. Caitlin mapped the distribution of Carthaginian coins found in Britain; significant numbers have been found around coastal and riverine sites, with high numbers found in around Thanet.

It seems that the substratum theory has led us back to the beginning; to the 'Orientalist' Colonel Charles Vallancey, who derived Irish from Punic. His wonderful theories are full of facts that deserve more attention.

Colonel Vallancey - Irish are Phoenicians.

Charles Vallancey came to Ireland as a young man. He joined the Royal Engineers and became a lieutenant-general in 1798 and was promoted to general in 1803. He fell in love with Ireland and became absorbed in its history, archaeology, and language, which was unusual since he was a British colonial officer.

Vallancey was strongly opposed Lhuyd's attempts to connect Irish with Basque:

> the learned Lhuyd has in my humble opinion, succeeded little better in his collation of Irish language with Basque between which I do have there is no affinity, but between Irish and Punic I think I may affirm there is a greater affinity than between the Irish and any other ancient language whatever. [p14, Charles Vallancey, An Essay on the Antiquity of the Irish Language, 1772]

Vallancey was very persistent with his view on Basque, he writes 'Irish partakes not the least of the Biscayan [Basque].'

He aimed to prove the existence of Punic-Celtic. He acknowledged the arrival of the Fomhoraigh or African pirates:

> 'In Ireland at several periods, they introduced the art of

> building with stone and lime, astronomy, and over-ran the country and made complete conquest, drove out the Nemedians and laid the island under tribute', proclaims Vallancey.

In Vallancey's 'Collectanea De Rebus Hibernicis (volume V)' - the opening page makes the reader aware that he is not 'conservative' in his approach to Irish history:

> By the assistance of Irish documents, we traced their mixing with the Bologues (the Fir Bolg of Irish history), according to some authors, were a race of Arabs of long standing, that had penetrated thus far to the eastwards. Some think further vindication think they were ancient Persians: Mr. Wilford judges they were Tartars. We showed their alliance and colonization with the Dedanites and Omanites, the Tuatha Dadan and Fir D'Omhan of Irish history, proceeding together, under the name of Feni and Phoenicians, to Tyre, from whence they moved down the Mediterranean to Crete, Malta, & to Spain, while others returned to Scythia, that is, to Colchis, and soon after sailed down the Sea of Islands, of the Aegean Sea, to Spain, and from thence to these Western Islands.

He is not afraid to suggest an Oman connection for the Tuatha De Danaans - which he brings out of Scythia and into the Arabian Peninsula and into Ethiopia; before eventually crossing the Mediterranean Sea (through Crete and Malta) to Western Europe.

Malta and Crete seem to play a major role in the history of the Gaels. It is quite likely that the Milesians formed part of the Sea People, a warlike coalition of tribes, that initially attacked ancient Egypt during the reign of Ramses II (c. 1290-1224 B.C.). The Sea People consisted of the Lukka, Sherdana, Siculi, Dardanians. Lebu (Libyans), Tjerku, Lukka, Peleset (Philistines) and Weshesh.

Some of these tribes such as the Sherdana and Siculi were recruited as mercenaries by the ancient Egyptians. Under the pharaoh Merneptah (c. 1224-1214 B.C.), a new coalition of the Sea People attempted a complete take-over of Egypt; they advanced from their island hideouts and jointly attacked Egypt. Pharaoh Merneptah was able to defeat this coalition. But only a few decades later another attempt was made by the Sea People to take over Egypt again. Ramses III (c. 1194-1162 B.C) was faced with a massive enemy on his boarders. The Sea People coalition had already destroyed the great

Hittite Empire, and devastated the Levantine coast of Syria.

The Lebor Gabhála gives an account of the Milesians assisting the ancient Egyptian during this period. Milesius, the son of Bile, the eponymous ancestor of the Irish Milesians, became the ruler of Iberia - attacks the Scythians, and then settles in Egypt for 7 years, marries Scota the Egyptian, and then makes his way back to Iberia. Could this explain the numerous links between Ireland, Morocco, Malta, Lebanon and Syria (Assyria), and Egypt?

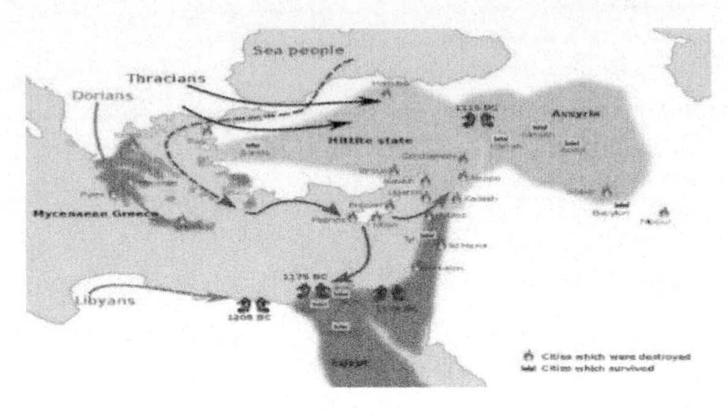

Map showing the Bronze Age collapse (conflicts and movements of people) (attributed to Lommes creative commons via Wikimedia Commons.)

Oriental Emigration of the Irish Druids

Vallancey is not the only one to bring the Druids out of the East. Gerald Massey in his 'Book of Beginnings' firmly places Africa as the source of all civilizations and interestingly mentions the African origin of the Swiss lake villages:

> As Karl Vogt says, "Our civilisation came not from Asia, but from Africa, and Heer has proved that the cultivated plants in the Swiss lake villages are of African, and to a great extent, of Egyptian origin." According to Logan/ the pre-Aryan civilization of southern India had a partially Egyptian character. The oldest races, he asserts, were of a variable African type who spoke languages allied to the African. Egypt, and not India is the common cradle of all we have in common, east, west, north, and south, all round the world. The language, beliefs, rites, laws and customs went out to India, but did not return thence by means of the apocryphal Aryan migrations. The Indian affinity with our European folklore and fairyology is neither first nor final, 'tis but the affinity of a collateral relationship. Egypt supplied the parent source, the inventive mind, the propagating migratory power. In Egypt alone, we

> shall find the roots of the vast tree, whose boughs and branches have extended to a worldwide reach.

The most intriguing work produced by Charles Vallancey is his thesis - 'On the Oriental Emigration of the Irish' - which is a remarkable piece of work. It shows a great understanding of the ancient trade routes:

> the ancient inhabitants of Ireland were the Cothi (as they denominate themselves) or Indo-Scythian, who, Mr. Wilford has proved from the Paranas, were the Palis, Balls, or Bils from that part of Hindoostan, bordering on the Indus, who, according to Irish history, did afterwards settle in Oman, on the Arabian Gulf, where, mixing with the Dedannites, they became the carriers by land and by sea, of the trade from Ethiopia to India, still preserving the name of shepherds. Mr. Bruce found their descendants in the same spot a few years ago, following the same employments, making the Args, or wicker vessels, covered with hides, for crossing the Red Sea and the Carbh, or planked vessels for longer voyages. "These people," says he, "were in Hebrew," called Phut, and in all other languages, shepherds; they are so still, for they still exist...they subsist by the same occupation. never had another....and therefore cannot be mistaken. They are called Belous, Bagla, Beloucee Berberi, Barabra, Zilla, and Habab, which all signify but one thing, namely, that of shepherds it is very probable that some of these words signified different degrees among them, as we shall see by the sequel. In these names we discover the Palis or Balis, the Buacal or Shepherd, and the Seal, all Irish words for sheep-grounds and shepherds, or flocks of sheep---in Arabic, Seleh, a flock; even at this present hour, it is the custom in the mountains of Scotland, that some people remove to feed their cattle on the hills, dwelling, during that season in huts, called sealans, or shepherds' huts, and in winter retire to their warmer habitations in the valleys. The name Berberi may probably be the Irish Fearbaire, a cowherd, to distinguish him from the shepherd." Letters too," adds Mr. Bruce, 'at least one sort of them, and arithmetical characters, we are told, were invented by this middle part of the Cushites, while trade. and astronomy, the natural history of the winds and the seasons were what necessarily employed the colony".

Now we can see why O'Flaherty made his statement that 'the Formorians whether they were the aborigines of Ireland or not, were not the descendants of Phut, son of Ham.' He was obviously reacting to Vallancey's thesis which proclaimed that 'the Formorians were descendants of Phut, son of Ham.' O'Flaherty denies such a relationship without having the courtesy of quoting Vallancey by name.

The Berbera or Barbara, mentioned by Vallancey, is another name for the Trogodytes or Shepherds described in the Periplus of The Erythraean Sea, *(written in the 1st century AD)*. These nomadic tribes inhabited much of East Africa and had vast herds. The northern Trogodytes lived in southern Egypt and along the Eritrean coast; while the southern Barbara Trogodytes dominated the spice trade - they had a complete monopoly on the export of Cinnamon. The Carthaginian Phoenicians once dominated the Atlantic trade routes; especially the secret trade links with the Cornwall tin mines. The Phoenicians knew that Senegal was parallel to the Cinnamon producing lands of the east (i.e., Horn of Africa), but surprisingly, they did not have a clue as to the real source of cinnamon (i.e., Sri Lanka and Indonesia).

The Cinnamon land was part of Trogodytica; it was inhabited by nomadic tribes. However, starting at Zeila, the name Berbera or Barbara is used in the Periplus of the Erythraean Sea. This region was famous for exporting frankincense, myrrh, cinnamon, and other spices. The ancient Egyptians referred to this land as Punt (Phut of the Old testament) - the most famous expedition was by Hatshepsut, the fifth pharaoh of the Eighteenth Dynasty of Egypt. Vallancey accurately described the East African Barbara and their dominance of the trade routes.

These African Barbara are described by Buzurg Ibn Shahriyar of Ramhormuz (930 AD) as an aggressive tribe. He said, *'the Barbara coast was very dangerous because the inhabitants castrated any strangers who fell into their hands.'* According to the Arab geographer Ibn al Mudjawir, the African Barbara drove the Romans and al Qumr (Indonesian/Madagascans) out of Aden, Yemen. The Chinese also mention the African Barbara (9th century AD) as being in conflict with the Arabs. This nation, they state, had never been occupied by other nations.

It is worth mentioning that Strabo mentions a branch of the Troglodytes living in eastern Europe near the Scythians. They are said to have inhabited the region around the ancient town of Callatis, now the modern city of Mangalia, Romania. This area was called Thrace in ancient times, and it should be noted that a significant proportion of Thracian DNA belongs to the African E1b1 (E-V13, E-M123):

After the country of the Scordisci, along the Ister, comes that of the Triballi and the Mysi (whom I have mentioned before), and also the marshes of that part of what is called Little Scythia which is this side the Ister (these too I have mentioned). These people, as also the Crobyzi and what are called the Troglodytae, live above the region round about Callatis, Tomis, and Ister. Then come the peoples who live in the neighbourhood of the Haemus Mountain and those who live at its base and extend as far as the Pontus — I mean the Coralli, the Bessi, and some of the Medi and Dantheletae. Now these tribes are very brigandish themselves, but the Bessi, who inhabit the greater part of the Haemus Mountain, are called brigands even by the brigands. The Bessi live in huts and lead a wretched life; and their country borders on Mount Rhodope, on the country of the Paeonians, and on that of two Illyrian peoples — the Autariatae, and the Dardanians. [Geography, of Strabo Vol. III, 1924]

Examples of Vallancey's Language Comparisons

Punic and Irish Compared: Grammatical Examples	
Punic	Irish
Num. *a dar, the house*	**N.** *an dae, the house*
Gen. *mit ta dar*	**G.** *meud na dae (the biggest of the house)*
Dat. *la dar*	**D.** *la dae, with or to the house*
Voc. *Ya dar*	**A.** *a dae, O house*
Abl. *fa dar*	**Ab.** *fa dae with or by the house*

Vallancey's comparison of Punic and Irish Grammar

The grammatical connections are explained by Vallancey as follows:

It is very remarkable, that all the Irish grammarians ancient and modern, have followed this method of expressing the genitive, by the substantive meud prefixed as in the example above. In the dative, la in old manuscripts is equal to dona or don, as leighios Canoin la German, i.e., legt Canones ad Germanum, vita. S. Patricii. Fiach apud Colganum. In the plural, dar is turned into dior, by the addition of the vowel I; the same rule exists in the Irish language. [p38, Charles Vallancey]

Comparison between Maltese (Hamito-Semitic/Afro-asiatic) & Irish	
Maltese (Hamito-Semitic/Afro-asiatic)	Irish
Allo (God)	*All (mighty,omnipotent)*
Samem (the heavens)	*Samh (the sun)* *Samhra (summer)*
Allo bier (God bless you)	*Ioll beiro dhuit (may you repent, God forgive you)*
Tummin (truly)	*Tam ann (that's true, Truly)*
Bin or ben (a son)	*Ban or bar, as banscath (son-in-law)*
Baghda (hatred, strife)	*Bagh (a contest, a fight)*
Dar, dir (desire, will)	*Deoir (will,pleasure)*
Ghana (to sing)	*Canadh (to sing)*
Ghamt (an aunt)	*Gean (a woman)*
Bir (a well, a fountain)	*Bior, bir (a fountain, a well)*
Iva b'allo, a curse	*Jobhadh (pronounced iva) bi a Allo, may death come from the Almighty*
Ara!	*Arah! An interjection*
Ardu, the end or summit	*Ardha, high, haughty* *Ard, a hill*
Barra, besides, at the bottom	*Barr, over and above, besides, the end*
Beit, a house	*Bath, baith, a cottage, hut*
Ghuscio, a place in Malta but properly a sorcerer, a conjurer	*Gu-sighe; gu a lie - sigh demon, a familiar spirit, geasa, sorcery.*
Hhabba, corn.	*Arbhar, corn.*
Ias-cese, shrivelled with age.	*Avis-caiseac, wrinkled with age.*
Ghana, to sing.	*Canadh, to sing.*
Ka-vi, strong, valiant, robust.	*Cath-f-hir, warriors.*
Sara, to combat, to fight.	*Svagha, conquest, victory.*
Sahta, wasted, destroyed.	*Sachadh, to sack, to destroy.*
Och, a nun.	*Ogh, a maid, a virgin.*
Ba schar, good tidings.	*Ba-sceal, good tidings.*
Q'al, speech.	*Agall, speech.*
Q'elp, hounds	*Cu-ealb'a, a pack of hounds.*

Vallancey's Comparison of Maltese and Irish

On a final note, concerning the comparison between Irish, Maltese, and Punic, Vallancey gives numerous examples which cannot be ignored. These linguistic connections lend support to the theory that the Irish migrated from the Libyan coast. The theory of so-called 'Insular Celts' from central Europe falls apart and seems to lack any evidence. If the Gaels and Cymry migrated from the African coast and Mediterranean islands, surely it is reasonable to presume they spoke a non-Indo-European language. How else can these connections be explained?

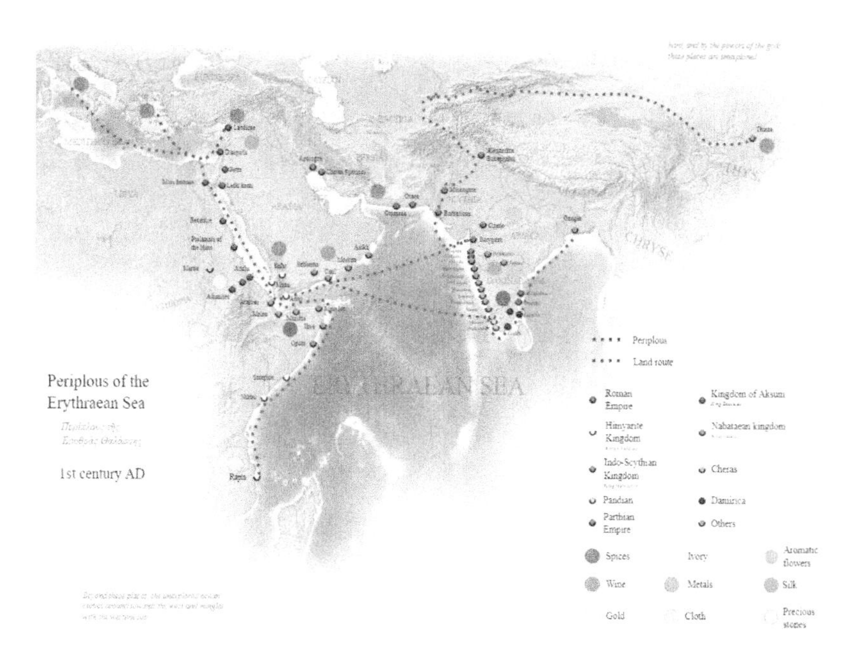

Map to Illustrate the Periplus of the Erythraean Sea 60 A.D.
(Attributed to George Tsiagalakis,
CC creativecommons via Wikimedia Commons)

King Arthur, Excalibur, and Merlin: An Arabic Substratum?

The tale of King Arthur, Camelot, and the mystical druid Merlin are known all around the world. But what do we really know about these popular semi-historical characters? The origin of these characters is not the focus of this section. A brief analysis of the names associated with the most famous character in British (Cymric) folklore leads straight back to the African Substratum Theory. Could the name Arthur and other names mentioned in these post Roman medieval tales be Arabic names? Was King Arthur an African, a Moor, a Kushite, or an Arabian?

King Arthur and his son Amir (أمير)

The identity of King Arthur has been debated for many centuries. However, the controversy over the origin of his name is not widely known. The oldest historical documentation of Arthur can be found in the Historia Brittonum ascribed to Nennius, who lived around 828 AD.

Arthur's *(son of Uther Pendragon)* journey towards becoming the King of the Britons is well known:

> King Arthur. of him, as a veritable and historical personage, nothing can be said. But he is the idealized and idolized hero of British and Welsh legend........ He is as real, or, if you please, as mythical, a character as William Tell. He is the reputed son of a reputed king, Uther Pendragon (dragonhead), a surname, Ritson says, taken possibly from the form of his helmet or his crest. From him Arthur inherits the title, Arthur grew up ignorant of his high birth, was taken to London, and, there drawing from a stone, in which it was embedded, a sword on which was inscribed, "Whoso pulleth this sword out of this stone is right wise born King of England," was crowned King of Britain. [Baron Alfred Tennyson, The coming of Arthur and The passing of Arthur, 1893]

The legendary Arthur had a son called Amir (Amr). William L. Jones gives an account of how he is remembered:

> Here, we are told, is a mound of stones, on the top of which is one stone bearing the mark of a dog's foot. This mark was made by Cabal, " the dog of Arthur the warrior " (*Arthuri militis*), when he was hunting ' the boar Troit " (*porcum Troit*). The pile of stones was put together by Arthur, and is called Cam, or the Cairn of Cabal. .... There may be found a tomb close by a spring which is called the Source of the Amir, — juxta fontem qui cognominatur Licat Amir, after the name of the man who was buried there. This Amir was the son of " Arthur the warrior," who himself killed, and buried him, on that spot. The "marvellous" property of this tomb was that, when men came to measure it, at various times, they never found it of the same size; "'and," the writer ingenuously adds, "I have made proof of this by myself" (et ego solus probavi). These two miracula, as he calls them, are all that Nennius, or his authority, has to tell us of the mythical, as distinguished from the historical, Arthur. [William Lewis Jones, King Arthur in History and Legend, 1914]

It becomes immediately apparent that Arthur's son, Amir (أمير), has an Arabic or Semitic name. It is quite apparent that the name Amr (or Anir in Welsh) cannot be explained in terms of Indo-European. In Welsh traditions, Arthur had three children. Arthur's son Amr is the first son ever mentioned in the literature - he is mentioned in the Historia Brittonum written by Nennius (828 AD). According to early Welsh folklore, Mordred is not regarded as

Arthur's son. In the Arthurian legends, as recorded by Geoffrey of Monmouth, Arthur kills Mordred who is not his son.

Mordred makes an alliance with Saxons, Picts, and Scots - and wages war against King Arthur:

> Geoffrey of Monmouth is the first to give us elaborate details about Arthur's encounter with Modred, and his motley army of Saxons, Picts and Scots, on the banks of "the river Cambula," or Camel. The river, according to Geoffrey, is in the west country, and the battle is popularly supposed to have been fought near Camelford, in Cornwall. [p27, William L. Jones, King Arthur in history and legend, 1914]

Arthur and Mordred came face to face in battle; Mordred is killed, and Arthur is wounded but survives. Arthur is placed in a boat and taken to the Isle of Avalon, where the faeries attempt to heal him. The story ends with Arthur laying beneath the Tor [a mound], waiting for the day Britain will need him to rise again. [Note the word Tor, a hill, mound, a cairn, etc., occurs in most Hamito-Semitic languages in various forms].

Ad Putter in his 'Arthur's Children in Le Petit Bruit and the Post-Vulgate Cycle' explains the inconsistencies in the story of Arthur and the killing of his son Amir:

> In Nennius, as we have seen, Arthur is said to have killed his own son (Amr or Anir). Another possibility is that the author or authors of the Vulgate Cycle were Arthur's Children influenced by the Charlemagne tradition. In some versions of the Charlemagne legend, of which the earliest extant representative is the Old Icelandic KarJamagntis saga (c. 1240)

An important development in the narrative, in later accounts, is that Mordred morphs into Arthur's son, a consequent of Charlemagne committing an unmentionable sin - they confront each other in battle at Camlann. The story changes with time with many additions made and modifications. [see Ad Putter]

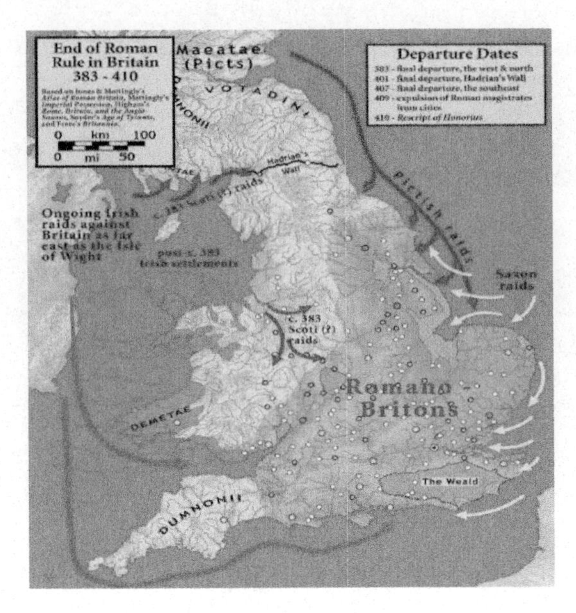

End of Roman Rule in Britain
(attributed Notuncurious, creative commons via Wikimedia Commons)

Regardless of the constant changes and additions made to the story of Arthur, the origin of the names used in the story fit comfortably within the Hamito-Semitic language family, especially Arabic; and lends support to the African Substratum Theory.

Toby D. Griffen in his paper, '*Arthur's Name, Celtic Studies Association of North America' [April 8, 1994, Athens Georgia]*, makes some interesting observations about the name Arthur:

> **the -ur ending is not a Latin termination for a masculine noun, particularly one adapted as the name of an individual. The normal ending -us (second declension masculine nominative singular) would have been necessary.**
>
> Our next problem is with the *-th-*, which is not Latin at all.
>
> Given the form Arthur as it first appears in the British/Welsh Gododdin, we are faced with the same problem we found in Latin: The ending *-ur* does not occur elsewhere, in spite of Rhŷs's argument from the speculated name of a god **Artor* (Rhŷs 1891:48). Nor can we simply add a British ending and solve the problem.

> Any Briton hearing the word *Artur* (or possibly *Arturos* with a nominative masculine ending would have heard someone saying the equivalent of English Bear-man
>
> Why was there no Arthur before Arthur?
>
> Why were there many Arthurs after Arthur?
>
> In all things, Arthur could be neither Briton nor Romano-Briton; rather, he and his name had ever to be both. [Toby D. Griffen]

The name Arthur cannot be found before the end of Roman rule in Britain. Griffen put forward the idea of Artur signifies Bear-man, others have *Arnthur* (Etruscan), *Arcturus* (bear star), or from *Artorius* (Roman). These explanations are not convincing. We know that Arthur had a son called *Amir* or *Amr*. A name that cannot be explained by Irish or Welsh. Amir is clearly Arabic (أمير) and is derived from the Arabic root a-m-r, a commander, a leader, or a prince. The name is also used as a tribal name such as the Beni Amr (Sudan's Red Sea Province) and Banu Amr bin Auf (بنو عمرو بن عوف) an Arabian tribe from the vicinity of Mecca.

The word Amar was used by ancient Egyptians to describe parts of Lebanon and Syria, The Amorites were known as the *Amurru* or *Amar*: again, more evidence for a connection with Semitic.

A very convincing explanation of the name Arthur can be found in Arabic:

> Ar- is a common prefix in Arabic and North African naming conventions, meaning "the" Ar-Rumi, for example, the name of an early Arab poet means "the Greek." Ar-Rahman is "the Most Gracious," Ar-Rabi, "the Master, and Ar-Rashid "the Right-Minded." [VI] Many of these are traditional names of God's servants in pre-Islamic religion. If we take Arthur's name as Semitic or Arabic or Kufic Arabic it may be a corruption of his father's name: Ar-Uthr. As to what Uthr might have meant originally, however, we will not venture an opinion here.[dnaconsultants.com/north-Africans-early-Britain/]

These Arabic derivations make a lot of sense - the prefix *ar* occurs frequently: *ar*-Rahman (الرحمان merciful), *ar*-Rahib (the monk), and *ar*-Rakkab (The All-Observing). Coupled with the fact that Arthur's first son Amr or Amir is obviously Arabic; a strong connection with Arabic becomes apparent.

It is also worth considering some of the following examples: على الأثير *ealaa al'athir* (on the air); Ibn Athīr the family name of three famous 12th century brothers (Majd ad-Dīn, Diyā' ad-Dīn, and Ali ibn al-Athir). Ali ibn *al-Athir* wrote 'The Complete History' (al-Kāmil fit-Tārīkh) - an important historical work, produced around 1231 AD.

Even Arthur's sword has an Arabic name. The name Excalibur has an Arabic origin. It is derived from the Arabic *qalaba* (قَلَب), which is derived from *qalb* (قلب) heart. The word *qalaba* can used in several ways: *qalib tasmim* (قالب تصميم design template), *qalib sabun* (قالب صابون soap mould), *qalib al'ahadhia* (قالب الأحذية) shoe mould. The word calibre (quality, or standard) is derived from the Arabic *qalb*; in the 16th century it passed from French into Italian calibro.

The story of Excalibur seems to have many parallels with the Islamic account of Zulfaqar (اَلْفَقَر), the sword of Ali ibn Abi Talib. Middle Eastern, scissor-like, double bladed swords were commonly inscribed with a reference to Zulfaqar. Islamic traditions say, *'lā sayfa ʾillā Ḏū l-Faqāri wa-lā fatā ʾillā ʿAlīyun'* was proclaimed aloud by prophet Muhammad (pbuh) - at the Battle of Uhud. He praised Ali's successful achievement of splitting in half the shield and helmet of Mecca's strongest warrior. Ali is said to have shattered his own sword as a result, of this conflict. Prophet Muhammad (pbuh) is said to have given Ali his own sword Dhu-l-Fiqar (Zulfiqar*). [see wikipedia.org/wiki/Zulfiqa]*

The Battle of Camlann was the final battle fought by King Arthur. Even this name cannot escape the African Substratum Theory. It could be derived from the Arabic *Khamila*, from the root *Kamil* (كامل k-m-l) - perfect, whole, or complete - also *Kamlan*, *Kamalah*, *Kamilan*, etc.

Muslims in Offa's England 8th century AD

Islamic merchants and travelers settled in post-Roman Britain. The influence can be seen during the reign of King Offa of Mercia who came to rule between 757 AD and 796 AD. During his reign King Offa produced his own gold coins, based on coinage from the Abbasid caliph al-Mansur (754-775 AD.), with the inscription Offa Rex and the Islamic *shahadah* - the Islamic declaration of faith:

> ašhadu ʾan lā ʾilāha ʾilla -llāhu, wa-ʾašhadu ʾanna Muḥammadan rasūlu -llāhi
>
> [I bear witness that there is no deity but Allah, and I bear

witness that Muhammad is the messenger of Allah.]

Offa King of Mercia 757 AD to 793 AD Gold dinar.
Copy of dinar of the Abbasid Caliphate 774 AD.
(British Museum, Public domain, creative commons via Wikimedia Commons)

Why did Muslim coins suddenly make an appearance in Anglo-Saxon England, northern Italy, and the Carolingian Empire?

Sherif Anwar, et al., explains:

> Muslim gold coins and the Muslim term mancus suddenly appeared in parts of northern Italy and occasionally elsewhere, such as Anglo-Saxon England and the Carolingian Empire. Based upon the medieval sources, the term mancus appears over 100 times in the 8th and 9th centuries in Latin documents from Italy, including Venice, Rome, and Milan. "All this shows that Arab gold coins were known in Italy, and that they saw limited use for certain kinds of transactions. They supplied a recognized standard of value, they were the kind of reserve coinage that wealthy individuals held in relatively small numbers, and they were familiar enough to supply a recognized and painful standard for penalty." .... the term also appeared in England during the reign of King Offa as the official language for the payments promised to the papacy. In addition, an actual Muslim coin struck in 157 A.H. (773 – 74 C.E.) must have reached England by 786, which was copied by an Anglo-Saxon die cutter. Therefore, the most prestigious gold coin in the late 8th century central Mediterranean world was the Muslim dinar or, as it was known in Latin, the mancus. [p17, Sherif Anwar and Jere L.

> Bacharach, The Prestige of Muslim Coins: An Eight-Century English Imitation of a Muslim dinar]

This research has uncovered the intimate connections between post Roman Britain, Africa, and the Islamic world. Something that Bob Quinn ingeniously unearthed decades ago. It gives a glimpse of a highly civilized cosmopolitan culture in Britain - where immigrants settled and transformed every aspect of society. All this shows a complex society that had different ideas of what it meant to be British. It again raises the question, **'how do we define who is British or Irish?**

> We have high status graves of individuals born in Africa, that have been identified using strontium isotope analysis; Arthur's name and that of his son Amir has been identified as being Arabic; and numerous skulls have sub-Saharan affinities (Ivory Bangle Lady and Beachy Head Lady).

19 CONCLUSIONS

In the past, my efforts were focused on Neolithic migrations from Africa and the Near East that introduce farming and new technology. These African and Near East tribes left remnants of their language within 'Celtic'.

However, when I started to write this present volume, I was determined to change my focus and find out if the 'Celts' ever existed at all in Iron Age Britain.

My familiarity with the phenotypes of Siluria and many parts of these islands seemed to indicate there was no 'Celtic' invasion at all.

This raised the important question, 'Who were the Belgic tribe?'

Since I was very familiar with the skeletal evidence from areas said to have been inhabited by the 'Celtic' Belgic tribes; my suspicions were raised. The new science of isotope analysis has confirmed what I had written over 20 years ago. The evidence is overwhelming and also confusing.

The DNA evidence will be left for volume 2. However, it is worth briefly mentioning the research by Turi E. King, et al., 'Africans in Yorkshire? - the deepest rooting clade of the Y phylogeny within an English genealogy,' Eur J Hum Genet 2007. The research revealed:

Y chromosomes belonging to the deepest-rooting clade of the Y phylogeny, haplogroup (hg) A, are regarded as African-specific, and no examples have been reported from Britain or elsewhere in Western Europe. We describe the presence of an hgA1 chromosome in an indigenous British male; comparison with African examples suggests a Western African origin. Seven out of 18 men carrying the same rare east-Yorkshire surname as the original male also carry hgA1 chromosomes....... Our findings represent the first genetic evidence of Africans among 'indigenous' British and emphasize the complexity of human migration history as well as the pitfalls of assigning geographical origin from Y-chromosomal haplotypes.

Not only were the Iron Age people of Britain and Ireland very closely related to the African Guanches of the Canary Islands, Egyptian Copts, Etruscans, and Pompeiians; they had no 'racial' connection with 'Celtic' Hallstatt people of central Europe.

The myth that the inhabitants of Iron Age Britain and Ireland were related to the Continental 'Celts' has been completely disproved by a comparison of dental affinities.

The innovative research undertaken by Mallory J. Anctil delivers the final coup de gras to the 'Celts' of Britain and Ireland model. The final death blow is inflicted by an unusual study, the analysis of dental affinities. Anctil's paper, 'Ancient Celts: myth, invention or reality? Dental affinities among continental and non- continental Celtic groups, (2016), finally proves that there was NO migration of Hallstatt or La Tene 'Celts' into the British Isles.

Mallory J. Anctil's unusual thesis, completed at the University of Alaska Fairbanks, explored the dental anthropology of the proto-Celts, continental, and non-continental Celtic tribes from the Iron Age. This was the first-time dental anthropology was applied to the 'Celts', with the aim of estimating biological affinities of different tribes.

Samples were collected from different regions:

> *The continental proto-'Celtic' samples, representing the Hallstatt D Culture (650-475 BC), came from a cemetery located in the Salzkammergut region of Austria.
>
> *The continental 'Celtic' samples came from the well-known La Tene cemetery of Munsingen-Rain (420–240 BC) in Switzerland.
>
> *The non-continental 'Celtic' samples were taken from Iron Age cemeteries from Yorkshire, England. The samples collected were associated with the Iron Age Arras culture. The cemeteries involved in the study were Rudston makeshift, Garton Station, Burton Fleming, Wetwang Slack, and Kirkburn.

The comparative sample (7th-4th century BC) came from cemeteries in Pontecagnano, southern Italy. Pontecagnano sits on the site of the ancient Etruscan city of Amina.

The thesis proves beyond doubt that 'Celts' did not settle in Britain:

> There is no evidence for population continuity between La Tene population at Munsingen-Rain (Switzerland) and those from Yorkshire. The Celts, as defined by the Munsingen-Rain population, were not present in Yorkshire during the Iron Age....... there is no archaeological, genetic, or linguistic evidence for the presence of the continental Celts (from Munsingen-Rain) in Yorkshire......... The population discontinuity evident between the British and Munsingen-Rain cemeteries indicates that the non-continental Celts were a distinct population compared to the continental Celtic populations possessing La Tene culture. [Mallory J. Anctil, Ancient Celts: myth, invention or reality? Dental affinities among continental and non- continental Celtic groups, 2016]

This thesis also proved that there was population discontinuity between the Hallstatt D (proto-'Celtic') and Munsingen-Rain (La Tene). The spread of La Tene culture was as a result of cultural transmission and not through population movements. The author of the study found that 'the Yorkshire tribes were non-'Celtic' and there is no evidence of the presence of continental 'Celts.' The indigenous Yorkshire population adopted 'Celtic' material culture through trade This also implies that the populations labelled 'Celtic' in Iberia are most likely 'non-Celtic' - the transmission and adoption of 'Celtic' language and culture occurred through trade, without any significant population movements.

Mallory J. Anctil's thesis concludes with the listing of six principals:

> * the La Tene=Celtic paradigm is not supported by the dental data.
>
> * there is notable heterogeneity among the samples.
>
> * there is population discontinuity from the proto-Celtic Hallstatt D period to the continental Celtic La Tene period.
>
> * the association between the inhabitants of Yorkshire during the Iron Age and the Celts is nominal.
>
> * there is no single specific dental complex that serves to unite the continental and non-continental Celts.
>
> * the continental Celts represented by Munsingen-Rain (La Tene, Switzerland) represent a biologically distinct population.

The dental study was able to confirm that 'large-scale migration throughout the continental 'Celtic' region is not supported, nor is large-scale movement into the 'Celtic' expansion area.'

If Anctil research had expanded his study to include the African Guanches and Egyptian Copts, he would have been able to see the African origin of the indigenous British and Irish Iron Age tribes. The MMD analysis of samples from the Canary Islands (D. Guatelli -Steinberg, et al., 2001) indicated a close similarity to the Shawia, Kabyle, Bedouin tribes, and Carthaginians. The study also showed that the population of La Gomera, Gran Canaria and Tenerife were very similar to each other - suggestion a single foundling population.

At the beginning of this book, I proposed the African Substratum theory and put forward the following points:

> * The old Hallstatt-La Tene model - a migration of so-called 'Aryans' from Central Europe into Britain and Ireland should be abandoned.
>
> * 'Celtic from The West' proposed by professor Cunliffe, et al., places the 'Celtic' homeland in Iberia. However, the evidence presented in this book has shown that there was a spread of 'Celtic' cultural material with no significant population movements.
>
> * The African Substratum Theory brings the Gaels and Cymru out of Africa. They initially spoke a Hamito-Semitic (Afro-asiatic) language, or a closely related proto language. The increase in trade during the Iron Age resulted in the gradual adoption of a new 'hybrid' language consisting of both Hamito-Semitic (Afro-asiatic) and Indo-European elements. There was no large-scale migration of Indo-European speakers until the Angles and Saxons crossed over, around the 5th and 6th century AD.

Today's so-called 'Celtic' languages developed and spread due to the growing commerce with the Atlantic Fringe countries. The analysis of skeletons from Iron Age Britain have fail to show the presence of any 'Celtic' population; - instead, we see a strong coefficient of racial likeness with the African Guanches, Copts of Egypt, Pompeiians, and the Etruscans of Italy.

Ancient Britain and Ireland can be described as a very cosmopolitan, diverse society. This raises the interesting question of 'how do we define Britishness and Irishness?'

I will leave it up to the reader to decide.

A Challenge for the Reader

Phyllis Jackson developed a new branch of ethnoarchaeology. Her pioneering work on foot outlines has increased our knowledge of human migrations.

Why not add your foot outline to my research, and contribute to the understanding of human migrations across the world? Please include the origins of both paternal and maternal grandparent (if known) and where they lived. Any further identifying features such as place of origin and genealogical data (including clan and tribal affiliations) would be helpful.

Wherever you live, I would love to hear from you.

Ibrahim Ali –
May 2021
blackcelts2016@gmail.com

20 SILURIAN GALLERY

This impressive mural was sculpted by Frank Abraham, a local artist, and was commissioned by Cardiff Council. The artist finally completed the mural in 1983; it took three years to complete. Frank Abraham captures the striking phenotypes that is frequently encountered amongst the Valleys population of South Wales.

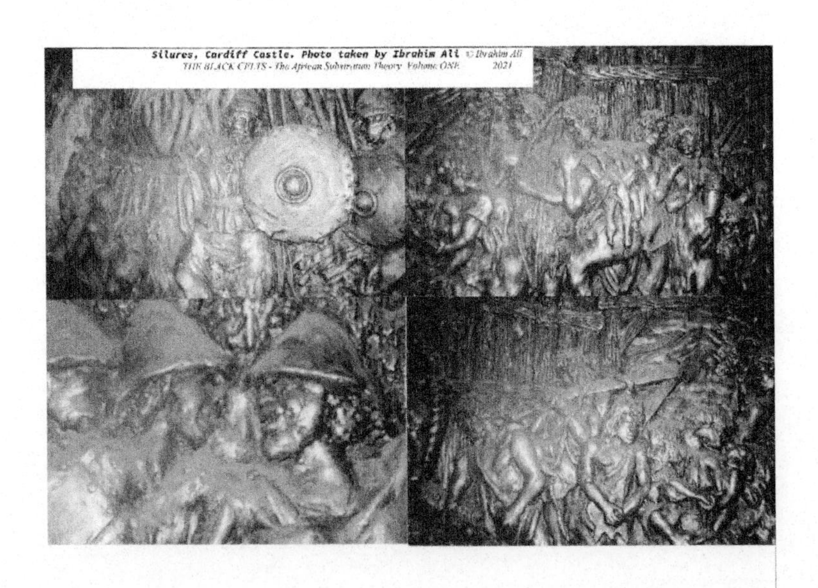

Silures, Cardiff Castle.
Photo taken by Ibrahim Ali
The Black Celts - African Substratum Theory

Silures, Cardiff Castle. Photo taken by Ibrahim Ali

Silures, Cardiff Castle. Photo taken by Ibrahim Ali
© Ibrahim Ali
THE BLACK CELTS - The African Substratum Theory Volume ONE
2021
Ibrahim Ali

Silures, Cardiff Castle.

Silures, Cardiff Castle.
Photo taken by Ibrahim Ali ©Ibrahim Ali
THE BLACK CELTS - The African Substratum Theory
Volume ONE
2021
©Ibrahim Ali

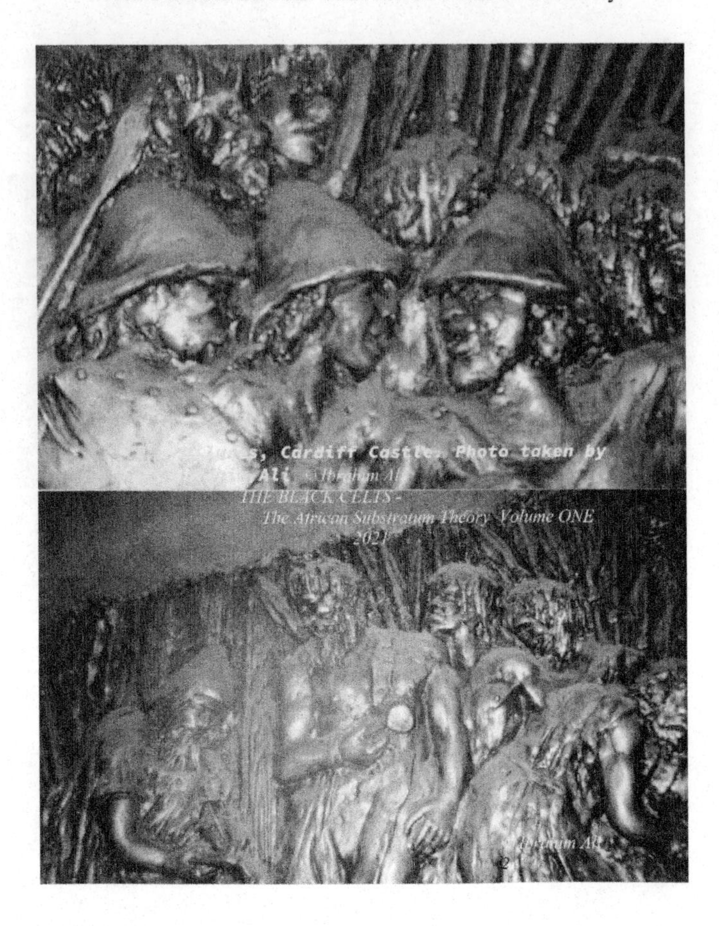
Cardiff Castle. Photo taken by
Ali
THE BLACK CELTS -
The African Substratum Theory Volume ONE
2021

21 APPENDIX

Pre Indo-European-Syntax in Insular 'Celtic'

[John Morris Jones University College, Bangor, March 1898.]

> Otto Schrader [1855-1919] said, "The notion of a 'mixed language' must have more weight assigned to it than has heretofore been allowed." [Prehistoric Antiquities p.113]

The syntax of Welsh and Irish differs in some important respect from that of the languages belonging to the other branches of Indo-European, Professor Rhys suggested many years that these peculiarities are due to the influence of a pre-Indo-European language; this suggestion led to make the comparison summarized in this paper. The substance of that part of the paper which deals with Egyptian was communicated to Professor Rhys in April 1891; the other comparisons were made later; but hitherto they have all remained unpublished. I now gladly avail myself of the opportunity kindly offered to publish them in the pages of "The Welsh People."

When one language is supplanted by another, the speakers find it comparatively easy to adopt the new vocabulary, but not so easy to abandon the old modes of expression; and thus, whilst the old language dies, its idioms survive in the new. The neo-Celtic languages, then, which are Indo-European in idiom, appear to be the acquired non-Indo-European speech of a population originally speaking a non-Indo-European language. The view does not necessarily imply that the ancestors of the Welsh and Irish belong almost exclusively to the conquered pre-'Celtic' race; we may suppose that the invading armies of Celts destroyed a large part of the male population, and took possession of their wives, thus producing an amalgamated race, who, however, learnt their speech from their non-Celtic mothers.

These non-Celtic inhabitants of Britain are believed by anthropologist to be the same race as the ancient Iberians, and to have migrated through France and Spain from North Africa, where the race is represented by the Berbers and the Ancient Egyptians. "The skulls of the pure Iberian race, such as those found in the long barrow of Britain, or the Caverne de l'Homme Mort, are of the same type as those of the Berber and the Guanches and bear a considerable resemblance to the skulls of the Ancient Egyptian."

Again, on the linguistic side, M de Rochemonteix has shown in his "Rapports grammaticaux entre l'egyptien et le berbere," that a relation exists between the Berber languages and Ancient Egyptian, which are now usually included in one family, called Hamitic. If the Iberians of Britain are related to the speakers of these languages, it is natural to expect that their language also belonged to the Hamitic family - in other words, that the pre-Indo-European idioms which still live in Welsh and Irish were derived from a language allied to Egyptian and Berber tongues.

And if there is evidence that this is so - if we find, on comparison, the neo-Celtic syntax agrees with Hamitic on almost every point where it differs from Indo-European, we have linguistic complement of the anthropological evidence, and the strongest corroboration of the theory of the kinship of the early inhabitants of Britain to Africa.

Ancient Egyptian preserves a very ancient form of Hamitic speech, and we can assume with confidence that it approaches much nearer to the primitive Hamitic type than Berber tongues which we are acquainted with only through their modern form. Ancient Egyptian may therefore be expected to agree more closely in general structure with our hypothetical pre-Celtic dialect; and it will be convenient first those parallels which are offered by it.

The Order of Words in The Sentence

As the relationship of words in an Indo-European sentence are sufficiently shown by the inflexion, the order of words may vary; but normally the verb comes last. In Welsh and Irish the verb comes first; thus, in Welsh, Darttennod Ifan y llyfyr, "Evan read the book"; in med. Irish, Aliss Patrice Dubthach, "Patrick requested Dubthach."

O'Donovan in his "Irish Grammar" (p.357) says, "In the natural order of an Irish sentence the verb comes first, the nominative, with its dependents, next after it, and next the object of the verb." Compare with the above the following rules given by Renouf in his "Egyptian Grammar" (p.57); "The order of the words in an Egyptian sentence is constant. When the verb is expressed, it precedes the subject. If both the nearer and the remote objects of a verb are nouns, the former is placed after the subject and the latter comes last."

But there appears in Welsh another form of sentence in which the nouns come first. No distinction is made in any of our Welsh grammar between this and the simple form of sentence in which the verb comes first: and the Welsh translators of the Bible constantly misuse it for the simple form; as Job a atebod, instead of atebod Job, for "Job answered." The misuse of the construction is absolutely unknown in the spoken language; and such a phrase as Job a atebod is never heard except when someone having answered is known and the doubt in the hearer's mind is as to who it was that answered. In short, the verb "to be" is understood with Job, and a is the relative pronoun; thus Job a atebod means "(it was) Job who answered." In Egyptian, says Renouf (p.57), "a noun at the beginning of a sentence implies the ellipsis of the verb 'to be.'"

But a noun may also stand quite independently at the beginning of a sentence. In Irish, writes O'Donovan (p.357), "when the noun is placed before the verb, it does not immediately connect with the verb, but rather stands in an absolute state." So Renouf, speaking elsewhere of a noun coming first, says: "The noun is not the grammatical subject of the verb, but what grammarians call the 'nominative absolute'" (p.47).

In Welsh and Irish an adjective or noun in the genitive case is placed after the noun which qualifies; as, Welsh, gwr mawr, Irish, fear mor, "vir magnus"; Welsh, Can Selyf, "the Song of Solomon"; Irish, inghean Shaidhbhe, "the daughter of Sabia." So, in Egyptian pa netar á a (Welsh, eithafoed daear), "the great god", t' ruu ta (Welsh, eithafoed daear), "the ends of the earth." Of course, the same order is preserved when the relation of the genitive is expressed by means of a preposition. Now, M. Bergainge has shown that in the primitive Indo-European sentence the qualifying word, whether adjective or genitive, came before the word qualified. In Welsh and Irish, then, we have a divergence from the primitive Indo-European order, and an adoption of the same as found in Egyptian.

Personal Suffixes

In Egyptian the suffixes representing the different persons are:

Singular		**Plural**	
1st person	*a*	1st person	*n*
2nd person masc.	*K*	2nd person masc.	*ten*
3rd person fem.	*T*	3rd person fem.	*sen*
3rd person fem.	*s or set*	3rd person fem.	*set, u, or un*

These suffixes (which, with one exception, do not exist independently) are added to verbs, prepositions, and nouns. In Welsh and Irish they are represented (1) by inflexional personal endings already existing in Indo-European; (2) by agglutinative personal pronouns. In what follows, I use an asterisk * between an inflexion and root in writing Welsh and Irish, thus gwel*af, "I see"; and a hyphen between a suffixed pronoun and the word to which it is attached, thus gwel-hi, "she sees."

Welsh grammarians say that in Welsh, usually at any rate, the verb agrees with its subject in number and person; and most writers, notably the translators of the Bible, have attempted to some extent to observe the rule. But natural spoken Welsh knows nothing of such an agreement; the verb is always put in the third person singular (which is thus virtually an impersonal form), except when the subject is the personal pronoun implied by the inflexion; thus, daethat is "they came," but "the men came" is daeth y dynion. This principle was stated as follows, in an article contributed by me to the Welsh quarterly Y Geninen, October 1890, before I was aware of the existence of anything analogous to it outside 'Celtic': "The 'inflected' forms daethum, daethoch, daethant, and the like, may be called pronominal forms, and they should not be used except when the pronoun is the subject of the verb. If the subject is a noun, the simple impersonal form daeth should be used: daeth y dynion, not daethant y dynion. The meaning of daethant y dynion, if it has any meaning, is 'the men they came.'" I now quote the rule of Egyptian grammar as given by Renouf (p.47): "The suffixes stand for pronouns, and as such take the place of the subject when the latter is not expressed. When the subject is expressed, the suffix must be omitted, We say anx-sen, they live; but anx netaru, the gods live. Netaru anx-sen would signify 'the gods, they live.'"

The coincidence is absolute. The pronominal suffixes in Egyptian are not mere signs of relation; each has a substantial meaning of its own and must not be used when that meaning is already expressed by another word. In Welsh, the idea of pronominal suffixes has been completely transferred to Indo-European inflexions of the verb.

It is the same in Irish. "It must be confessed, however, says O'Donovan (p.357), "that in the Irish language, ancient or modern, no agreement is observed between the nominative case and the verb, except in the relative and third person plural, and that even this agreement would appear to have been originally adopted in imitation of the Latin language." Indeed, in Irish, the impersonal form of the verb, besides being used when the subject is a noun, may be employed with a suffixed pronoun form. This, of course, represents the Egyptian method still more faithfully; and it has almost wholly supplanted verbal inflexion in Scotch Gaelic.

In Irish, an ending of an inflexional character may be used to denote the object of the verb. "These are the same pronominal elements," says Windisch, in his "Irish Grammar" (Eng. trans. p.57), meaning the elements attached to prepositions, "also become suffixed to verbal forms in the sense of subjects and objects; thus, ainsiunn, protegat nos (ainis, protegat), taithiunn, est nobis (taith, est)." Renouf says of Egyptian (p.48): "The suffixes appended to verbs, either directly or with the intervention of particles, may represent the object as well as the subject of a verb; thus, mas-sen, superat eos, tes-nek, nectit tibi." In Welsh, the object is expressed by the ordinary suffixed pronoun; thus, the Egyptian nehem-ten-ua, "defendite vos me," may be rendered literally into Welsh diffynn*wch-fi.

The neo-Celtic passive voice is more properly an impersonal verb; is inflexional ending, which is the same for all persons, stands for the indefinite subject, and the suffixed pronoun denote the object; the Welsh cer*ir-fi, "on m'aime." In Egyptian, the passive is formed by the suffix tu, which also means the same as the French "on"; thus i-tu-er tet, "on vint pour dire," Welsh deu*wyd i ddywedyd. The Egyptian tu is feminine in form; and in Welsh, when the indefinite subject is denoted by a suffixed pronoun, that pronoun is the third person singular feminine hi; as mae-hi yn glawio, "it is raining."

In Welsh and Irish, when the object of a preposition is a personal pronoun, it takes the form of pronominal suffix which is so fused with the preposition as to be indistinguishable from an inflexion; thus, in Welsh, "for us" is not er ni, but erom. In Welsh, three "conjugations" of prepositions may be distinguished - those in which the first-person singular ends in af, -of, -yf. It is needles to point out how un-Aryan [Indo-European] this conjugation of prepositions is; but, as above stated, in Egyptian the endings which form personal verbs are also affixed to prepositions. Thus, Egyptian em, "in" (am in combination), Welsh yn, Irish in; Egyptian am-a, am-ek, am-ef, "in me, in thee, in him," Welsh ynn*of, ynn*ot, yn*do, Irish, ind*ium, ind*iut, ind*id.

The Egyptian suffixes are attached to nouns in the sense of possessive: thus, tfe-a, "my father"; tfe-f, "his father." I believe we have in Welsh a few nouns taking pronominal suffixes, which, like those attached to prepositions, are of the same form as verbal inflexions. Hyd means "length," hyd hyn, "the length of this," i.e., as far as this: ar hyd Gwy, "on the length of the Wye," i.e., along the Wye (Zeuss-Ebel, p.685). Now, "along me" may be expressed by ar fy hyd, in which hyd is plainly a noun, or by ar hydof, or simply hydof: and so for all persons. With hyd, "length," and hydof or ar hydof, "along me," compare the Egyptian xeft, "face," and xefta or em xefta, "before me." The Welsh noun eido, "property," has not hitherto been satisfactorily explained. It may have prefixed to it a possessive pronoun, as fy eido, "my property"; or it may take a personal ending, with or without the article yr prefixed; thus, eidof, or yr eidof, "my property"; eidot or yr eidot, "thy property." It is usually explained as a possessive pronoun, and equated with the Irish ai, "his" or "her"; so that eidof means "my his." This explanation, though not impossible, leaves something to be desired, especially as he old first and second persons plural are einym, einwch, which again cannot be explained from the first plural possessive ein, since this was invented by Salesbury in the sixteen the century, the old form being an. But even if eidof is a pronoun, it is like no ~Indo-European pronoun; rather it resembles the Coptic series of pronouns: poi, "il mio"; pok, "il tuo"; pof, "il suo"; or the Berber oua-i, "le mien"; ouak-k, "le tien."

But instances of nouns with personal inflexions are rare in Welsh; and (unless eidof be one) are confined to prepositional phrases. his, indeed, is only what we should expect: for in the Aryan [Indo-European] languages acquired by our Iberians the noun had other endings for which personal inflexions could be substituted only in very exceptional cases. The possessive pronoun is usually prefixed to the noun in Welsh and Irish (which may also be done in Egyptian); but a suffixed pronoun is frequently added to the noun, as if it had been felt that the force of the old suffix ought not to be altogether lost. In written Welsh, as rule, this suffixed pronoun is artificiality suppressed; but it is always heard in spoken Welsh, except when i is reflexive: thus, Pan wel-o i dad, "when he sees his (son) father"; but Pan wel*af i dad-o, "when I see his father"; and Pan wel-o i dad-o, "when he sees his (ejus) father."

Periphrastic Conjugation

Speaking from the point of view of word-building, one may say that the base of the verb in Egyptian consists of a verb noun or indefinite, as anx, "living" or "to live"; but it becomes a verb by the addition of a subject, as in the instance above quoted, anx netaru, "the gods live," or of a pronominal suffix, as anx-a, "I live," anx-ek, "thou livest." The element n or an added to root form a ense-stem, whose meaning, however, seems to be somewhat vague: meh-na or meh-an-a, "je remplis (pres. or pret. Brugsch), rex-na, "io ho sapuo" (Rossi). There is no other simple form of verb, but a large variety of tenses can be expressed periphrastically.

(a) Perhaps the most common form of periphrastic conjugation is the following: (1) verb "to be," with personal suffix or other subject; (2) preposition; (3) crude form of verb as verbal noun. In Welsh and Irish, although these languages retain many of the Indo-European tenses, this construction is extremely common; and, in Welsh any rate, has long tended to supplant the synthetic form of conjugation, as being more precise, though weaker. The three prepositions commonly used for this purpose in Egyptian are em, "in," er, "to," "for," her, "above," "upon," indicating the present, future, and perfect respectively. These correspond in use with the Welsh proposition yn, "in." am, "for," wedi, "after."

Thus:

Egyptian: auk em meh
Welsh: wy*t yn llanw
English: art thou in filling, i.e., thou art filling.
Egyptian: au a er sem er ta ant.
Welsh: wy*f am fynd I 'r mynyd.
English: am I for going to the mountain, i.e., I shall go.
Egyptian: au f her kem taif hemet.
Welsh: mae-ef wedi cael ei wraig.
English: is he (upon/after) finding his wife, i.e., he has found, etc.

A very large proportion of simple assertions heard in spoken Welsh, probably about a third of the total number, are cast in this form. In the present sense we have in English a similar construction: he is a-coming (i.e., on coming). This is not Germanic; is it not borrowed from 'Celtic'? In the present sense it has been transferred from the Irish into Irish-English; as when an Irishman says, "I am after having my dinner," meaning that he has had it. Of course, the English comic paper always mistake him to mean that he is in quest of it, which shows how foreign the construction is to English.

(b) There are also in Egyptian periphrastic verbal forms without prepositions, of which the following are the most common types, "he knows" may be expressed: (i) au rex-ef, literally "is knows he"; (ii) au-f rex ef, "is-he knows-he"; (iii) au-f rex, "is-he knows." With (i) may be compared the use in medieval Welsh of the impersonal proclitic form ys of the verb "to be" before a finite verb, e.g., ys attebwys Owein, "is answered Owen," i.e., Owen answered, ys ethyw gennyf deuparth vy oet, "is went with me two parts of my life," that is, two-thirds of my life spent. With (ii) and (iii) the use of sef (ys -ef, est is) or syd (ys-yd, est id) at the beginning of a sentence, e.g., sef yw hwnnw, "est-ist ille"; yssyd yssit cussul a rodaf itt, "est-id est-id consilium quod do tibi." The verb "to be," which serves only to mark an assertion, would be liable to drop, leaving behind its affixed pronoun; and this is possibly the explanation of the fact that the verb in simple assertions in spoken Welsh has usually a pronominal element before it: fe wnaeth ef hyn, "he did this"; yr oed ef yno (yr = medieval yd), "he was there." At any rate, this is what actually took place in Egyptian itself, where the old auxiliary frequently disappears in Coptic, leaving its personal affix to stand at the beginning of the verb. It may be objected to this explanation that the pronoun is always followed by the relative in medieval Welsh, mi a welaf, ef a daw. Medieval prose writers certainly had a tendency to reduce everything to this form; but in these cases, the a is mostly artificial. In the oldest piece of written Welsh now in existence, the Juvencus fragment, we have Ti dicones, not ti a dicones; and in the Gododin, Ef diodes gormes, ef dodes ffin; ti disgynnut, and so throughout; so also in the Black Book, mi disgoganafe. In some cases, however, the a may be legitimate, slightly modifying the sense; ac yssef a dygyrch, "and is-he that snatches," i.e., and he snatches. This seems to be similar in form to the Egyptian au-f pu mer, "is-he that loves," i.e., he loves, "egli ama."

Periphrastic forms with the verb "to do" are very simple in Egyptian: ari-a-mer, Welsh gwnaf*f garu, "I do love"; ari-k mer, Welsh gwne*i garu, "tu ami." In Welsh, the verbal noun is very commonly placed first, followed by a and the auxiliary verb; thus, mynet a oruc Kei y 'r gegin, "go that did Kay to the Kitchen," i.e., Sir Kay went into the kitchen. Compare:

> Egyptian: seper pu ar-nef er paif pe
> Welsh: dyfod a wnaeth-ef i 'w dy
> English: come that did he to this house.

The Preposition Yn

The syntactical similarity of the Welsh preposition yn, in all its uses, to the Egyptian reposition em is so remarkable that it deserves a section to itself.

(1) Like other prepositions, both take pronominal suffixes:
Egyptian: au-k
am-a, au-a am-ek
Welsh: wy*t ynn*of, am I in thee
Thou is, "thou art in me, I am in thee."

(2) In periphrastic conjugation both mark the present tense, as above noted; au-f em meh, mae-ef yn llanw, "he is filling."

(3) Renouf says (p.56): "The usual sense, however, of the [crude form of the] verb preceded by em is participial or gerundive." Similarly, few Welsh grammars omit to say that the present participle is formed by prefixing yn to the infinitive: as Dr. Davies, "ex Infinitis fiunt participia, praeposita yn, vt yn caru, amans."

(4) Both are used in the sense of "in" before the name of a place, e.g., Egyptian em Abu, "in Elephantine," Welsh yn lLundain, "in London"; Egyptian em tet-a, Welsh yn (fy) llaw-i, "in my hand." Also, before a noun of time: Egyptian em kerht, Welsh yn (y) nos, "at night," In this sense both form a large number of prepositional expressions: Welsh yn ol, Egyptian em sa,

"derriere, apres, d'apres, selon, par suite de."

(5) The Egyptian em and the Welsh yn are used to introduce the complement after the verbs of being, becoming, & c. Thus, "I am a child," "thou art a god," "he is a servant of Osiris":

Egyptian: au-a em sera. au-kem neter.
Welsh: wy*f yn blentyn. wy*t yn duw.
English: am I child. art thou god.
Egyptian: unn-ef em ses en Asar.
Welsh: mae-ef yn was I Asar.
English: is he servant of Osiris.

No English word can represent the preposition ere; occasionally it may be rendered approximately by "as," thus xa em neter cyfod yn duw, "rise as a god"; but it means more than "as" or "like": it implies absolute identity. It is true that into, etc., may occur sporadically in Aryan [Indo-European] languages in a similar manner after verbs of "making"; but the peculiarity of the Welsh construction is that the preposition introduces every kind of complement, and to omit it is the exception, not the rule. It comes, like Egyptian em, before an adjective as well as a noun, e.g., "thou art might"; Egyptian: unn-ek em user. Welsh: wy*t yn gadarn. English: art thou mighty.

(6) Allied to the above construction, but sufficiently distinct from it, is the use of yn before any adjective to form an adverb. This is the only way in which adverbs can be formed from adjectives in Welsh, and the same method is always employed in Egyptian. Thus, Egyptian em next, Welsh yn gryf, "strong"; Egyptian: aq-es er pet em sexen. Welsh: aeth-hi i nef yn ebrwyd; English went she to heaven suddenly.

The use of this preposition yn before an adjective has long puzzled writers on Welsh grammar; but the difficulty disappears if we suppose that the idiom was taken over from a language in which, as in Egyptian, no line could be drawn between an adjective and an abstract noun.

The preposition yn in Welsh is followed by different mutations of initial consonants; but these differences imply no more than that the word in constructions (5) and (6) was originally similar in form to the archaic Latin indu, as Zeuss saw it must have been in construction (1). It is not, however, upon the sameness of the preposition that I wish to lay stress: the preposition may, and does, vary; thus, in Egyptian, er is used as commonly as em in construction (6). But the remarkable thing is that every one of these constructions, all of which, except the fourth, are more or less peculiar, should have its exact counterpart in Egyptian.

These constructions are also found in Irish; but the preposition in (2) and (3) is oc, ag, and in (6) co, go, though in, ind, appears in the older periods;

while the "in" of (5) has been made into "in his," partly perhaps on account of the aspiration after it corresponding to the Welsh soft mutation, but chiefly from an attempt to make it logical. At any rate, it does not seem to be old in this form.

We should expect the parent Berber language to form a link between Egyptian and Iberian, and to have developed in common with the later certain features not found in the former. This is, indeed, what the evidence seems to indicate; for, though the modern Berber dialects have been greatly modified by early contact with Semitic, they furnish parallels to most of the peculiarities of neo-Celtic syntax which we have not matched in Egyptian.

(1) The Berber dialects agree with Egyptian and neo-Celtic in the arrangement of the different parts of the sentence. "Il semble que la construction la plus generale soit la suivante: le verbe, puis le sujet, enfin le regime: Chekkadh a tue un lion, inr'a Chekkadh ahar"; in Welsh lladod Chekkadh lew."

But, as in Welsh, a noun or its equivalent may come first (as complement of an implied verb "to be") followed by a relative pronoun (expressed or implied) with the verb and the rest of the sentence. The pure relatives so used are a (=Welsh a), (=Welsh yd, y).

Tamashek': midden a nemous ourger tidhidhin.
Welsh: gwyr yn nid gwraged.
English: (it is) men that we are not women.
Tamashek':s Tamachek' as isioul ourger's tarabt.
Welsh: yn Tamachek' y sieryd nid ynArabeg.
English: (it is) in Tamashek' that he speaks not in Arabic.
Tamashek': s takouba as t inr'a.
Welsh: a chledyf y 'I lladod.
English: (it is) with (a) sword that him he killed.
Tamashek':nekkou a t inr'an.
Welsh: myfi a 'I lladod.
English: (it is) I that him killed.
Tamashek':entenidh at inr'an.
Welsh: hwyntwy a 'I lladod.
English: (it is) they that him killed.

The form inr'an is called a participle in the grammars; but there seems to be no reason for such a name. "En realite, il n'y a la rien qui ressemble au participe francais ou arabe"; it is an impersonal form of the verb used when the relative is subject. Tamashek' has feminine and plural forms of it, not known in Kabyle; but the last two instances show that even in Tamashek; the simple form is used after the pure relative, just as in the Welsh rendering given the third person singular, or rather the impersonal; lladod is used after the expressed subject a, although its antecedent is in one case first person singular and in the other third plural. In spite of our grammars, no Welshman would venture in speaking to say lladsant for lladod in such a sentence as the last quoted, for fear of being laughed at. So, we have in the Gododin Gwyr a aeth Gattraeth (not aethant), "the men who went to Cattraeth." So in Egyptian also:

> Egyptian: na rotu a sem er t'est.
>
> Welsh: y gwyr a aeth i (r) wlad.
>
> English: the men who went into (the) country.

It is worthy of remark that the so-called participle of the Tamashek' verb "to be," illan, corresponds in use to the Welsh syd, "who is," "who am," etc. The third person singular, illa, corresponds to the Welsh mae; as illa r'our-i aiis, Welsh mae genn*yf geffyl, "is with me horse," that is, I have a horse; and imous, Welsh gwas (a) yw, "servant that he is," i.e., he is a servant; ma imous aoua, Welsh pwy yw hwn, "who is this?"

I am tempted to think that the resemblance between illan and syd goes deeper than the surface, for the final n of illan seems to be, like the yd of syd, a pronominal suffix. When the verb is preceded by a particle, the suffix n (as is usual with Berber suffixes) becomes attached to the particle; so, they say in Tamashek', for "which is not," not our illan-n elli, just as we say in Welsh, not na s-yd, but na-d oes. Thus, the Tamashek' ma illan, ma our n-elli? "what is, what is not?" i.e., what news/ would be in Welsh beth s-yd, beth na-d oes?

Sydd is the only distinctively relatival form in Welsh; but in Irish the regular verb has a relative inflexion, with singular and plural forms, used like the Tamashek' "participe." These forms, as Professor Rhys has pointed out, are derived from Indo-European present participle with some (probably pronominal) suffix. Thus, the Berber relatival verb with its pronominal suffix, which suggests a "participe" to the grammarians, corresponds to the Irish relatival verb formed from the Indo-European participle apparently with some such suffix.

With regards to the preposition of the adjective and the genitive, it will suffice simply to mention that they follow the noun, as in Egyptian.

If we adopt Professor de Lacouperie's ideoligical notation, the above observations on the order of words in these sentences may be summarized thus: "the syntactical indices of primitive Indo-European are 1,3,5,8, III.; those of neo-'Celtic', 2,4,6,7, IV.; of African Hamitic, 2, 4, 6, 7, IV. Thus neo-'Celtic' differs from primitive Indo-European on every point and agrees on every point with African Hamitic.

(2) The suffixed pronouns in Tamashek' are the following: - Singular: I, i, ou; 2, mas. k, fem. m; 3, s, t. Plural: I, ner'; 2, mas. koun, fem. kemet; 3, mas

sen, ten, fem. senet, tenet.

The suffixes are added to the preposition and noun in the same manner as in Egyptian, and the Celtic parallels need not be repeated. But it may be noted here that "to have" expressed in Berber, as in Welsh and Irish by means of the verb "to be" and a preposition with the necessary suffix; thus, Tamashek' illa r'our-ek, Welsh mae genn*yt, Irish ta le*at, "is with thee," i.e., thou hast. So also Coptic, ou-nta-i, "io he (e di mi)," ou-nta-k, "tu hai (e di tu)." The verb "to be" is usually omitted in the present tense in Kabyle; it may be omitted in Tamashek'; it may also be omitted in Irish.

In the Berber languages the suffixes are not used to form finite verbs, but a conjugation with purely inflexional prefixes and suffixes has been evolved, evidently under the influence of Arabic aorist to have been developed independently. It is perhaps due to the same influence that the habit has grown of making the verb agree with the subject; and even when the subject is a plural noun following its verb "l'accord peut n'etre pas absolu en apparence entre le verbe et son sujet."

The pronominal suffixes in Berber are added to the verb to denote the object direct or indirect; thus, Kabyle izera-thent, Welsh, gwelod-hwynt, "he saw them"; Tamashek' ekfet-i-tet, Welsh rhowch-imi-hi "give (pl.) to me her," give her me.

When the verb is preceded by a particle or a relative or interrogative pronoun, the pronominal suffix which denotes the object is attached, not to the verb, but to the particle or pronoun. This is also the case in Welsh and Irish; and the suffixes so placed between the particle and the verb are called by Zeuss "infixed pronouns." Thus, Berber and neo-Celtic absolutely agree in the rendering of such phrases as the following:

Tamashek': iouout-I but our-K eouiter'.

Welsh: trawod-FI, but ni-'TH drewais.

English: he struck me, not the struck I.

Kabyle: izera-TH but anou-a ITH izeran.

Welsh: gwelod-EF, but yrhwn-a 'I gwelod.

English: he saw him, he who him saw.

Three examples of this suffix with a relative are given, with their equivalents, in I above. Examples of the suffix so placed as indirect object are common in older Welsh and Irish, e.g., Welsh ni'M oes, "non mihi est."

The objective suffix does not seem to be added to the particle in Egyptian, so that the construction was developed in Western Hamitic only. But the detachability of the suffix results in a very similar construction in Egyptian, where the subjective suffix is attracted by negative and some other particles, "de maniere que les pronoms se trouvent parfois ajoutes a la particule au lieu d'occuper leaur apres le verbe."

Of course a suffixed pronoun can only be used where there is something to support it; and as a pronoun is often required to stand in an absolute state or as complement of an implied verb "to be," Welsh and Irish, like Egyptian and Berber, have series of independent pronouns to be sued for this purpose; as Welsh mi, minnau, myfi, myfinnau, Tamashek' nek, nekkou, nekkounan, nekkouder', "I." Sometimes, in Berber, "nous avons affaire a un redoublement du pronoun lui-meme": in Welsh, we have a whole series of these pronouns formed by reduplication, myfi, tydi, myni, etc. The grammatical resemblance between neo-Celtic and Hamitic is strikingly shown in the classification of personal pronouns. Zeuss in his great "Grammatica 'Celtic'" distinguishes three classes in 'Celtic', which he calls absoluta, infixa, suffixa, but as the infixa are only a variety of the suffixa we have really two classes, absoluta and suffixa. So, the Berber personal pronouns are classified into isoles and affixes, and the Egyptian into assoluti ans suffissi.

(3) Berber conjugation has only one form, which is commonly used in a part sense, but it may be present by internal vowel change. The deficiency of tense-form is supplemented party by periphrastic conjugation, but chiefly by prefixing a particle to the simple verb.

The more common method of periphrastic conjugation is that in which the personal verb is preceded by a personal form of the verb "to be," as ellir zrir, "was-I saw-I," i.e., I had seen. This form is discussed under 3 (b) above. Traces of the form with the preposition are also found, in which, however, the verbal noun after the preposition is replaced by a personal verb, as ellir d'a zerrer' "I was seeing." The alternative, and by far the most common, method of denoting time may originally have been the last-mentioned form without its verb "to be"; but in effect it is merely the prefixing of a particle to a personal verb; thus, erser, "I descended," ad erser, "I shall descend." The particles so used are, in Kabyle, ad and r'a to mark the future, and ai to specially mark the past.

Although Welsh and Irish with their Aryan [Indo-European] tenses have little need of such helps, tense-particles are familiar phenomenon in these languages also, especially in older periods - such is the persistence of old habit of speech. In Irish no is the sign of an incomplete action and is used before the present and future tenses; ro and do denote complete action and are generally found with past tense: "ro gives a preterite signification to the present indicative and to the present habit." In mediaeval Welsh dy is occasionally met with, and ry very frequently. Thus, Kabyle ai zrir is Welsh ry weleis, "vid."

These tense-particles in Berber, like other particles, attract the objective pronominal suffixes, which are thus placed between them and the verb. This is also the case in Welsh and Irish, where tense-particle may be followed by Zeus's "pronomina infixa." Thus Tamashek' ad-I-inhi, "he will see me," ad-AS-enner, "I shall tell him." Compare Irish, No-T-alim, "I beseech thee," ro-M-gab, "he seized me"; Welsh ry-Th-welas, "saw thee."

(4) As the Berber verbal system, has been probably modified under Semitic influence, the equivalent of the Egyptian em is hardly to be found in it, though some of the verbal particles have often a distinct prepositional force. The equivalent of em before an adjective must also be rare, since statements such as "thou art mighty" (Egyptian unn-ek em user) are usually expressed by turning the complement into a verb, as can also be done in Egyptian (user-ek). But we have a distinct trace of the old preposition in d, "in," placed before the adjective in such expressions as aa oud iou agui d amellal, Welsh (mae'r) ceffyl hwn yn wyn, "this horse is white"; or in comparative statements such netta d ar ezfan-fell-i, Welsh (mae) efe yn fwy na-mi, "he is bigger than I."

The whole of the structure of the neo-Celtic sentence and nearly all its distinctively non-Indo-European features are embraced in the principles discussed above and have been shown to have parallels in Hamitic. There are many minor points of resemblance which are important only as supplementing the above general principles. A few of these may be mentioned here.

(5) The pleonastic use of a pronominal suffix after a preposition governing a relative, e.g., Irish, an fear A raibh tu ag caint LEIS, "the man whom thou art wert talking to him." This is considered incorrect by O'Donovan, but it is common to Irish, Welsh, Berber, and Egyptian. In the Welsh, "the relative will stand alone at the commencement of the clause, and the preposition will follow the verb with a proper pronominal suffix"; Egyptian, "il relativo preced la frase, e la preposizione e rimandata alla fine, e spesso ricongiunta col soggetto per mezzo di un affisso pronominale."

(6) The omission of the copula which is also characteristic of Hamitic, especially after a pronoun. Egyptian, nuk Hor, "I (am) Horus"; Tamashek', nekk-ou Mohamed, "I am Yscolan" (the last two in answer to an inquiring stranger); Irish, tu ar g-cruthuightheoir, "thou (art) our creator"; Welsh, pwy y marchawc, "who (is) the knight."

(7) The amplification of the negative by a noun placed after the verb, like French pas; thus, Kabyle OUR-k zerir ARA, Welsh literally N1 'th welais DIM, "je ne t'ai pas vu." This is common to Irish, Welsh, Berber, and Coptic; and may not the French construction have the same origin.

(8) The numerals in Welsh are usually followed by a singular noun, tri dyn, "three man." This is probably an extension of the original construction as found in Irish, where all plural numerals take plural nouns, except twenty and

higher multiples of ten, which take the singular. Most of the Berber dialects have adopted the Arabic numerals; I have been able to examine only two in which the ancient system of numeration is preserved and in these all-plural numerals take the plural, except twenty and other multiples of ten, which take the singular in Zenaga and the genitive singular (with a preposition) in Tamashek'.

In the above comparison I have confined myself strictly to syntax and have not ventured to suggest any phonetic equation. But there is one point of contact which is not easy to pass by. Perhaps the most remarkable fact of 'Celtic' phonology is the total disappearance of Indo-European p in Welsh and Irish, In Berber, le p est excessivement rare, et ne se rencontre qu'en Zenaga." There are difficulties in the way of connecting the two things, but coincidence is certainly striking.

The occurrence in Semitic of many of the modes of expression above is due to the relation which undoubtedly exists between Semitic and Hamitic languages. Of the precise nature of this relation, it is difficult to form a clear connection; but it seems to involve an intimate connection of some kind between families of speech in the prehistoric period, though they are probably not actually cognate. It is with Hamitic, however, rather than Semitic, that Celtic syntax is in agreement; for, as we have seen, it agrees with Egyptian where both differ from Arabised Berber, it also agrees with Berber where the latter differs markedly from Arabic, as, for instance, in the shifting of the pronominal suffix from the verb to a proceeding particle.

The case for the derivation as opposed to the independent development of these idioms in neo-Celtic is strengthened rather than weakened by their appearance in Semitic, since the connection between Semitic and Hamitic is generally admitted. Some connection can probably be traced wherever any of them occur; thus, in Persian, the pronominal suffixes attached to nouns and verbs, and the pleonastic pronoun after the relative (construction 5 above) may be due to Semitic influence. Is the influence of Hamitic substratum to be discovered in the simultaneous development on the analytical lines of French, Spanish, and Italian, in their use of infixed and postfixed pronouns?

So far as I have been able to examine Basque, I have discovered little syntactical similarity between it and either Hamitic or 'Celtic'. Some attempts have recently been made to connect it with Berber: there seems to be no reason why Basque should not contain a number of Iberian words; Van Eys doubts that it is related to Iberian, and Prince Lucien Bonaparte and others have tried to show that it is allied to Ugric, in which family Sayce is inclined to class it. Taylor suggests that it is the language of the broad-headed French Basques, who chiefly belong to the Auvergnats or Savoyards are the same stock as the Lapps.

The pre-Celtic inhabitants of Britain were an offshoot of the North Africa race is shown by the cranial and physical similarity between the long-barrow men and the Berber and Egyptian, and by the line of megalithic monuments which stretches from North Africa through Spain and the west of France to Britain, marking the route of the tribes migration. It is not the object of this paper to dwell upon the anthropological evidence, but one further point may be mentioned. Schrader has proved beyond doubt that primeval Indo-European family was purely agnatic, counting every relationship through the father; and Zimmer, in his remarkable paper "Das Mutterrecht der Pikten," has shown that the early inhabitants of Britain were cognatic; "Auf einnen Piktenherrscher und seine Bruder folgt nicht etwa der Sohn des altesten, sondern der Sohn der Schwester." This state of things has come down to our own time among the Berbers: "Quand le roi meurt ou est depose, ce qui arrive assez souvent, ce n'est pas son fils qui est apple a lui succeeder, mais bien le fils de se soeur."

The idea of comparing neo-Celtic with Hamitic was suggested to me by the view just mentioned as to the origins of the Iberians. If they are the same people as those who speak Hamitic languages, then the explanation of neo-Celtic syntax which Basque had failed to supply was to be sought for, it seemed to me in Hamitic. The appositeness of this comparison of this comparison of idioms may be illustrated by supposing a parallel case. If Irish, like Iberian, had been irretrievably lost, and we were led by anthropological or other reasons to infer a relationship between this lost language and Welsh, a comparison of Irish English with Welsh would suggest the derivation of the phrase, he is after coming from the Irish equivalent of mae ef wedi dyfod. Now, as Irish is fortunately not lost, we know this to be actually the case. Further, the persistence of idiom as compared with vocabulary is shown by the fact that, although each word in this phrase agrees in meaning in Welsh and Irish, not even the word for "after" is etymologically related (Welsh, wedi; Irish, iar n-); and this goes some way to show that they are both translations of a pre-Celtic word. These two languages have diverged considerably in the matter of phonetics; it is likely that they would have independently evolved syntactically forms identical in the two languages but differing from anything previously existing. The answer must be these forms are not independently evolved, and do not differ from anything previously existing. The prevalence in Welsh and Irish of the very same analytical expressions shows that analysis, which is usually regarded as a modern development, goes back in these languages to a primitive period. It is the characteristic of the language of the people and has been supposed to be modern only because it is not apparent in the earlier literary language, besides being largely artificial, was based upon the dialect of a more or less Indo-European aristocracy.

[John Morris Jones University College, Bangor,March 1898.]

22 ABOUT THE AUTHOR

Ibrahim Ali has spent over two decades investigating the connections between Africa and the so-called 'Celts'. He is a trained scientist and a holistic, intuitive Sufi therapist and life coach, specializing in problem solving using alternative healing techniques.

He has developed the use of psychometry in archaeology, helping to unveil hidden histories. He is also an avid traveler and has explored many ancient ruins in Ireland, Wales, and East Africa.

Printed in Great Britain
by Amazon